François Couperin le Grand

Wilfrid Mellers

François Couperin

and the
French Classical Tradition

DOVER PUBLICATIONS, INC.

This Dover edition, first published in 1968, is an unabridged republication of the work originally published in 1950 by Denis Dobson Ltd. The *Discography*, which was out-of-date, has been deleted.

This edition is published by special arrangement with Denis Dobson Ltd., 80 Kensington Church Street, London, England.

Library of Congress Catalog Card Number: 68-19894

Manufactured in the United States of America
Dover Publications, Inc.
180 Varick Street
New York, N. Y. 10014

Contents

Contents

Illustrations

The design on the title page is Couperin's coat-of-arms

To Vera
and to the illustrious memory
of François Couperin le Grand

Preface

So far as I am aware, this is the first book on Couperin le Grand in English; indeed it is possibly the first comprehensive study of his work in any language, for of the three French books on him known to me, that of Bouvet is purely biographical while those of Tessier and Tiersot do not claim to be more than introductory monographs. (As such, they are both admirable.)

I have divided this study of Couperin into three sections. The first gives the facts of his life and some account of the nature, values, and standards of his community. Of the facts of his life, little is known, and I have not indulged in speculation. For most of the information contained in my introductory chapter I am indebted to the biographical sections of the previous books on Couperin referred to above, with the addition of some documentary evidence more recently published by M. Paul Brunold.

The chapters on the values and standards of the *grand siècle* do not pretend to offer a revolutionary approach. My general attitude to the period is influenced by the miscellaneous writings of Mr Martin Turnell, published in *Horizon*, *Scrutiny*, and elsewhere[1]—especially those on Racine, Molière, Corneille, and *La Princesse de Clèves*, and by a most interesting essay by Mr R. C. Knight also published in *Scrutiny*, which was in part a criticism of Turnell's account of Racine. I have also found many hints worth following up, and much useful information, in Mr Arthur Tilley's two books, *From Montaigne to Molière* and *The Decline of the Age of Louis XIV*. Most of the information in my chapter on the court theatre music is derived from the writings of the recognized authority on the period, M. Henri Prunières. These books are listed in the bibliography. In this chapter, as in the others, I am of course responsible for the critical

[1] Much of Mr Turnell's work on the period is available in book form. (*The Classical Moment*, 1948.)

comments on the music and for the various analogies between Lully and other artists.

In general I have tried where possible to base my remarks on contemporary documents, creative or critical, and perhaps I may claim as original my attempt to state and interpret the relationships between the various facets of *grand siècle* culture in manners, philosophy, literature, painting, architecture, and music. I am aware that comparisons between the arts are sometimes considered dangerous, but I cannot see that, providing some technical basis is given to them, they can be other than illuminating. One would certainly expect artists working in different media but in similar conditions, with a similar philosophical background, to have much in common. In any case my whole approach presupposes an interrelation between the arts, as manifestations of the human spirit, and life; and I have taken pains to establish by frequent cross reference the close dependence of the second part of the book on the first.

This second part includes some comment on everything Couperin wrote. Even at the risk of monotony, I wished the book to serve as a work of reference as well as a critical study. This section thus stands in lieu of a thematic index. But of course the primary intention of this part is not merely informative but also critical. It aims to assess Couperin's achievement in relation to his social and musical background.

In such an attempt it is always difficult to decide how a book may be most profitably arranged. Even if the dates of composition of Couperin's works were all definitely established, a chronological method would hardly be feasible if adequate consideration is to be given to the various styles and conventions which Couperin employs. I have thus dealt in separate chapters with Couperin's contribution to each of the genres current in his time, preserving some hint of chronological sequence in so far as I deal with each genre at the time in the composer's career when he showed most interest in it. Thus I discuss the violin trio sonatas after the organ masses because it was at that stage in his work that Couperin was most preoccupied with the problems of the sonata convention. But he wrote other violin sonatas late in his life, and these I have discussed in the same chapter, since only as a whole can one assess Couperin's contribution to this convention.

From some points of view it would have been more convenient to the reader if I had discussed Couperin's predecessors—not merely the theatre music but all that he owed to the past—in a preliminary chapter, instead of scattering the information throughout the chapters on each genre of his work. For instance, the reader who knows something about the lutenists is in a better position than the reader who knows nothing to approach any aspect of Couperin's music. Yet an account of them undoubtedly fits most cogently into the chapter on the keyboard music which thus views the evolution of the clavecin school as a continuous process from the early years of the *grand siècle* to Couperin le Grand. Moreover, by inserting a proportion of general information and theory into the chapters on particular branches of Couperin's work, I hope I have to some extent palliated the monotony of many continuous pages of technical comment and analysis. If in this arrangement some duplication and cross reference between the chapters is unavoidable, I do not think this is necessarily a liability.

For Part II my main sources are of course Couperin's music, in the Oiseau Lyre text (whose spelling and accentuation of titles is adopted in this book), and the music of other relevant composers in editions specified in the Bibliography. But I should mention that for much of the information contained in the chapter on the secular vocal works I have drawn on Théodore Gérold's study of *Le Chant au XVIIième Siècle*; and that I have found Paul-Marie Masson's comprehensive work on the operas of Rameau especially helpful with reference to the dances and the social background of the Regency.

On the third section of the book no comment is necessary except to remark that even in dealing with matters of theory and practice I have tried not to forget their relation to aesthetic and social values. One need hardly add that anyone who writes on eighteenth-century musical theory owes much to the work of Arnold Dolmetsch and to Dannreuther's book on Ornamentation.

Many people have helped me with comment and discussion. In particular I must mention Mr R. J. White of Downing College, Cambridge, and Mr Alan Robson of Oxford University, who have made many useful suggestions about the first part of the book. Mr Felix Aprahamian has lent me music from his library and has discussed seventeenth-century French organ music with me; Mr Eric Mackerness has made various incidental criticisms.

PREFACE

But most of all I must pay a tribute to Mr C. L. Cudworth, of the Pendlebury Library, Cambridge, and to Mr R. C. Knight, of the French Department of Birmingham University. Mr Cudworth has put his extensive knowledge of early eighteenth-century music at my disposal and has unerringly directed my attention to music in the Pendlebury, Rowe, and University Libraries which seemed, however remotely, relevant to my subject. He has also read the whole of the manuscript, making many pertinent criticisms; and has compiled the catalogue raisonné of Couperin's music. I cannot too strongly express my gratitude both for his erudition and for his enthusiasm.

Mr Knight has undertaken the arduous task of reading and checking the proofs, especially the French quotations. He has corrected me on several points of fact, and has discussed with me many of my opinions. Both his knowledge and his sympathy have proved invaluable.

Finally I must convey my thanks to my publisher for his unfailing courtesy and generosity in dealing with more than two hundred music type quotations and many not easily accessible illustrations, at a time when even the simplest kind of book production is beset with difficulties.

W. H. M.

CAMBRIDGE, *August* 1949

Part I

Life and Times

Rien n'est beau que le vrai.

BOILEAU

We Polish one another, and rub off our Corners and Rough Sides, by a sort of *Amicable Collision*.

SHAFTESBURY

I think, moderately speaking, that the Vulgar are generally in the wrong.

SHENSTONE

GENEALOGICAL TABLE OF THE COUPERIN FAMILY

CHARLES COUPERIN

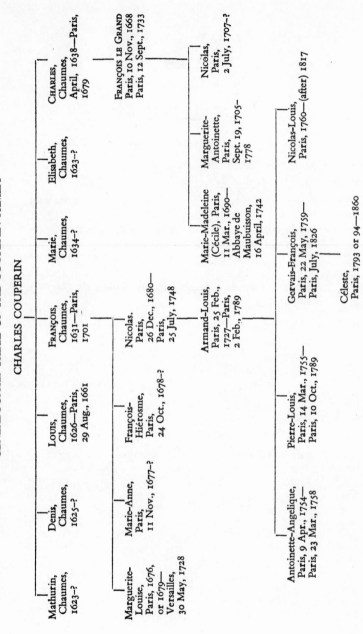

Chapter One

The Life

AFTER THE BACH family the Couperins are probably the most distinguished of all musical dynasties. Little is known about their origin though it is rumoured that there was foreign blood in their veins some time in the sixteenth century. At the beginning of the seventeenth a Mathurin Couperin was village lawyer at Beauvoir, in Brie. His son Denis succeeded him and eventually advanced to become a royal notary. Another son, Charles, set up as a tradesman in the neighbouring town of Chaumes. He was an amateur musician of some ability, playing the organ at the parish church and also at the Benedictine abbey in the town. He was the grandfather of Couperin le Grand. Three of his eight children became professional musicians, laying the foundations of the Couperin 'dynasty'. These three were Louis, born in 1626, François I, born some time between 1627 and 1633, and Charles, born in 1633.

The story of how the Couperins entered the fashionable musical life of Paris is well known, picturesque, and authentic—since it comes from the reliable contemporary chronicler Titon du Tillet. We may leave him to tell the tale in his own words:

Les trois frères Couperin étoient de Chaume, petite ville de Brie assez proche de la terre de Chambonnière. Ils jouoient du violon, et les deux ainez réussissoient très bien sur l'orgue. Ces trois frères, avec de leurs amis, aussi joueurs du violon, firent partie, un jour de la fête de M. de Chambonnière, d'aller à son chateau lui donner une aubade; ils arrivèrent et se placèrent à la porte de la salle où Chambonnière étoit à la table avec plusieurs convives, gens d'esprit et ayant du goût pour la musique. Le maître de la musique fut surpris agréablement de même que tout la compagnie, par la bonne symphonie qui se fit entendre. Chambonnière pria les personnes qui l'exécutoient d'entrer dans la salle et leur demanda d'abord de qui étoit la composition des airs qu'ils avoient jouez; un d'entre eux lui dit qu'elle étoit de Louis Couperin, qu'il lui présenta. Chambonnière fit aussitôt son compliment à Louis Couperin, et l'engagea avec tous ses camarades de se mettre à table; il lui temoigna beaucoup d'amitié, et lui dit qu'un homme tel que lui n'étoit pas fait pour rester dans un province, et qu'il falloit absolument qu'il vint avec lui à Paris; ce que Louis Couperin accepta avec plaisir. Chambonnière le produisit à Paris et à la Cour, où il fut goûté. Il eut bientôt après l'orgue de St. Gervais à Paris, et une des places d'organiste de la Chapelle du Roi.

The year of this musical tribute is not specified, but it was probably about 1650, or earlier.

The post of organist at St Gervais was one with which the Couperin family became intimately associated. Louis also played the viol and violin in the ballet music of the court. When the great Chambonnières incurred the King's displeasure, for some reason which we know nothing about, Louis was offered the much coveted post of Joueur de l'Epinette de la Chambre du Roi. He declined it out of a sense of delicacy, but that the offer was made testifies to the esteem in which he was held. It may have been as an alternative to this position that he was offered a post as one of the King's official organists; in any case he seems to have been affluent and highly successful. He was studying the work of Chambonnières and Gaultier, and composing energetically himself when, on the crest of his fortunes, he died This was in 1661, in his thirty-fifth year.

The second son, the elder François, came to Paris a few years after Louis. He too became a pupil of Chambonnières, and an organist and music teacher, but he does not seem to have shared either the talent or the fame of his brothers. He lived in the parish of St Louis en l'Ile and there is no evidence that he was ever organist of St Gervais, though he may have helped out occasionally during the interim period after Charles's death, when the busily fashionable La Lande was *locum tenens*. It is certain that he never occupied the St Gervais organist's house.[2]

Charles, the third son, followed Louis to Paris after an interval of a few years. He too became a pupil of Chambonnières, and one of the King's violinists associated with the ballet. When Louis Couperin died he succeeded to the organ of St Gervais, married, and installed himself in the ancient organist's house overlooking the graveyard. Here, after seven years, a son, François, was born on the tenth of November 1668. Eleven years later Charles, like Louis, died at an early age. The little François, although only a child, inherited the

[2] The question of the attribution of the great François's organ masses to the elder François is discussed in Appendix A.

organist's post from his father, and continued to live with his mother in the old house in the rue de Monceau. The church authorities arranged that until François grew up the brilliant La Lande should deputize for him on the organ, simultaneously fulfilling the duties of his two other Parisian churches. Meanwhile François had received a thorough musical training from his father, with some help perhaps from his uncle at St Louis en l'Ile and from the renowned organist, Jacques Thomelin. After Charles's death, Thomelin became, according to Titon du Tillet, a second father to François. He could not have been in better hands. It was undoubtedly from Thomelin that François learned the firm contrapuntal science, the mastery of the old technique which is conspicuous in his first work, the organ masses.

The contract made with La Lande had specified that he should carry out the organist's duties until Couperin was eighteen. Owing to the pressure of his commitments at court, La Lande was only too pleased to leave St Gervais somewhat before the stated date; he can have been in no doubt about the young François's proficiency either as an executant or theoretical musician. Couperin took over the St Gervais organ in his eighteenth year, in 1685 or early in 1686. Four years later he married Marie Anne Ansault, of whom little is known. In 1690 were born both his first child and the first fruits of his musical creativity. He obtained a *privilège du Roi* to enable him to publish, with La Lande's recommendation, his organ masses, but funds ran out and the plan had to be abandoned. Instead, he had several manuscript copies made, and bound them with an engraved title page saying that they were composed by 'François Couperin de Crouilly, organiste de St. Gervais'.

Two years later, in 1692, François thought he would show his mettle as a fashionable composer by writing some sonatas in the Italian manner. Many years afterwards, when he published the works with some new sonatas, Couperin revealed an innocent deception he had practised. The passage from the preface to the sonatas is worth quoting, if only because the prose has so Couperin-like a flavour:

La première Sonade de ce Receuil fut aussy la première que je composay et qui ait été composé en France. L'histoire même en est singulière. Charmé de celles de signor Corelli, dont j'aimeray les œuvres tant que je vivray, ainsi

que les ouvrages françaises de M. de Lully, j'hasarday d'en composer une, que je fis executer dans le concert où j'avais entendu celles de Corelli. Et me defiant de moi-même, je me rendis, par un petit mensonge officieux, un très bon service. Je feignis qu'un parent que j'ay, effectivement, auprès du Roi de Sardaigne, m'avoit envoyé une Sonade d'un nouvel Auteur italien: je rangeay les lettres de mon nom, de façon que cela forma un nom italien que je mis à la place. La Sonade fut dévorée avec empressement; et j'en tairay l'apologie. Cela cependant m'encouragea, j'en fis d'autres. Et mon nom italianisé s'attira, sous le masque, de grands applaudissements. Mes Sonades, heureusement, prirent assez de faveur pour que l'équivoque ne m'ait point fait rougir.

It is clear however that by this time François was becoming famous in his own right, without recourse to anagrams; for in the next year, 1693, he entered the King's service as one of the organists of the Chapelle du Roi, having been chosen by Louis himself as 'le plus experimenté en cet exercice'. Four organists shared the royal chapel between them, officiating for periods of three months yearly. Couperin succeeded his old master Thomelin; his colleagues were Le Bègue, Buterne, and Nivers. Once he had established this link with the court, François progressed rapidly. In 1694 he was appointed Maître de Clavecin des Enfants de France, teaching the Duke of Burgundy and almost all the royal children, at the same time as Fénelon. He must by now have been in very comfortable material circumstances; he was also gaining confidence in his creative work which, although conceived in the Italian fashion, had already revealed a decisive personality.

About this time, probably in 1696, Louis paid a tribute to Couperin's distinction and celebrity by ennobling him. It was an honour that was well deserved, for no man has had a more innate aristocracy of spirit than François le Grand. Characteristically he showed a touchingly innocent delight in the compliment, and was still more overjoyed when, a few years later, he was made a Chevalier of the Lateran order. He devised a coat of arms for himself, incorporating a golden lyre as a symbol of his muse, and signed himself, with a flourish at once baroque and precise, Le Chevalier Couperin, at the baptism of his daughter Marguerite-Antoinette in 1705.

During the first decade of the eighteenth century he was engaged on the production of music which would soothe the King's increasing melancholy. A considerable part of his output was church music written for Versailles. In much of it, very high and delicate soprano parts were written for his cousin Marguerite-Louise, a daughter of François the elder, who must have been a singer of remarkable accomplishment, if we are to judge from the words of Titon du Tillet:

> Une quantité de Motets dont douze à grand choeur ont été chantés à la Chapelle du Roi, devant Louis XIV, qui en fut fort satisfait de même que toute sa cour. La Demoiselle Louise Couperin, sa cousine, musicienne pensionnaire du Roi, y chantait plusieurs versets avec une grande légèreté de voix et un goût merveilleux.

The motet *Qui dat Nivem* was the first of Couperin's works to be published except for a few slight *airs de cour* and clavecin pieces in miscellaneous collections. It appears that at this period he also wrote some secular cantatas, including one on the theme of *Ariane abandonée*, but these are lost.

In addition to the church music Couperin also regularly produced chamber music for the *concerts du dimanche*. Couperin's position as a court musician is not very clear, for the Ordinaire de la Musique at the beginning of the century was officially d'Anglebert the younger, and François did not succeed him until 1717. It is certain however that Couperin was virtually in charge long before that date, and probable that he presided at the clavecin from 1701 onwards. D'Anglebert's ill-health and defective eyesight are possible reasons for his failure to fulfil an office he ostensibly held; the *galant* sense of delicacy and moral scrupulousness are possible reasons for his being allowed to keep a title which he did nothing to justify. In any case Couperin had some of the most celebrated musicians of the day in his charge. Forqueray the violist and Rebel the violinist were among those who played with him at the *concerts*, and it may have been at these entertainments that Marguerite-Louise sang the lost cantatas. We know too that at this period of his life Couperin became the intimate friend of the organist Gabriel Garnier, to whom one of the loveliest of his early clavecin pieces is dedicated.

By 1710 Couperin was already known to his contemporaries as Le Grand. Monteclair, Siret, Dornel and many other disciples dedicated works to him, expressing their recognition of his pre-eminence. François himself seems to have been serenely conscious of his powers, though this does not mean that his urbane irony, as revealed in his

21

prefaces, did not extend to himself. He had the true humility of genius, and was always willing to pay deference to others when he recognized genius in them. He had a profound respect for La Lande, and in the case of the great Marin Marais went so far as to hold up the production of one of his works because, 'ayant tous deux le même graveur', the publication of his work would have interfered with the publication of Marais's. The only two musicians of consequence who seem to have distrusted François were Lecerf de la Viéville and Louis Marchand. Lecerf de la Viéville, author of a famous book on the conflict between the French and Italian styles, suspected Couperin of a dangerous partiality for Italianism—a rather unreasonable charge when one recalls Couperin's often reiterated desire to mate the two styles, and his many tributes to his 'ancêtres' and to the incomparable Lully, 'le plus grand homme en musique que le dernier siècle ait produit'. Marchand seems to have been a difficult person on any count. He was hostile to Couperin not because he regarded him as a fanatical adherent of any musical cause but through jealousy, partly professional, partly personal. The legend that there was a woman in the case, recounted by the unreliable son of d'Aquin de Château-Lyon, is not otherwise authenticated. Significantly, if the stories about him are true, Marchand seems to have felt about Bach very much as he felt about Couperin. A man of remarkable talent[3] and originality, he wrote music which is in some ways frustrated and unresolved; it may well have been the lucidity, the objectified quality, of Bach's and Couperin's music that so exasperated him. Most probably his exasperation has been grossly exaggerated with the passing of the years.

During the period of his court activities Couperin returned to Paris periodically to teach and to direct the services at St Gervais. He had moved from the old organist's house as early as 1697 and lived in a succession of Parisian houses up to 1724, each dwelling growing more majestic as his reputation advanced. On the fourteenth of May 1713, he took out a *privilège du Roi* to publish his

---

[3] Cf. Dr Burney: 'Marchand was one of the greatest organ players in Europe during the early part of the present century. Rameau, his friend and most formidable rival, frequently declared that the greatest pleasure of his life was hearing Marchand perform; that no one could compare with him in the management of a fugue; and that he believed no musician ever equalled him in extempore playing.' (*A General History of Music.*)

work, and this time was able to carry it through. He first printed
his first book of clavecin pieces, which had been written intermittently over the last ten or fifteen years; in the next year he began to
publish his *Leçons des Tenèbres*, but this project was unfortunately
never completed, so that only three out of nine survive. In 1716
appeared his theoretical work, *L'Art de toucher le Clavecin*; and the
second book of clavecin pieces in 1717, in which year, on the fifth of
March, he at last officially inherited the post of Ordinaire de la
Musique. He was still writing concert music for the king's evening
entertainment during these years, and after Louis's death continued
to act as Maître de Clavecin aux Enfants de France. (He taught the
little princess, the wife-to-be of Louis XV, from 1722 to 1725.)
Couperin was forty-seven when Louis XIV died. During the
Regency he published his third book of clavecin pieces, and some
of the Concerts, under the title of *Les Goûts Réünis*. The success of
these encouraged him to publish some of his early Italian violin
sonatas, adding a 'French' suite to each of them to redress the
balance and incorporating one completely new work. The whole
collection, called *Les Nations*, appeared in 1726.

For two years the Couperins had now been settled in a beautiful
new house in the rue Neuve des Bons Enfants. We know almost
nothing about the last ten years of his life. In 1728 he published the
suites for viols and also a *Benedixisti* which seems to have been a
revival of a work dating from 1697. The fourth book of clavecin
pieces, put together with the help of his family, was published in
1730. Never very strong, he was intermittently ailing from his early
forties; the preface to the fourth book is valedictory in tone:

Il y a environ trois ans que ces pièces sont achevées, mais comme ma santé
diminue de jour en jour, mes amis me conseillent de cesser de travailler et je
n'ay pas fait de grands ouvrages depuis. Je remercie le Public de l'aplaudisse-
ment qu'il a bien voulu leur donner jusqu'icy; et je crois en mériter une
partie par le zèle que j'ai eu à lui plaire. Comme personne n'a guères plus
composé que moy, dans plusieurs genres, j'espère que ma Famille trouvera
dans mes portfeuilles de quoy me faire regretter, si les regrets nous servent
à quelque chose après la vie, mais il faut du moins avoir cette idée pour
tâcher de mériter une immortalité chimerique où presque tous les Hommes
aspirent.

The tinge of irony in this gravely measured prose only makes its
cadence the more poignant; in much of the music which follows

this preface we may find a comparable union of melancholy with an objectified precision, a detachment from the merely personal. The last two clavecin *ordres*, perhaps the most civilized music that even Couperin ever wrote, are his farewell to civilization and the world. In 1723 he had handed over the St Gervais organ to Nicolas, a son of François l'aîné; in 1730 he relinquished his remaining posts, his daughter Marguerite-Antoinette becoming Ordinaire de la Musique for the interim period until d'Anglebert died.

Couperin died on the twelfth of September 1733, in the big, elegant house in the rue Neuve des Bons Enfants. Another daughter, who was also a musician, became a nun. A son, Nicolas-Louis, born in 1707, presumably died in infancy, for nothing is known of him. Six months before his death Couperin had taken out a second *privilège du Roi*, on the expiration of the period of twenty years covered by the *privilège* of 1713. His intention, referred to in the preface to his fourth book, that his wife and relations should undertake the production of his unpublished works, was not fulfilled. His wife, a shadowy figure throughout, possibly had little business sense or initiative; his nephew Nicolas, to whom the task was entrusted, seems to have been irresponsible. Whatever the reason, nearly all Couperin's music apart from that which he himself published is lost. The missing manuscripts include a considerable amount of church music and 'occasional' concert music, but probably not any important clavecin works.

After François's death the musical direction of St Gervais remained in the hands of the Couperin family for several more generations. Nicolas's son Armand-Louis, and then his grandsons Pierre-Louis and Gervais-François, followed in the succession. They were all reputable musicians, both as executants and composers, but their distinction declines progressively with the civilization that produced them. The Revolution meant the end of the world that had made the glory of the Couperins possible; perhaps they were ill-adapted to survival in the strange new world which was inevitably emerging. Gervais-François died in 1826 in circumstances that were a bathetic reversal of the great days of the first Louis or of François the great. His daughter Céleste was given the thorough musical education habitually accorded to members of the family and seems to have been a competent organist. But her father was the last of the

24

St. GERVAIS.

The Church of St Gervais

Veue de la Grande et Petite Escurie et des Deux Cours

Couperins to officiate at St Gervais; Céleste declined to the status of a second-rate piano teacher. In 1848, in indigence, she was obliged to sell the family portraits to the state; the Couperins had become a museum piece. She never married; and that was the end of the Couperin dynasty. At least it would have been the end had not the Couperins of the *grand siècle* and of the age of the *Roi Soleil* left an imperishable monument to their name in their music.

We have little direct evidence as to the kind of man the great François was. No correspondence survives—a regrettable fact since we know that Couperin had a long correspondence about musical matters with Bach; the letters not unnaturally disappeared after being used as lids for jam-pots.[4] We know that Bach copied out several of Couperin's scores for himself and Anna Magdalena, and admired him above all French composers for 'l'élégance et la mélancolie voluptueuse de certains motifs, la précision et la noblesse dans le rythme, enfin une sobriété qui n'est pas toujours forcée, mais témoigne parfois d'une louable discrétion' (Pirro). From his prefaces and other writings one gathers that Couperin was, as one might expect, habitually courteous and urbane though capable of an acidulated irony. Clearly he suffered fools, but did not suffer them gladly. The beautiful portrait by André Bouys gives to Couperin a characteristically compact and neat appearance; it does not surprise us that this man wrote the music he did, or that he should have taken such scrupulous pains over the engraving of his works and have left such detailed instructions for their correct performance. In particular Couperin's hands seem appropriate to the delicately lucid appearance of his printed scores. But of course there is more to the portrait than this; the essence lies not in the precision which belies any hint of ostentation in the Louis XIV perruque, but in the large, rather melancholy eyes, at once intelligent and sensitive. It is here that we see the real Couperin, who is not so much a representative of his age as its moral and spiritual epitome.

We know very little about the facts of Couperin's life. There are speculations in plenty which can all be read in the largely hypothetical biography of Bouvet. But the essential facts I have given, and they are not many. When one has said that, one has only to look at

---

[4] This story was related to Charles Bouvet by Mme Arlette Taskin, who claimed that it was handed down in her family from an ancestor who was a relative of Couperin.

Couperin's portrait to realize that the chain of facts, the sequence of events, is not very important. We may have little evidence as to what, on any specific occasion, was going on in Couperin's mind, what he said or thought on this occasion or the other, what other people said to him. But if we have little particular information, we have a great deal of *general* evidence. As M. Tiersot has pointed out, in the *concerts* and clavecin *ordres* we have Couperin's memoirs, a microcosm of the world in which he lived. There are movements, such as *L'Auguste* or *La Majestueuse*, which reflect the gallant bearing of the King himself, and an easy familiarity with the great ones of Society. There is the gracious gallery of portraits of noble ladies, proud, tender, languid or coquettish. There are pieces, such as *Les Plaisirs de St. Germain en Laye*, which tell of the exquisite pleasures of the *fête champêtre*. Other movements reflect the sights of the Parisian streets which Couperin observed from his window in the rue Neuve des Bons Enfants—the martial glitter of soldiers (*La Marche des Gris-Vêtus*), the comic antics of acrobats and strolling players (*Les Fastes de la Grande et Ancienne Ménestrandise*). Other movements again tell of his love, as urbanely civilized as that of La Fontaine, for the country, with memories of days spent in his youth in the pastoral gentleness of Crouilly (the piece with that name, *Les Moissonneurs*, *La Muséte de Choisy*). And yet all these reflections of a world which to Couperin was immediate and actual, are universalized in the pure musicality of his technique. A world of life has become a world of art.

For it is not the surface of the pictures that matters; it is the moral and spiritual values which the pictures represent. Though we know little about the facts of Couperin's life, we know much about the ways people living in his society felt and thought; similarly we know a good deal about the ways *he* felt and thought if we can listen intelligently to his music. Knowledge of the values and standards of his time will help us to listen intelligently; conversely, listening to his music is one of the ways, together with reading Corneille, Racine and Molière and looking at the pictures of Poussin and Claude, whereby we learn what the values of his time were. In any case we do not listen to Couperin's music merely to re-create the past; we re-create this aspect of the past because we believe that it is of significance for *us*. Apart from Racine and Molière, no artist presents the

26

values of his time, purified of all merely topical pomposity, with as much precision as Couperin. If we can listen to his music adequately we shall experience one of the most profound conceptions of civilization which music has to offer. It can hardly be disputed that, the conditions of the contemporary world being what they are, anything which helps us to understand what the term Civilization might mean is worth investigation.

It may be that Couperin's civilization seems hopelessly remote from the problems with which we are preoccupied. If so, that is not anything for us to be proud about. He still stands as a criterion; he serves as a reminder of things we are rapidly forgetting. That we shall be any the wiser for the loss of them, few would have the temerity to claim. For myself, I do not even believe that we shall be any the 'freer' or the happier.

Couperin's culture was a minority culture, and it was doomed from the start; many things about it were foolish, and some were wicked. This does not alter the fact that it entailed values and standards which no serious conception of civilization can afford to ignore. In the first part of this book we shall discuss in general terms what these values and standards were. In the second part we shall discuss their manifestation in the technique of Couperin's music.

Chapter Two

Values and Standards in the Grand Siècle

Chaque heure en soi, comme à notre égard, est unique: est-elle écoulée une fois elle a péri entièrement, les millions de siècles ne la rameneront pas: les jours, les mois, les années, s'enfoncent et se perdent sans retour dans l'abîme des temps; le temps même sera détruit; ce n'est qu'un point dans les espaces immenses de l'éternité, et il sera effacé. Il y a de légères et frivoles circonstances du temps, qui ne sont point stables, qui passent et qui j'appelle des modes: la grandeur, la faveur, les richesses, la puissance, l'autorité, l'indépendence, le plaisir, les joies, la superfluité. Que deviendront ces modes, quand le temps même aura disparu? La vertu seule, si peu à la mode, va au delà des temps.

Les extremités sont vicieuses, et partent de l'homme; toute compensation est juste, et vient de Dieu.

LA BRUYÈRE

THERE WOULD NOWADAYS, one imagines, be few dissentient voices to the suggestion that the France of Louis XIV is one of the supreme glories of European civilization. Yet if this opinion is now a commonplace, it was not such at the end of the last century. To artists and critics of the nineteenth century, Versailles was anathema. The romantics loved solitude, bosky nooks, and nature picturesque because confused: the people of Versailles liked company, were apt to be afraid of solitude, and regarded the *confusion* of nature as an unmitigated evil. They would do what they could to mitigate it; they would chop down trees, open up vistas, clip lawns, marshal avenues, arrange their gardens and houses with geometrical precision. Since the King was the Sun, they must see that their world rotated around him. In a very literal manner, they planned the axis of the park and gardens of Versailles so that it should run from the Avenue de Paris

in the east, through the centre of the Palace, through the middle of
the King's bedchamber, out at the Parterre d'Eau to Latona, and
from there through the Tapis Vert to the Fountain of Apollo. They
knew that nature had dark corners, and they knew that there were
dark corners in the mind. But they believed, with all the conviction
of which they were capable (and they were nothing if not self-
assured), that the dark corners, where possible, should be illuminated;
and where that was not possible, should be left alone.

The romantics loved shadowy corners and regarded order as
suspect. It is therefore not surprising that they saw, in the attempt of
the *grand siècle* to order and illuminate, nothing but the superficies.
The elaborate code of values which Versailles evolved to regulate
human behaviour was to them always silly and inhumanly obstruc-
tive; to them the whole of life at Versailles seemed to *périr en
symétrie*, to use the phrase which Mme de Maintenon permitted her-
self, thinking petulantly of the draughts which whistled through the
carefully balanced windows. The finical code of manners which
involved such unjustifiable emotion, such petty jealousy and such ob-
sequious flattery (for instance the business of the King's *lever*) was to
to them merely absurd. The geometrical plan of the gardens was to
them not the consummation, but the denial, of art. The ceremonial
stylization of the literature, painting, sculpture, architecture and
music was to them a confession of bankruptcy, as frigid and 'artificial' as the menageries, the grottoes, the fountains, the temples *à
l'antique*, the hydraulic organs that imitated the carollings of birds.

It is only with the passing of the 'romantic' attitude to life that we
have been able once again to see what is there, in the art of the *grand
siècle*. And the renewed response to the art has brought with it a
revaluation of the society that produced it; for we are not naïve
enough to suppose that this remarkable crop of artists in almost
every medium—Corneille, Racine, Molière, La Fontaine, Le Nôtre,
Poussin, Claude, Watteau, Lully, La Lande, Marais, de Grigny,
Couperin, to mention merely the more obvious names—occurred
together by accident. If we admit the greatness of the art, we must
look with a modified eye on things that in social intercourse might
otherwise appear pernickety, affected, foolish. We come to see that
when the men of the *grand siècle* referred to an entertainment as
'galant et magnifique' they meant something that had a whole

29

philosophy—a view of the nature and destiny of man—behind it. We see that the unity with which artists in different media worked together is a factor of profound social significance; we see, from many a passage of Saint-Simon for instance, that even the insistence on deportment may not be a trivial thing:

> Jamais homme si naturellement poli, (he is speaking of Louis) ni d'un politesse si fort mesurée, si fort par degrés, ni qui distinguât mieux l'âge, le mérite, le rang, et dans ses réponses, quand elles passoient le *je verrai*, et dans ses manières. Ces étages divers se marquoient exactement dans sa manière de saluer et de recevoir les réverences, lorsqu'on partoit ou qu'on arrivoit. Il était admirable à recevoir différemment les saluts à la tête des lignes à l'armée ou aux revues. Mais surtout pour les femmes rien n'étoit pareil. Jamais il n'a passé devant la moindre coiffe sans soulever son chapeau, je dis aux femmes de chambre, et qu'il conoissoit pour telles, comme cela arrivoit souvent à Marly. Aux dames, il ôtoit son chapeau tout à fait, mais de plus ou moins loin; aux gens titrés, à demi, et le tenait en l'air ou à son oreille quelques instants plus ou moins marqués. Aux seigneurs, mais qui l'étoient, il se contentoit de mettre la main au chapeau . . .

One can well believe, with Mlle de Scudéry, that Louis played billiards with the air of a master of the world.

In English Augustan civilization too we can observe how standards of correctness may be inseparable from standards of value. Though the romantics did not like Pope any more than they liked Corneille and Racine, it is clear that when Pope and his contemporaries talked about Reason, Truth and Nature they were speaking of socially tested values which their readers would immediately recognize as such. And it is an inestimable advantage for an artist if he can accept the sanctioned values of his time without being ashamed of them; for although, if he is a good artist, he will lend an additional depth and subtlety to the conventional valuations, he can always be sure that what he says will be the richer for having the endorsement, not merely of his own convictions, but of a civilization. Moreover, he will have the advantage that the terms he uses will mostly be comprehensible to his audience.

If the Augustan civilization of Pope and Johnson was a fine one it had, however, obvious limitations; significantly it produced no vital tragic poetry and no great music. Though Reason, Truth, and Nature were values that meant much to Augustan society, to the society of Versailles, or at least to the more sensitive spirits in it, *raison, honneur,*

30

honnêteté, le galant, la gloire meant rather more. They were perhaps a series of counters; but the counters mattered because they were imbued with moral significance. Naturally, the balance was precarious; the code was always in danger of becoming divorced from its moral implications. But this society was great because at its best the code was an incarnation of life, not a substitute for it; because it was related to the complex of human passions, desires and fears; because it referred not only to the formal integration of society but also to the integration of the individual as a part of that society. The simultaneous preoccupation of the *grand siècle* both with *Caractères* (human nature) and with *Maximes* (behaviour and morality) is not an accident.

It is hardly too much to say that seldom if ever in a civilized, as opposed to a primitive, society has 'living' been so highly developed an art, and art and life more closely connected. And almost all the significant art of the period, in social intercourse as well as in poetry, theatre, music and painting, depended on the moral tension involved in, on the one hand, feeling deeply, and on the other hand preserving that self-control which, through reference to an accepted standard, makes civilization possible. Nothing could be more beside the mark than to accuse the people of the *grand siècle* of a deficiency of passion; the evidence of passion is there not only in Racine and Couperin but everywhere throughout the copious memoirs of the period. When they proclaimed as their ideal the *honnête homme* they did not mean that they advocated that last refuge of the spiritually craven, indifference; they did mean that the individual ought to realize that his own passions are not the be-all and end-all of existence. Probably, in the long run, it was best for his own spiritual health, as well as society's, if he admitted that he had obligations to the people among whom he lived. So the creed of *bienséance*, in the heyday of the Hôtel de Rambouillet, maintained that the *honnête homme* should have *un cœur juste* and *un esprit bien fait*. He should be considerate of other people's *amour-propre*, solicitous for their pleasure, alert to spare them pain or distress, prompt with his sympathy if pain cannot be avoided; and he should never impose his personality on others. To these people, *Raison* was both a personal and a social virtue; both an intellectual ideal and an emotional attitude of poise and moderation. They were far too intelligent to imagine that *la raison* could necessarily be equated with *la verité*; they knew that falsehood and wickedness and egoism would exist as long as man remained fallible and a sinner. But they believed that these evils were more manageable if one acted reasonably; and that one's chance of acting reasonably was better if one acted in accordance with the tested wisdom of civilization than if one trusted implicitly to one's own whims and fancies. This is why *le moi est haïssible*.

This moral tension between passionate feeling and personal self-control, with its attendant social implications, functions at widely different levels. At a fairly frivolous level we may cite Mme de Sévigné's description of how one behaves at the end of a love affair. The Chevalier de Lorraine visits a one-time mistress of his, La Fiennes, who promptly plays the forsaken nymph for him. Is there anything extraordinary in what has happened? he asks. Please let us behave like ordinary people, in a grown-up fashion. And as a final comment he adds, That's a pretty little dog you've got there. Where did you get it? Mme de Sévigné adds that that was the end of that *grand amour*. The story of course is funny; but there is no need to depreciate the girl's feeling, or the sincerity of the Chevalier's desire to put her at her ease. And the remark about the little dog is an achievement of civilization.

Similarly Bussy-Rabutin's comments to Mme de Sévigné on the war of the Fronde are not only brilliantly witty; they place the war in the perspective of civilization. It is odd to think, he says, that we were on different sides in this war last year, and are so still, even though we have both changed over. But your side seems to be the better one, because you manage to stay in Paris. I've come from St Denis to Montrond, and it looks as though I'll end by going from Montrond to the devil. Keep gay and lively, he says, and never take things too solemnly; then you will live at least another thirty years (they were both quite advanced in years when he wrote this), and I can talk to you and write to you and love you. After that, I shall be happy to wait for you in Paradise. He says he is never serious; yet beneath the poised urbanity with which he says it, we feel the affection which, despite many violent upheavals, must have existed between these two. The passion is there, though it is not expatiated on. It is interesting to note that the only passion which Mme de Sévigné seems to have been unable to cope with was her love, almost pathological in its intensity, for her daughter.

A more subtle case is the celebrated affair of Vatel, on the occasion of the King's visit to the Duke of Condé at Chantilly in 1671. This is worth quoting in full:

> Le roi arriva hier au soir à Chantilly; il courut un cerf au clair de la lune; les lanternes firent des merveilles, le feu d'artifice fut un peu effacé par la clarté de notre amie; mais enfin, le soir, le souper, le jeu, tout alla à merveille. Le temps qu'il a fait aujourd'hui nous faisait espérer une suite digne d'un si agréable commencement. Mais voicy ce que j'apprends en entrant ici, dont je ne puis me remettre, et qui fait que je ne suis plus ce que je vous mande; c'est qu'enfin Vatel, maître d'hotel de M. Fouquet, qui l'était présentement de M. le Prince, cet homme d'une capacité distinguée de toutes les autres, dont la bonne tête était capable de contenir tout le soin d'un Etat; cet homme donc que je connaissais, voyant que ce matin à huit heures la marée n'était pas arrivée, n'a pu soutenir l'affront dont il a cru qu'il allait être accablé, et en un mot, il s'est poignardé. Vous pouvez penser l'horrible désordre qu'un si terrible accident a causé dans cette fête. Songez que la marée est peut-être arrivée comme il expirait. Je n'en sais pas davantage présentement; je pense que vous trouvez que c'est assez. Je ne doute pas que la confusion n'ait été grande; c'est une chose fâcheuse à une fête de cinquante mille écus . . .
>
> M. le Prince le dit au roi fort tristement: on dit que c'etait à force d'avoir de l'honneur à sa manière; on le loua fort, on loua et l'on blama son courage. Le roi dit qu'il y avait cinq ans qu'il retardait de venir à Chantilly, parce qu'il comprenait l'exces de cet embarras. Il dit à M. le Prince qu'il ne devait avoir que deux tables, et ne point se charger de tout; il jura qu'il ne souffrirait plus que M. le Prince en usât ainsi; mais c'etait trop tard pour le pauvre Vatel. Cependant Gourville tâcha de reparer la perte de Vatel; elle fut reparée; on dîna très bien, on fit collation, on soupa, on se promena, on joua, on fut à la chasse; tout était parfumé de jonquilles, tout était enchanté.

This is no doubt a most amusing story; but one may observe that it involves a very complex tissue of emotions. There is of course the contrast between the tragedy of Vatel's suicide and the bathetic circumstances that occasioned it. But the real reasons for his suicide were not trivial at all; they indicate in a remarkable manner how the moral values of the society of Versailles permeated all its manifestations, from highest to lowest. On top of this there is Mme de Sévigné's attitude to be taken account of. Her appreciation of the element of the ridiculous in the situation (it was a shocking thing to happen at a fête that cost 50,000 crowns), even a suggestion of callousness in the way she seems to regard such tragedies as inevitable if unfortunate incidents in the running of an ordered society; these should not lead us to underestimate her sensibility to the issues involved. In this case, after all, the tragedy was only the result of a misunderstanding; for the fish may have arrived, just too late. It was the consequence, society decided, of too nice a sense of honour, which is a good thing. Vatel's action, some thought, showed courage; which is also a virtue. Others thought his response a little in excess of the object; and excess is bad. Even a person as exalted as the King showed delicacy in realizing that his visit was bound to cause trouble one way or another; and the pressure of feeling which poor Vatel must have laboured under can only be imagined. There is plenty of emotion all round; but the admirable maître d'hotel is dead, and tears will not bring him back to life. Meanwhile civilization must go on; so the scent of the jonquils is everywhere, and in short all is delightful.

Some considerable space has been devoted to this apparently unimportant incident because it has so representative a value. Something comparable with its peculiar balance of feelings is observable in the most profound manifestation of the culture of the time. The writings of Sain -Simon are a case in point. He was a man whose creed was guided by *la raison* and *la loi*. However aware he may have become of the imperfections of the *ancien régime*, of its failure to live up to its standards, he none the less believed in those standards profoundly. His preoccupation with details of court etiquette may even prove exasperating to modern readers (for instance his tedious account of *l'affaire de la quête*); and yet his concern for the letter of the law and the urbanity of his mode of expression do not disguise, but serve rather to reinforce, the intensity of his loves and hates. His prose has a colloquial flexibility and sinuosity within its sophistication. The orderly precision of the words, the psychological acumen, acquire an almost reptilian venom; for all the *galanterie* and the *politesse* the words came out like pistol shots:

De ce long et curieux détail il resulte que Monseigneur était sans vice ni vertu, sans lumières ni connoissances quelconques, radicalement incapable d'en acquerir, très paresseux, sans imagination ni production, sans goût, sans choix, sans discernement, né pour l'ennui, qu'il communiquoit aux autres, et pour être une boule roulant au hasard par l'impulsion d'autrui, opiniâtre et petit en tout à l'excès . . . livré aux plus pernicieuses mains, incapable d'en sortir ni de s'en apercevoir, absorbé dans sa graisse et dans ses ténebres, . . . sans avoir aucune volonté de mal faire, il eût été un roi pernicieux.

No one can say that this lacks feeling, or that the feeling is not intensified by the razor-sharp edge of Saint-Simon's mind; just as his criticism is the more valid because we know that when he speaks of *vertu, goût, choix, discernement* and so on, he is not merely using words.

The incident of Vatel is a part of contemporary life; the memoirs of Saint-Simon are perhaps half-way between life and art. With the poets we are a stage further towards the objectifying of the values of life in art, and all the significant poets show the same union of deep and delicate emotion with formal discipline. La Fontaine, for instance, has many qualities in common with Saint-Simon—the sharp intelligence, the slightly acidulated wit, the diction that is close to polite conversation, but still more tautly disciplined; and he has many qualities in common with Mme de Sévigné—the urbanity and poise, together with great nervous sensitivity. He has a sensibility to nature and a sympathy with animals such as are usually supposed to be foreign to his age but these qualities are always subservient to his prime interest in human behaviour. The more one reads La Fontaine, the more he reveals himself as a great traditional *moral* poet. He is witty and charming, of course; but in all his most representative work (we may mention *Le Chêne et le Roseau*) his sensitivity combines with the lucidity of his mind to create a noble emotional power and grandeur. In *La Mort et le Mourant* the passion rises to the heights of tragic art.

But it is in the dramatic poets that the relation between poetic technique and moral values is most clearly indicated. In all of them the formal alexandrine, like Pope's heroic couplet, is an achieved order in poetic technique which corresponds to an achieved order in civilization. The stylized vocabulary is also, as we have seen, indicative of moral values, sanctioned by society; and in each case, to varying degrees, the poet is concerned with the tension between this criterion and personal sensibility—with some kind of conflict between passion and social obligations.

The 'tension' is least marked in the earliest of the writers, Corneille; or at least in his work there is the minimum of ambiguity as to what ought to be the issue of the conflict. His early plays were written in the reign of Louis XIII, and represent a consolidation of values, an attempt to arrive at, to win to, a conception of order and stability:

> *Je suis maître de moi, comme de l'univers.*
> *Je le suis, je veux l'être.*

35

The famous lines splendidly express the connection between personal and social integration, the proud assurance with which it is held, and also the effort of will-power involved ('je veux l'être') in achieving it. But if Corneille was aware of the effort, he had no doubt as to what ought to be its outcome:

> Sur mes passions ma raison souveraine
> Eût blâmé mes soupirs et dissipé ma haine.

He never for a moment doubted that reason ought to dominate passion, and could do so. In a dedicatory epistle to La Place Royale he says:

C'est de vous que j'ai appris que l'amour d'un honnête homme doit être toujours volontaire; que l'on ne doit jamais aimer en un tel point qu'en ne puisse jamais n'aimer pas; que si on en vient jusque-là, c'est une tyrannie dont il faut secouer le joug.

He is quite unequivocal; and his superb conviction echoes through the clang of his alexandrines, through the lucidity with which each word 'stays put', without emotional overtones. He did not advocate a passive acceptance of the code; but he was convinced that the code represented the wisdom of civilization, and that it must withstand all threats from within and without. It was greater than the individual; but it was for individual men to keep it alive as the safeguard of their sanity and happiness, and not to seek to destroy it. Though this was an attitude which could easily droop into complacency, within its limits its nobility, its heroic quality, was authentic.

The above is the conventional account of Corneille; it has not gone unchallenged. One interesting account of his work has suggested that his world, far from being unambiguous, is assailed by fundamental uncertainties and doubts; that his characters, particularly in the later plays, are wilfully living on error. The human will is prized for its power to impose order on chaos, independently of ethical considerations; there might almost seem to be, in Corneille's obsession with the power and the glory of absolutism, an element of psychological compensation for the timidity of his nature and the relative lowliness of his origin. If this account is accepted it gives a slightly different stress to, but does not radically alter, our case. For it would then appear that Corneille regarded order as so important that he was prepared to uphold it even if it entailed in some respects the substitution of error for truth. Such a view of the world must no doubt be considered a confession of failure, in so far as it sacrificed the *grand siècle*'s ideal of a harmonious balance between collective and individual morality. It is, however, a failure that has an element of proud and impressive greatness.

Both Molière and Racine come at the zenith of the reign of the Roi Soleil. They accept the values that Corneille lived by and helped to create, and also the alexandrine and the stylized vocabulary that help to express them; but the tension between these values and the demands of personal sensibility is now more complex. This is demonstrated in the *use which they make* of the alexandrine. Their language has not the ceremonial precision of Corneille's, the rhythms are more flexible, the imagery 'suggests' more; just as, in the paintings of Poussin and Claude, the precise architecture of the proportions, the grouping of tones, the sculpturesque treatment of the figures with their stylized heroic gestures, are enriched by the sensuously evocative quality of the colour. In Molière's case this increased flexibility goes alongside the fact that he wrote comedy rather than heroic tragedy; the language, though still urbane, is less consciously stylized, more close to *galant* conversation. We may observe in this connection that the conversation of so ordered a society slides into art almost without one noticing at what point the metamorphosis happens.

This great plasticity of rhythm and metaphor parallels a deeper psychological interest in the workings of the mind—of the personal consciousness. In Corneille the insistence is primarily on the moral *order*; in Molière the stress is on the complexity of the relations between the moral order and the personal sensibility. This tendency reaches its climax in Molière's greatest play, *Le Misanthrope*, in which the balance between the two groups of interests is maintained with consummate subtlety. To a degree, we are clearly meant to sympathize with Alceste in his attack on the idiocy and potential wickedness of *empty* social conventions; in so far as Célimème represents them they are obviously unsatisfactory. But on the other hand we are clearly meant to feel that the intensity with which Alceste denounces is not altogether admirable; that it springs from a lack of 'integration' in his own personality, and is in a sense adolescent. The poise is held by Philinte, the *honnête homme*, who continually brings Alceste's transports to the bar of *raison*:

37

La parfaite raison fuit toute extrémité,
Et veut que l'on soit sage avec sobriété.

When Alceste breaks out desperately:

Et parfois il me prend des mouvements soudains
De fuir dans un désert l'approche des humains,

Philinte replies:

Mon Dieu, des mœurs du temps mettons-nous moins en peine,
Et faisons un peu grace à la nature humaine.

All the satire of the frivolous time-serving courtiers, the play seems to say, is justified, and the imperfections of society are manifold. But society *is* human life, and it is for human beings to make it work; running away into deserts is no answer at all. In no play of Molière, however, is the difficulty of the issues more subtly indicated. Mr Turnell has even suggested that Molière himself was beginning to grow doubtful about his positives; for nobody in the play seems to find Philinte's reasonable advice either helpful or convincing. This is a point to which we shall return later.

Molière was less roughly handled than Corneille by nineteenth-century critics because he wrote comedy rather than tragedy, and therefore had more excuse for not being sufficiently 'poetic'. Racine is a heroic writer, like Corneille; but his verse, which is tragic in a sense which the earlier poet did not attain to, has emotional overtones in plenty. Perhaps the nineteenth-century critics vaguely realized this when they invented the legend of the 'tender' Racine; though in some ways this may have been an even more damaging misrepresentation. Couperin, as we shall see, has suffered from something similar.

In Racine, as in Molière, the stress is centred on the threat to organized society occasioned by the unruly impulses of the individual. But whereas Molière emphasizes the folly involved in submission to the passions, so that his work is both serious and funny, Racine emphasizes the evil. The intensity of passion in his characters, especially Phèdre, sometimes breaks down the conventional norm; but it is only because of the existence of the norm that the effect of the passion is overwhelming. The sudden glimpses of an unsuspected world in the dark reaches of the mind which the imagery and movement reveal to us, are the more terrible because they appear against the background of 'les bornes de l'austère pudeur'; we have learned afresh in the last forty years that in a world of violence, violence may cease to shock. Racine's psychological penetration and his poetry are one and the same. They suggest that he is a greater poet than Corneille not because he believed less in Corneille's positives, but because he relates these positives to so very much wider a range of experience.

Phèdre is an analysis of evil—or of the effects of evil—more comprehensive and profound than anything attempted by Corneille, who was not much interested in evil as a problem of the individual. But Racine's greater subtlety is revealed still more remarkably in his last play *Athalie*, which deals not only with the consequences of sin in relation to man and society, but for the first time with the relation between man and God. That this play can so identify *la loi* with spiritual sanctions is a testimony to the greatness of his civilization; it is paralleled only in the greatest work of Couperin and La Lande. But while this spiritual interpretation of *la loi* was a possible one, it was not habitual. It was also possible for *la loi* to become synonymous with brute force; it was possible for it to destroy the very things it had been intended to preserve.

La Bruyère cynically remarked that a *dévôt* is a man who under an atheist king would be an atheist; and Mazarin advised his nieces to hear Mass for the world's sake, if not for God's. Yet although there was, particularly in the latter part of the reign after Louis's conversion, a good deal of purely fashionable religion, one would not say that the average religion of the time was insincere. If there was an increasing tendency for convents to become homes for the unmarriageable but unvicious, and if there was a large number of priests, like Cardinal de Retz, who were really politicians, there were also good priests like the Jesuit Bourdaloue, who with genuine piety stressed the potential ethical significance of the values of the time. In the sermons of Bourdaloue and Bossuet and in the writings of Fénelon, there is a mixture of qualities—of imaginative passion, psychological penetration and abstract logical argument—very similar to that in the higher manifestations of the poetry and drama. But perhaps one could say that it was the mastery of logical argument, among these qualities, which excited such remarkable enthusiasm in congregations during the great days of the classical epoch, and in this

39

connection we may note this significant comment of Mme de Sévigné: 'Le maréchal de Gramont était l'autre jour si transporté de la beauté d'un sermon de Bourdaloue, qu'il s'écria tout haut, en un endroit qui le toucha, *Mordi, il a raison!*'

The religion of the age, that is, did not normally signify much in purely spiritual terms. It is certainly legitimate to suggest that Racine's *Athalie* entailed a conception of spiritual, even of mystical values which, although not unique, was exceptional. It is probable that Racine saw some analogy between the persecution of the Israelites and that of the Jansenists in his own day. And although there is no *necessary* connection between the spirituality of *Athalie* and Racine's conversion to Jansenism, none the less *Athalie* does help us to appreciate the significance of the Jansenist movement in the world of the Roi Soleil. Corneille's heroic plays suggest that through reason and the human will order may be attained and preserved; Racine's tragic plays suggest that reason and the human will are helpless without the intervention of God's grace. Whereas the Cornelian hero believes that he is 'maître de moi comme de l'univers', Racine's heroine says 'je crains de me connoître en l'état où je suis'. Implicitly, Racine makes the same point about the corruption of the world in which he lived as Mme de Maintenon makes when she says:

Otez ces filles qui ne respirent que le monde. . . . Otez ces beaux esprits qui dédaignent tout ce qui est simple, qui s'ennuient de cette vie uniforme, de ces plaisirs doux et innocents et qui désirent de *faire leur volonté.* (My italics.)

Implicitly, Racine offers a criticism of the Cartesian view of the destiny of man to which Corneille in the main adheres.

Descartes's mechanical view of nature, his belief in the sovereignty of reason as the only means of obtaining knowledge of material things, presented the *grand siècle* with a philosophical formulation of the values it lived by. 'The whole is greater than the parts' is a creed reflected no less in social behaviour than in the administration of Colbert, the gardens of Le Nôtre, the theatre music of Lully, the buildings of Mansart, the decorations of Lebrun; and the aesthetic theories of Boileau are an exact counterpart of Cartesian philosophy, for both attempt to interpret nature through reason, deprecate enthusiasm, start empirically from the present moment, and are completely non-historical. (To Molière, Gothic cathedrals were odious monstrosities of the ignorant centuries.) Moreover, like most of the people of his time, Descartes reconciled his instinct for rationality and order with a profound interest in the workings of the human mind, expressed in the *Traité des Passions de l'âme*. Here he demonstrates that the passions are good in themselves; that evil consists in the wrong or immoderate use of them; and that only through reason can one decide which use is justified, which is not. Descartes, like Lully and Corneille, remained formally a Catholic, and his theories of the absolute and infinite Thought which our individual thoughts presuppose were much exploited by Catholic theologians as a 'rational' proof of God's existence. Even the Jansenists found in the pre-determinist aspects of his thought something which seemed superficially to support their beliefs. But in the most important respects Descartes's thought was fundamentally non-religious. Bossuet, the exponent of Catholic orthodoxy, perceived that the insistence on the pre-eminence of reason inevitably led to free thought; Pascal, more profoundly, realized that Descartes's teaching was inimical to the concept of Grace.

In some respects a man of the new world, a brilliant mathematician imbued with the spirit of scientific curiosity, and at first himself a Cartesian, Pascal was at the same time of a fervently religious temperament rather alien to the outlook of his age. It was his intellectual equipment that disposed of the Cartesian proof of God's existence; it was his religious temperament that, when once he had exposed the fallacies which in his opinion made Cartesianism not a bulwark of Christianity but its potential destroyer, led him to develop his notion of the dual reasons of heart and mind. The heart has its reasons, of which *raison* knows nothing. Descartes, he said, would much have preferred to have dispensed with God in the whole of his intellectual system, but had to bring Him in to set his mechanistic universe in motion; that done, Descartes had no further use for Him. But to Pascal, whose natural proclivities were encouraged by the Jansenist preoccupation with St Augustine and by his long brooding over the stoicism of Montaigne, the opposition between good and evil cannot be explained in purely rational terms; and the proof of the existence of God lies in the misery of man without Him.

Such an attitude goes to enforce a peculiar gloom. The proofs of

Original Sin and of the Fall are all around one in cynicism, scepticism and folly; only through the crucified Christ can sin be redeemed. Crucifixion, in one form or another, is the only hope of life to come, and by inference the only tolerable form of life here and now. Beneath the suave lucidity which characterizes not only the prose of the *Lettres Provinçiales* but even the casual epigrammatic jottings of the *Pensées*, the mystic's ecstasy of self-immolation burns with unquenchable passion. We can see something similar in the tautness of line which gives such tension to the apparently tranquil paintings of Pascal's and Arnauld's friend, Philippe de Champagne.

Naturally, the group of Solitaries who met and meditated at the Cistercian nunnery of Port Royal did not normally carry their religious fervour as far as Pascal's Augustinian abnegation; but their outlook did have a two-fold relation to the life of the time. In a positive sense it was a recognition that there were aspects of experience which the values of the contemporary world were apt to neglect. From this point of view it is not, of course, to be considered in narrowly sectarian terms. Jansenism did not necessarily involve religious partisanship. The Jesuit Bourdaloue and people such as Mme de Maintenon and Mme de Sévigné who were the intimates of Jesuit circles were impregnated with Jansenism; just as the cleric Fénelon, who took the side of the Jesuits in the controversy over efficacious grace, could support the case of the later quietist sect in the affair of Mme Guyon.

And then in a negative sense, it was a reaction from the world of Versailles, with its absolute identification of Church and State; it was not so much a search for new values as an admission that the vitality of society depended on a balance between organization and human impulses which seemed in danger of growing lop-sided. So elaborately organized a world, calling for so much unity and conformity, could exist only under a despotism. Racine had dreamed that that despotism might be the rule of the Holy Spirit; Saint-Simon, looking back, saw clearly that it had become the despotism not of God, but of an arrogant man, self-deified, so afraid of *la vérité* that he had to surround himself with an army of sycophants who would tell him what he wanted to believe, and nothing else. In Racine's attitude there was still something of mediaevalism; the course of history represented the triumph and the tragedy of the Cornelian ideal of 'maître de moi'. The identification of King and God is revealed in a famous passage from La Bruyère:

Qui considérera que le visage du prince fait toute la félicité du courtisan, qu'il s'occupe et se remplit pendant toute sa vie de le voir et d'en être vu, comprendra un peu comment voir Dieu peut faire toute la gloire et tout le bonheur des Saints;

while in a sermon on the occasion of the Dauphin's birth, Senault compared Louis with God the Father and the Dauphin with Christ. Louis himself said, 'Celui qui a donné des rois aux hommes a voulu qu'on les respectât comme ses lieutenants'. We must remember however that the King's absolutism obtained an enormous popular support; and this was partly due to the fact that the peasants and bourgeoisie felt that the only alternative was the anarchy of the nobility and the horrors of the Fronde.

It is easy to exaggerate the degree to which the court culture was removed from everyday life; we shall later note plenty of evidence that it preserved some contact with popular elements. Most of the great artists of the time were not professional courtiers, and many of them never even visited Versailles. Yet there is some truth in the conventional account that the artificial removal of the court from the centre of French life in Paris has a quasi-symbolical significance. In a sense, it was only because the court was self-enclosed and homogeneous that it could evolve such lucid moral values, and achieve such subtlety and depth within them. But it is interesting that a person of such exquisite nervous adjustment as Mme de Sévigné can write with callous indifference of the sufferings of people outside her circle; that she can cheerfully describe the breaking on the wheel of an itinerant musician involved in a provincial rebellion, casually remark that the hanging of sixty scapegoats is to begin tomorrow, and conclude with the pious reflection that this will no doubt serve as a lesson to any others who might be thinking of throwing stones into their betters' gardens. Significantly, it is only after the midsummer of the culture that a humane sympathy with other spheres of life begins—in the painting of Chardin for instance—to manifest itself. As we shall see, there is perhaps an anticipation of this in some of Couperin's later clavecin pieces.

Towards the latter end of the reign the appreciation of the dangers latent in its autocracy assumed, in many of the most acute minds of the time, the proportions of a social conscience. Saint-Simon criticized the absolutism of the King, the cult of *la gloire* and war, the misery it brought in its wake, and the ultimate stupidity of it:

C'est donc avec grande raison qu'on doit déplorer avec larmes l'horreur d'une éducation uniquement dressée pour étouffer l'esprit et le cœur de ce prince, le poison abominable de la flatterie la plus insigne, qui le déifia dans la sein même du christianisme, et la cruelle politique de ces ministres, qui l'enferma, et qui pour leur grandeur, leur puissance et leur fortune l'enivrerent de son autorité, de sa grandeur, de sa gloire jusqu'à le corrompre, et à étouffer en lui, sinon toute la bonté, l'équité, le desir de connôitre la verité, que Dieu lui avoit donné, au moins l'émoussèrent presque entièrement, et empêchèrent au moins sans cesse qu'il fît aucun usage de ces vertus, dont son royaume et lui-même furent les victimes.

Fénelon is no less severe:

Quelle détestable maxime que de ne croire trouver sa sûreté que dans l'oppression de ses peuples. . . . Est-ce le vrai chemin qui mêne à la gloire? Souvenez-vous que les pays où la domination du souverain est plus absolue sont eux où les souverains sont moins puissants. Ils prennent, ils ruinent tout, ils possèdent seuls tout l'Etat; mais tout l'Etat languit. Les campagnes sont en friche et presque désertes; les villes diminuent chaque jour, le commerce tarit. Le roi, qui ne peut être roi tout seul, et qui n'est grand que par ses peuples, s'anéantit lui-même peu à peu par l'anéantissement de ses peuples dont il tire ses richesses et sa puissance. . . . Le mépris, la haine, le ressentiment, la défiance, en un mot toutes les passions se réunissent contre une autorité si odieuse.

This sombre vision is reinforced by La Fontaine's moving fable of *La Mort et Le Bûcheron*, and by La Bruyère's terrible picture of life in the country districts:

L'on voit certains animaux farouches . . . répandues par la campagne, noirs, livides, et tout brûlés de soleil, attachés à la terre, qu'ils fouillent et qu'ils remuent avec une opiniâtreté invincible. . . . Quand ils se lèvent sur leurs pieds, ils montrent une face humaine; et en effet ils sont des hommes. Ils se retirent la nuit dans des tanières où ils vivent de pain noir, d'eau, et de racines;

though we must remember that conditions in the countryside varied enormously, and that in many parts a rural folk culture was still very vigorous. We must remember too that the mere fact that Saint-Simon, Fénelon, La Bruyère and many others can write such astringent criticism is itself testimony to the intellectual honesty which their society permitted them. Their account must be qualified by the manifest achievements of Versailles, which they not only appreciate, but represent. None the less, the weakness is there; and how inseparably it is linked with the virtues is demonstrated most subtly in Mme de La Fayette's great novel, *La Princesse de Clèves*.

The world here described by Mme de La Fayette is one in which the existence of absolute values is accepted as unquestionably as are standards of manners; the characters speak of *la vérité*, *l'honneur* and so on without any conscious ambiguity. The theme of the book is the analysis, within this scheme of values, of the passions of personal relationships, particularly sexual passion. With great subtlety we are shown how, in such a closely ordered society, personal life is inevitably mixed with public; how *amour* merges into *intrigue*, and that into *affaires*. Between private and public life a balance ought to be maintained. But what in fact seems to happen is that *amour* reveals a fatal disparity between public affairs and the ideal absolute values that are supposed to give them meaning. Order is meaningless apart from what, in human terms, is ordered; yet in practice society does not regulate *amour*, but *amour* proves that the pretensions of society are not what they seem. It destroys tranquillity of mind, and ultimately, therefore, civilization:

L'ambition et la galanterie étoient l'âme de cette Cour (the book is ostensibly set in the court of Henri II, but this is no more than a tactful disguise for the contemporary court) et occupoient tous les hommes et les femmes. Il y avoit tant d'interêts et tant de cabales différentes, et les dames y avaient tant de part, que l'amour étoit toujours mêlé aux affaires, et les affaires à l'amour, Personne n'étoit tranquille ni indifférent; on songeoit à s'élever, à plaire, à servir, ou à nuire; on ne connoissoit ni l'ennui ni l'oisiveté et on étoit toujours occupé des plaisirs ou des intrigues.

This attitude is similar to that expressed in more dolorous terms by La Bruyère:

Il ya un pays où les joies sont visibles, mais fausses, et les chagrins cachés, mais réels. Qui croirait que l'empressement pour les spectacles, que les éclats et les applaudissements aux théâtres de Molière et d'Arlequin, les repas, la chasse, les ballets, les carrousels couvrissent tant d'inquiétudes, de soins et de divers intérêts, tant de craintes et d'espérances, des passions si vives et des affaires si sérieuses?

and broadly parallel to that expressed by Molière in *Le Misanthrope*; and while possibly Molière and certainly Racine would have said that the remedy was not to have less love but to have more wisdom in dealing with it, there is here a paradox by which many sensitive and intelligent people of the time must have been bewildered. There is no easy solution to it. The end of the book, the woman's entry into the convent, is as much an evasion of the issues as Alceste's threat to run off into the desert, since there is no evidence that the Princess has experienced any spiritual conversion. Such a religious solution almost certainly calls for some special aptitude, and a type of mind similar to that of Racine, Pascal or Couperin. The Jansenists, one imagines, must have been composed partly of people like Pascal, partly of people whose motives resembled those of the Princesse de Clèves; and there can be no doubt that in the society as a whole the Princesses de Clèves must greatly have outnumbered the Racines and the Pascals.

In some ways comparable with the entry of Mme de La Fayette's heroine into the convent is Louis's own belated religiosity—as opposed to the religious emotion of the Jansenists, whom the God-King persecuted as being rebellious to the State Church and to his absolute authority. The great age of the Roi Soleil was over, internal corruption was increasing, *la gloire* was not what it had been. The succession of military triumphs began to be succeeded by an equally monotonous series of defeats. Despondency echoed hollowly through the corridors of Versailles, and the King pathetically pretended, perhaps even believed—for he was not consciously insincere—that *la gloire* was not what he had lived for; that his nature, at least under the influence of Mme de Maintenon, was essentially religious; that he liked nothing so much as to be alone with God. So this King of the Sun, who abhorred limited horizons, retired to a damp, forest-enclosed house in a mean valley at Marly ('un méchant village, sans clôture, sans vue, ni moyens d'en avoir, un repaire de serpents et de charognes, de crapauds et de grenouilles', Saint-Simon called it); rather like—to descend from the sublime to the tawdry—another addict of power, Henry Ford, who in his old age became a passionate antiquarian, buying up quaint old pubs, rebuilding the old farm home stead just as it was when he was a lad, trying to put everything back, as Dos Passos put it, 'as it was in the days of horses and buggies'. It almost seems that Louis himself came to accept the irony of La Bruyère; 'Un esprit sain puise à la cour le goût de la solitude et de la retraite'. The deeper irony of the position is that Louis could not escape his self-imposed destiny. He ended by transforming his successive retreats from pomp and circumstance into the very thing he had been seeking to avoid. Marly grew into a miniature Versailles; just as Ford's rural homesteads glittered with Every Modern Convenience.

It was in the more melancholy latter end of Louis's reign that Couperin's genius matured. Of course the gradual changes cannot have been very perceptible to someone working within that self-enclosed circle; and it would be utterly erroneous to find anything valedictory in Couperin's classical, positive, and on the whole serene art. But we might be justified in saying that the conditions under which he worked influenced his outlook in two unobtrusive, connected ways. They imbued some of his music with a sensuous tenderness and wistfulness beneath its elegant bearing which, like the comparable quality in the painting of his great contemporary Watteau, springs from an apprehension of transience; from a recognition that all this graciousness and beauty must pass away, perhaps quite soon. And they encouraged him to develop the religious aspect of his genius which produced his greatest work and is as much more 'spiritual' in conception than Lully's ceremonial art, as Racine's late work is more spiritual than that of Corneille. (I shall hope in the course of this book to demonstrate, in terms of the technique of music, what I mean by these generalizations.)

Couperin's music thus gives an oddly subtle impression of being simultaneously of his world, and not of it; just as the world of Watteau's pictures is simultaneously the real world, and a golden, idealized, never-never land of the spirit. In one sense, Couperin may still be the *galant homme*, the symbol of civilization painted competently if not very profoundly by men such as Mignard and Hyacinthe Rigaud. In another sense, he is the black-robed figure who, in some paintings of Watteau, beside the merry throng discoursing and flirting with such gracious urbanity, stands quietly in his corner, seeming to suggest not that the junketings are meaningless, the gestures empty, the urbanity a sham, but that, though the company may be delightful, one may be lonely, still. This is something much more complex and valuable than the emotion of nostalgia; it is an achieved equilibrium which, for being sensitive, is no less strong. It was because Paris, 'le théâtre des scènes tendres et galantes', seemed to be becoming a place where 'chacun y est occupé de ses chagrins et de sa misère', that many sensitive spirits sought in a mythical Ile de Cythère a civilization that was not subject to calumniating Time,

47

where age and bitterness and the complexity of human emotions did not destroy the qualities that make civilization possible:

> Venez dans l'île de Cythère
> En pélerinage avec nous,
> Jeune fille n'en revient guère
> Ou sans amant ou sans époux,
> Et l'on y fait sa grande affaire
> Des amusements les plus doux.

This was not merely an escape. It was an attempt to achieve in art something which the real world could not give. The world which Watteau and Couperin present to us is one in which the codes and the values of the time are not frustrated—as they so painfully were in real life—by people's wickedness or stupidity; in which there is no disparity between intention and realization. In this connection it seems to me no accident that in the last years of the seventeenth century appeared the work of the King and Queen of fairy-tale writers, Charles Perrault and Mme d'Aulnoy. It is important to remember that, at their very much slighter level, these tales are not unallied to the religious aspects of the art of Couperin and Racine.

The society of Louis XIV was not unique in producing some of its most consummate artistic manifestations when its end was near; one could say almost as much of Shakespeare's society. But in approaching Couperin it is not the decline we should think of; we should remember the beauty and magnificence of the achievements of this society rather than the gossip and intrigue, and the more idiotic affectations of court etiquette.[5] It was in the walks of the Tuileries that Racine absentmindedly declaimed his tragedies to a group of labourers on the waterworks; it was in the theatres and salons of this community that Lully and Molière talked over their latest enterprise, that La Fontaine told his immortal fables, and Perrault his no less immortal tales. Make all the qualifications you like, but how many times has there been a better environment for an artist to be born into? Perrault was justified when he said of Versailles:

> Ce n'est pas un Palais, c'est une ville entière,
> Superbe en sa grandeur, superbe en sa matière,
> Non, c'est plutôt un Monde, où du grand Univers
> Se trouvent rassemblez les miracles divers.

[5] It was a popular saying that courtiers had three things to remember: speak well of everyone, ask for everything that is going, and sit down when you get the chance.

Chapter Three

Taste during the Grand Siècle

La belle Antiquité fut toujours vénerable,
Mais je ne crus jamais qu'elle fust adorable.
Je voy les Anciens, sans plier les génoux,
Ils sont grands, il est vray, mais hommes comme nous:
Et l'on peut comparer sans craindre d'être injuste,
Le Siècle de Louis au beau siècle d'Auguste.
        PERRAULT: *Le Siècle de Louis le Grand.*
            Parallèle des Anciens et des Modernes

IN THE LAST chapter we have tried to give some idea of the values
and moral concepts of the world which Couperin inherited. In a
general sense these values conditioned the ways in which he felt and
thought, and therefore the nature of his music; but we can adequately
assess their influence on his art only if we supplement our general
remarks on the values of the time with some more particular comments on the evolution of taste and on the relation between the artist
and the *grand siècle* audience. For it is not too much to say that the
taste of Couperin's day was the consequence of a long maturing
which had gone on more or less continuously since the beginning of
the seventeenth century. Only against this background are some
aspects of Couperin's art intelligible.

The classical conception of a lofty, noble, and heroic art, apposite
to a heroic mode of life, was originally associated with the Renaissance attempt to establish a finer discrimination in social tone. The
civilizing influence of women in the early years of the century did
more than create a taste for the exquisite. The tremendous vogue
for Honoré d'Urfé's interminable pastoral romance *L'Astree* was
attributable not so much to its literary merits—though it was not
devoid of graciousness—as to the fact that it offered a primer of good
manners; a chivalric code going back not only to French, Spanish

49

and Italian pastoral romances of the sixteenth century, but still more to the troubadours. Women, the ornaments of the world, were to be served and worshipped; and in the pages of *L'Astrée* men could learn how to serve them, the phrases to use, the gestures to indulge in, the refinements of approach and response. If at one level this seemed frivolous enough, it offered opportunities for civilized intercourse which the more intelligent and sensitive were quick to seize upon. Soon Mme de Rambouillet's Blue Room was providing an environment in which men and women could meet together to discuss seriously, within a scheme of conventional courtesies, not only the etiquette of love, but all aspects of human behaviour and psychology, the values and standards of art, even grammar. The Hôtel de Rambouillet offered a series of rules for living, and a rallying point where artists could meet to discuss their work, as members of society honoured by virtue of their calling. Moreover, it provided for those artists an audience which, though not large, had high discrimination and an adult morality. Mme de Scudéry's fictional description of such a society was not so far from the reality in its heyday:

On y voit sans doute, comme ailleurs, des gens qui ont une fausse galanterie insupportable; mais, à parler généralement, il y a je ne sais quel esprit de politesse, qui regne dans cette cour, qui la rend fort agréable et qui fait qu'on y trouve effectivement un nombre incroyable d'hommes fort accomplis. Et ce qui les rend tels est que les gens de qualité de Phénicie ne font pas profession d'être dans une ignorance grossière de toutes sortes de sciences, comme on en voit en quelques autres cours où on s'imagine qu'un homme qui sait se servir d'une épée doit ignorer toutes les autres choses; au contraire il n'y a presque pas un homme de condition à notre cour qui ne sache juger assez délicatement des beaux ouvrages, et qui ne cherche du moins à se faire honneur en honorant ceux qui savent plus que lui.

This was not a society of specialists, but of people whose 'education' covered every aspect of their lives.

From the early years of the century, the civilizing tendency in social behaviour is accompanied by a civilizing classicism in literature. Both the salon of Mme de Rambouillet and the aesthetic of Malherbe banned 'low' words and provincialisms; and Malherbe's insistence on lucidity and purity of style in poetry was influenced by the growing tendency for men of fashion, the representatives of the *salons*, to intermingle with the professional men of letters. The nobility increasingly dabbled in literary and musical composition, and the professional writers and musicians were increasingly accepted in aristocratic society; most of the leading artists in the great classical period were to come from bourgeois stock, later to be ennobled by Louis. In general, Malherbe's critical aesthetic is a remarkable anticipation of full-flown classicism, as is Richelieu's transformation of a polite literary circle into the Académie française. Balzac's polishing of the cadences of his prose, and Vaugelas's work on the dictionary and his *Remarques sur la langue française*, aimed to regulate language not in accordance with an abstract system of rules, but with the usage of 'la plus saine partie de la cour et des écrivains du temps'. We may note as an example of the centralizing tendencies of the time, that whereas Malherbe had said that the language of poetry ought to contain no phrase that an educated Parisian could not understand, in Vaugelas's prescription the model is narrowed to that of the court.

None of these men was himself remarkable for creative genius; their formalizing influence was, however, of as great an importance as was that of Mme de Rambouillet in the field of social conduct. In the works of the minor but truly creative poets who, though they jeered at Malherbe, would not have written as they did but for his work, we can find a combination of exquisite sensibility with nobility of bearing which is the product of a high degree of civilization. And this is something which survives in La Fontaine and, despite many cultural upheavals, well into Couperin's day. We can trace some relation between the simultaneous exquisiteness and gravity of one of Couperin's pastoral pieces and, say, a lyric of Tristan l'Hermite, for 'exquisiteness' is not a characteristic of the classical age itself. Perhaps, too, the measured nobility of the great chaconnes of the clavecinists has something of the lofty purity of the odes and elegies of the early years of the century.

The society of the Blue Room had created a public with standards both of technique and morality. It was perhaps inevitable that as it grew in size it should decline in quality. The great days of the salon were over by 1650; its material growth outpaced its moral growth, and its standards were overlaid by a veneer of immature sophistication. Something of this is expressed in a passage from La Bruyère:

Voiture et Scarron étaient nés pour leur siècle, et ils ont paru dans un temps où il semble qu'ils étaient attendus; s'ils s'étaient moins pressés de venir, ils arriveraient trop tard, et j'ose douter qu'ils fussent tels aujourd'hui qu'ils ont été alors: les conversations légères, les cercles, la fine plaisanterie, les enjouées et familières, les petites parties où l'on était admis seulement avec de l'esprit, tout a disparu. Et qu'on ne dise point qu'ils le feraient revivre; ce que je puis faire en faveur de leur esprit est de convenir que peut-être ils excelleraient dans un autre genre; mais les femmes sont de nos jours ou dévotes, ou coquettes, ou joueuses, ou ambitieuses, quelques-unes même tout cela à la fois; le goût de la faveur, le jeu, les galants, les directeurs, ont pris la place, et la défendent contre les gens d'esprit.

Of course the excesses of the *précieuses*—the ultimate inability to call a spade a spade—were the development of elements which were present in the society of Mme de Rambouillet. In the salons of Mlle de Scudéry and of the other successors of the original Hôtel de Rambouillet, however, the conventional stylizations of language and behaviour gradually came to have a less intimate relation to life. Mlle de Scudéry's super-subtle attempts to define *la galanterie* are an indication of the atmosphere of the precious mid-century:

Cependant cet air galant dont j'entends parler ne consiste point précisément à avoir beaucoup d'esprit, beaucoup de jugement, et beaucoup de savoir, et c'est quelque chose de si particulier et de si difficile à acquerir quand on ne l'a point, qu'on ne sait où le prendre ni où le chercher. Car enfin je connois un homme que toute la compagnie connoît aussi, qui est bien fait, qui a de l'esprit, qui est magnifique en train, en meubles et en habillements, qui est propre, qui parle judicieusement et juste, qui de plus fait ce qu'il peut pour avoir l'air galant, et qui cependant est le moins galant de tous les hommes. . . . Je suis persuadé qu'il faut que la nature mette du moins dans l'esprit et dans la personne de ceux qui doivent avoir l'air galant une certaine disposition de le recevoir; il faut de plus que le grand commerce du monde et de la cour aide encore à le donner; et il faut aussi que la conversation des femmes le donne aux hommes . . . je dirai encore qu'il faut même qu'un homme ait eu, du moins une fois de sa vie, quelque légère inclination amoureuse pour acquérir parfaitement l'air galant.

The epics and romances of such writers as Chapelain and Madeleine de Scudéry, with their jargon of *galanterie*, their ludicrously flattering portraits of commonplace people, were an inflation beyond the bounds of sense of qualities which had once been admirable. They were the result of the too rapid growth of a reading public, for they appealed to a public which was educated enough to toy with the externals of the *galant* conventions, without being sufficiently educated to understand what, for the original circle, those conventions had stood for. La Bruyère gives a trenchant account of this bogus education:

Avec cinq où six termes de l'art, et rien de plus, l'on se donne pour connoisseur en musique, en tableaux, en batîments, et en bonne chère; l'on croit avoir plus de plaisir qu'un autre à entendre, à voir, et à manger; l'on impose à ses semblables et l'on se trompe soi-même. La cour n'est jamais dénuée d'un certain nombre de gens en qui l'usage du monde, la politesse ou la fortune tiennent lieu d'esprit et suppléent au mérite; ils savent entrer et sortir, ils se tirent de la conversation en ne s'y mêlant point, ils plaisent à force de se taire, et se rendent importants par un silence longtemps soutenu, ou tout au plus par quelques monosyllables; ils payent de mines, d'un geste, et d'un sourire. Ils n'ont pas, si je l'ose dire, deux pouces de profondeur: si vous les enfoncez, vous rencontrez le tuf.

The members of Mme de Rambouillet's society wanted to purify language as well as behaviour, but they did not deliberately put the stress on the *difference* of their language from that of ordinary people, as did the *précieuses* of the mid-century, according to Somaize's *Grand Dictionnaire des Prétieuses*, published in 1661. Moreover, the very last thing that members of the Blue Room would have said was that, even in matters of pleasure and entertainment, they valued imagination more than truth.

At the same time we cannot regard the *précieux* phase of the middle years of the century merely as the decline of a highly developed civilization. The cheaper sophistication prevalent during the early years of the Fronde, after the retirement of Mme de Rambouillet and of Julie d'Angennes, was an inevitable consequence of the expansion of a homogeneous group, and the part it played in moulding the taste of the time was far from ephemeral. At its best the *précieux* vocabulary was as much a part of Corneille's moral code as was the neo-Platonic conception of love he inherited from *L'Astree*. Even Molière, who delivered a frontal assault on the affectations of the *Précieuses Ridicules*, assimilated much of the love-etiquette of *préciosité* and employed its stylized vocabulary not only in verse but in prose as well. In a musical form it appears, we shall see, in the technique of the lutenists, and Chambonnières' ornamentation may be considered a manifestation of it. Even as late as Couperin's day its influence is still discernible.

One literary form which the cult of *préciosité* assumed was a consciously naïve, archaizing, pseudo-popular style of occasional poetry, invented by the celebrated wit of Mme de Rambouillet's salon, Vincent Voiture. About the middle of the century, this type of 'marotic' verse—so called because of its deliberate introduction of archaisms mostly taken from the work of Clément Marot—became highly fashionable, and it was perfected by La Fontaine in the early part of his career. The work of the Jesuit Du Cerceau, one of the most admired humorous poets of the day, proves that in Couperin's time the marotic line was still vigorous; Du Cerceau wrote a preface to the first re-edition of Villon in 1723, in which he treats Villon as a forerunner of the marotic vein. Certainly there is an aspect of Couperin's work—a consciously popular manner, a sophisticatedly naïve interest in 'old' French things which are regarded as at once *naturels* and *ingénieux*—which relates back to this tradition: and we may mention too the elegantly rustic *galanteries* which Bodin de Boismortier composed for flutes, bagpipes, and hurdy-gurdy.

Closely associated with this type of occasional verse was the burlesque tradition, an outpouring of sophisticated high-spirits which were irresponsible because uncritical. Practised mainly by Scarron and d'Assoucy, burlesque was a travesty of classical literature in an affectedly 'low' language, a smart game intentionally inverting the precepts both of Malherbe and of Mme de Rambouillet.[6] Spanish and Italian drama and literature, particularly Marini, were absorbed into a local convention, devised to meet a popular demand. The nobler spirits protested against it; Poussin for instance dismissed Scarron's *Typhon* as 'dégoûtant'. None the less, the burlesque manner influenced the outlook of the century. Couperin's pieces 'dans le goût burlesque' are not unrelated to it; certainly they have an oblique connection with it through the *commedia dell'arte*.

The Italian players, with their stylized and yet improvisatory art, had been cultivated in France all through the sixteenth and early seventeenth century. There is a reference to a 'Maistre André italien' and his company as early as 1530, the celebrated Gelosi troup were in France in 1571, and Isabella Andreini, as cultured and distinguished as she was beautiful, died in France in 1604, her memory being fêted all over Europe. During the first half of the seventeenth century, the

[6] The burlesque tradition is later found in theatre music, as well as in literature and the drama. A parody of the Lully-Quinault opera *Phaéton* was extremely popular in Paris, towards the end of the century. It may have had some bearing on the growth of the English ballad opera.

companies of the Accesi and the Fedeli were in repeated demand in France. But it was not until the mid-century that the vogue reached its height, and until 1660 that the Italian players, at the instigation of Mazarin, founded a permanent Parisian group. The great Scaramouche Fiorilli at one time lodged and worked in collaboration with Molière himself, at the Petit Bourbon; the story of the friendship between them, and of the way Molière incorporated many aspects of the Italian theatre into the French comedy, is well known. Other celebrated Italian players, including Biancolelli as Harlequin, were intermittently in the French company, and the conventional *commedia* characters soon became a part, not only of the French theatre, but of French popular culture. As Louis, swayed by Mme de Maintenon, grew more sober-minded with advancing years, the vogue of the Italian players declined, until in 1697 they were expelled for having made some tactless witticism at the expense of *la fausse prude*. But their reign had lasted long enough to make a profound impression on the sensibilities of the young Couperin and Watteau. There is a moving picture of their farewell by Watteau; and in all his work, and in Couperin's pantomime, harlequin and other pieces *dans le goût burlesque*, the old stylizations are rarefied and immortalized. Here we can gain some notion of the beauty, pathos and wit that the improvization of such highly cultured and imaginative artists as Isabella Andreini, Fiorilli, and Biancolelli must have given to the conventional framework, in the heyday of the *commedia*. Like Shakespearean tragedy, the *commedia* appealed at a number of different levels. It was of course a popular entertainment; but for those who had eyes to see and ears to hear, that was not the whole story.

Here however we are not concerned with what the *commedia* meant to a Couperin or a Watteau; we are concerned with it as an aspect of taste during the middle years of the century; and in this respect one might legitimately correlate the hardening of the official attitude to its frivolity with Boileau's attack on the various facets of *préciosité*. There are certainly many signs, round about the sixteen-sixties, that a fresh start was considered necessary; we may perhaps best appreciate the significance of, for instance, La Rochefoucauld's rather sentimental (*mélancolique*) cynicism if we see in it a recognition that the conventional counters of etiquette were becoming divorced from their moral implications, so that *la vérité* began to look suspiciously like self-interest. Within the narrow range of experience which he allowed himself, La Rochefoucauld had an acute insight, typical of his time; none the less he is, despite the metallic precision of his comments, the product of a phase of relative decadence. The Great Age might have countered his arguments with the words of Vauvenargues: 'Le corps a ses grâces, l'esprit a ses talents; le cœur n'aurait-il que des vices, et l'homme capable de raison, serait-il incapable de vertu?'

Boileau has been much castigated for his inadequate appreciation of the great poets of his time, yet his pedestrian approach has value in so far as it sums up ideals and opinions from which even the greatest, consciously or unconsciously, profited. His critical aesthetic had two main, interlinked purposes. One was to establish a criterion of naturalness and lucidity, in opposition to the unreality of *préciosité*; in this he was the climax of the tradition which had been established by Malherbe. The other was to insist on the relationship between aesthetic and moral standards. He wanted to give the growing and comparatively irresponsible reading public a standard of reference by reminding it of classical achievements. Roughly speaking, this phase lasted from about 1660 to the publication of the *Art Poétique* in 1674, when it attained a resounding European success.

We have seen in the last chapter that Boileau's aesthetic was in some ways a reduction into literary terms of the Cartesian philosophical outlook, and thus a seminal creation of the time; and we have seen that most of the great writers show some kind of conflict between Boileau's ideal of Nature ordered by Reason, and the complexity of human passions. What ultimately matters is how the great artists use the conventional framework; but in this chapter, concerned as we are with the fluctuations of taste, it is the nature of the framework itself that interests us. Boileau did not object to the *précieux* style *per se*; he accepted it, with reservations, in Corneille for instance. He objected to it only in so far as it had become, in such works as Mlle de Scudéry's novels and Scarron's plays and burlesques, frivolous and irresponsible. This is why he insisted on themes of a high moral elevation and of general, as opposed to topical and local, interest; and the best way to achieve such a generalized significance seemed to him to be through the imitation of

56

classical antiquity. He did not advocate pastiche; he recommended the use of a convention which liberated the author from the ephemeral. The artist should aim to interpret man in his general and eternal, rather than in particular, aspects. He should exercise his powers of selection in determining what is important, what is not, remembering always that 'tout ce qu'on dit de trop est fade et rebutant'. Above all he should avoid triviality, even in comedy.

While Boileau's attitude is in some respects so closely rooted in the Cartesian outlook, in others it is clearly irreconcilable with Cartesianism. For if one fully accepts the supremacy of reason and the irrelevance of history, art, like human nature, ought to be growing progressively less imperfect, so that to study the ancients, even in order to reinterpret them, would be absurd. This latent paradox became more evident in 1688, in the famous quarrel of the Ancients and Moderns, in which Fontenelle, Perrault (the author, strangely enough, of the fairy tales), and Malebranche took the progressively 'modern' scientific view, whereas the leading artists on the whole defended the Ancients. Boileau himself was reduced to a feeble compromise, maintaining that perhaps the Ancients were better at some things, the Moderns at others. But even this confusion is a part of Boileau's representative significance, for a mingling of reverence for antiquity with a progressive modernism is found repeatedly in the outlook and culture of the time. The classical ideal came to have a very direct bearing on contemporary life, as we may see from, among many possible examples, this passage in which Fénelon recommends

aux jeunes filles la noble simplicité qui parait dans les statues . . . qui nous restent des femmes grecques et romaines; elles y verraient combien des cheveux noués négligemment par derrière, et des draperies pleines et flottantes à longs plis sont agréables et majestueuses. Il serait bon même qu'elles entendissent parler les peintres et les autres gens qui ont ce goût exquis de l'antiquité. . . . Je sais bien qu'il ne faut pas souhaiter qu'elles prennent l'extérieur antique; il y aurait de l'extravagance à le vouloir; mais elles pourraient, sans aucune singularité, prendre le goût de cette simplicité d'habits si noble, si gracieuse, et d'ailleurs si convenable aux mœurs chrétiennes.

Here we see Boileau's literary precepts translated into terms of social etiquette. Their rational belief in their own standards gives to these people their self-confidence; their habitual reference to a criterion outside themselves—in this case antiquity—preserves their humility, their sense of the mean. It is this union of self-confidence with humility which is so impressively demonstrated in La Bruyère's essay *Des Jugements*. It still survives in Couperin's attitude to his art, and the part played by the classical ideal in achieving it should not be lightly estimated.

Classicism begins and ends with the distinction of genres which is an expression in art of a refinement of social approach. Everything is well in its proper place; 'tout poème est brillant de sa propre beauté'. The generation that lived on after Boileau's death into the Regency marked in some ways a return once more to the precious, a softening of the outlines, a loosening of the tension between etiquette and morality. And yet all this veering and tacking between the noble and heroic, the naïve and ingenious, the archaic and popular, the pompous and intimate is a part of the gradual maturing of public taste. If the values and standards are becoming less clearly defined, they are also becoming operative for a wider public. The autocracy of Versailles is decaying and the life of Paris is beginning to take its place. A tendency towards decentralization is manifested in every branch of social entertainment. Art, expressing the ideal of *douceur de vivre*, becomes easier and more familiar. Architecture changes from the 'official' grandeur of Mansart to the style of a Robert de Cotte, which preserves something of the external magnificence, but inside is gracious, elegantly ornamented, comfortable, suited to the intercourse of a more amiably intimate society.[7] In painting the propagandist Lebrun is succeeded by the more personally emotional Watteau; in music Couperin follows Lully. The history of the opera and ballet during the last years of Louis's reign and the early years of the Regency reveals the changing outlook most clearly. But this is a subject of such crucial importance for the understanding of the musical culture that Couperin inherited that it must be dealt with in a separate chapter.

[7] For a minor but very revealing illustration of the changing cultural atmosphere compare the grandly proportioned case of the *buffet* of the St Gervais organ, which dates from the great age of Louis XIV, with the more graciously elegant case of the Versailles organ, which is the work of Robert de Cotte. See Plates VIII and IX.

Chapter Four

Music, the Court, and the Theatre

On trouve dans ses récits, dans ses airs, dans ses Chœurs, et
dans toutes ses Simphonies, un caractère juste et vrai, une
variété merveilleuse, une mélodie et une harmonie qui
enchantent, et il mérite avec raison le titre de Prince des
Musiciens François, étant regardé comme l'inventeur de cette
belle et grande Musique Françoise.

TITON DU TILLET (of Lully)

So FAR WE have tried to give some account of the values and the
taste of the society into which Couperin was born, mainly through
reference to the memoirs, literature, and painting of the period. The
musical counterparts of these fluctuations in taste will be discussed in
detail when, in Part II of this book, we examine the various branches
of Couperin's musical activity. There is, however, one aspect of
court music—the ballet and opera—which Couperin did not touch
upon, but which none the less influenced profoundly both his sensibility and his technique. In this chapter we shall therefore give some
general account of the rise of a courtly musical-theatrical art in
France during the *grand siècle*, and suggest some reasons why
Couperin did not make any specific contributions to the theatrical
genre, even though the whole temper and character of his work is
impregnated with the Lullian spirit.

In order to understand French theatrical music in the seventeenth
century it is necessary to consider briefly the relations between
French and Italian culture during the period and, to a lesser degree,
during the preceding century. There is nothing surprising in the fact
that Italy should have evolved a sophisticated secular art, founded on
aristocratic patronage, earlier than any other European culture. The
breakdown of the social and economic framework of the Middle
Ages occurred in Italy sooner than elsewhere; indeed the fifteenth

and even the fourteenth century are often referred to as the 'Italian renaissance', rather than as the end of the Middle Ages. And although Burckhardt's tendency to attribute everything vital in the Middle Ages to a premature renaissance is to be deprecated, it is true that the brilliant fifteenth-century Florentine culture in some ways anticipates developments normally associated with the next century. It demonstrates that, while the church had always provided opportunities for spectacle of a ritualistic order, a relatively unstable economy is apt to encourage a heightened humanism, to give a vigorous impetus to the instinct for rhetoric and dramatization. In the Florentine cities, as later in Elizabethan England, feudalism was dying and a national, commercial outlook was becoming more obtrusive. Both because man's economic position was more precarious, and because his relation to a universal Order was less clearly defined, the claims of the individual seemed more important, and the relation between the individual and the community more complex. This heightened personal and social consciousness found expression in a great outburst of pageantry and spectacle; we may note that it was the guild movements that brought pageantry out of the aegis of the church. This pageantry in turn gave a fillip to the theatrical aspects of the arts attendant on it. It is no accident that it was in Italy, which already had so long a tradition of spectacle and theatre, that the tremendous humanistic passion of the chromatic madrigal and of early baroque opera was first manifested.

When the musical-spectacular dramatic art of the Italian renaissance spread to France in the sixteenth century, it was rapidly modified by the native French tradition. Considerably before the full flowering of Italian baroque opera, the sophisticated court society of Henry II saw in the Italian masquerades, intermedii, and balletti a type of entertainment which could be adapted to local court functions. *Mascarades à grand spectacle*, held in the open air on a lavish scale, and *mascarades de palais*, held less magnificently in a room or small garden, became the customary accompaniment to the complimentary speeches to the King and nobility which graced all court festivities.

French composers had no difficulty in providing a stream of dance movements for these entertainments. The French tradition had always been rich in dance music. The folk music is itself remarkable for its sense of physical movement; and although men such as Josquin and Lassus exhibit in their religious polyphony a rhythmic variety no less subtle than that of Byrd or Victoria, there flourished too, all through the sixteenth century, an elegant homophonic choral tradition which is linked to folk dance. The symmetry and precision of this secular line, from Adam de la Halle to Jannequin, to Guillaume de Costeley, gives to French folk dance a super-civilized reincarnation. The combination of melodic and rhythmic simplicity with a delicate economy of craftsmanship gives the music a quality, at once naïve and sophisticated, which is not paralleled by the English madrigalists, who are either more complex and profound, or else less sophisticated, more directly in touch with a folk culture. Even some sixteenth-century French religious choral music, for instance the Psalms of Mauduit, uses a technique of homophonically built-up choral masses which almost anticipates the majesty of Lully.

Now the instrumental dance music is complementary to this elegant choral homophony. Many of the dances were published in the famous collection of Attaignant in 1557. Some were modelled on imported Italian dances, for instance the corantos, though the French soon developed their own version of the dance also. Others, such as the various types of branles, were a direct transference of folk dances, indicating that the sophisticated court culture had not yet lost contact with 'the people'. Others again, such as the pavanes and galliards, were a compromise between sophisticated and popular elements. The music, scored for strings, oboes, bassoons, and *cornets à bouquins*, had similar qualities to the vocal chansons; the implicit connection with a vocal tradition lent the rhythm plasticity, without any sacrifice of verve. The clarity of texture, the sharp definition of line and rhythm and orchestration, make the music still entrancing to listen to; it is entertainment music which is admirably designed for its function, and is also an enlivening of the spirit. The string parts probably included violins rather than viols, for a version of the violin more resembling the Italian *lyra da braccia* than the modern violin was introduced in France as early as 1530, well before the appearance of violins in Italy. The characteristic tone colour of the instrument must have enhanced the music's vivacity and *allure*. The following quotation from Philibert Jambe-de-Fer, dated 1556, would seem to indicate that in the mid-sixteenth century

61

the attitude of cultivated musicians to the violin was still somewhat patronizing:

Le violon est fort contraire à la viole. . . . Il est en forme de corps plus petit, plus plat, et beaucoup plus rude en son. . . . Nous appellons *violes* celles desquelles les gentilz hommes, marchantz, et autres gens de vertu passent leur temps. L'autre sorte s'appelle *violon*, et c'est celui duquel en use en dancerie communement et à bonne cause: car il est plus facile d'accorder pour ce que la quinte est plus douce à ouyr que n'est la quarte. Il est aussi plus facile à porter, qui est chose fort nécessaire, mesme en conduisant quelques noces, ou mommerie. . . .

But by the early years of the seventeenth century violins had become the rule in court festival music, having lost much of the social stigma attached to them. That their theatrical glamour was clearly recognized is attested by the appearance in the score of Monteverdi's *Orfeo* (1607) of *violini piccoli alla francese*; and by this passage from Mersenne's *Harmonie Universelle* of 1636:

Et ceux qui ont entendu les 24 Violons du Roy, aduouent qu'ils n'ont jamais rien ouy de plus rauissant ou de plus puissant; de là vient que cet instrument est la plus propre de tous pour faire danser, comme l'on experimente dans les balets, & partout ailleurs. Or les beautez et les gentillesses que l'on pratique dessus sont en si grand nombre que l'on le peut préferer à tous les autres instrumens, car les coups de son archet sont par fois si rauissants, que l'on n'a point de plus grand mescontentement que d'entendre la fin, particulièrement lors qu'ils sont mêlez des tremblemens & des flattemens de la main gauche. . . .

The brilliant French dance orchestras soon became famous all over Europe; some of them travelled to Germany, England, and even as far as Poland and Sweden.

The greater importance of the dance in art music was, however, only one aspect of the influence in France of the Italian renaissance. In both countries—and many Italian musicians were, in the second half of the sixteenth century, resident in France—it was felt that the figured dances of the court entertainments contained latent aesthetic possibilities which had not been adequately explored. Just as Peri and Bardi tried to combine the arts of music, dancing, painting, and poetry into an organized whole, in a manner which they imagined to be a marriage of modern civilization with the principles of classical antiquity, so, in France, Ronsard and the poets of the Pléïade group collaborated with the musicians to work out similar theories. From the start, the Italians had the drama in mind; the French, to begin with, were content to insist on the interdependence of music and poetry. Music was to be 'la sœur puisnée de la poésie'. Without it, poetry is 'presque sans grâce, comme la musique sans la mélodie des vers, inanimée et sans vie'. (Ronsard.)

The first product of this experiment was the *airs de cour* for solo voice and lute. A more detailed account of these will be given in the chapter on Couperin's secular vocal music. Here it is only necessary to say that, unlike the finest songs of the English Dowland, these airs have lute parts which were increasingly divested of polyphonic elaboration and reduced to a series of continuo-like chords. Le Roy interestingly contrasted the *airs de cour* with the chansons of Roland de Lassus, 'lesquelles sont difficiles et ardues'. In England, this desire for the simple and tuneful develops very much later.

It is hardly just, however, to suggest that the early *airs de cour* were lacking in subtlety. If they had a less delicate balance between melodic and harmonic elements than the English ayres, they were no less subtle in the way in which the extraordinarily free rhythm of the solo line reflected the slightest nuance of the text. Jodelle said 'Même l'air des beaux chants inspirés dans les vers / Est, comme en un beau corps, une belle âme infuse'. In the hands of a great man such as Claude Le Jeune, who is also a superb contrapuntist in his church music, these songs may achieve a limpid beauty which is a fitting complement to the poetry of Ronsard that Le Jeune so frequently set. Occasionally, through the introduction of the intense chromaticisms of the Italian arioso technique, the songs may rise to a considerable passion. Normally, however, such humanistic drama was left to the Italians; the effect of the *airs de cour* as a whole—we may take Du Caurroy rather than Le Jeune as typical—is of a witty entertainment of the spirit, or of a gently nostalgic melancholy that is somewhat emasculating. Mersenne, writing during the height of the fashion, summed up adequately both the airs' virtues and their limitations:

Il faut avouer que les accents de la passion manquent le plus souvent aux airs français parce que nos chants se contentent de chatouiller l'oreille et de plaire par les mignardises sans se soucier d'exciter les passions de leurs auditeurs.

Nothing could be further removed, both in intention and effect, from the Italian arioso at its best.

63

The French tradition of courtly theatre music developed through the mingling of these *airs de cour* with the instrumental dances discussed previously. In 1571 the poet Antoine de Baïf and the musician Thibault de Courville founded under royal patronage the *Académie Baïf de Musique et de Poésie*, to practise and propagate the new theories about music and prosody, to combine music and poetry with the dance by creating ballets based on Greek metres, and to circulate ideas among performers and audience. (There was often no sharp distinction between the two.)

> *L'entreprise*
> *D'un ballet que dressions, dont la démarche est mise*
> *Selon que va marchant pas à pas la chanson*
> *Et le parler suivi d'une propre façon*

was, with its insistence on Greek metres, perhaps a rather coldly academic prescription, but it was not rigidly adhered to. By the time the work of the *Académie* was interrupted by the Wars of Religion, it had impregnated French culture so deeply that its influence was felt for the next hundred and fifty years.

In 1581 Charles IX commissioned Ronsard, Baïf, and Le Jeune to produce *mascarades* to celebrate the marriage of the Duc de Joyeuse and Mlle de Vaudemont. Stung to emulation, Catharine de Medici ordered Balthazar de Beaujoyeulx to arrange an even grander affair, and although the King had already obtained the most distinguished artists, Beaujoyeulx compensated for the lack of glamorous 'names' in his production, by an element of novelty. He created *Circé, ballet comique de la reine*, which although not in any way profound, for the first time made a conscious attempt to link dance, music, and spectacle into a coherent whole through the introduction of a slender story. 'Je puis dire avoir contenté en un corps bien proportionné l'œil, l'oreille, et l'entendement'. *Circé* immediately created a furore. The *ballet comique* superseded the casual *mascarade* as the recognized entertainment for all big court festivities; even the smaller *mascarades de palais* were influenced by it, introducing more developed literary and musical elements.

The history of the French ballet through the seventeenth century is described in detail in Prunières's fascinating book on the subject, to which the reader is referred. Briefly, the ballet fluctuated between a literary and musical approach, the element of the dance remaining constant throughout. During the early years of the century, the presence of Rinuccini and Caccini at the French court encouraged a development of the musical elements; with the production of the *Ballet d'Alcine* in 1610 the dramatically inclined *ballet comique* reasserted itself. A new form, embracing dance, song, spectacle, pantomime and gesture, was created, and flourished from 1610 to 1621, when the Constable de Luynes, who had been in charge of it, died. Prunières refers to this type as the *ballet mélodramatique*. De Luynes's successor as master of the revels, the Duc de Nemours, had a partiality for the grotesque *ballet mascarade*; and the classical form of the *ballet de cour* was the offspring of a liaison between the *ballet mélodramatique* and the *ballet mascarade*.

The classical ballet was usually in five sections, each divided into several subsections. It opened with the dedicatory chorus to the King and court ladies, which was followed by a number of entries with characteristic dances, often of a grotesque nature. Then came the entry of quaintly masked musicians with lutes and viols to play instrumental interludes and to accompany the recitative and airs. Next came the climax with the entry of the King and nobles, masked; and the ballet concluded with a general dance and chorus. The songs included *airs de cour*, and *vaudevilles* or adaptations, some satirical, some amorous and pastoral, of popular songs and carols; another indication of the popular affiliations of this esoteric art. The one new element was the recitative, and this was a natural evolution from the freer type of *air de cour*, from which it differed only in being more consistently narrative and declamatory. One cannot say that this recitative is in the least dramatic; rather flat and characterless, it hardly attempts to solve the difficult problem of the relation between speech and lyrical song. But at least it was a step *towards* the opera; it was something that Lully could start from.

Musically, the most interesting section of the ballets would seem to be the *entrées de luth* which preserved some connection with the old polyphonic technique. They are not brisk like the conventional fanfares, but emotional and melancholy, dreamy and relaxed, obviously related to the elegiac tone of the lutenist music of the salons and *ruelles*. The other instrumental sections were not much more distinguished than the vocal parts—the recitative, solo airs, and choruses. Before Lully, the overtures do not extend beyond a few conventionally imposing gestures; and the dances appear to have been less rhythmically alert than those of the sixteenth century. Prunières warns us, however, that we have imperfect evidence as to the nature of the original ballet scores. Comparison of Philidor's early eighteenth-century transcriptions with the few examples which have survived in contemporary transcriptions for the lute, indicates that Philidor has emasculated the dances. In any case they must have been, in their original orchestration, a bright and colourful addition to the spectacle.

The dances made animated play with decorative and descriptive details; soldiers, battles, cock-crows and other bird-calls, 'national' dances, the more outlandish the better, were especially favoured. Ornamentation and the French dotted rhythm (which was not an invention of Lully), were employed to give vigour and point to physical gestures. Moreover, a case can be made out that the French were justified in putting the stress on the dance rather than the drama in creating a musical-theatrical art, because music and dancing are natural allies which move at the same speed. Music, on the other hand, is bound to take longer than poetry to make its emotional effect, and thereby produces a tricky technical problem which few opera composers have adequately solved. However this may be, the architectural quality of the French *ballet de cour* made an immense impression on foreign artists. It greatly influenced the later masques of Ben Jonson. Rinuccini studied it in detail, and determined to introduce it into his own country on his return; Monteverdi's magnificent *Ballo delle Ingrate* is one of the fruits of the French influence. If the French theatre music had originally sprung from Italian sources, it had certainly developed a character of its own which the Italians, among other European musicians, were eager to emulate.

During the early years of the seventeenth century the ballet had one composer of genius, Pierre Guédron. His dances have unusual virility, and his *airs de cour* a genuine pathos and dramatic power. One cannot say, however, that Guédron is the representative composer of the ballet of the *grand siècle*. It is his successor Antoine Boësset who, as the most fashionable ballet composer, was universally honoured and feted; whose work was studied by Heinrich Albert, one of the leading German composers for the solo voice, and, according to St Evremond, by no less a person that Luigi Rossi, the

Italian opera composer esteemed in France above all others. Boësset is a real composer, with a personal melodic gift, but he lacks—and would not, one imagines, have desired—Guédron's tautness and sinew. He is a 'génie de la musique douce', writing music that is sweetly mellifluous and often subtle. But the soft fluidity of his rhythms and the elaborations of his ornamentation get increasingly out of touch with the prosody they had originally been designed to illustrate. They are indulged in for their own sake, and become in the long run wearisome and enervating. By the time of the Roi Soleil the ballet appeared to be in decline. What was needed to weld its constituents into a musico-dramatic convention of classical maturity was an artist of commanding authority. He came in the person of Jean-Baptiste Lully.

Lully was, interestingly enough, himself an Italian, and the son of a miller. Born in Florence in 1632, he was brought up in the humanistic traditions of Italian music. At the age of fourteen he came to France as *garçon de chambre* and unofficial instructor in Italian to Mlle d'Orléans; by the time he was twenty his precocious musical gifts and headstrong temperament had carried him into the court ballet, where he excelled both as dancer and musician. He acquired a thorough grounding in the French traditions of composition from two men of the old school, Roberday and Gigault, and was himself soon composing, with equal fluency, ballet music in the French style, and Italian airs in the manner of Rossi and Carissimi. A brilliant fiddler, Lully had little use for the famous Vingt-quatre Violons du Roi; indeed of them he 'faisait si peu de cas qu'il les traitait de maîtres aliborons et de maîtres ignorants', in particular protesting against their habit of introducing unauthorized ornamentation into their parts. Lully's appeal for naturalness and simplicity applied of course to his vocal writing as well as to his instrumental. Lecerf de la Viéville reports him as saying: 'Point de broderie; mon récitatif n'est fait que pour parler, je veux qu'il soit tout uni.' It is worth noting that Lully's first appeals for dignity and lucidity in performance and composition correspond in date with Boileau's attack upon the excesses of *préciosité*.

That Lully's personality had remarkable power is indicated by the fact that the King listened to his complaints even though, at the time, Lully was not a person of much consequence. Louis put him 'à

67

la tête d'une bande de violons qu'il peut conduire à sa fantaisie'. Lully soon proved that the King's confidence in him was not misplaced; according to Lecerf de la Viéville, the new band, called Les Petits Violons, 'en peu de temps surpassa la fameuse bande des Vingt-Quatre'. Lully introduced many improvements into string technique, mostly for the purpose of achieving greater brilliance and more incisive rhythm. There can be no doubt that his experience of playing string music as an accompaniment to physical movement was of great value to him in his subsequent career as a theatre composer.

When Lully, with his Italian background, first came to France, Italian music, and in particular the opera, was in vogue among the French intelligentsia, largely because of Mazarin's insatiable passion for it. Mazarin's vindication was that he 'ne faisoit pas ces choses tant pour le public que pour le divertissement de leurs Majestés et pour le sien, et qu'ils aymoient mieux les vers et la musique italienne que la française'. (Perrin). It was at his invitation that Luigi Rossi and Carlo Caproli spent long periods in France, and through his efforts that in the sixteen forties Rossi's opera *Orfeo* was given a sumptuous Parisian production. It enjoyed a considerable *succès d'estime*, or possibly *succès de scandale*, among the dilettanti; and undoubtedly the aristocratic refinement and hyper-subtlety of both Rossi's and Caproli's music must have appealed to an audience which admired the sophistications of the lute music and the *airs de cour*. But it cannot be said that the perfervid Italians made any lasting impression on the French temperament. If the French liked the Italians' emotional subtleties, they distrusted their violence; the dolorous intensity of Rossi's music, its vehement chromaticisms, were admired less than its languishing elegance. On the whole the Italian musicians were regarded with suspicion. After Mazarin's death it was inevitable that the Italian influence should decline.

The much heralded visit of the great Cavalli in the sixteen sixties was thus somewhat of an anti-climax. His opera *Serse* passed, musically speaking, almost unnoticed, and when, a little later, his *L'Ercole Amante* was produced, it was the additional ballets written by Lully that aroused all the enthusiasm. Not unnaturally Cavalli was piqued that a composer of international celebrity such as himself should be ousted by a composer of pleasant dances—which were almost all
68

Lully had to his credit at that date. He returned to Italy, leaving Lully in full musical possession of the country of his adoption. But although opposition to things Italian was temporarily so strong that Cavalli's music was not generally appreciated, Lully himself was not slow to recognize its virtues. He was aware that, though the French might not know it, there were things in Cavalli's theatre music that the French tradition could use to its own advantage.

For while Cavalli could employ a passionate Italian chromaticism when he wanted, as in the famous lament from *Egisto*, the general tendency of his work was towards balanced periods founded on the integration of melody and bass, and simple diatonic harmony of the type that reaches its culmination in Handel. Rossi and Caproli were transitional composers in the sense that their dramatic harmonic audacities and sensuous glamour still have contact with the polyphonic methods of the past. Cavalli differentiates much more sharply between his supple but highly stylized declamation, and his formal arias. He has not Rossi's baroque imaginativeness, but he has dramatic power combined with a sense of architectural order and of the alternation of mood. Cavalli deliberately avoids the subtle harmonic effects of false relation and appoggiatura that Rossi delighted in; avoids, too, Rossi's contrapuntal complexities in choral and instrumental part-writing. He aims at a broad effect; and this was just what Lully wanted if he was to establish a criterion of order in music, as Boileau established it in poetic technique; if he was to discipline the floridity of *précieux* line and harmony, as Mansart regulated and stabilized the proportions of baroque architecture. After the production of *L'Ercole Amante* all Lully's ballets show an expansion of the traditional French technique (which he had helped to formulate with his *Ballet de la Nuit* of 1653) by means of the sense of harmonic proportion he had learned from the Italians, and from Cavalli in particular. This debt remains, even though Lully, having thrown in his lot with the French cause, came bitterly to resent any Italian interference.

To the traditional French methods Lully added, at the start, little that was new. But he gave the ceremonial dances and cortèges on the classical model a more organic unity with one another, and a more intrinsic elegance and zest. Early on he showed a clear understanding of the tonal principles on which a convincing homophonic

69

architecture was to depend; and he developed the ground-bass technique of the chaconne, that most primitive expansion of a symmetrical figure through the simple process of repetition, into a medium capable of an intense emotional expressiveness, exploiting the possibility of tension between the regularly repeated bass and the varied groupings of the melodies above it. This development of the chaconne is an example of how the seventeenth-century composer turned to his advantage a practical necessity—namely, the repetition of the symmetrical ballet tune as long as the dancers wished to go on dancing. The somewhat later development of the rondeau with couplets is a further example, as we shall see, of a technique of expediency turned to an expressive purpose. Both techniques are a compromise between a dance music for practical use and the *melodically* generative technique of the sixteenth century. Though the rhythmic conception is now more accentual, there is still a link between the chaconne and rondeau technique of Lully and Couperin respectively, and, for instance, the variation technique of the Tudor virginalists.

Important as was Lully's work in developing the dance element in the ballet, still more significant is his transformation into the theatrical overture of the formal introductory fanfares heralding the arrival of the maskers. This reconciles all the transitional elements of the technique of composition which were then current. The slow majestic opening harks back to the polyphony and false relations of the instrumental fantasia, the bouncing dotted rhythms and the ornamentation deriving from Lully's knowledge of the physical movements of the ballet, acquired when directing Les Petits Violons; while the quick fugal section is a compromise between polyphonic procedure and the regular rhythms and simple harmonies of the dance. If the Lullian overture is a transitional technique, it is none the less mature. It is not surprising that its influence spread far beyond the confines of the French court.

In addition to his expansion of the symphonic aspects of the ballet, Lully developed the vocal elements. His interest in vocal music was considerably encouraged when, in 1664, he entered into collaboration with Molière and produced a long series of *comédies-ballets*, *Le Mariage Forcé*, *La Princesse d'Elide*, *L'Amour Médecin*, *Le Sicilien*, *Le Ballet des Muses*, *Le Grotte de Versailles*, *George Dandin*, *Les Amans Magnifiques*, *Monsieur de Pourceaugnac*, *Le Bourgeois Gentilhomme*,

70

and, to complete the cycle, *Psyché*, in collaboration with Pierre Corneille. In all these, care is taken to relate the musical interludes to the action. Some of them, *La Princesse d'Elide*, *Les Amans Magnifiques*, *Psyché*, were heroic works in the grand style, with considerable choral passages, treated vertically in massive homophony, and with elaborate stage machinery; they were almost grand operas, but for the absence of dramatic recitative. The lighter works, on the other hand, *Le Mariage Forcé*, *L'Amour Médecin*, *Le Bourgeois Gentilhomme* and *Pourceaugnac*, led on to the French comic opera. Here, in the dance movements we find a crispness and bubbling zest which is enhanced by the scrupulously clean orchestration, a vein of exquisite pastoral elegance (*Le Sicilien* is the loveliest example) and a lyrical idiom sensitively moulded to the inflections of the French language. The line is unbroken from *Pourceaugnac* to Chabrier's *Le Roi Malgré Lui*. Moreover, in *Le Grotte de Versailles*, *George Dandin*, and *Les Amans Magnifiques*, Lully has gone far towards creating a recitative as well as a lyrical style which is a musical incarnation of the French language. All these *bergeries* and *comédies-ballets* are full of intimations of the later operas. The gay satirical scenes of *Pourceaugnac* and *Le Bourgeois Gentilhomme*, with their extravagant local colour, their serenades, drinking-songs and descriptive details, are already the creation of a mature comic genius which M. Prunières relates to Rossini. In *Les Amans Magnifiques*, the *sommeil* of Caliste and the scene of the *Jeux Pithiens*, with its ceremonial dialogues between choir and resplendent orchestra of trumpets, flutes, oboes, strings, and percussion, give a foretaste of some of the most impressive moments of *Cadmus* and *Thésée*.

The creation of *ballets comiques* continued from 1664 to 1671, the date of *Psyché*. In the following year, after complicated and unscrupulous legal negotiations, Lully obtained an exclusive privilege of founding an *Académie Royale de Musique*. As a result of this, he established a school of opera centred at the Palais Royal, and between 1673 and 1686 produced his famous series of operas, twelve of them in collaboration with Quinault, three with Campistron and Thomas Corneille, the brother of Pierre. If Lully had been fortunate in having the wit and urbanity of Molière at his disposal for his *ballets comiques*, he was hardly less fortunate in having for his tragic operas the services of a poet who, though not a genius, had habitual

71

distinction and good taste. We have already referred to the rewarding collaboration between artists in different media, as being indicative of the cultural unity and vitality of Versailles; in this case the
collaboration appears to have been especially intimate, for Quinault
was much influenced by Lully's ideas and allowed the composer a
considerable share in the shaping of the librettos.[8] The plan of the
operas was highly stylized. After the overture, a more spacious
version of the ballet overture already described, came the prologue
with complimentary speeches to the King and allusions to the latest
victories, followed by choruses and dances of patriotic intent. All
this was a direct survival from the masque. Then followed the
tragedy, usually concerned with sexual passion, and involving supernatural agencies which provided opportunities for complicated stage
mechanism.

The centre of interest, the unfolding of the story, lies in the
recitative; this is the principal difference from the ballets. This
recitative is far from the perfunctory declamation of the old ceremonial addresses. Lully modelled it with the greatest care, studying the
inflections of the great Racinian tragedians such as La Champmeslé,
trying to create a line which should be scrupulously attentive to the
effect of the spoken word, while at the same time having sufficient
musical interest to stand on its own feet. There is a good deal of
evidence, as Romain Rolland has shown, that Racine's own notion
of declamation was close to song: leaps in pitch as great as an octave
were encouraged in the more passionate passages. It is probable,
therefore, that Lully's recitative reflects fairly accurately the contour
of Racine's declamation. The latter was closer to song than are our
notions of declamation, whereas Lully's recitative was closer to
speech than our, or at least nineteenth-century, recitative. If today
Lully's recitative sounds dull, it is usually because it is sung too
stolidly and formally. It should have the flexibility of animated, if
always elegant, conversation; contemporary opinion insists repeatedly not only on its majesty, but on its liveliness and naturalness. If Lully studied the tragedians as a model for his recitative, it is
equally true that they in their turn studied his recitative as a model
for their declamation. It may have been the decay of this relation

[8] A most interesting account of Lully's method of work and of his association with
Quinault is given in Bonnet's *Histoire de la Musique*, vol. iii, p. 95 *et seq.* (1725 edition.)

between the dramatic and operatic traditions that led to the wide-spread misunderstanding of Lully's idiom.

Though never, like that of the Italians, dramatically violent, Lully's line attains a convincing Cavalli-like balance between melodic interest and harmonic elements, exemplified for instance in the line's use of diminished fifths and sevenths. Since the French language perhaps does not naturally lend itself to musical expression, Lully's achievement was, even on purely technical grounds, of no mean order; but what is most remarkable is the range of emotional expression he compasses within his restrained utterance. The use of melodic intervals is carefully graded according to the intensity of the emotion to be expressed; but the fact that the idiom is stylized, as are the values of Lully's civilization, does not mean that it is insincere. As he matures, Lully tends to make his recitative more lyrical without sacrificing its fluidity, while he tends to submerge his arias in the recitative. In the last operas he almost discards the late baroque differentiation between aria, arioso, and recitative in favour of the early baroque's continuous arioso which absorbs into itself both recitative and lyrical song. The arias now give the impression of being merely the overflow of the recitative's more passionate moments. They are infrequent—not more than two or three marking the high points of the opera; when they do occur, they are sometimes derived from the *air de cour* (and therefore still fairly close to speech), sometimes brief strophic melodies with refrain. In no case are they allowed to assume a self-subsistent importance or to interrupt the flow of the voice's intimate relation to the poetry and the orchestra.

The orchestra on the other hand is given a more independent function. The stylized action offers plenty of opportunities for the introduction of *bergeries*, dances, and interludes, treated in an expansive style by both chorus and orchestra. The vocal and symphonic elements are clearly differentiated in the early operas; through the succession of *Alceste* (1674), *Thésée* (1675), *Atys* (1676), and *Isis* (1677) we can observe that the recitative acquires a more lyrical swell and continuity, while the symphonic elements are more closely linked to the recitative.

With the great operas of the last years of the Lully-Quinault collaboration, *Proserpine*, *Persée*, *Phaéton*, *Amadis*, *Roland*, and *Armide*,

73

the French classical tradition comes musically to fruition. The heroic parts of the central characters are not only more lyrically rich, but roles of some psychological power. Moreover, while formal ballets, *bergeries* and marches in the line of the *ballet de cour* are still introduced these symphonic elements begin, too, to acquire psychological significance—to have bearing on the dramatic situations, on the desires and fears, joys and despairs, of the characters. Lully now frequently employs recitative accompanied by the orchestra, making the instruments underline the emotional implications of the scene; the battle pieces, thunder-storms and the like become less decoratively descriptive, more descriptive of 'states of mind'. In particular, the *sommeil* scenes in *Armide, Roland,* and *Amadis,* with their vague, vaporous murmur of muted violins, are almost impressionistic in effect, though the texture and structure remain meticulously clear and the effect does not depend on the confusion of line and timbre, as does late nineteenth-century impressionism.

The combination, in passages such as these, of grand symmetrical architecture in the *symphonies,* with intimacy in the inflections of the vocal line and the harmony of the inner parts, suggests some analogy with the gardens of Le Nôtre. For the broad, clear horizons of Le Nôtre's gardens are planned with geometrical precision, while within that lucid framework the detail is of extraordinary complexity; the total impression owes something to both the lucidity and the elaboration. A similar but still more significant analogy may be established between Lully's music and the painting of Poussin and Claude. Poussin, of course, died in 1665, before the great days of Louis XIV, and both he and Claude spent most of their careers in Rome—another instance of the relations between French and Italian culture in the seventeenth century. But we can regard them as more imbued with the Racinian spirit than the conventional court painters like Lebrun, who see only the surface *grandeur;* and Poussin at least was much admired at Versailles—Le Nôtre had a fine collection. Just as Lully groups his periods with ceremonial equilibrium, so the architectural proportions, the relations of part to part, in Poussin's classical mythology and Claude's landscapes, are calculated with mathematical exactitude. On the other hand, the quality of the colour has sensuousness and translucency, just as has Lully's harmony in such things as the *scènes de sommeil.* But these colours are placed in

74

Gardens of the Duc d'Orléans

Prosp: du Cours de La Reyne Mere

'Dans le Goût Pastoral': Cours de la Reine Mère

balanced groups, put on smoothly, with no gradations, no impressionist flowing of one shade into another; the colours, even the sharply defined shadows, are part of the architecture. We remember Louis Testelin's remark which became one of the key-phrases of the period—'Le dessin est intellectuel, tandis que la couleur n'est que sensible'; and Poussin's statement of principle, which stands as an epitome of the ideals of the *grand siècle*: 'Mon naturel me contraint de chercher les choses bien ordonnées, fuyant la confusion qui m'est aussi contraire et ennemie comme est la lumière des obscures ténèbres.'

Exactly comparable with Poussin's architectural use of colour is Lully's use of the sensuous colour of his harmonies and orchestration. These elements he employs not in the intentionally blurred manner of the nineteenth-century orchestra, but in clearly defined groups, as part of his tonal architecture. The effervescent and resilient orchestration of Lully or La Lande—consider for instance the latter's *Symphonies des Noëls* or the magnificent *Musique pour les Soupers du Roi* of which M. Roger Desormière has made a recording—is the polar opposite of Wagner's 'harmonizing with the orchestra'. Together with the sonorous brilliance which should characterize the chamber-music combinations of the time, it has been buried as deeply beneath the incrustations of nineteenth-century academic convention as the luminosity of Poussin and Claude was buried beneath the incrustations of begrimed varnish. The re-created classical mythology, the heroic gestures in the painting, seem to have as great a weight of traditional experience behind them as does the stylized vocabulary of the dramatic poets. If Lully's last operas were produced with a sensitive appreciation of his idiom and with adequate resources, it is possible that we should find a comparable sublimity in his heroic gestures and noble perorations. The argument which maintains that Lully's operas are impractical for modern performance because they depend on out-moded fashions, does not seem to me impressive; so do the plays of Corneille, and even Racine. A producer and audience that cannot appreciate a sense of stylization are not worth their salt. The plots of the operas, *qua* plots, are, like the plots of Shakespeare's drama, of little consequence; what matters is what the music, or the poetry, does to them. It is interesting that the most remarkable instrumental and colouristic development in Lully's work coincides

75

with the flowering of his lyrical speech. Compared with the Italians, the lines in the last operas are still quiet and close to speech; but we can hardly deny to the composer of the famous *Bois épais* the command, when he wanted it, of a melodic line of distinction.

Despite its restraint the work of Lully was considered, by the contemporary opinion of Bonnet's *Histoire de la Musique* of 1715, to be moving enough to melt hearts and to make the very rocks groan with him; while speaking of *Alceste* Mme de Sévigné remarked 'On joue jeudi l'opéra qui est un prodige de beauté, il y a des endroits de la musique qui ont mérité des larmes. Je ne suis pas seule à ne les pouvoir soutenir, l'âme de Mme de la Fayette en est alarmée.' It is also worth noting that when the last great operas were presented in Paris at the public theatre they enjoyed a spectacular popular success; *Phaéton* was even called '*l'opéra du peuple*'.[9] This certainly suggests that the court culture was not as out of touch with French life as is sometimes suggested; if it had been, it could hardly have given so triumphant a manifestation of vitality. It is precisely this zest combined with elegance that Lully expresses in his last work, *Acis et Galathée*, a return, after the cycle of tragic operas, to the pastoral convention. This beautiful work, the most obvious candidate for revival, unites the rhythmic exuberance and melodic *allure* of the early ballets with the linear subtlety and architectural gravity of the late operas. It is the ripe fruit of a great civilization; and it suggests the direction in which the opera is to tend after Lully's death. In its more amiable and intimate atmosphere it is also of all Lully's works the closest to Couperin.

From the start the opera had not been without opponents. To the logical French mind, absurdities which might be tolerated in a superficial entertainment were inappropriate in a music drama which purported to be a representation of life. La Bruyère, Boileau, and St Evremond, among other celebrated people, deplored the frivolity of the spectacles, the incredibility of the recitatives. Yet in many ways, as we have seen, Lully's aesthetic was complementary to Boileau's; and in general the classical stylization vindicated itself. Marmontel's defence that 'la musique y fait le charme du merveil-

[9] 'Et je vous apprends, mon petit cousin, qu' *Armide* est l'opéra des femmes; *Atys* l'opéra du Roi; *Phaéton* l'opéra du peuple; *Isis* l'opéra des musiciens. Mais enfin revenons au recitatif. C'est principalement par là que Lully est au dessus de nos autres musiciens. . .'

76

leux; le merveilleux y fait la vraisemblance de la musique', seemed convincing so long as the opera dealt with themes parallel to those of the classical drama. Lully's triumph was complete; even the acid St Evremond made an exception in his favour:

> Would you know what an opera is? I'll tell you, it is an odd medley of Poetry and Musick, wherein the Poet and Musician, equally confined one by the other, take a World of Pains to compose a wretched Performance. . . . It remains that I give my advice in general for all Comedies where any singing is used; and that is to leave to the Poet's discretion the management of the Piece. The Musician is to follow the Poet's direction, only in my opinion, Lully is to be exempted, who knows the Passions and enters further into the Heart of man than the Authors themselves.

When the opera finally fell out of favour it was not because it was stylized but because the stylization ceased to have a purpose. In the last years of Louis's reign, *la gloire* was in decline, festivities were no longer officially in fashion. In the circumstances the patriotic celebrations with which the opera had always been associated were hardly in the best of taste. Mme de Maintenon encouraged Louis to regard the opera as frivolous; it became so when it no longer had the backing of the quasi-religious cult of the state.

As soon as the King had definitely thrown over the opera, the rationalist Boileau and the devout Arnauld and Bossuet came out into the open with their moral denunciations of it. Despite its generic and structural relation to the noble classical tragedy, the opera was regarded with disapproval by these men because it tended to idealize love at the expense of duty. The main theme was considered to be lubricious; while the incidental divertissements were condemned because they were frivolous and trivial. Ironically enough, when the opera decayed with the *grand goût* of the Roi Soleil, it was precisely the divertissement that once more took its place. As culture became more decentralized, the divertissement became more a private party than a state function; entertainments were less sumptuous, but more exquisite. The revival of the opera-ballet, instead of the tragic opera, 'sympathise', as a contemporary writer put it, 'avec l'impatience française';[10] the 'moral' implica-

---

[10] Roy: *Lettre sur l'opéra*, in *La Nouvelle Bigarrure*, quoted by Masson in *L'Opéra de Rameau*.

With reference to the changing cultural atmosphere, the title of one of the *entrées* in Campra's delightful *Fêtes Venitiennes* of 1710 seems especially significant; it is called *Le Triomphe de la Folie sur la Raison.*

77

tions of the theatre music of the classic age had been lost because 'le public n'est plus ouvert à une certaine sensibilité et il est bien plus flatté des choses agréables à ses yeux que de celles qui touchent le cœur.'

Yet this new phase is not simply, or at all, a decline, as the above rather extravagant quotation from Destouches would suggest. For it goes together with the other manifestations of a more intimate and familiar culture which we mentioned in the last chapter; if it means a loss in some of the virtues of Versailles's autocracy, it is also a gain in so far as it applies to a wider, more centrally Parisian, public. So the vivacious pastoralism of the opera ballet of Campra, Mouret and Destouches is the link between the court opera of Lully and the next great opera composer Rameau who, in the early part of his operatic career at least, wrote for the Parisian public.

Campra is especially interesting from this point of view, for although his music has plenty of aristocratic finesse it has also a popular *allure*, a sun-baked vitality, which seems to spring from his Provençal origin. His exuberant sense of physical movement and of orchestral colour makes him perhaps the most enchanting of all dance composers. Something of this resilience is found even in his fine religious motets, which resemble Couperin's in mating the French and Italian *goût*. Mouret, 'musicien des Grâces, si gai, si vif,' as Daquin said, was also a Provençal and manifests, in his *Divertissements pour la Comédie Italienne* and his *Suites des Simphonies pour des violons, des hautbois et des cors de chasse*, a comparable popular buoyancy of rhythm and glittering clarity of orchestration. De Noinville, in his *Histoire de l'opéra en France* of 1767, said that 'tant des ouvrages de Mouret ont un goût de légèreté qui semblent répondre à son tempérament, et ils ont toujours plu extrèmement aux connoisseurs.'

Destouches has less vigour, but the seductive emotionalism of his harmonies likewise testifies to the more relaxed atmosphere. His originality is his charm, though his unconventional harmonic progressions may often be due to his technical inexperience. He was a rich dilettante and a pupil of Campra; his work shows a slender but remarkable talent exactly suited to the temper of his age. These three composers have an easy geniality which is seldom found in the music of the great days of Louis XIV's reign; and of Couperin, as of

Rameau after him, we may say that the highest point of French musical culture since the late Middle Ages comes at a time when it is not too late to remember and live by the old classical virtues while avoiding, in the new more intimate environment, the dangers of autocratic rigidity.

The first twenty years of Couperin's working life correspond with the last twenty of Louis's reign. During this period, therefore, he was called upon to provide music that could soothe in the relative quiet of chamber or salon, that could enliven the ceremony of eating, that could elevate or inspire in the ritual of the church. Thus he did not follow Lully in composing ballets and operas. He concentrated on domestic music, concert music, and church music, fields which had been cultivated in Lully's day only as accessories to the all-important theatre music. By the time of the Regency he had discovered that the forms of chamber music suited him best, for he made no attempt to follow Campra and Destouches into the more relaxed delights of the ballet-opera. It is hardly necessary to add that, while Couperin did not write any theatre music, all his musical thought is influenced both by the divertissement and by recollections of Lully's art. The pastoral and mythological subjects, the dances, the sonorous texture of Lully's orchestra, Lully's combination of architectural dignity with subtle sensuousness of detail—all these are latent in Couperin's work. The clavecin *ordres* might even be considered as a series of miniature ballets, expressed in absolute instrumental form.

But the change from a technique of theatre music to a chamber music idiom involved certain developments which Lully had not fully anticipated. The elder man had shown how it was possible to weld the heterogeneous elements of a theatre music into a convincing organism. He had created the structure of the operatic overture, and shown a grasp of tonal relationships, somewhat before the comparable work of Alessandro Scarlatti; his influence is unmistakable both in the early overtures of Scarlatti and in those of Cesti. But it was the Italians again who, at the end of the century, were to make the classically final reconciliation of Italian harmonic drama with the French sense of physical movement and architectural proportion. It was the Italians who were to indicate with classical economy how dances could be imbued with intense emotion, how dramatic harmony could be given formal discipline, and how the two could be

79

combined in an entity which could stand by itself as 'absolute' music without reference to a theatrical framework.

Here we see the significance of the vogue for the Italian violin sonata, which was at its height when Lully's death in 1687 removed the main impediment to a renewed enthusiasm for things Italian. For the Italian sonata might be said to summarize in instrumental microcosm the technique of baroque opera. It is fitting, therefore, that our survey of the position as Couperin found it should close with this brief reference to a convention to which composers all over Europe felt obliged to pay homage. For the moment the reference must suffice. We shall have occasion to discuss the technique in detail when we come to Couperin's own experiments in the idiom. His first work, on the other hand, does not greatly depend on this 'modern' Italian technique. It is rather a tribute to his forebears, a recognition of the nature of his inheritance.

Part Two

THE WORK

Mon naturel me contraint de chercher les choses bien ordonnés, fuyant la confusion qui m'est aussi contraire et ennemie comme est la lumière des obscures ténèbres.

POUSSIN

La clarté orne les pensées profondes.

VAUVENARGUES

Polissez-le sans cesse et le repolissez: soyez-vous à vous-même un sévère critique.

BOILEAU

THE WORK

Chapter Five

The Organ Masses

STARTING JUST AFTER the heyday of French classical civilization, and in his youth at least unaware of the impending collapse, Couperin can never have been in any doubt as to the kind of music he wanted to write. His first work, however, partly owing to the circumstances in which it was written, pays a tribute to the long tradition which lay behind him by being deliberately an exercise in the manner of the past. The two organ masses were composed when Couperin was twenty-one, four years after he had become organist of St Gervais. The first of them, *À l'usage ordinaire des paroisses pour les fêtes solemnelles*, was presumably employed by Couperin at St Gervais; the other, *Propre pour les Convents* (sic) *de Religieux et Religieuses*, was probably written for some specific community. These works do not betray much conscious modernism; but like Purcell's string fantasias, composed at the same age, they reveal more about their creator and the society he lived in than he may have realized. Though their modernism is implicit rather than explicit, it is none the less real.

Like most of the work of the seventeenth-century organ schools, the masses were intended as music for religious ritual. Yet as far back as the early years of the century we are aware of a gradual change in instrumental church music. The supreme figures of the baroque organ school, Titelouze, Sweelinck, Frescobaldi, Bull, and Gibbons, all follow Cabezon in starting from the vocal conventions of sixteenth-century polyphony. But their use of a keyboard, and of a technique derived from the fingers, suggests harmonic and figurative developments which, despite the experiments of a Gesualdo, were beyond the scope of the human voice. Bull, Frescobaldi, and Sweelinck exhibit this passionate intensity in harmony and figuration more consistently than Gibbons or Titelouze; they are closer in spirit to the violent humanistic genius of Monteverdi. But all the

83

early baroque organ composers used this technique because the impulses behind them were changing. The crowning glory of European organ music—the line stretching unbroken from the early baroque composers to Buxtehude and Bach—appeared when vocal music was forced to learn a new technique. Though they did not know it, the early organists were on the way from a religious outlook to the ethical humanism of the eighteenth century; from polyphony, to diatonic harmonic structures founded on the dance, not the voice. And beyond those harmonic structures lies the instrumental 'drama' of opposing key centres, and the great world of classical symphonic music.

If one compares Gibbons's string fantasias with those of Purcell which are modelled on them, one may observe a clear example of this tendency. Gibbons's harmonies are often audacious enough; but he remains sixteenth-century in approach in that he is primarily interested in the flow of his lines and regards the harmonies as a consequence, albeit not a fortuitous one, of that flow. Purcell tends to use shorter, more easily memorable, phrases so that the grouping of his themes in sequence produces a more rhetorical effect. The fourth four-part fantasia creates, through its chromaticisms, dissonant suspensions and overlapping false relations, a more directly 'personal' and dramatic effect than anything in Gibbons. It might be a lament from one of Purcell's operas; it has even been called Wagnerian! The balance between melodic and harmonic organization, characteristic of sixteenth-century polyphony, is being superseded by a preoccupation with the poignant phrase and expressive harmony per se. These harmonic elements could be given coherence only through some new type of organization, such as we discussed in general terms in the last chapter, involving the dance and the stage.

Purcell did not succeed, for reasons for which he was not personally responsible, in establishing such a system. When Couperin started work in Paris the form had already been developed in the opera of Lully. Purcell's fantasias represent the more or less unconscious emergence of impulses which the composer, during the remainder of his short life, must attempt to subdue and organize. Couperin's organ masses may start from a similar point, but they contain other elements that help us to understand why, in France, a great classical and operatic tradition survived; whereas, after Purcell, the English tradition withered.

Besides containing much lovely music, the two organ masses are thus a case-book demonstrating the growth of the French classical tradition. They amalgamate, without any immature experimentalism, the many different tendencies observable in seventeenth-century French organ music. Basically, there is the austere, religious polyphonic technique of the plainsong fantasia, inherited from the great Titelouze; it was from the German Protestant complement to this tradition that J. S. Bach started. Then there are passages which use chromaticism and dissonant suspensions to convey a peculiar impression of the dissolution of the senses. This technique is more extremely employed by Gigault and Marchand, and we have already referred to its appearance in Purcell. It is significantly used by the subjective and emotional Frescobaldi to accompany the most mystical moment of the Catholic ritual, the Elevation of the Host. The greatest and most celebrated of all examples of the technique is, of course, the Crucifixus of Bach's B minor Mass.

At a further extreme from these chromatic passages there are movements showing a lively sense of physical movement, which Couperin learned from the ballet. This links up with the more naïve popular type of *air de cour* such as the *vaudevilles*; as one may see more obviously in the relatively unsubtle work of Nicolas Le Bègue. From the more sophisticated aspects of the *air de cour*, and from the clavecinists and lutenists, Couperin and the other organ composers derived a symmetrical graciousness in their melodies and some conventions of ornamentation. And over all there is a concern for the proportions of the whole which he learned from the theatre music of Lully. Most of these contributory features will be discussed in more appropriate contexts in later chapters of this book. In this estimate of Couperin's start, it is the synthesizing process that we are most interested in.

The form of the masses is simple. Since they were intended for liturgical use, any elaborate musical development would have been unsuitable. The Catholic Church in France did not allow the organ the importance it came to have in Protestant Germany; unpretentiously, it had to fill in any gaps in the service with brief comments or variations on the liturgically important plainsong motives.[11]

---

[11] This convention still survived in 1770, as we may see from Dr Burney's patronizing description of a service at Notre Dame: 'Though this was so great a festival, the organ accompanied but little. The chief use of it was to play over the chant before it

Couperin's couplets on the Kyrie, Gloria, Offertory, Benedictus (Elevation), Sanctus, and Agnus Dei have, like those of his contemporaries, mostly lost their connection with the plainsong base; they are short pieces, headed by a phrase of the Latin text, some in the old fugal idiom, others more operatic in technique. Most of the couplets in the minor end on the dominant, suggesting their functional position as a preparation for some part of the service. We may note that Couperin and his contemporaries usually employ the term couplet for the episodes of the rondeau. The use of the term in the organ masses would seem to imply that the pieces are episodes in the liturgy. The (normally unstated) theme is the plainsong melody.

In discussing the music we shall in the main follow the catalogue of its constituent elements, given earlier in the chapter. All the real plainsong fantasias, those directly rooted in the old technique, occur in the bigger work, the *Messe Solemnelle*. Of course, Couperin's plainsong pieces are not monumental music like the tremendous hymns of Titelouze. Those are the culmination of a great religious age; their polyphonic embroideries around the plainsong stem attain great intensity, but even at their most baroque they remain cathedral music as much as the masses and motets of Lassus, with never a hint of theatricality. Some of the finest movements in Titelouze's *œuvre* (and he seems to me one of the most profound and noble of all keyboard composers) have a pure, other-worldly suavity in the vocal contours of their lines which is almost medieval in feeling, closer to Josquin than to anything in the later sixteenth century.[12] We may mention as one instance a truly celestial fantasy on

---

was sung, all through the Psalms. Upon enquiring of a young abbé, whom I took with me as a nomenclator, what this was called, "C'est proser" ('Tis prosing), he said. And it should seem as if our word prosing came from this dull and heavy manner of recital.' (*The Present State of Music in France*.)

[12] From this point of view, it is interesting that Titelouze deprecated modal alteration and encouraged rhythmic freedom as a means of achieving variety: 'Quant au changement du mode, je croy qu'il faudroit plustot changer de mouvement, haster aux paroles violentes et furieuses et tarder aux tristes et pesantes, car pour le changement de mode il est défendu par les lois musicales en même ouvrage, et le changement de mouvement est permis et a un grand effet par la variété qu'il y apporte.' (Correspondence with Mersenne, 1622.)

Titelouze must have acquired a thorough grounding in the old style vocal polyphony of the Franco-Flemish school at the Walloon Jesuit College of St Omer, where he received his elaborate education. On the other hand he would also have become familiar with more advanced instrumental techniques. The college was much frequented by English Catholics escaping persecution, and it seems reasonably certain that Titelouze must have met Bull and Peter Phillips.

Ave Maris Stella, which employs a more or less continuous pedal point:

Nowhere does he indulge in the chromaticisms and recitative-like rhapsodic passages that we find in, say, Frescobaldi's toccata elevations. It is noteworthy, however, that although Titelouze adheres always to the medieval plainsong-variation convention, and theoretically at least to the scholastic basis of the church modes, his concern for an effective keyboard technique constantly leads him into devices (chains of suspended sevenths, for instance), which give a curiously rich and 'modern' tonal impression:

Now it is this polyphonic-harmonic aspect of Titelouze's technique which Couperin develops in a more extreme form in his plainsong pieces and fugues. The rich sequential sevenths in the last few bars of the tiny *Deo Gratias* that forms the epilogue to the *Messe Solemnelle* are a beautiful example of this; and the yearning upward lift of the diminished fourth in the little fugato motive illustrates the more 'harmonic' nature of Couperin's linear writing:

A comparable and highly impressive example of this harmonic-contrapuntal technique is contained in the four organ fugues on one subject, by d'Anglebert, with their powerful false relations, parallel sevenths, and appoggiaturas:

Another composer who was partial to the sequential technique was the organist of Chartres, Giles Jullien, who employed it sometimes with nobility, as in the *Prélude du Premier Ton*, sometimes with a rather cloying pathos:

Couperin, however, never loses his balance. Later, a merging of this harmonic-contrapuntal idiom with the overlapping suspensions which he learned from the Italian violin sonatas is to produce beautiful results not only in chamber music but also in church motets and elevations.

These passages represent the basis of Couperin's technique in organ music; and they are, as we have seen, half-way between polyphony and harmonic thought. We next come to the passages and movements which are ostensibly harmonic in effect, depending mainly on chromaticisms and dissonant suspensions. They are perhaps best regarded as an intensification of the basic contrapuntal-harmonic technique, since although they are not usually fugal, they are always the product of fluent part-writing. The point of departure is the same; only the harmonic impact of the passage takes the centre of the stage, ousting the linear element.

The couplet *Et in Terra Pax* is a fine example from the *Messe*

89

Solemnelle, almost identical with a passage in one of Purcell's fantasias; one chromatic chord resolves on to another until they sink to rest on a serene major third:

Still more remarkable is the whole of the Benedictus elevation from the same mass. There is nothing here which is astounding in the manner of the contemporary organist Louis Marchand, whose suspended dissonances are so elliptical as to produce an almost Tristanesque dissolution of tonality, paradoxically violent in its emotional effect, considering that the piece is so consistently quiet:

But Couperin's idiom is as a whole more coherent and mature. Though Couperin's dissonances are intense, there is nothing emotionally virulent in his style, as there is in the work of Marchand and Gigault, or in the earlier generation, Bull, Sweelinck, or Frescobaldi. The acridity of Couperin's dissonances is rounded off in the flow and the warm spacing of the parts. Those of Gigault are uncompromising, and at times even ferocious, as witness this coruscation of sevenths, ninths, and seconds:

Even quite unimportant composers such as Boyvin, or elegiac ones such as Dumont, occasionally have a similar muscular quality:

What counterbalances the emotional harmonies in Couperin's
organ music is the lucid diatonicism of his melodies, which have a
simplicity and freshness perhaps derived, deep down, from French
folk song and its relation to the French language. The elegance of
the clavecinists here meets the austere passion of the organ composers, so that the 'linked sweetness' of the double suspensions is
reconcilable with the sonorous simplicity of a wonderful little piece
like the *Qui tollis peccata mundi* of the *Messe des Convents*. The poise
of this—the pure yet flexible line, the clear yet fluid part-writing—
gives the music a luminosity which is, if possible, a refinement on
the most fragrant triple-rhythmed melodies of the lutenists and
Chambonnières. The tender strophic tune and the diatonic harmonic
period appear to be related to the Italian operatic aria; yet how completely different is its mood from that of the slow airs of Handel:

This music has a spring-like innocence, a *premier matin du monde*
atmosphere which is also supremely civilized; we may compare it,
perhaps, with Racine's *Esther*. The couplet is interesting, too, in that
it shows how Couperin's voluptuous delicacy, which like Lully's is
capable of a theatrical interpretation, is not irreconcilable with the
religious roots of his art in sixteenth-century polyphony. Both spiritually and technically he stands between the melodically (and reli-
giously) founded Titelouze and the harmonically (and socially)

92

centred Rameau. We shall note a more significant instance of this compromise when we examine Couperin's vocal church music.

The chromatic harmonic technique of emotional drama, in the organ pieces of Marchand no less than in the madrigals of Gesualdo, had been disruptive of the old conception of tonality rather than re-creative. It was assimilated into a coherent form of theatre music only through a preoccupation with harmonic clauses based on the symmetry of the dance such as we find principally in the works of Rameau and Handel. Couperin is neither Handelian, nor disruptively baroque. His methods of achieving a balance between melodic flexibility and harmonic symmetry are more mature than those of Purcell, and in some ways comparable with those of Bach.

Some couplets, particularly the trumpet pieces such as the delightful fourth couplet of the Gloria of the *Messe Solemnelle*, are simply symmetrical in their dance rhythm, although their lucid harmonic periods are enlivened by contrapuntal treatment. But more subtle pieces, for instance the beautiful eighth couplet of the same Gloria, achieve an equilibrium between the calm fluidity of the part writing, the melancholy of the chromaticisms which the flexible parts create, and the regularity of the underlying metrical pulse. As in so much of Bach, the level flow of the rhythm and the tranquil arching of the lines 'distances' the melancholy of the chromaticisms, divests them of any subjective emotionalism which would be inapposite to a music conceived for religious ritual:

In other pieces the symmetry of the pulse is counteracted by the unmetrical flow of a baroquely ornamented solo line, the ornaments playing an integral part in the line's expressiveness. (See the Benedictus elevation of the *Messe des Convents*.) In the complementary movement from the other mass, both elements, fluid chromaticisms and ornamented solo part, are combined together with a regular rhythmic pulse:

This method is more maturely developed in many of the greatest of Bach's choral preludes and in the finest of Couperin's later church music. Significantly the technique is less used during Couperin's most Italianate period.

The way in which these elements can be brought together to make a musical-theatrical form on a fairly extensive scale is revealed in the two *Offertoires*, the biggest pieces in the collections. That from the *Messe Solemnelle* is especially remarkable. It is modelled on the operatic overture, with a massive introduction embodying chains of harsh suspensions, rooted in vocal technique but much more aggres-

94

sive in their instrumental form; a plaintive fugal section, with piquantly dissonant entries; and a virile, contrapuntally treated gigue to conclude. This last movement uses clear dominant-tonic key relations, but its contrapuntal treatment of them is less harmonically formalized than the dance movement structure of the eighteenth-century suite. In this respect the piece as a whole is closer to the keyboard suites of say, Kuhnau, which resemble Lully's overture in that they occupy with dignity and beauty a position somewhere between fugal polyphony, operatic lyricism, and the dance. It lives without confusion in both a religious and an operatic world.

Nicolas de Grigny, the greatest of Couperin's contemporaries in the French organ school after Titelouze, shows the same compromise between religious polyphony, fluid baroque ornamentation, and clear architectural period; so does the powerful if less profound Du Mage, and the subtly refined Roberday. It is interesting that the organ composers who come out 'progressively' on the side of the new, secular, dance-like elements are musically the least satisfying. They have relinquished the old tradition without having learned how to deal adequately, in a purely instrumental form, with the new. Even a composer with a boldly experimental talent such as Marchand displays in the slow chromatic piece previously referred to, or in the richly dissonant *Plein Jeu* with the double-pedal part, fails on the whole to achieve a coherent idiom; while Gigault, who has a really impressive technique and a vigorous personality, makes no attempt to reach the paradoxical mingling of voluptuousness and spirituality which is the subtlest feature of the work of Couperin and de Grigny. The lesser men, such as Le Bègue, can substitute for the old polyphonic craftsmanship nothing but sequences of (often very charming) dance tunes. The final secularization of the tradition occurs in the Noëls and other pieces of Claude Balbastre, which although often in two parts are unequivocally dances built on symmetrical harmonic periods, with figuration and ornamentation as appropriate to the harpsichord as it is inapposite to the organ. The lutenist school declined when the clavecin composers took over many of the essentials of lute style. The clavecinists absorbed some features of organ polyphony also, but in this case there was little direct continuity because the technique of the organ, unlike that of the lute, is fundamentally opposed to that of the clavecin. Thus

Couperin is the last of the French organ school and even he wrote all his work for the instrument in his early twenties.

But Couperin was a man of the future as well as of the past. It was for him to show what the dance tune could be made to yield, for him to develop his work towards a classical stability. It was with this in mind that he turned, after the composition of the organ masses, to a deliberate study of the technique of the Italian trio sonata for violins and continuo.

Chapter Six

The Two-Violin Sonatas

Il faut écouter souvent de la musique de tous les goûts. . . .
Embrasser un goût national plutôt qu'un autre, c'est prouver
qu'on est encore bien novice dans l'art.

RAMEAU

AT THE END of the seventeenth century the Italian trio sonata was
accepted everywhere as the supremely fashionable musical convention. If it was 'modern', however, it was not revolutionary. There
was no element in it that was altogether new; its importance lay in
the fact that it provided a synthesis of tendencies which had been
developing all through the century. These trends towards technical
lucidity accompany, of course, the trend towards an autocratic,
highly stylized order in society.

There were two types of instrumental sonata, the sonata da chiesa,
and the sonata da camera. As its name suggests, the former had the
closer links with the past. It was normally written for violins, lute,
and organ, and comprised a slow prelude, a fugal *allegro*, a lyrical
grave, and a more dance-like *presto*. All the movements inclined to
imitative treatment; and the very fact that the composers favoured
the two-violin medium rather than the solo violin suggests a reluc-
tance wholly to relinquish polyphonic methods in favour of the
homophonic continuo.

There are still frequent passages, in the classical Corelli as well as
the more intrepid Purcell, in which the lines produce the most
dramatic intensity through chromaticisms, false relations, and overlapping figurations, similar to those in the toccata technique of the
brilliant Frescobaldi or Gabrieli. In general, however, the tendency
which we have already noticed in the organ masses, for the polyphony to be ordered by harmonic considerations rather than itself

97

producing the harmony, is here more explicit. The polyphonic element is represented by the solo instruments, the homophonic element by the continuo which articulates the harmonic periods not, as in the opera, in accordance with a series of events on a stage, but with a musical logic of its own. This logic graded all diatonic chords in accordance with their distance from a tonic centre, distance being measured by reference to the cycle of fifths. Certain harmonic procedures—such as the use of chains of suspended sevenths and to a lesser degree 6 : 3 chords, or the use of the dissonant diminished seventh chord to gather tension before the resolving dominant-tonic cadence —gradually became accepted methods of defining tonality. To this definition the soloists' polyphony had to be adjusted.

Gabrieli had used a melodically generative technique whereby the initial subject grows into other themes, so that the movement often ends with five or six related motives. The sonata composers employ a basically similar technique, but seek for greater unity and cogency, usually restricting themselves to a mono- or bi-thematic treatment. It is true that they sometimes, when they use two themes, suggest a contrast of mood between them, thus remotely anticipating the development of 'shape' music in the second half of the eighteenth century. They never attempt, however, to investigate the possibilities of contrasted tonalities. Even to music of the late baroque period the dramatic tonal contrasts associated with the Viennese sonata are entirely foreign. The late baroque sonata still functions by way of a continual melodic generation and expansion; it differs from the early baroque principle of *division* and variation mainly because the continuous expansion of the initial motive or motives is now ordered by the scheme of tonal relations based on the cycle of fifths. The growth of the figuration moves through a series of fresh starts in different keys, usually the dominant, sub-mediant, sub-dominant, super-tonic, and relative minor or major, the dominant having an importance equal with but not greater than the other keys. The structure is essentially architectural rather than dramatic.

The other type of sonata, the sonata da camera for one or two violins usually with harpsichord continuo and string bass, was not radically different from the current dance suite. This will be discussed in detail in a later chapter; here we must note that the dance movements in the sonatas showed an increasingly mature understanding of the principles of tonal relationship and, as a corollary, an increasing independence of the dance itself. In achieving this independence the sonata da camera borrowed many characteristics from the sonata da chiesa, into which convention it in turn introduced a more dance-like secularity. The two types soon became but vaguely differentiated. The sonata da chiesa acquired airy dance elements and lyrical passion from the theatrical inclinations of the sonata da camera, and the latter stiffened its backbone with some of the contrapuntal vitality of the sonata da chiesa; just as baroque opera incorporated many elements of religious polyphony and was then reabsorbed into the church. By Corelli's time the two sonata conventions though still flexible had more or less settled down as follows: Sonata da chiesa; slow overture (majestic and inclined to the polyphonic), free fugal movement (canzona), slow air (usually in 3 : 2 with some imitation and smooth chordal progressions), and finally a fugued dance. Sonata da camera; slow overture, canzona or allemande or coranto (the dance, particularly if an allemande, inclining to contrapuntal treatment), slow air or sarabande, quick dance (often a gigue, and often quasi-fugal). In his works for solo violin Bach applies the term sonata only to the sonata da chiesa; the da camera sonatas he describes as partitas. His solo violin works thus offer a neat illustration of the difference between the two types.

As the two kinds of sonata merge into one another, one sees that the sonata owes its historical importance to the fact that it mates the technique of voice and dance. The violin can do things which the voice cannot, yet it is not anti-vocal in conception. The violin line modifies the traditional vocal phrases by the introduction of intervals, such as the diminished seventh or augmented fourth, which have a high degree of tension and passion; but it does not deny vocal principles. All the contemporary commentators refer to the cantabile character of Corelli's playing; Martinelli points out in his *Lettre familiari e critiche* of 1758 that Corelli's unenterprising partiality for the middle register of his instrument was due to his desire to preserve a singing sweetness and naturalness of tone. He wanted his violin to sound like someone singing with ease and purity; the very high and very low registers of the instrument were used only rarely and for some special effect, as an opera composer might, in exceptional circumstances, demand from his singers a shriek or a growl.

99

One might almost say that during the later baroque period the violin became the moulding influence on operatic vocal line itself. In the operatic arias and the bel-canto-like slow movements of the violin sonatas, the ornaments with which violinist and virtuoso singer embellish their lines both counteract the rigidity of the harmonic periods and help to build up the climax in the line itself; there is a beautiful example in the largo of Handel's D major sonata.

Only gradually did the violin composers overcome a deep-rooted distrust of the simple symmetrical 'tune', which had for so long been regarded as unworthy of inclusion in a serious composition. But even in fugal movements a more dance-like symmetry becomes noticeable. Fugal entries increasingly concentrate on a simple metrical motive with clear harmonic implications, and there is a leaning towards the 'thematic development' of a pithy phrase in place of the technique of lyrical growth. This procedure may have been suggested by the operatic splitting up of words for dramatic effect. On the other hand, the violin composers of Corelli's school do not approach the harmonically systematized fugue of the middle eighteenth century. Their fugal subjects are 'harmonic' in character, but their method of treating the subjects preserves much of the seventeenth-century freedom. Perhaps one might say that there is about an equal proportion of old-fashioned, quasi-vocal fugues 'instrumentalized', and of bright symmetrical dances 'fugued'.

Formally, as we have seen, the sonatas usually start from the old method of melodic generation and expansion. The influence of the dance, however, leads to frequent phrase-groupings in sequence, to repetitions of phrases in related keys, and, still more important, to a repetition of material at the ends of the sections. From this point of view there is an interesting development in the dance forms. The majority are in binary structure, state their melodic material and develop it with contrapuntal passage-work to a close in or 'on' the dominant, thus concluding the first section. The second section repeats the material in the same order, only starting from the dominant and working back to the tonic. On the other hand, a later type of dance movement, much favoured by Domenico Scarlatti, has a similar first section, then a section of development or mild contrast in related keys, then a restatement of the original material in the original key at the end. This is a remote anticipation of the 'inveterately dramatic' sonata form of Haydn and Mozart. In both Bach and Couperin the more archaic convention still holds its own with the new. This latter type of ternary structure should not be confused with ternary *da capo* form, which has a first section ending in the *tonic*, middle section of development in related keys, and restatement of the original material in the original key. The conclusion of the first section in the tonic deprives the *da capo* form of any sense of progression, and makes it more suitable for reflective and meditative, than for dramatic, expression; many of Bach's arias in the cantatas are a case in point. The sonatas have a few movements constructed on this relatively static principle, but they are not frequent.

The technique of the violin sonata is usually associated with the name of Corelli, though he did not 'invent' it—it was rather an autonomous growth. Fine sonatas of the da chiesa type by Marini and Mezzaferratta, and by composers of other nationalities such as Biber and Rosenmüller, had appeared some years before Corelli's famous volumes. It is perhaps pertinent to mention the extremely beautiful French H.M.V. record of Rosenmüller's E minor sonata, both because the performance, with its solo violins and organ, harpsichord and string continuo, gives a convincing notion of the baroque richness of sonority which should characterize these works, and which is so pitifully misrepresented by the usual performance with piano; and because the work itself is of such superb quality. It illustrates all the features of the early baroque sonata, having a massive slow introduction, a lovely second movement which is half-way between vocal polyphony and the operatic aria, a strange, rhapsodic transitional movement derived from operatic recitative, and a fugued dance to conclude. It demonstrates clearly—with its long, finely balanced lines which at the same time do not make much use of crude repetition—the compromise which we have remarked on between the soaring polyphony of the solo lines and the homophony of the continuo.

If Corelli did not invent the sonata, however, there is some excuse for associating it with his name in that he did, in his scrupulously pure and polished examples, give it its classical form. His work has both lyrical ardour and incisive precision; and this union of qualities prepares the way for the great classical baroque composers whose work for his instrument and in an idiom in part derived from him, may be said to surpass his work in sublimity and power. These composers are Vivaldi, J. S. Bach, Leclair, and the Couperin of *L'Impériale*.

There were three main reasons why Corelli's sonata attained so remarkable a popularity in France. One reason, as we have seen, was that its technique could not be ignored by any European composer who wished to create a vitally 'contemporary' music. Another reason was intellectual snobbery, for even people who could not understand the implications of the sonata realized that so advanced and sophisticated a society as the French could not afford to be musically behind the times. And the third reason was that there was much in Corelli's sonatas that the French could recognize as a native product. It is hardly surprising, considering the high point to which Lully had developed the forms of theatre music, that Corelli should have made use of many facets of Lully's work in his classical sonata. Many of Corelli's gavottes and minuets have a flavour of the French theatre, and, particularly in the concerti grossi, there are movements —for instance the largo and allegro of the third concerto—which derive directly from the Lullian overture. Corelli acquired a thorough knowledge of Lully's work from the francophile Muffat, and cannot himself have approved of the animosity which was later shown by the partisans of both the French and Italian cause.[13]

We have seen that during the *grand siècle*, in France as in England, the violin had been regarded as a somewhat ribald instrument; as Peter Warlock pointed out, the attitude of cultivated musicians to the violin was similar to the attitude of such people to the saxophone today. The viol, lute, and clavecin were the instruments of polite society; the violin could be used for dance music, on festive occasions, and in operatic tutti when a considerable noise was required. But even as late as 1682 Father Ménestrier referred to the violin as 'quelque peu tapageur', while six years earlier, in England, Mace had written: 'You may add to your Press a Pair of Violins to be in Readiness for any Extraordinary, Jolly and jocund Consort Occasion: *But never use them, but with this Proviso*'. We should remember,

[13] It can, however, have been only in his late work that Corelli was *conscious* of the influence of Lully. We remember the well-known story of Handel's exasperation with Corelli, when the Italian performed with inadequate passion one of Handel's works; Handel is said to have snatched the fiddle out of Corelli's hands; whereupon Corelli retorted, 'Ma, caro Sassone, questa musica è nel stilo francese, di ch'io non m'intendo.'

of course, that Mace was a valetudinarian in his attitude to contemporary music.

It was by way of the church that the violin became respectable in France; for an instrument that could be used to accompany the cantatas of a Carissimi was clearly worthy of serious attention. The cantata was related to the sonata da chiesa, which could also be performed in church; when once the French public had observed the dignity which Corelli could give to the instrument there was no more ground for suspicion. Then, in 1705, even Lecerf de la Viéville, the bitterest opponent of Italianism, could admit that although the violin 'n'est pas noble en France, mais enfin un homme de condition qui s'avise d'en jouer ne déroge pas'. The vogue spread with phenomenal vigour. 'Quelle joie, quelle bonne opinion de soi-même n'a pas un homme qui connoît quelque chose au cinquième Opera de Corelli', complained Lecerf de le Viéville, in despair. Couperin's innocent deception in producing his early sonatas under an Italian name, as described previously, had shown which way the wind was blowing. Soon, 'cette fureur de composer des sonates à la manière italienne' obsessed almost all French composers, and from 1700 a continuous stream of sonatas appeared, culminating in the four volumes of the great Leclair's sonatas from 1723 to 1738, the last two violin works of Couperin in 1724 and 1725, and the noble sonatas of Mondonville in 1733.

In 1692, two years after the composition of the organ masses, Couperin wrote four sonatas in the Italian da chiesa manner. In 1695 he added two more. Nearly thirty years later, in 1724, he added to three of the original four sonatas, sets of dances or partitas in the French manner, thus producing a series of diptychs analogous to the Bach violin sonatas and partitas. He then rechristened them; (*La Pucelle* became *La Françoise*, *La Visionnaire* became *L'Espagnole*, and *L'Astree* became *La Piemontoise*); added another double sonata called *L'Imperiale*, the da chiesa part of which may have been written about 1715; and published them all together under the title of *Les Nations*. In these double works we can thus see the French and Italian manners placed side by side. Finally, in the two *Apothéose* sonatas which he composed in 1722 and 1725, we can see the two manners mated. We shall examine these works more or less in chronological order, first dealing with the Italian sonatas of 1692 and 1695, then with the partitas added to them, then with the two parts of *L'Impériale*, which

103

are both manifestations of Couperin's maturity, and lastly with the two *Apothéoses*.

As though to emphasize its experimental nature at this stage of his career, *La Steinquerque*, one of the earliest of the 1692 group of sonatas, is the work that most reminds us, not only of Corelli, but also of Handel. In these sonatas Couperin is investigating some of the possibilities of the harmonic 'shape', as opposed to the melodic texture; so, whereas the organ masses had been to a considerable degree polyphonic in impetus, he here produces a work which relies mainly on the balance of spacious harmonic clauses, in which even the fugal subjects are, like so many of Handel's, built largely out of the notes of the common triad. The result is an Italianized version of Lully's battle musics, a work in the grand manner, befitting a ceremonial occasion—the piece is in honour of the victory at Steinkerque. But compared with the mature reconciliation of polyphonic and harmonic principles which we find in Couperin's later work, or in Bach, or even in the earlier organ masses, its spaciousness is achieved at the expense of subtlety. Being in some ways a ceremonial piece, and in others a technical experiment, the music lacks personality; it has few of the unmistakable Couperin touches.

Its form is a free descriptive version of the sonata da chiesa, with a strong dance influence. It opens with a vigorous overture constructed out of the martial fanfares of the introductory flourishes to the ballet; the interest centres almost entirely in the massive march of the harmonies. This is followed by a simple symmetrical air, on the model of the airs of Lully, though perhaps with a slightly Handelian solidity. A powerfully harmonized *grave*—musically the most interesting section of the sonata—makes extended uses of overlapping suspensions and leads to a jaunty, but not very sustained, fugue. An interlude of fanfares, impossible to perform convincingly on the piano, introduces a swinging theme in 3 : 2, fugally treated, but very harmonic in character. There is a further *grave* passage, and then the movement bounds in triple rhythm to a joyous close, the violins playing in consistent homophony in thirds and sixths.

The E minor sonata, finally called *La Françoise*, is of deeper musical interest than *La Steinquerque*, but it is still hardly representative of Couperin's intrinsic quality. This time it is closer to Corelli than Handel, though the opening *grave* displays an almost lush 'Italian' indulgence in chromaticisms, such as the classical Corelli himself did

104

not often sanction. Though short, the movement rises to a most impressive climax:

(Reduction)

etc.

The atmosphere is refined, elegant, and *mélancolique*; it has possibly something of the elegiac self-indulgence of La Rochefoucauld. The briskly contrapuntal second movement is quite elaborately developed, and makes jocular use of a little descending scale passage. Here too the atmosphere is highly charged and emotional; the brisk rhythm is counteracted by some extraordinary passages in dissolving sequential sevenths:

Violins

Continuo
&
Bass

The other movements are not at the same level as these two. A simple, quasi-operatic air half-way between Lully and Corelli, two measured *grave* interludes, and a couple of very Corellian gigues (the second of which has an agile cello part), are all beautifully made but compared with Couperin's finest work are lacking in character.

L'Espagnole sonata, in C minor, opens with a very fine *grave* which produces a dark sonority through frequent use of augmented intervals, and dissonant appoggiaturas and suspensions:

The quick section into which the *grave* leads also has tension and excitement, and mounts to its B flat climax in the first-violin part, with inevitable momentum. The air in siciliano rhythm makes fascinating use of the opposition of solo voices and a quasi-tutti effect. It often uses a falling scale passage, diatonic or chromatic, in the bass, grouping above it melodic patterns, decorative figurations, and seductive harmonies of sevenths and ninths:

The feeling, at once noble and pathetic, suggests the *lamento* of seventeenth-century baroque opera; one is reminded of Purcell, or even of the airs on a chromatic bass in Monteverdi. A merry canzona is notable for the whirling descending scale passages in the bass part, combined with chains of suspensions in the violins and continuo. A brisk, rather 'harmonic' and Handelian gigue is followed by a chromatically accompanied air, and the work concludes with a powerful double fugue on a stable, diatonic theme, with a chattering countersubject.

The opening *grave* of *La Piemontoise* sonata, in G minor, is perhaps the most Purcellian movement in Couperin's work. In this passage

it is not merely the chromatically moving bass, but the long arch of
the lines, the habitual syncopations, the augmented fourths and
diminished fifths, which remind us of Dido's lament:

Reduction

Something of this operatic passion is preserved in the elaborately
syncopated quick fugal movement, where the part-writing has an
agility and rhythmic independence which is common in Bach, but
rare in Handel or Corelli; in this respect it presages Couperin's most
mature work. The next *grave* is in the mood of the opening, and has
some acute dissonant suspensions. Here, too, the level flowing
movement, the dissonances, and the sudden change to the major
anticipate some of Couperin's most characteristic effects in later
work. The delicate canzona is based on two instrumental figurations
derived from the common triad and the major scale. Two quasi-
operatic airs, one in the major, the other in the minor, are gently
symmetrical and have a more personal voice than the similar movements in the other 1692 sonatas; the suspensions and ornamental
resolutions in the inner parts suggest the influence of the clavecinists,
and may be compared with the similar devices in the sarabande of
Chambonnières, quoted on page 198. A return to Purcellian intensity occurs in the brief *grave*, with its chromatic progressions and
energetic *marqué* dotted rhythm, in ascending and descending scales.

It leads without break into a simple Corellian gigue, charming, but
not especially significant.

The two 1695 sonatas, *La Sultane* and *La Superbe*, use the same
idiom as the 1692 group, but within their deliberate Italianism they
allow for a much freer expression of Couperin's sensibility. Here
Couperin absorbs the Italian convention into the French tradition as
consummately as Purcell adapted it to the linear and harmonic
vigour of the English. *La Sultane*, in particular, is conceived on a
grand scale, and is remarkable not only for its extensive development but also for the fact that it includes two more or less independent cello parts. It thus has four free string parts in all; the second
cello sometimes, but by no means habitually, doubles the bass of the
continuo.

The first *grave* is on a much bigger scale than any of the overtures
to the earlier sonatas. It is more than twice as long, and, over a level
flowing crochet pulse, imitatively develops proud, spacious themes
in overlapping suspensions which reinforce the majestic progression
of the harmonies. In passages such as this:

persistent suspended seconds have a sinewy power, balancing the richness of the harmonies, which we meet with for the first time in Couperin's work—for the comparable passages in the organ masses have not this linear vigour. It is the first intimation of that union of solidity with subtlety which relates Couperin's finest work more closely to Bach than to any other composer. This controlled but highly emotional prelude also includes a remarkable, dark-coloured passage for the two cellos, over long-sustained dominant and tonic pedals.

The second, quick contrapuntal, movement is thematically related to the *grave* and is also designed on a broad scale. It is notable for its close, Bach-like rather than Handelian, texture, both in its harmonic progressions:

and in its linear organization:

The *air tendre* is a dialogue between the two cellos, dark-hued in the minor, and the two violins, softly glowing in the major. It leads into a *grave*, built on drooping appoggiaturas, wherein Couperin, for the first time in his Italianized music, recovers the quintessential Couperin of the finest movements of the organ masses. Predominantly harmonic in effect, the chains of appoggiaturas are suavely sensuous, and yet paradoxically create an unearthly feeling that the ego (*le moi*) and the will (*la volonté*) are dissolving away. Note the insistent dotted rhythm; the caressing ninth; and the augmented fifth chord which almost suggests that the tenderness of the emotion is about to break into tears:

The words of Fénelon—'C'est dans l'oubli du Moi qu'habite a paix'—are relevant to this aspect of Couperin's music. We shall discuss it in detail in the chapter on the church music, and shall then have occasion to note many examples of the technical features referred to above. The two remaining fast sections of this sonata are less personal, though the gigue has some typical harmonic acridities and rhythmic surprises. It provides, in any case, an appropriately festive note to conclude this most beautiful work.

The A major sonata, *La Superbe*, though this time for the normal resources, also has a certain *ampleur* of conception. It opens with a *grave* and canzona which have a maturely experienced majesty com-

parable with Handel's finest work, and far removed from the more
naïvely noble gestures of *La Steinquerque*. None the less, these movements are not among Couperin's most representative work. The
next section, *très lentement*, is, however, one of his finest inspirations,
combining the *superbe* Handelian manner of this sonata with a subtle
use of false relation reminiscent of the organ masses. Through the
dotted rhythm and the hushed progression of the harmonies it
evokes a tremulous quietude similar to that of the *grave* interlude of
La Sultane. The harmonies are often of a most unconventional
nature—for instance, this 'sobbing' use of the diminished fifth in an
interrupted cadence, followed by the melting sequence of seventh
chords; the last of them produces one of those 'catches in the breath'
that we have had occasion to refer to once or twice before:

Reduction

The canzona and final gigue are sprightly and well developed, but
have not the closely wrought texture of Couperin's best work in
this manner. The *air tendre* is one of the simplest and most beautiful
of Couperin's pieces in the triple-timed *brunete* convention.

The dance suites which Couperin added to three of the 1692
sonatas in 1724 are identical in technique with his *concerts royaux*,
published about the same time. In some ways it would thus be
logical to discuss them together with the *concerts*, as the most
central expression of the French instrumental tradition. By con-

sidering them beside the sonatas to which they were attached, however, one can understand more clearly how the classically developed
form of the French suite approximated to the binary convention of
the Italian partita or sonata da camera. We shall therefore leave
detailed consideration of the suite until the chapter on the *concerts*;
and in this context we shall say on the subject only so much as is
necessary to indicate the relationship between the French and Italian
genres. The two-violin suites all date from the last years of Couperin's
life, and may stand with Bach's cello, violin and keyboard partitas as
examples of an apparently limited convention used with the maximum of imaginative significance.

As with Bach—and in conformity with tradition—the allemandes are, apart from the chaconnes, the most musically extended
movements, and often have considerable polyphonic complexity.
Couperin's more discreet sensibility does not often call for the
whirling linear arabesques typical of Bach's most baroque work, as
exemplified in the great allemande from the D major cello suite, or
those from the D major and E minor harpsichord partitas; but there
is something of Bach's disciplined melodic profusion in the treatment of the aspiring scale passage in the allemande of the first
(E minor) suite. The C minor allemande is less free melodically, but
more involved harmonically; it is at once richly chromatic and
gravely elegiac. This quality is found, too, in the allemande of the
G minor suite, perhaps the finest of the three, very subtle in its
phrase groupings.

Each suite has two courantes, the first of which (the French type)
carries the traditional rhythmic ambiguity of the dance to an extreme
point. Couperin rivals Bach in the complexity of the alternations
and combinations of 3 : 2 and 6 : 4 which he extracts from his
material. These movements are usually highly ornamented, the
ornamentation being an integral part of the line and harmony:

These rhythmic and harmonic elaborations of a simple dance structure testify to the high degree of sophistication in Couperin's community. The second courante is usually more airy and flowing,
more dance-like; though Couperin does not confine himself to the
6 : 4 Italian form, and never gives the courante the straightforward
harmonic treatment of Handel.

Couperin writes two types of sarabande. One (like that of the G
minor suite; it is actually in the major) is *tendre* and *cantabile* in
character, of exquisite refinement and fragilely ornamented, in the
manner of the theme of Bach's Goldberg Variations. This type of
sarabande, as we shall see in a later chapter, is a part of Couperin's
legacy from Chambonnières, who in his turn inherited it from the
lutenists. The other type is grave and powerful, congested in harmony, like that of Bach's E minor partita; it often uses dissonant
appoggiaturas and acciaccaturas, and employs a slow but strenuous
dotted rhythm, conventionally performed with the dots doubled.

Couperin's gigues are sometimes of the amiable Italian type in a
lilting 6 : 8 (that for instance from the G minor suite); sometimes of
a French type in 6 : 4, more complicated rhythmically than those
of Corelli or Handel. This type of gigue Couperin derives from
Chambonnières and the lutenists; he treats the dance with a tautness
which is again suggestive of Bach, though his gigues are usually
slight and rather frothy. They are scherzo movements, and he has
no crabbed, almost ferocious gigues such as Bach writes, in a contrapuntal style, in the E minor partita. The little gavottes, bourrées and
minuets are not much more than occasional music, and do not call
for comment in this chapter.

The crowning glories of the suites are the rondeaux and the
chaconnes—both being a further development of Lully's treatment,
which we have already discussed, of the ballet dances. The rondeau
of the C minor suite is suavely melancholy but not especially re-

markable; the rondeau in G, from the fourth suite, is on the other hand a delightful example of Couperin's sophisticated-rustic manner, producing a silvery flute-like sound through canonic overlapping and dulcet thirds:

This mode is even more beautifully expressed in the rondeau of *L'Impériale*, which we shall describe shortly.

In the chaconnes, the regular flow of the repeated bass (with the accent on the second beat of the traditional 3 : 4) provides a foundation over which the lines and figurations grow cumulatively more impassioned until they break into quicker movement. The opening suspensions across the bar, in the E minor chaconne, have a tone of noble melancholy; the level crochet pulse splits into quaver movement, then into a vigorous dotted rhythm with great animation in the bass part, and finally into resplendent staccato descending scale passages combined with extended trills. The chaconne of the C minor suite is an even grander work. The opening statement (*noblement*) is itself massively harmonized, with appoggiaturas suggesting an anguish almost comparable with that of the great B minor clavecin passacaille. There is an exquisite couplet for the two violins unaccompanied, in canon, and then the movement begins to build up a remorseless crescendo of excitement. A *vivement* couplet is founded on trumpet fanfares; the bass acquires greater animation, while the violins chant long chains of suspensions. Tentatively, the bass introduces chromatic elements, and the climax is reached in the mingling of the chromatic version of the bass with triple suspensions in the continuo and a powerful duo in double-dotted rhythm for the two violins:

115

The Bachian quality which we have noticed in our account of the suites finds its most consistent manifestation in the two parts of *L'Impériale*, a work in which both the da chiesa and da camera sections have an equal maturity. The classical ripeness is demonstrated most clearly in the power and length of the melodic structure. The opening *grave* has a melodic span that one finds but seldom outside Bach's work; its amplitude of structure is combined with subtlety in its linear and harmonic details:

The contrapuntal movement that follows is fiery, with acute dissonant suspensions. The second three-time *grave* is a *galant et magnifique* piece over a pulse in dotted rhythm. Its subsidiary chromaticisms have a dignified restraint, compared with the more fervid chromaticisms in the first two movements of the early *La Françoise*. This piece is in the relative major, as is the next, a gracious minuet in rondeau. A return to the triple rhythm provides a lyrical transition back to D minor, and the sonata ends with a vigorously developed fugue on this muscular subject, with its prominent tritonal sequences:

This is music of tremendous power, even ferocity, with a Bachian closeness of texture. This one movement is sufficient to dispose of the legend of Couperin the 'exquisite'.

The sonata da camera has a deliciously tenuous gigue and a massive sarabande, but is notable chiefly for its two big movements, the rondeau and chaconne. The rondeau has a theme of a tender diatonic simplicity which, in conjunction with the level rhythm, like a quietly breathing pulse, suggests a sense of light, space, and tranquillity comparable with the emotional effect of the ordered landscapes of Claude:

Like so much of Couperin's finest work, this music sounds as though it was written to please, to entertain, and yet is at the same time, in its purity, a spiritual rejuvenescence. The mood of the chaconne is similar, though the piece is on a grander scale. The broken rhythm and violently contrasted sonorities of the couplet in the minor key have an unexpected dramatic force, and, as in the graver C minor chaconne, the gradual introduction of chromatic elements gives the piece a cumulative momentum:

It ends, however, in happy tranquillity.

Couperin's last word in the sonata convention is contained in the two *Apothéoses*, dedicated to Corelli and Lully respectively; and there is no more effective demonstration of the distance Couperin has travelled than to compare the prelude of the Corelli *Apothéose* of 1722 with that of *La Steinquerque* of 1692. In the late work there is no sacrifice of majesty in the proportions. The balance of the movements as wholes is preserved, as is the lucid sequence of tonalities which do not adventure far beyond the dominant, sub-dominant, sub-mediant, and relative major and minor. But the incidental vitality and subtlety of melodic life have increased enormously. The lines are more nervously sensitive, so the polyphony is more flexible; and, as a consequence of this flexibility, the harmony has an added

118

richness. Such a passage as this, with its eloquent augmented and diminished intervals, indicates admirably this interior vitality, which is on the one hand so much more supple than the rather beefy homophonic texture of *La Steinquerque* and is on the other hand so much more mature than the chromaticisms of *La Françoise* (see next page). Something of this quality is found, too, in the fugal movement that expresses Corelli's joy at his reception on Parnassus; the tight harmonic texture is enhanced by fascinating syncopations. In such passages—we shall meet them throughout Couperin's work—the music, like the painting of Watteau, achieves a moving union of strength with sensitivity. The sensuous quality of the harmony parallels Watteau's glowing use of colour, which he in part derived from Rubens, and to a lesser degree from Titian and Veronese; the supple precision of the three string lines parallels Watteau's nervous draughtsmanship, the most distinctive quality of his genius, which he in part inherited from the Flemish and Dutch genre painters; while the stable sense of tonality in the movements as wholes corresponds to Watteau's instinct for proportion and 'composition', which was in part encouraged by his study of the noble serenity of Giorgione and the Venetians.[14]

The tranquil movement describing Corelli drinking at the spring of Hypocrene is one of those quintessential Couperin pieces which, however often one hears them, strike one anew with their freshness. The material—a level quaver movement proceeding mainly by step, accompanying serene minims which form quietly dissonant suspensions—is simple; yet the result has a spirituality which is perhaps Couperin's unique distinction. The piece is a still more rarefied distillation of the serenely 'dissolving' movements in the early *La Sultane* and *La Superbe* sonatas. It produces the same feeling of the dissolution of the ego and the will, and thus may, not altogether extravagantly, be termed 'paradisal'. In particular we should mention the modulation to A minor which comes at the end of the movement after two pages of unsullied D major. In the fluidity of the har-

[14] This account of Watteau's work indicates how he reconciles the two opposing parties of the *Poussinists* and the *Rubenists*. The conflict between the two schools, led by Felibien and De Piles respectively, was not dissimilar to the quarrel between the Ancients and the Moderns. For the contending factions, Poussin stood for draughtsmanship and the classical ideal, Rubens for colour and a 'modern' sensuousness. Both Watteau and Couperin—and for that matter Poussin himself—showed that the two conceptions need not be opposed, but could mutually enrich one another.

Violins

Bass
&
Continuo

monic transitions here, we have a reminiscence of the technique of
the organ masses—the paradox of a voluptuous purity. Note for
instance the heart-rending false relation in the penultimate bar,
before the tender resolution on to the major third:

The reminiscence of the earlier technique in no way compromises the music's integrity. Couperin no longer feels it necessary, as he did in *La Steinquerque*, to insist on his command of the modern homophony.

Another movement in this radiant manner is the *sommeil* music, one of the few intrusions into this Italianate work of an element intimately associated with Lully, even though originally derived from the Italian opera. It is remarkable for its delicately intertwined figuration. The progression of the lines by conjunct motion, in even quavers with a crochet pulse, was the accepted musical stylization of the idea of repose. The two sections flanking it, describing Corelli's enthusiasm and his awakening by the Muses, have a gaily glittering texture. In the first, Corelli's happiness bubbles and swirls in rapid scale passages and florid arabesques for the violins unaccompanied; in the second, the French dotted rhythm bounces through some closely wrought modulations from D to A, to F sharp and C sharp minor. The work concludes with an elaborately developed fugue on this excitingly syncopated subject:

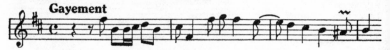

This also breaks into florid passages for the violins towards the end. We are a long way from the rather perfunctory, chordally dictated fugato passages of *La Steinquerque*.

Despite the interpolation of descriptive movements suggested by the ballet, the structure of the Corelli *Apothéose* is basically that of the sonata da chiesa; or it is the Italian sonata modified by Couperin's long experience of the French tradition. In the Lully *Apothéose* Couperin first gives, as it were, a summing up of the tradition on which he had been nurtured; and then demonstrates how he has, through his career, managed to incorporate the Italian sonata into it The *Apothéose* begins with a suite of pieces which are a microcosm in instrumental form of the Lullian opera; only when Corelli appears on the scene in the second part does the sonata technique become obtrusive. Then it is not merely in such superficialities as the quaint device of making Lully and Corelli fiddle in the 'French' and 'Italian' clefs respectively that we see how their two idioms have merged into one another.

Couperin's preface explains that the work is not conceived for violins exclusively; it may be performed on two clavecins, or on various appropriate combinations of instruments. This is true to some extent of all the sonatas; but it is interesting that it should be this explicitly theatrical work which prompts Couperin to say so. The Overture (Lully in the Elysian fields) moves with grave simplicity in a regular crochet pulse, achieving a noble pathos through groupings of a falling scale passage. It is a theatre piece which is more consistently homophonic than the Corellian da chiesa prelude usually is, but the relationship between the two types is clear enough. The airs of the *ombres liriques*, the *Vol de Mercure*, the *Descente d'Apollon* (contrapuntal but dance-like), and the *Rumeur souteraine* of Lully's contemporaries and rivals, are all chamber music versions of operatic devices. The *Tendres Plaintes* of Lully's contemporaries, which Couperin specifies should be performed by flutes or by *violons très adoucis*, is a beautiful instance of Couperin's rarefied sensuousness, built on a faux-bourdon-like procession of 6 : 3 chords. Again it differs from the 'rarefied' movements in earlier sonatas in being entirely homophonic. The *enlèvement de Lully* to Parnassus for the first time introduces the contrapuntal method of the Italian canzona, and makes fascinating play with a syncopated rhythm.

When Lully reaches Parnassus he is met by Corelli and the Italian muses who greet him with a *largo* strictly in the da chiesa manner, majestically proportioned, with acrid augmented fifths:

The *Remerciement de Lulli à Apollon* is a symmetrical operatic aria which illustrates the absorption of the Lullian air into the tonally more developed Italian arias of Handel; note the solid sequences and the figuration. The ornamentation remains, however, more French than Handelian:

Next Apollo persuades Lully and Corelli that the union of *Les Goûts françois et italiens* would create musical perfection; so the two muses sing together an *Essai, en forme d'ouverture, élégamment et sans lenteur.* This opens with a brilliant fanfare in dotted rhythm, which is followed by a 3 : 4 tune in flowing quavers, making considerable use of arpeggio figures. Then come two little *airs légers* for the violins without continuo; in one of them Lully plays the tune and Corelli the accompaniment, in the other the roles are reversed. And the whole work is rounded off with a full-scale sonata da chiesa, in which Lully and Corelli play together, the Italian technique being finally, as it were, translated into French.[15]

Musically, this sonata is the finest part of the Lully *Apothéose*. The *grave* is in the main Italian, with astringent augmented intervals and a Bachian closeness of texture. But the canzona, *Saillie*, is French in spirit and worthy to be put beside Couperin's best pieces in the burlesque vein. (We shall discuss this in detail in the chapter on the clavecin pieces.) The 3 : 2 *grave, rondement*, recalls the fragrance of the *Messe des Convents*, though it has now a more Italian amplitude. The last movement combines a Corellian contrapuntal technique with the dotted rhythm of the French theatre, and includes some interesting modulations, such as this from G to the minor of the dominant (see next page).

Although the Lully *Apothéose* is one of the most important of Couperin's works from a documentary point of view, it seems to me musically inferior to the Corelli *Apothéose*. The latter work, with the *Impériale* sonata, perhaps represents the highest level of Couperin's achievement in this convention; and both impress by their Bachian maturity. From this point of view, Couperin offers an interesting comparison, and contrast, with Purcell. Both experimented in the Italian sonata technique in the early sixteen-nineties, and for the same reason—they knew that if their country's music was to have a future, they had to take account of the new directions which the Italian sonata stood for. When they started to compose their sonatas, Purcell

[15] For an interesting anticipation of this mating of a 'French' and 'Italian' melody, see J. J. Fux's *Concentus Musico-instrumentalis*, published at Nuremburg in 1701. The seventh Partita of this work includes a movement in which an *aria italiana* in 6 : 8 is played simultaneously with an *air françois* in common time. Most of the pieces have French titles (*La joye des fidèles sujets, Les ennemis confus,* etc.); the *Sinfonia* combines a French triple rhythmed middle section with an Italianate contrapuntal opening. See Chapter xi for a general account of the French influence in Germany.

had behind him the Tudor tradition and the seventeenth-century baroque polyphonists such as Lawes and Jenkins; Couperin had behind him the organists, the lutenists, the ballet, and the theatre music of Lully. Purcell's more direct relation to the 'inflectional' methods of the sixteenth century was in some ways an advantage, for through it he was able to create those bold modulatory and harmonic effects which are the glory of his finest sonatas, such as the F minor or A

126

minor. But if Couperin's early sonatas have not Purcell's fiery originality, their relatively polite urbanity brings its own reward. Purcell, without a developed theatre music behind him, was unable to establish an English classical tradition; Couperin, with Lully behind him, had merely to modify in a contemporary manner a tradition that was already there.

This is why Couperin was able in later years to create sonatas, such as *L'Impériale* and the Corelli *Apothéose*, which in their classical poise are beyond anything which Purcell attempted in this style; this is why Couperin was able to produce music that can seriously be related to the work of Bach. It is not so much a question of the comparative degree of genius with which nature endows a particular composer; this is always difficult to estimate, since so many contributory factors have to be taken into account. It is a question of the value of a tradition; and while Couperin, like Bach, could have made nothing of the tradition without his genius, it is possible that, without the tradition, his genius might have been frustrated.

Chapter Seven

The Secular Vocal Works

IN DISCUSSING COUPERIN'S concern with 'les Goûts réunis', we have broadly equated the French 'goût' with the style of Lully. This style, however, incorporated a number of elements from French traditions of domestic music for the solo voice; and to these traditions Couperin himself made a modest contribution. Intrinsically his secular vocal music is of no importance; but the conventions which he employed in it have a direct bearing on his church music, and an implicit bearing on almost everything he wrote. In this chapter we must therefore offer some account of French conventions of solo vocal music in the seventeenth century, in order that we may understand how, in his church music, Couperin was able to translate Italian techniques into French terms; in order that we may have a more adequate appreciation of the native traditions to which he belonged.

During the *grand siècle* there were in French song two main lines of evolution, which are not always sharply differentiated. The first of these is the sophisticated *air de cour*, on which a few preliminary remarks have been made in Part I; the second is the more popular *chansons à boire*, *vaudevilles*, and *brunetes*. In the early years of the century there was not much difference between the two lines. Both were variations of the simpler homophonic madrigal in which the melodic interest was centred in the top line, so that the under parts could be with equal effectiveness either sung or played upon instruments; and both were associated with the dance, whether folk dance or the sophisticated ballet. The collection of *airs de cour* made by Adrien le Roy in 1597 makes no attempt to delineate the characteristics of the genre, beyond indicating that simplicity and a gentle graciousness were prerequisites of it.

Under the influence of *précieux* society, the *air de cour* became explicitly monodic and more sophisticated. It was not an attempt to embrace the Italian humanistic passion, but the deliberate creation of a refined, virtuoso stylization. It is true that the greatest of the early *air de cour* composers, Pierre Guédron, showed, under the influence of the *ballet mélodramatique*, some influence of the methods of Caccini, and in some of his airs attained to an almost operatic intensity:

but such passages are exceptional. In general the *air de cour* composers remained recalcitrant to the Italian style not because they were ignorant of it—they themselves composed 'Italian' settings of Italian words—but because they sought a different effect. Like every artist of the salons, they wanted a certain proportion and refinement combined with a highly charged emotionalism of a sweetly '*mélancolique*' order. The atmosphere is indicated by this quotation from Sorel's novel *Francion*:

Alors il vint des musiciens qui chantèrent beaucoup d'airs nouveaux, joignant le son de leurs luths et de leurs violes à celui de leurs voix. Ah, dit Francion, ayant la tête penchée dessus le sein de Laurette, après la vue d'une beauté il n'y a point de plaisir qui m'enchante comme fait celui de la musique. Mon cœur bondit à chaque instant; je ne suis plus à moi; les tremblements de voix font trembler mignardement mon âme.

The date of this passage, 1663, places it in the second florescence of the *air de cour*; it is quoted here because it demonstrates so clearly the impulse from which the *air de cour* grew. The concentration on an esoteric emotionalism, the deliberate cultivation of sensuous subtleties, is found also in the contemporary lutenists; it produced a kind of escape art which links up with the pastoral convention of the highly fashionable *Astree*. This pastoralism had itself been borrowed from Italian sources—from Guarini, Tasso, and Sannazar; it was not surprising that it prospered in the hyper-sophisticated French community. The pastoral life became an ideal because it was supposedly free of complications, free of *intrigue*; because it seemed to offer, regressively, a simpler mode of existence. From this point of view we can see the significance of Mersenne's remark:

Il faut premièrement supposer que la musique et par conséquent les airs sont faicts particulièrement et principalement pour charmer l'esprit et l'oreille, et pour nous faire passer la vie avec un peu de douceur parmi les amertumes qui s'y rencontrent.

This is an ambiguous attitude which we have met before—in La Rochefoucauld, for instance. The self-protective irony should not lead us to underestimate the degree to which the authors meant what they said.

In terms of musical technique, the sense of proportion was realized in the very simple formal structure which the composers adopted —the strophic tune in two parts, both with repeats (AA, modulation to dominant; BB return to tonic). The emotionalism and sensuousness within this formal framework were achieved partly by the incidental rhythmic subtleties, suggested by the text and by the composers' experiments in Greek prosody:

Ces Nymphes hos-tes-ses des bois,   Bravant les a - mou-reu - ses loix

and partly by the ornamentation which, with increasing complexity, embellished the vocal line. The elegant emotionalism was thus almost entirely a rhythmic and linear matter; the composers were not greatly interested in the Italian harmonic audacities, and were content if their lute parts 'accompanied' with flatly homophonic chords.

Even in the early days of the *air de cour*, the ornamentation was thus an integral part of the *préciosité*, of the *mignardise* which all the artists of the salons cultivated. It gave the line its suppleness of nuance; it made hearts tremble. Some of the ornaments were suggested by sixteenth-century conventions, particularly those of a descriptive nature. Thus references in the text to upward or downward movement, to flight, to flames literal or metaphorical, to pain or distress, are accompanied by appropriate melodic stylizations:

si la mort fié-chi - roit

and there is some approach to a scheme of musical symbols, analogous to the conventional vocabulary of the poems of a Tristan l'Hermite. There was, however, a growing tendency to indulge in ornamentation for its own sake—as a virtuoso exhibition of *mignardise*. Formulae such as the following were sometimes appropriate to the words:

Que n'es - tes vous las - sé - es,

at other times purely conventional:

D'un si doux trait,

In either case they rubbed any sharp corners off the lines and provided some compensation for the melodies' unenterprising range, which seldom exceeded an octave, was often restricted to a fifth, and, except in the case of Guédron, avoided leaps with any degree of harmonic tension. The ornaments helped to create a stylization suitable for the expression of *douceur* and *mollesse*.

Between 1630 and 1640 the *airs de cour* seemed to be in decline. A new impulse came from Pierre de Nyert, a wealthy dilettante, born in 1597 and educated in musically 'progressive' circles. He lived in Rome for a while, and made a study of the Italian theatre and Italian song: Maugars tells us that de Nyert himself announced that he wished to 'ajuster la méthode italienne avec la française'. He must have been a singer of virtuoso accomplishment; Bacilly remarks that the great Luigi Rossi 'pleuroit de joie de luy entendre exécuter ses airs'. He must also have been a man of some force of character, for all the composers followed his lead in attempting to reconcile the French and Italian techniques. La Fontaine's famous epitaph:

> Nyert, qui pour charmer le plus juste des Rois,
> Inventa le bel art de conduire la voix,
> Et dont le goût sublime à la grande justesse,
> Ajouta l'Agrément et la Délicatesse,

does not seem hyperbolical when compared with the mass of contemporary tributes to de Nyert's 'génie prodigieux, discernement merveilleux', and so on. His schools for singers, teaching voice production, pronunciation, style and gesture, soon became nationally celebrated: and it was partly through de Nyert's work, which encouraged a more declamatory technique and a more systematized harmonic sense, that the *air de cour* became one of the constituents of the classical opera.

Perhaps the most impressive evidence of de Nyert's influence is the re-emergence of Antoine Boësset, after a silence of some years, during which he was presumably studying the new techniques. The work of Boësset's old age has a lyrical vitality which cannot be found in the cloyingly 'sensitive' music he wrote in the first part of the century; we may note, for instance, his use of melodic progressions which have a clear harmonic basis:

It is also worth noting that the final volumes of Boësset's work are still published with lute tablature. Henceforth, the songs are published occasionally with lute tablature, more often with an instrumental bass, sometimes with a bass intended to be sung. The more modern methods increase at the expense of the old.

The leaders of the new movement were men of a later generation than either de Nyert himself or Boësset. Le Camus, de la Barre, and Michel Lambert (whom Lecerf de la Viéville called 'le meilleur maître qui ait été depuis des siècles') wrote their airs consistently with figured bass, and are more interested in problems of form and proportion than were the composers of the first half of the century, though they preserve much of the traditional rhythmic freedom. Their *air serieux* is the old *air de cour*, modified by Italian harmony and virtuosity. None of them has a talent of the order of Guédron, but they can create melodies which have a genuine dignity and pathos, as we may see from Lambert's setting of Jacqueline Pascal's poem, *Sombre désert, retraite de la nuit*. Although Mazarin imported Italian singers, and encouraged Italianism in every way, the native tradition was not swamped. Italianate violence was never allowed to imperil propriety, good taste, and *mignardise*. The distinction made by J. J. Bouchard, in a letter to Mersenne, was still upheld:

Que si vous voulez sçavoir mon jugement, je vous dirai que, pour l'artifice, la science, et la fermeté de chanter, pour la quantité de musiciens, principalement de chanteurs, Rome surpasse Paris autant que Paris fait Vaugirard. Mais pour la délicatesse et une *certa leggiadira e dilettevole naturalezza* des airs, les François surpassent les Italiens de beaucoup.

Mersenne himself makes the same point:

Les Italiens . . . représent tant qu'ils peuvent les passions et les affections de l'âme et de l'esprit, par exemple la colère, la fureur, le dépit, la rage, les défaillances du cœur et plusieurs autres passions, avec une violence si extraordinaire que l'on jugeroit quasi qu'ils sont touchez des mêmes affections qu'ils représentent en chantant, au lieu que nos Français se contentent de flatter l'oreille et qu'ils usent d'une douceur perpetuelle dans leurs chants, ce qui en empesche l'énergie.

Even the Italians themselves seem to have been susceptible to the virtues of the French idiom, while recognizing its limitations, if we may judge from J. B. Doni's *Traité de la Musique* of 1640:

Où est-ce que l'on chante avec tant de mignardise et délicatesse et où entend-on tous les jours tant de nouvelles et agréables chansons, même en la

bouche de ceux qui sans aucun artifice et étude font paroistre ensemble la
beauté de leurs voix et la gentillesse de leurs esprits; jusqu'à tel point qu'il
semble qu'en autres pays les musiciens se font seulement par art et exercice,
mais qu'en France ils deviennent tels de nature.

It may seem a little odd that Bouchard should break into Italian in
attempting to describe the characteristics of the French style, and
that Doni should find this most highly stylized technique remarkable for its naturalness. But all the authorities are agreed as to the
general character and value of the French convention; and it is
interesting that Cambert, who of all French composers approached
most nearly to the Italian cantata technique, was considered crude
compared with the most civilized French standards. 'Les sentiments
tendres et délicates lui echappaient', said St Evremond; and a disciple
of *préciosité* could hardly make a more damning comment than
that.

The second generation of *air de cour* composers not only systematized the formal and harmonic structure of the genre, they also
organized the haphazard decorative techniques of the early part of
the century into a fine art. The elaborate system of ornamentation
which they evolved was partly an extension of traditional practice—
the *port de voix*, the *coulé*, the *flexion*, the descriptive vocalise and
the *tremblement* had all appeared in the airs of Guédron and Boësset.
But now the various resources are systematized, and the system is
more or less synonymous with the invention of the *double* or
diminution. This ornamentation was the basis of the ornamentation
of Couperin and the clavecinists, and it is therefore important that
we should have some notion of what it was like, and of what the
composers thought they were doing when they used it. A detailed
account of Couperin's own ornamentation will be reserved until
our consideration of his theoretical work, in the third part of this
book.

The origins of the *double* are obscure. It is said that Bacilly may
have invented it, through singing embroidered versions of airs by
earlier masters such as Guédron and Boësset, though in so doing he
may merely have been imitating an Italian fashion. Titon du Tillet
seems to suggest that Lambert—celebrated equally as composer and
singing teacher—was responsible for the development of the
technique:

On peut dire qu'il est le premier en France qui ait fait connoître la beauté de la Musique et du Chant, et la justesse, et les grâces de l'expression; il imagina aussi de doubler la plus grande partie de ses airs pour faire valoir la légèreté de la voix et l'agrément du gozier par plusieurs passages et roulades brillantes et gracieuses, où il a excellemment réussi.

In any case, it soon became the custom to compose and to sing one's airs more or less 'straight' in the first stanza, adding increasingly complex passage work in subsequent verses. Bacilly himself offers a somewhat unconvincing analogy with painting as an explanation of the method:

Tout le Monde convient que le moins qu'on peut faire de passage dans un premier Couplet c'est le mieux, parce qu'assurément ils empeschent que l'on entende l'Air dans sa pureté, de même qu'avant d'appliquer les couleurs qui sont en quelque façon dans la Peinture, ce qu'est dans le Chant la Diminution, il faut que le Peintre ait premièrement désiné son ouvrage, qui a quelque rapport avec le premier Couplet d'un air.

The strophic build of the air is, as it were, the draughtsmanship; the ornamented couplets are the sensuous elements of colour applied to the linear structure.

The *port de voix* was the simplest and most common of the ornaments. It was an upwards appoggiatura, a slide up a major or minor second, or sometimes a third, fourth, or even a fifth; it was widely employed for 'les finales, médiantes, et autres principales cadences'. An extremely complicated set of rules conditioned its employment: its purpose was to enhance the plasticity and delicacy of the line, and its correct application called not only for a sound technique but also for good taste. As Bacilly said:

Que le port de voix soit le grand chemin qui les gens qui chantent doivent suivre, comme estant fort utile, mesme pour la justesse de la voix . . . mais . . . il y a des coups de maistre qui passent par dessus le règle, je veux dire que les sçavans par une licence qui est en eux une élégance du chant, obmettent quelquefois de jetter le note basse sur la haute par un doublement de notte imperceptible.

A hardly less important grace was the *tremblement*, by which the composers meant a rapid alternation of two notes, corresponding to the Italian *tremolo*. (The Florentines' *trillo* consisted of rapid repetitions of the *same* note.) More complicated was the *cadence*, 'un des plus considérable ornamens, et sans lequel le chant est fort imparfait'.

This took the form of a variously elaborated preparation, followed by a *tremblement*, followed by a resolution:

Another ornament was the *tremblement étouffé*, in which 'le gosier se présente à trembler et pourtant n'en fait que le semblant, comme s'il ne vouloit que doubler la notte sur laquelle se devoit faire la cadence'. This appears to correspond with the Germans' *Pralltriller*. *La flexion de voix* was a quick mordent.

All these ornaments and many subsidiary divisions of them were executed on the long syllables. Another group of ornaments, called *accents* and *plaintes*, was used on the short syllables. Bacilly defines them as follows:

> Il y a dans le Chant un certain ton particulier qui ne se marque que fort légèrement dans le gosier que je nomme accent ou aspiration, à qui d'autres donnent assez mal a propos le nom de plainte, comme s'il ne se pratiquoit que dans les endroits où l'on se plaint.

Mersenne also speaks of the 'accent plaintif' performed 'sur la notte accentuée, en haussant un peu la notte à la fin de sa pronunciation et en lui donnant une petite pointe, qui passe si viste, qu'il est assez difficile de l'apercevoir'. All the ornaments were sung with considerable rhythmic freedom; groups of decorative notes were conventionally sung in a *pointé* dotted rhythm, not liltingly in the manner of the gigue, but 'si finement que cela ne paroisse pas, si ce n'est en des endroits particuliers qui demandent expressément cette sorte d'exécution'.

The performer was thus called upon for a considerable degree of creative artistry, if he was to interpret sensitively the ornaments which the composer had marked in the score, and at the same time to know where to add ornaments which the composer had not troubled to indicate because he regarded them as conventionally understood. For both performers and audience, the ornaments are introduced partly to enhance the music's expressive *préciosité*, partly to show off the skill which made these people a musical, as well as a social, elect. The ornaments make the music more subtle and *tendre*, and less approachable by the common rank and file. While some of the ornaments are suggested by the words in the manner of the sixteenth century:

Je pleu — — — re et gé - mis nuit et jour

it is significant that this realism is less in evidence than in the early part of the century. Bacilly insists on the importance of stylization for its own sake and pokes fun at the exponents of descriptive realism, which he considers childish and unsophisticated:

De dire que par exemple sur le mot *onde* ou celui de *balancer* il faille expressément marquer sur le papier une douzaine de nottes hautes et basses pour signifier aux yeux ce qui ne doit s'adresser qu'à l'oreille, c'est une chose tout à fait badine et puérile.

Lully himself disapproved of the hyper-subtle ornamentation of the *doubles* as being of Italian extraction and inimical to the French tradition of naturalness and grace. He underestimated the degree to which the ornamentation had become a local product; in any case he is to Lambert and Le Camus a direct successor. They had written much music, both vocal and instrumental, for the ballet, and it is their sense of proportion and of harmonic progression that Lully, in his theatre music, more impressively developed. In his work, the esoteric *air de cour* meets the popular elements in French song which complemented it.

Before we turn to examine this more popular tradition, however, we should note that French religious song, during the *grand siècle*, became virtually indistinguishable from secular song; a fact which is sociologically as well as musically interesting. The *chants religieux* of a man such as Denis Caigret, who started from the lute song convention of Le Jeune and Mauduit, are relatively simple and homophonic in technique, since they were intended for amateur performance; but in essentials they are the same as the secular pieces. Of the religious songs of the mid-century Bacilly roundly declares that 'Il faut que ces sortes d'airs soient si approchés des airs du monde pour être bien reçus, qu'à peine on en puisse connaitre la différence': and Gobert's preface to his settings of versified psalms takes care to warn

137

the performer not to 'obmettre à bien faire les ports de voix, qui sont les transitions agréables et les anticipations sur les notes suivantes. On doit observer à propos les tremblements, les flexions de voix . . . etc.' De Gucy, in his settings of psalm-paraphrases published in 1650, wrote fully developed *doubles* to the psalms, and blandly admitted that one had to 'faire des chants sur le modèle des airs de cour pour estre introduits partout avec facilité'.

Both in the music and in their words the *airs de cour* were a sophisticated art form. Bacilly, in his *Remarques*, describes songs of the *air de cour* type as *airs passionés* (he means that they are full of feeling, not passionate in the modern sense). His other main division of *airs de mouvement* includes all the more 'popular' types of seventeenth-century French song. During the second half of the century, the sophisticated and popular elements tended to become more sharply differentiated; Perrin, after defining the *air de cour* as a song which 'marche à mesure et à mouvement libres et graves', adds that 'la chanson diffère de l'air en ce qu'elle suit un mouvement réglé de danse ou autre'. All the lighter songs—*chansons*, *vaudevilles*, *airs à boire*, *brunetes*, and *airs champêtres*—had some affiliation with the dance and were, as Lecerf de la Viéville says, 'articles considérables et singulières pour nous'. Most of them fall into one of two groupings; songs in which both words and music have a popular character, and those in which sophisticated words are adapted to popular or quasi-popular tunes.

The songs which are popular in both words and music are comparatively few, and are almost all *chansons à danser*, survivals from the sixteenth-century technique of homophonic sung dances. Their technique and purpose had not greatly altered since Mangeant's description of them in 1616:

Il n'est point d'exercice plus agréable pour la jeunesse, ny qui soit plus usité en bonnes compagnies que la danse; voire en tel sorte que le plus souvent au défaut des instruments l'on danse aux chansons.

Another charming contemporary account suggests that they were sometimes preferred to instrumental dance music:

Il y avait des violons, mais ordinnairement on les faisait taire pour danser aux chansons. C'est si joli de danser aux chansons.

The chansons were symmetrical in construction, 'simples et naturelles'.

138

Much more frequent, in Ballard's collections of the airs, are the songs in which sophisticated words are written to popular tunes. Some of these are in dance rhythms. It became a fashionable pastime to write verses in sarabande, gavotte, and bourrée form, and so on. Normally, however, the songs are not meant to be danced to, and the more serious ones such as the sarabandes are often indistinguishable from the simpler *airs de cour*. More characteristic of the sophisticated adaptations of popular tunes are the *vaudevilles* (or *voix de villes*); it is interesting that in defending them against the charge of vulgarity, Bacilly points out that popular tunes are in essence *naturels*, 'qui est une qualité fort considérable dans le chant'. 'Les François sont à peu près les seuls qui aient entendu cette brièveté raisonnable qui est la perfection des vaudevilles et cette naïveté qui en est le sel.' De Rosiers, in the preface to his collection *Un Livre de Libertés*, explains why he thinks *vaudevilles* are an important part of *musique de société*:

Un homme toujours sérieux serait insupportable et sa conversation ne serait bonne que quand l'on est endormi; le rire dissipe l'humeur mélancolique, c'est pourquoi la pratique en est nécessaire;

and he goes on to say that though his music may appear somewhat frivolous, none the less to compose it calls for considerable cunning:

Ceux qui font profession de mettre au jour quelque musique sçavent bien que la naïveté des chansons à danser ne demande point l'artifice et l'étude des airs de cour; néanmoins s'ils considéront bien mes chants ils verront que ma plume les fait voler assez haut pour en acquérir le titre.

We may note that, just after the middle of the century, when the *air serieux* was reaching its highest point of esoteric elaboration, there was a complementary increase in the numbers of trivial and facetious *chansons* and *vaudevilles*. At the same time, sophisticated ornamentation was tentatively introduced into the more popular songs, 'qui veulent estre exécutées avec plus de tendresse', as Bacilly characteristically put it. This desire to 'get it both ways'—to enjoy the advantages of a civilized society while avoiding social responsibility through a consciously naïve retreat to a simpler mode of existence—also connects up with the pastoralism of *L'Astree*.

A more extreme instance of this is provided by the *chansons à boire*, which also flourished most vigorously during the period of the *air de cour*'s greatest refinement. (We may compare the development of the English tavern catch, during the reign of Charles I, beside the highly sophisticated music of Jenkins and William Lawes.) The phenomenon of the *chanson à boire* parallels the growth of burlesque literature. At the beginning of the century, the *chansons à boire* are not distinct from other chansons of a light character; they fall into a period of triteness and vulgarity, and then, in the second half of the century, gain a more self-conscious elaboration, ultimately becoming songs which demand considerable virtuosity from the performer:

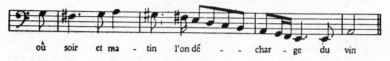

où   soir   et ma - tin   l'on dé - - char - ge   du   vin

The *chansons à boire* were more often for two voices, in canon, accompanied by two violins as well as continuo; though examples for a single voice and for various other combinations with continuo are plentiful. Lully composed some sprightly examples in the classic form with violins, and approved of them strongly because they 'sont des pièces propres à la France que les Italiens ne connoissoient pas—l'art de faire des jolis airs, des airs d'une gaïté et facilité qui cadre aux paroles est un point que l'Italie ne nous contestera pas'. (Lecerf de la Viéville.) Despite its bacchic and dionysiac associations, the *chanson à boire* was not remote from the other popular manifestations of the air. The *air tendre et à boire* was a frequent compromise, the implication being that the wine would titillate the amorous palate, leading it not to intenser passion, but to greater subtlety and *préciosité*.

The *brunete* did not materially differ from the *vaudeville*, except that it tended to use less spicy texts, and a more elegantly Platonic version of the love theme. The proportion of pseudo to real folk songs was also rather larger. Some of the more melancholy *brunetes* thus merge into the *airs serieux*, and Ballard reprints the simplest *airs de cour* in his *brunete* collections. *Brunetes* were for one, two, or three voices, accompanied by theorbo lute, or sometimes sung unaccompanied. The singers took great pride in singing the songs unaccompanied, *à la cavalière*, with the appropriate ornamentation and nuance; the habit also had practical advantages:

On sçait que l'accompagnement aide et adoucit la voix: cependant une belle voix, qui n'est point accompagnée, ne devient pas insupportable . . . il y a des moments où l'accompagnement est presque incommode. La conversation languit; on prie quelqu'un de chanter un Air, on l'écoute et on recommence à causer. S'il avait proposé d'envoyer chercher une basse de viole, on se seroit separé. A la fin du repas, dans l'émotion où le vin et la joie ont mis les conviez, on demande un air à boire à celui qui a de la voix; l'accompagnement aurait là quelque chose de gênant, qui serait hors de saison . . . Nos François les plus amoureux de leurs voix ne font pas non plus difficulté de chanter sans théorbe et sans clavescin et . . . c'est faire le précieux ou la précieuse de se piquer de ne point chanter sans Théorbe. (Lecerf de la Viéville.)

These little pastoral songs—called *brunetes* after the pseudo-shepherdesses who sang them or about whom they were sung—enjoyed a phenomenal popularity throughout the seventeenth century, and it was a song of Lully in this manner (*Sommes-nous pas trop heureux*), which inverted the normal relation between folk music and art music, and entered French folk song as a carol.

Lully also carried the *brunete* into the opera where, under the title of *air tendre*, it preserved its national identity, 'ce caractère tendre, aisé et naturel, qui flatte toujours sans lasser jamais, et qui va beaucoup plus au cœur qu'à l'esprit'. Not *too* much to the heart, however, for it is only 'un *peu* d'amour' that is 'nécessaire' and 'un charmant amusement'. Here, as always, one must preserve a balance between emotion and a sense of propriety, if only because it is more comfortable to avoid emotional complications. By the early eighteenth century the term *brunete* was being used rather indiscriminately to cover most varieties of the pastoral. But it was still a living reality, and perhaps more than anything, preserved the French tradition from the encroachments of Italianism. In Couperin's work it was a counterpoise to the Corellian sonata; he must have felt about it much as did Lecerf de la Viéville when he wrote:

Et toutes ces Brunettes, toutes ces jolies airs champêtres, qu'on appelle les Brunettes, combien ils sont naturels. On doit compter pour de vraies beautés la douceur et la naïveté de ces petits airs—les Brunettes sont doublement à estimer dans notre musique, parce que cela n'est ni de la connoisance, ni du génie des Italiens, et que les tons aimables et gracieux, si finement proportionnés aux paroles, en sont d'un extrême prix.

It is rather surprising that Couperin's specific contributions to the *brunette* collections are so few. If we discount the numerous arrangement of his harpsichord pieces in vocal form, we have left only three *airs serieux*, and half a dozen or so songs in the semi-popular, semi-sophisticated vein. The earliest of the *airs serieux*, *Qu'on ne me dise plus*, is dated 1697. It is a gravely melancholy piece in E minor, with first section ending in the relative major. The groupings of the melodic clauses are varied, and the line mounts to a quite impressive climax:

The second *air serieux*, *Doux liens*, was published in 1701, and the words are a French translation of an Italian poem already set by Alessandro Scarlatti. The music, however, is French in its rhythmic fluidity, and is perhaps closer to the *air de cour* of the first half of the *grand siècle* than is the more architecturally balanced *Qu'on ne me dise plus*. The third *air serieux*, explicitly called *Brunete*, is dated 1711. The most developed piece in Couperin's secular vocal music, it is an *air de cour* with five *doubles* or couplets. The air itself is in the usual two sections, with repeats, the first section modulating from G to the dominant with some piquant intimations of D minor. Exquisitely stylized, the melodic arabesques of the *doubles* have no obvious descriptive intent, although the pliancy and *douceur* which they give to the line are a part of its expressiveness. As in the earlier *airs de cour* the convolutions of the ornamentation counteract the rigidity of the harmonic structure:

142

The harmonies remain constant while, through the succession of couplets, the complexities of the ornamentation increase. However much the influence of de Nyert may have encouraged the French to experiment with this kind of melodic filigree, the soft fluidity of the line is germane to the French tradition. One can observe reflections of it all through Couperin's work. As a whole, this song is a most beautiful example of musical *préciosité*.

These three songs are sophisticated pieces in the esoteric manner of the *air de cour*. Another sophisticated song, of a simpler, more harmonic type is *Les Solitaires*, a piece of amicably self-indulgent melancholy, written for two voices, moving note for note, and continuo. Then there are a few songs in the semi-popular vein, *La Pastourelle*, *Muséte*, *Vaudeville*, and *Les Pellerines*, all published in

143

1711 or 1712. The *vaudeville* is for three voices and bass, the other songs for two voices, the parts in every case moving note for note. *Les Pellerines* also exists in a clavecin version in Couperin's first book of keyboard pieces. Despite their popular flavour, the tunes seem to be original, not adaptations of folk-songs. They are all charming, but indistinguishable from innumerable other songs in the *brunete* tradition; Couperin here makes no attempt to use the *brunete* convention, as he does later, for his own ends.

More interesting than these characterless pastorals is Couperin's *air à boire*, a setting of La Fontaine's *Epitaphe d'un Paresseux*. The two vocal parts follow convention in being freely canonic; there are some contrapuntal jokes on the words *Deux parts en fit*, and the canonic parts are throughout neatly dove-tailed. Finally, there are three unaccompanied songs in three parts. Two of them are canons, the second being an entertaining *chanson à boire*, *A moi, tout est perdu*, which parodies operatic recitative. The declamatory theme gives prominence to the notes of the major triad. Appoggiaturas in the ornamentation create some effectively odd parallel seconds:

The three-part unaccompanied parody, *Trois Vestales et trois poliçons*, is one of the most personal of the secular pieces, and suggests the kind of modification of the pastoral convention which Couperin introduces into his most significant work. There may not be much in a passage such as this:

144

Quel bruit sou - dain vient troub - ler nos re - trai - tes?

to indicate that it is by an important composer but it is illuminating to consider it in relation to, say, the quick sections of the *Leçons des Ténèbres*.

For clearly, our account of the *brunete* tradition, comparatively detailed as it is, could not be justified simply as an introduction to Couperin's few trifling exercises in this style. We need to understand the pastoral tradition because it is one of the points from which Couperin starts. His contributions to the idiom are insignificant; what is important is the manner in which he uses elements of the *brunete* in all his most important work. We shall find subtle transmutations of the *brunete* repeatedly throughout his clavecin music and concerts; while in the relatively Italianate period of the church music, it is the *brunete*, even more than the opera of Lully, which stands for Couperin as the central line in the French tradition.

Chapter Eight

The Church Music

La Musique d'un Motet, qui en est, pour ainsi dire, le corps,
doit être expressive, simple, agréable. . . . La Musique de
l'Eglise doit être expressive. Les régles que nous nous sommes
établies la mènent là bien certainement. N'est-il pas évident que
plus ce qu'on souhaite est doux, plus ce qu'on craint est
terrible; et plus nos sentiments veulent être exprimez d'une
manière vive et marquée? Or où est-ce qu'on craint et qu'on
souhaite de si grandes choses? Les passions d'un Opéra sont
froides, au prix de celles qu'on peint dans notre Musique de
l'Eglise.

BONNET, *Histoire de la Musique*, 1725

THE SECULARIZATION OF church music during the seventeenth
century was not an isolated phenomenon, but a part of the drift of
European culture from the church to the stage. Secular music
evolved from Orazio Vecchi's latently operatic treatment of the
madrigal, to Monteverdi's explicitly narrative and dramatic version
with soloists and instrumental ritornelli; and thence to the solo
cantata itself. (For instance, such works of Monteverdi as *Il Combat-
timento di Tancredi*, and the baroquely emotional cantatas of Rossi.)
Similarly, in the field of ecclesiastical music, the monumental polyphony of the Venetian school of Giovanni Gabrieli gave to the religious technique a glamour which almost suggested the humanistic
passion of the chromatic madrigal. When once the chromatic idiom
entered the church, it was only one step further to introduce the
operatic aria and recitative.

The first years of the century show an extraordinarily rich fusion
of techniques. The Vespers and Magnificat and other church music
which Monteverdi composed for St Mark's, Venice, have a grounding in the old counterpoint, combined with monumental colouristic
effects, brilliant instrumentation, baroque figuration, madrigalian

146

chromaticism, and passages of operatic aria and recitative. And there is a mature fusion, not a confusion, of styles. Even when the homophonic theatre style had been unequivocally accepted in the church, there are still traces of continuity with the old methods. The opening of this solo cantata of Schütz, who was at one time among Monteverdi's pupils, recalls the placing together of unrelated triads typical of the chromatic madrigal:

and this passage suggests both the chromatic madrigal, and the contrapuntal technique of the baroque organists:

But the key-figure with reference to the future of church music is not Monteverdi, nor Schütz, but the Italian Carissimi. His life stretches across the century from 1605 to 1674, and his work is intimately linked with the religious life of Rome. No doubt the enthusiasm of Pope Urbino VIII for the new monodic style encouraged Carissimi to develop Cavalieri's attempt (in his *Rappresentazione di anima e di corpo*) to adapt the operatic technique to a religious use; but in so doing he was following the direction in which his sensibility led him. In 1630 he was appointed musical director of the Jesuit college of St Apollinaire, for German students, and it was in this environment that he composed his long series of sacred histories and oratorios. He accepted in his technique the operatic recitative and aria, madrigalian chromaticism, and the 'monumental' homophonic style of choral writing: his music is by no means devoid of the Bernini-like qualities, the declamatory passion and emotional chromatic progressions which characterize the secular cantatas of Rossi:

The essence of his achievement, however, lies in the more sober stylization of baroque exuberance which he introduces. Like Cavalli in the opera, he employs an almost consistently homophonic style in his large-scale choruses; in his solo cantatas he is as much interested in the balance of clauses, the alternation of mood, as in lyrical expressiveness. In these smaller works he substituted for the glittering baroque orchestra the more intimate combination of solo voices, with two obbligato violins, and a rich but subdued continuo of organ, harpsichord and theorbo lute. There is thus some analogy between the chamber cantata and the baroque violin sonata.

Some of Carissimi's arias have a lyrical suavity and balanced elegance which reminds one of Lully, or even Handel:

and there is a very moving choral passage at the end of *Jephtha* which anticipates the technique of tranquilly sensuous suspensions in dotted rhythm which we have already observed in some of the slow movements of Couperin's violin sonatas:

In any case, it is not difficult to understand why Carissimi's music, with its aristocratic disciplining of baroque passion, made so immediate an appeal to his contemporaries who were in search of an autocratic stylization; the virtues of his work were such as were bound to interest, in particular, the adherents of the Roi Soleil. By the time of Lully, Carissimi's influence on French church music was of an importance which was hardly to be exceeded even by Corelli's influence on the instrumental school. Lecerf de la Viéville, who was the last person to flatter an Italian, said:

> Quoique Carissimi soit antérieur à cet age de la bonne musique italienne, j'ai toujours été persuadé qu'il est le plus grand musicien que l'Italie ait produit et un musicien illustre à juste titre, plein de génie sans contredit, mais, de plus, ayant du naturel et du goût; enfin, le moins indigne adversaire que les Italiens ayent à opposer à Lully.

It seems probable that at the height of his popularity this 'homme d'un mérite extraordinaire s'était longtemps formé en faisant chanter ses pièces aux Théatins de Paris.'

In 1649 a French youth of fifteen, Marc-Antoine Charpentier, went to Rome to study painting. He seems to have had precocious musical gifts also, for, hearing some of Carissimi's sacred histories, he decided that his life's work must be to create music such as that. The legend has it that he memorized several of Carissimi's works and carried them back to France in his head. However this may be, there is no doubt that his efforts and those of Michel Farinel did much to encourage the vogue for Carissimi in France. Most of Charpentier's own work is sacred music in Carissimi's convention; though his *Médée* suggests that he might have been a successful opera composer also, but for Lully's monopoly. His compositions include masses, psalms, and *leçons des tenèbres* for the Dauphin's private chapel, sacred histories and motets for the Jesuits of the rue St

Antoine, and even a few small works for Port Royal. In Charpentier's music, the lyrical suavity and architectural gravity of Carissimi acquire a rather more pathetic and introspective tinge, as they merge into the French line of Lullian recitative. The declamation itself is a compromise between Lully and the Italian baroque flourish:

Per-cu - ti-am pas - to - rem, percu - ti-am pas - to - rem   et dis-per-
- gen - - - - - - tur

and the tone of his work has an elegiac quality comparable with that of the lutenists. If he has less power and variety than Carissimi, he has possibly greater subtlety and depth, and certainly he preserves a closer contact with the polyphonists; Titon du Tillet called him 'un des plus sçavants et des plus laborieux Musiciens de son tems'. In the wonderful closing section of his finest work, *Le Reniement de St Pierre*, he attains to a sustained purity of line, mated with a dissolving sensuousness of harmony, which rivals the finest work of Couperin himself:

There is nothing that more recalls Couperin's flavour, unless it be a few passages in the cantatas of Henri Dumont.

Of all the church composers of the *grand siècle* Henri Dumont has perhaps the closest link with the polyphonic art of the previous century. Indeed he continued to compose contrapuntal music in the old *a capella* tradition until the end of his life in 1684, and he was the only composer of his time to write masses directly based on plainsong themes, even though these themes were mensurated and tonally modernized. He is however chiefly remembered for his fine motets in the new style for solo voices and continuo, many of which date from the middle of the century. These have a sinewy power which is at once fervent and devotional. They suggest a development which was finally consummated in the work of La Lande, unquestionably one of the greatest religious composers of the seventeenth century, though his work is, in this country at least, little known. With his

152

habitual good taste Louis personally chose La Lande to be Du Mont's successor[16] as Superintendent of the Royal Chapel. He had picked a man who was able to create in church music a worthy counterpart to the grandeur of Lully's achievement in secular music. The general tenor of La Lande's work is noble and Handelian, but the contrapuntal vitality of his lines gives great nervous force to his rich and sonorous harmonies. We cannot deny that a work such as his *De Profundis* conveys a spiritual illumination which makes it perhaps the most impressive musical instance of the strain of mysticism that we have seen to be latent in this ostensibly hedonistic society.

Now while Couperin in his church music does not attempt to emulate La Lande's massive dignity he rivals, perhaps even excels him in the ability to express an intimate spirituality, a purity of feeling and a sense of wonder which are the prerequisites of a religious view of experience. From this point of view both Couperin and La Lande differ essentially from Lully. Sometimes, it is true, there is an unexpected tenderness, as well as nobility, in the drooping suspensions of Lully's motets:

and the magnificent early *Miserere* (1664) that so moved Mme de
Sévigné achieves its lacerating intensity by a La Lande-like fusion
of harmonic and contrapuntal elements. His more typical, later
church works, however, such as the *Te Deum* or even the nobly
passionate *Dies Irae*, are massive, ceremonial, festive, deriving not
from the intimate sacred histories of Carissimi but from his homophonic choral pieces. There is nothing specifically religious about
these bold lines and monumental harmonies, any more than there is
about Corneille's ostensibly Christian play *Polyeucte*. Some analogy
may be established between Lully's harmonic and architectural
majesty, and the noble resonance of Corneille's heroic couplet. They
both have few emotional overtones; they deal in the social values of
civilization.

Compared with Lully's ceremonial homophony, the church music
of Couperin, like that of La Lande, shows a greater fluidity of line
and freedom of harmony; we see in his finest religious music perhaps the most remarkable demonstration of his compromise between
polyphonic and homophonic technique. If Lully's homophony may
be related to Corneille's alexandrine, perhaps we may see, in the
more flexible line and harmony of Couperin, some analogy with the
depths of meaning which imagery and rhythm reveal beneath
Racine's ostensibly conventional language. Ultimately, this plasticity corresponds to a deeper interest in the workings of the human
mind and to a more spiritual conception of values than is common
to the gallantry of Lully and Corneille. We can adequately understand Couperin's Molière-like sanity and humour only if we realize
that it is modified by a tragic sense of the implications of *Le Misanthrope*; we can appreciate his classical poise only if we see it in relation to the ferocity of *Phèdre*; and we can most clearly understand
his spiritual radiance if we see it in relation to the *extrême douceur* of
Racine's *Athalie*.[17]

For central representative of the *grand siècle* though he is, Racine
has, especially in *Athalie*, a spiritual purity which seems to refer back
to the great days of French medieval civilization. Couperin's church
music has a similar quality. He accepts the Italianized, secularized

[17] The music for the choruses in Racine's *Athalie* and *Esther* was in fact composed by
J-B. Moreau who also set three of Racine's *Cantiques Spirituels*. While not in the class
of Couperin's finest work, his music has an exquisite grace which is worthy of *Esther*,
if not of *Athalie*.

convention of the motet and cantata in the manner of Carissimi, but
he manages to reconcile this with a purity and simplicity of technique and feeling which reminds one of Josquin, or even Dufay. In
this he more maturely develops an element which we shall later note
in the work of Chambonnières. Of course, apart from the linear
nature of his idiom—closer to Bach than to Lully or Handel—there
is in Couperin's work no direct technical heritage from the fifteenth
and sixteenth centuries. But there is a certain temperamental affinity,
and it is this which gives him so central a position in the French tradition. While he belongs without ambiguity to the age in which he
lived, and cannot be said to live, like Bach, culturally in the past,
none the less he has something of Bach's transitional significance.
What was clearly true of the organ masses is more subtly true of all
his representative work. He looks backwards rather than forwards;
he stands between the medieval and the modern world.

The church music of both Couperin and La Lande was composed
between 1695 and 1715, during the last melancholy years of Louis's
reign, and for that reason it is perhaps understandable that a more
intimately spiritual tone should be discernible in it, if it be compared
with Lully's worldly splendour. This more spiritual quality is not,
however, present in the earliest example of Couperin's work for the
Chapelle Royale, the motet *Laudate pueri Dominum*, dated 1697. This
is an exercise in Carissimi's cantata technique, comparable with the
experiments in Corellian sonata technique which Couperin had
made a few years previously. Although an impressive piece, it is not
a work of mature personality.

The 'Symphony' is designed in the Carissimi manner for two
violins and continuo, though Couperin is not specific about the
instruments to be employed. The melodic parts are freely canonic,
with many overlapping suspensions, as in the two-violin sonatas.
The solo instruments anticipate the material of the vocal sections,
but are used only during the interludes or ritornelli, not in conjunction with the voices. The next movement, *Sit nomen Domini benedictus*, uses voices and violins together in imitation, in a solemn 3 : 2
pulse. The piece corresponds to the *grave* sarabande of the da chiesa
sonata. The harmony is rich and massive, though not especially
personal.

A solis ortu is a brilliant virtuoso section in the Italian fashion, a fugal movement on a 'harmonically' centred subject incorporating a rising arpeggio and falling scale passage:

A so - lis or - tu us - que ad oc - ca - - sum

Here the two instrumental parts have a continuously animated share in the counterpoint, and include much glittering passage-work in thirds. The *Excelsus super omnes gentes* section is in a simple symmetrical rhythm resembling the French *air tendre*. Echo effects are obtained in dialogue between voices and violins, and the gentle rhythm and limpid diatonicism provide the first intimation of an effect which Couperin is to develop in later church works:

et su-per coe - los glo - ri-a e - jus

Then follows a passage of arioso, making use of sequential figurations:

in coe-lo et in ter - ra, in coe-lo et in ter - ra, in

A charming Lullian dance in a dotted triple rhythm accompanies the words *Suscitans a terra inopem*, and leads into an Italianate arioso duo on the words *Ut collocet eum*. The work concludes with a long canzona on a brisk dance tune:

involving the two violins and three voices in continuous contra-puntal dialogue. The voices are called upon for considerable virtuo-sity; Handelian baroque passages in the bass are frequent:

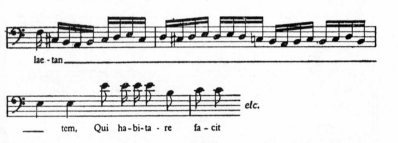

The movement is brilliant and effective, if not very typical of Couperin.

The *Quatre Versets d'un Motet chanté à Versailles*, 1703, to words from the psalm *Mirabilia testimonia tua*, marks the emergence of the authentic Couperin manner in Latin church music. It opens with a remarkable arioso passage (*Tabescere me fecit*) for two unaccompanied sopranos, treated in free imitation. The tenuous purity of the two voices, pitched high in their register, evokes the atmosphere of the whole work, which is of a 'celestial' radiance such as we have met before in parts of the violin sonatas and organ masses. The unaccom-panied opening—Couperin's direction that it 'se chante sans Basse Continue ny aucun Instrument' is unequivocal—has flexible lines and subtle effects of ellipsis. The instruments enter with a delicate theme embracing a rising fifth and a little repeated falling scale figure in quavers. The texture resembles that of the gayer, more ballet-like fugal sections of the organ masses, though when the voice appears it exploits a more Italian technique, with long roulades suggested by the words:

The quaver scale passage is used here sequentially to the *doux* accompaniment of drooping octaves on the violins. It appears fairly consistently throughout the movement: towards the end, a more emotional chromaticism is introduced into the bass.

The next verse, *Adolescentulus sum*, is in the major, scored for soprano, two flutes, and continuo played on violins. This limpid sonority accords with the innocent diatonicism of the lines, with the caressing passing notes, and with the simply symmetrical rhythm. This conscious naïveté could not have been created but for Couperin's relation to the *brunete* tradition. It is, however, much more than that, for it is in such effects as this intertwining of soprano and flute that we may find a purity, a spiritual innocence, more reminiscent of Josquin and Dufay than of the sensual emotion of Carissimi and the *grand siècle*. In this instance we may even see some slight technical similarity between the dissolving effect of the passing notes in the Couperin:

158

and those in some of the simpler, more homophonic work of Josquin.

This movement leads into a lightly dancing setting of *Justitia tua* for two sopranos, with a continuo of violins. The leap of a tenth gives the theme a lilting airiness:

There are piquant canonic entries producing dissonant suspensions:

The last section, *Qui dat nivem,* is scored for the same combination as the *Adolescentulus sum,* and likewise proceeds in a gentle crochet

159

pulse. Passing notes and appoggiaturas again create a glowing, radiant quality:

At the end the voice and flute dissolve away in triplets and then semiquavers in silvery thirds. Throughout, the texture of the work has a filigree-like delicacy, and no one but Couperin could have written it.

After this ethereal work, the *Sept Versets du Psaume Benedixisti Domine* of 1704 strike a different note. This piece has grandeur and intensity. The first section is a bass aria with flute obbligato. Although meditative and withdrawn, with a quiet regular rhythm like some of Bach's Passion arias, it is remarkable for its spacious proportions, linear complexity, and powerful sense of climax. The vocal phrases are of great length, with Italian descriptive flourishes:

Chromatically rising figures create a sense of urgency and pleading, but the emotion is always controlled by the even pulse, and by the grave proportions of the whole. Note for instance how in this passage the upwards aspiring line is counterbalanced by the falling sequences of the last two bars:

160

The texture has here a Bachian richness. The flute is subtly used both in imitation of the voice and, in a highly effective passage, in unaccompanied duplication at the tenth.

The next section, in the relative major (B flat), is a duo for tenor and bass with independent obbligato parts. The words *Numquid in aeternum irasceris nobis* suggest a contrapuntal treatment, highly baroque and Italianate, though with a French graciousness. The vocal parts indulge in rapid scale passages and virtuoso roulades. A passage of arioso for the *Ostende nobis Domine* leads into one of Couperin's hushed, contemplative movements in a swaying triple rhythm, for tenor with instrumental obbligato, probably flute. An atmosphere of naïve wonder is obtained through some odd processions of unresolved 6 : 4 chords:

The tonality changes to a clear G major and a passage of recitative flows into a gentle aria on a crochet pulse. Sometimes the part-writing creates tender dissonances similar to those in the *sommeil* movements of the *Apothéose* sonatas:

more commonly the texture is as transparently diatonic as that of the organ *Messe des Convents*:

The next verset is a duet for two tenors, again in the minor, and elegiac in tone, with Italian arabesques, mainly in thirds. *Veritas de terra* is a brief *da capo* aria in D, with ritornello. The theme starts with the notes of the major triad ascending, and again the solo line has an Italian floridity. The harmonies, however, attain a certain acerbity, during a prolonged modulation to the minor of the dominant. This motet ends quietly with a duet between two pairs of oboe and flute in unison without continuo; after the instrumental prelude, the voices double the first oboe and flute parts. As in the Versets of the previous year, this tenuous finale seems to suggest that the worldly glory of the Roi Soleil is dissolving away into eternity. In this sense, it is not altogether extravagant to say that Couperin's delicate sensuousness has merged into an attitude that can be called transcendental. To this music, as to the hushed, dissolving passages in the violin sonatas, the massive Handelian full close would be utterly inappropriate.

The *Qui regis Israel* versets of the next year, 1705, show a further development of the graver Bachian manner of the 1704 work. A triple-rhythmed prelude exploits echo effects between the solo instruments and the continuo instruments. The two voices, countertenor and bass, move mainly note for note in a nobly cantabile manner. The *Excita potentiam tuam* is one of Couperin's jaunty 3 : 8 movements, with the voices this time treated imitatively. The main theme has a sprightly rising scale figure:

The *Vineam de Aegypto* section is a bass aria in B flat, with a Lullian dance lilt underlying its Italianism. It leads into a lively 3 : 8 air for bass and double chorus, accompanied by groups of oboes and flutes, and violins. All these quick movements are of a somewhat secular frivolity. An altogether deeper note is sounded with the two magnificent arias for counter-tenor with obbligato flutes. These are in F minor—according to Rameau the conventional key for *chants lugubres*. The *Operuit mentes umbra ejus* section employs wild, whirling scale passages in the instrumental parts, similar to those adapted

163

from Lully's overture by the violists and lutenists in their *Tombeaux* movements. The piece as a whole has a most impressive union of the violist's ceremonial grandeur with Monteverdian dramatic fire—note for instance the big leaps, the diminished sevenths and tritones in the proudly declamatory line:

The second air, *Extendit palmites suos*, is in a steady triple rhythm, warm in its harmonic texture. It includes extended passages for voice with flutes and violins unaccompanied by the continuo. Here again we find the characteristically disembodied, unearthly effect.

The last section returns to C minor for a grave aria for counter-tenor with flute and viol obbligato. The regular rhythm and independent part-writing once more suggest a more ethereal Bach, especially in certain sequential effects in the obbligato parts:

The harmony, however, often inclines to an un-Bachian, if delicate, voluptuousness.

With the *Motet de Ste Suzanne* we reach one of the peak points of Couperin's church music. Here the paradox of a sensuousness of harmony that is united with a virginal spirituality of line finds its loveliest expression. The opening is Italianate and Handelian, yet the impression it produces is remote from Handel's solidity. The material is founded almost entirely on this little phrase:

The expressive wriggle on *coronaberis* later attains a lilting exuberance:

and is bandied about between the counter-tenor and obbligato violins. Couperin's sensuous sevenths and ninths introduce a more introspective tinge into the minor episodes, but the movement never loses its innocently smiling, almost playful, quality.

This playfulness is a part of the music's innocence and there is nothing superficial or irreverent about it. The seriousness of the work is revealed in the following duo for counter-tenor and soprano, *Date serta, date flores*, one of the most fragrant of all Couperin's movements in this manner. We may compare its ninth chords and melting suspensions with those in the *sommeil* movements of the *Apothéose* sonatas, or with the less mature examples in the organ *Messe des Convents*. The counter-tenor is the upper part and sounds an octave lower:

Nowhere does Couperin more cunningly exploit the effect of voices in thirds and sixths, high in their register. This air leads into a chorus, *Jubilemus, exultemus*, transparent in sonority, though gay. There are some exquisite overlapping scale passages, and naïve arpeggio figurations and chordal effects at the words *resonet coelum plausibus*.

The 3 : 2 aria, *O Susanna, quanta est gloria tua*, is related to the *grave* sarabande of the Italian violin sonata. It is superbly moulded in the Carissimi or Handelian manner, but voluptuously tender. We may regard it as the consummation of the little *Qui tollis peccata mundi* couplet of the *Messe des Convents* referred to in the chapter on the organ works. It has the same spiritual fragrance, but has too a classical amplitude in its proportions, particularly in passages in which the two obbligato violins sing in company with the soprano. This quotation gives an idea of its calm lyrical beauty, its richly tranquil harmony:

A change to four rhythm introduces the *Voluit Dominus sacrificium*
for bass, obbligato instruments and continuo. This is a harmonically
treated fugal movement in which voices and instruments use an
imitative technique more or less consistently. The theme makes play
with an octave leap, and the soloist has some eloquent descriptive
flourishes:

After a repetition of the *Jubilemus* chorus comes a duet for soprano,
bass, and continuo, the two voices being treated canonically. The
gently rising theme, with its elliptical entries, and the suspended
sevenths and ninths of the continuo again suggest an emotional
warmth, mingled with naïve wonder:

167

Here too the feeling resembles that of the organ *Messe des Convents*. A brief ritornello and a passage of not particularly distinguished recitative is then rounded off by a second repetition of the *Jubilemus* chorus.

Probably Couperin would have claimed no more for the *Ste Suzanne* motet than that it was a simple, sensuous act of veneration, dedicated to a saint who was also a pretty girl. Yet in the very simplicity of the sensuousness—the candour of the feeling—a spiritual experience is involved. The *douceur* and quietude of this music touch on a realm of emotion which we find in all Couperin's most significant work, and which has perhaps been most adequately described in verbal terms by Fénelon:

L'état passif est celui où une âme, n'aimant plus Dieu d'un amour mélangé, fait tous ses actes délibérés d'une volonté pleine et efficace, mais tranquille et désintéressée. Tantôt elle fait les actes simples et indistincts qu'on nomme quiétude ou contemplation; tantôt elle fait les actes distinctes des vertus convenables à son état. Mais elle fait les uns et les autres également d'une manière passive, c'est à dire, paisible et désintéressée. . . . Cet état passif ne suppose aucune inspiration extraordinaire; il ne renferme qu'une paix et une souplesse infinie de l'âme pour se laisser mouvoir à toutes les impressions de la grâce. . . . L'eau qui est agitée ne peut être claire, ni recevoir l'image des objets voisins; mais une eau tranquille devient comme la glace pure d'un miroir. . . . L'âme pure et paisible est de même. Dieu y imprime son image et celle de tous les objets qu'il veut y imprimer; tout s'imprime, tout s'efface. Cette âme n'a aucune forme propre, et elle a également toutes celles que la grâce donne. . . . Il n'y a que le pur amour qui donne cette paix et cette docilité parfaite.

The phrase 'tranquille et désintéressé' is the key to all Couperin's most characteristic music, and, indeed, to the most significant art of

168

his time. It is not a matter of any 'inspiration extraordinaire'; it is a matter of simplicity and honesty of response, and if one can achieve that, says Fénelon, the grace and the peace of God will be added unto one. It is purity of heart that leads to a *docilité parfaite*, which is greater than *le moi* or *la volonté*. We may recall also a passage from one of Fénelon's letters to the Comtesse de Montbaron:

L'amour-propre malade, et attendri sur lui-même, ne peut être touché sans crier les hauts cris. L'unique remède est donc de sortir de soi pour trouver la paix.

There is no more beautiful testimony to this than Couperin's music; and even in the nineteenth century we can, from this point of view, see Gabriel Fauré as Couperin's successor. His music, too, has purity of line, combined with a subtle sensuousness of harmony; and his *Requiem*, like Couperin's *Ste Suzanne* motet, is 'so near to God that it is without revolt, cry, or gesture'.

The motets which we have so far considered are all constructed on a plan similar to that of Bach's cantatas, with arias, recitatives of a lyrical arioso character, instrumental ritornelli, and obbligato parts. Unlike Bach and unlike Lully, Couperin makes little use of the chorus. When he does employ it, as in the *Ste Suzanne* motet, it is with discretion. The series of *Elévations* that follow the 1706 versets are all essentially music for soloists, with organ continuo. With one exception, they have no solo obbligato parts. Their form, like that of Carissimi's cantatas, is closely related to the sonata da chiesa. They are, as it were, 'chamber' cantatas, and in writing them Couperin was following the lead given by the beautiful *Elévations* of Lully.

The first elevation, *O Misterium ineffabile*, is the only example of Couperin's church music which was published in a modern edition before the appearance of the Lyrebird edition. It sets the temper of most of the elevations; a flexible vocal line flows over smooth harmonic progressions, in an even crotchet pulse. Some rather surprising modulations give the piece a restrained fervour—for instance this typical modulation to the minor of the dominant:

This quality is particularly noticeable in the 3 : 2 aria, in which long sustained suspensions on the exclamation 'O' combine with chromatic progressions and false relations to convey a quietly ecstatic yearning:

The second elevation, *O Amor, O Gaudium*, is for three male voices, and is in a similar mood. The opening 3 : 2 *grave* is not remarkable; an *affetuoso* 3 : 4 is a delightful air with cross-rhythmed exultations in the solo part:

The return to 3 : 2 takes us richly through the relative minor, and includes some imitative treatment of a *tendre* phrase built from descending fourths.

The third Elevation, *O Jesu Amantissime*, for counter-tenor, is perhaps the finest in this elegantly fervid manner. Its 3 : 2 aria has a spacious gravity, with effective melisma on the word *aeternitas*. It is chiefly notable, however, for its intense arioso—note this treatment of the word *crudelis*:

et cru - de — lis et cru - de — lis

The triumphant aria in the major provides a florid Italianate conclusion, but is hardly an adequate resolution of the more melancholy parts.

The *Venite exultemus Domino* elevation is more strenuous, and tauter in harmony. Its rising scale opening phrase expresses a more active yearning, compared with the relaxed emotion of the preceding works:

Ven - i - te ex - ul - te - mus Do - mi - no

A more vigorous homophonic treatment is also given to the ecstatic exclamations in the phrase *O immensus amor*:

O immensus a - - mor O O O O *etc.*

The final 3 : 4 aria has some chains of suspended sevenths. This more
powerful manner is developed further in the next elevation, *Quid
retribuam tibi Domine*, which is also in E minor. Here even the bass
line has considerable rhythmic animation. The counter-tenor's arioso
line is ardently lyrical, and the words' reference to the perils of
material existence suggest some exciting roulades:

Later the words *crudelis* and *salvasti* produce a plaintive chromaticism
and melisma:

With the *Audite omnes*, also for counter-tenor, we come to the
only elevation which has a 'symphonie' of obbligato parts. The
instrumental lines are in the main restricted to echo effects in
dialogue with the voices. The final 3 : 2 aria uses sequential sevenths
in a way that recalls the *Ste Suzanne* motet; but as a whole the work
is not very interesting. This is the last of the pieces specifically called
Elévation. The other motets in the collection are not substantially
different in form, though they possibly cover a wider range of feeling. The first of them, *Motet pour le Jour de Pâques*, at once strikes
a new note, being one of the most brilliant works Couperin ever
wrote. Its florid theme is developed with Handelian exuberance,
with many resonant thirds between the two voices. The *Christo
resurgente* section is ripely harmonized, and has elaborate descriptive
arabesques:

172

in qua sur - re _____ xit

The change to a four pulse brings some powerful Handelian decorated suspensions to *Alleluya*. Throughout, the alterations in rhythm
for the different sections build up a cumulative sense of climax. The
concluding alleluyas in 6 : 4 are a paean of triumph, again with effective syncopated suspensions:

The lengthy Magnificat also has some rousing exultations in 6 : 4,
and some typically sensuous seventh chords:

A brief passage marked *Lentement*, to the words *Suspecit Israel puerum suum* introduces one of Couperin's sudden shifts from major to minor, followed by dissolving sevenths; and an aria of glorification exploits a sprightly rising scale figure. As a whole, however, the work lacks direction. Most unexpectedly, for a work of Couperin, it is rambling rather than economical.

The next two motets are also pedestrian. The triumphant flourishes of the *St Barthélemy* motet have little of Couperin's imprint; though a reference to the Cross leads to some lovely drooping dissonances:

and the victorious conclusion interestingly reiterates its conventional penultimate suspended fourth. In the *Motet de Ste Anne* the regularity of the rhythm is not used to any expressive purpose. The *Memento O Christe* section has, however, an agile arioso line, and there is some neat contrapuntal writing for the three soloists in the final setting of *concedat nobis filius gratiam et gloriam*.

After these two relatively dull works, we come to two which are, in different ways, among the finest. The *O Domine quia refugium*, for three basses and continuo, is a dark-coloured, majestic piece, though without, perhaps, the sinewy vigour of the E minor *Quid Retribuam*. The opening 3 : 2 *grave* is in C minor. A noble homophonic movement with modulation to the relative major and simple return to the tonic by way of G minor, it contains no surprises, but impresses as being the opening of a work of some grandeur and solemnity. The change to a four pulse brings a more contrapuntal treatment, and the words *Dum turbabitur terra et transferentur montes in cor maris* suggest a semiquaver melisma, and then a surging arpeggio figure which is echoed between the three voices, to the accompaniment of a sustained major triad:

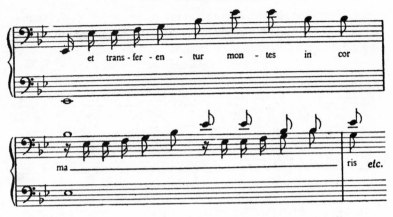

The *Propterea in Deo laudabo* shifts to the major and has an animated
bass in quavers, reinforcing the soloists' laudatory flourishes. At first,
the treatment is homophonic, interspersing a solo line with passages
of three-part note for note writing. Later there is some close canonic
imitation, and the parts demand an increasing virtuosity. The growth
of contrapuntal elements and of lyrical decoration builds up an imposing climax, until the motet ends in a blaze of diatonic counterpoint to the words *psalmos cantabimus*.

The *Motet de St Augustin* is in A, and returns to the radiant manner
of the tribute to Ste Suzanne. The opening phrase, with its tenderly
resolving 6 : 4 chord, has a soft glow which, if most un-Augustinian,
is quintessentially Couperin. The resolving 6 : 4 is later developed
into this delicious lilting phrase, with the persistent A as pedal in the
bass:

A fine passage of arioso in the minor has a highly decorated solo line, with a flexibly melodic bass which occasionally introduces chromaticisms. The return to the major again brings one of Couperin's smiling diatonic phrases, imitatively treated:

The words *coronatus immortali gloria* are set to quietly rising scale passages in imitation, combined with a sustained pedal E. The conclusion has some of Couperin's warm suspensions in dotted rhythm.

The *Dialogus inter Deum et hominem* is one of the most successful of the longer motets, and like the Versets of 1705 and 1706 offers some comparison with the technique of Bach. The opening aria is unpretentious, but the *Accede fili mi ad fontem* section, which changes the tonality to the major, is conceived on a grand scale. Much use is made of sequential figures, and the counter-tenor's line has a baroque luxuriance. A passage of arioso is interesting both melodically and harmonically, and the next 3 : 4 aria, in the minor, combines the grace of the *air de cour* with a Bach-like closeness of texture. A rising scale figure in the continuo gives the air a sense of urgency which is counterbalanced by the fact that the scale passage is grouped in *falling* sequences:

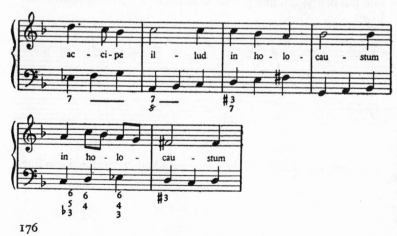

The last section, *Totum ardeat et consummatur flamma,* is a magnificent piece of baroque contrapuntal writing over a steady crochet beat. The melismata suggested by the word *flamma* gather momentum, and linear arabesques combine with sustained minims to create processions of suspended sevenths:

None of Couperin's motets has a more organic sense of growth to an inevitable end.

With the three *Leçons des Tenèbres* for one or two voices with organ and viol continuo we reach the highest point of Couperin's church music, and one of the peaks of his music as a whole. They were written between 1713 and 1715, possibly at the request of a convent. These are the works which justify the tentative comparison, made early in this chapter, between Couperin's achievement in church music and Racine's *Athalie.* While always preserving a civilized decorum, they attain to an intensity of passion which Couperin attempts but seldom. The Latin words of the prophet Jeremiah are interspersed with ritualistic Hebrew phrases which are used by

177

Couperin as an excuse for vocalises of remarkable elaboration. Here the Italian aria technique is reinterpreted in terms of the French tradition; the *port de voix, tremblement*, portamento and other ornamental devices of the *air de cour* lose their fragility and enervating nostalgia, and are transformed into a line which reconciles subtlety with strength.

The opening of the first *Leçon* indicates admirably this breadth of line, and also shows how the ornamentation is both an expressive part of the line's contour, and a concomitant of the harmony:

In the first arioso passage, the freedom of the lines creates supple key changes, for instance this transition to E minor:

The ornamentation of the *air de cour* is again in evidence, with great lyrical intensity. At the end of this section there is a beautiful instance of Couperin's progression to the flat seventh, followed by the rise to the sharp seventh to form the cadence. We are here in the re-created world of the organ masses.

The second section of vocalise is even more elaborate than the first. Long held suspensions are resolved ornamentally, and there is a subtle use of false relation in the cadence. The minor passage of arioso, *Plorans ploravit in nocte*, is one of the most extraordinary and poignant pieces in the whole of Couperin's work. The vocal line is an impassioned lament, in which dissonant *ports de voix* convey a heart-rending sorrow. Both the contour of the lines, and the harmonies, are of extreme boldness:

A little chromatically altered phrase for the word *lachrymae*, accompanied by suspended sevenths, is simpler, but hardly less moving.

The second passage of recitative-arioso, *Migravit Juda*, is also powerful. Here the chromatically rising phrase, followed by a falling fifth, is particularly expressive; so is the characteristic cadence to the major.

Double appoggiaturas and diminished intervals are conspicuous in the F minor arioso, and the last passage of recitative introduces some painfully dissonant *ports de voix* and some chromatically ornamented resolutions in which the emotionalism is balanced by the *grave* arch of the line:

This 'weeping' chromatic resolution is then taken over by the continuo, becoming the main motive in the concluding aria. The swaying chromaticism imbues the line with a yearning quality, comparable with that of the earlier *Elévations*. Here, however, the lilting line is never limp, but has great nervous vitality. And this vitality is enhanced by the supple interplay between the voice and the viol of the continuo:

As a whole, the work seems to me one of the most impressive examples of linear organization and harmonic resource in late baroque music.

The second *Leçon* is also for one high voice, with organ and viol continuo. Again it opens with a rhapsodic vocalise in D major. The first recitative has drooping suspended sevenths; the second vocalise, in triple time, flows mainly in conjunct motion with *air de cour* ornamentation. Acute double suspensions and chromatic progressions in the bass occur in the second arioso, in the relative minor. Again the ornamentation of the vocal line increases the dissonance, while the balance of the phrases guards against any emotional instability—note the mingling of conjunct motion with figures built from the minor triad:

The subsiding chromaticisms of the conclusion have a Purcellian pathos, though the air as a whole is more classically 'objective'.

The next two passages of vocalise are nobly diatonic, with suspensions in the continuo. Some effective portamento falling sevenths are grouped in sequence, in the *Peccatum peccavit* arioso. A change to the minor occurs for the *Sordes ejus in pedibus ejus*, a section having considerable dramatic power, with tritones prominent in the vocal line, and harsh dissonances in the continuo:

The work concludes with an extremely beautiful aria, also in the minor, *Jerusalem convertere ad Dominum*. It is built on a simple phrase rising up a fifth, and then serenely falling. *Ports de voix* are again used to give harmonic intensity and at the same time to smooth off the contour of the line. The final statement of the theme is in an ornamented version, accompanied by canonic entries in the continuo. The subtlety and sensitivity of the ornamentation never destroys the music's architectural quality, while the noble architecture gives power to the sensitivity:

If the third *Leçon* impresses one as being the greatest, it is largely because, being conceived for two soloists instead of one, it offers opportunities for a combination of the vocalise technique with polyphony. The opening vocalise uses the familiar soaring line in effective dissonant suspension, after the manner of the two-violin sonata. Here the winged, disembodied lines, moving mainly by conjunct motion, are vocal in conception, while the terseness of the dissonances is instrumental; this is the representative compromise between religious and secular technique:

The vocalise is repeated in artfully varied forms between each arioso section.

The first arioso incorporates Couperin's favourite modulation to the minor of the dominant; the second begins with a strange chromatic deliquescence:

The chromaticism is, however, defeated by the trumpet-like call of the voices in dialogue on the words *Vide Domine*; and the duo flows without break into a supple ornamented version of the vocalise in canon.

The *O vos omnes* section of recitative also balances a speech-like freedom of line and acute dissonances in the continuo, against trumpet-like phrases in rising fourths and sixths on the word

184

Attendite. The tonal transitions still have a seventeenth-century plasticity:

The pace quickens on the words *Quoniam vindemiavit me*, and the voices proceed note for note until, with the words *irae furoris sui*, a climax is reached on a diminished seventh chord[18] The section concludes with a beautiful version of the vocalise, even freer in rhythm and longer in melodic span:

[18] Such a use of the dramatic diminished seventh is not common in Couperin's work. The French were inclined to regard the chord with suspicion as being essentially Italian.

The next section of recitative is notable for its dramatic falling sixth and dissonant appoggiaturas on the words *posuit me desolatam*:

and the following vocalise has one of Couperin's pathetic false relations:

An arioso on *Vigilavit jugum* leads to another homophonic section in quicker movement; this has a delicate grace which reminds one, even in this spiritual work, of Couperin's relation to the *brunete* tradition:

The work ends with a full-scale statement of the vocalise, developed canonically, but now adapted to the Latin text of the

Jerusalem convertere. Over a level crochet movement, the aria evolves with conventional architectural modulations to the dominant and sub-dominant. The contrapuntal writing is of great purity, and uses a phrase—a rising fourth followed by a descending scale—which had been common property among the sixteenth-century polyphonists. This clear counterpoint, mated with this equally lucid tonal architecture, shows us that in his last and greatest church work Couperin is still, like Bach, poised between two worlds, and making the best of them both.

Chapter Nine

The Clavecin Works

IN TUDOR ENGLAND, the relation between the secular and ecclesi-astical keyboard schools was always intimate, and Bull and Gibbons are equally remarkable as composers of polyphonic organ fantasias and as composers of virginal pieces which, however complex they may become, at least start from secular song and dance. This close connection between the religious and the secular was one of the secrets of the extraordinary richness of English music at the turn of the century; and we have already seen that something rather similar was true of contemporary French musical culture. But whereas the French were aware of the implications of the 'modern' elements in musical style, and were prepared to sacrifice the old to the new, the English accepted the old and the new on equal terms. They were hardly aware, perhaps, that they had to make a choice; and their relative lack of self-consciousness is their strength. But it also means that their keyboard music—which is of a variety and subtlety not exceeded by any period of European history, and certainly not by the contemporary French schools—is an end as much as a beginning. Byrd, Gibbons, Farnaby, and Bull were not followed by a 'classical' keyboard composer, as Titelouze was followed by Chambonnières, and Chambonnières by Couperin. Between sixteenth-century poly-phony and the classical age, there was a break in England's cultural continuity; and this break has, of course, social and economic causes which are summed up in the phenomenon of the Civil War. In French culture there is no such break in continuity. For the claveci-nists the connecting link between sixteenth-century polyphony and the classical age is the work of the lutenist composers.

All through the sixteenth century, in France as in England, the lute had been a musical maid-of-all-work analogous to the modern piano. It had been used as a makeshift, for playing polyphonic vocal music in transcriptions that were literal apart from slight modifications and decorations suggested by the nature of the instrument; it had been used for playing homophonic dance music—pavanes, galliards, branles and so on—usually as an accompaniment to the dancing. In this way, it was in close touch with both the social and religious aspects of sixteenth-century music, and beyond them with many of the traditions of folk art; so that when the lute composers began to grow into an independent school, they had behind them a consciousness of many centuries of French musical history—religious polyphony, secular harmonized chansons, court dances, and the dances of the people.

It was in the early years of the seventeenth century that a personal, expressive element became noticeable within music that had previously been of an 'occasional' order. In the dances of a man such as Antoine Francisque, a vein of sophisticated sensuousness appeared parallel to the growth of *précieux* elements in the verse of a St Amant or Théophile. The influence of the passionate Spanish vihuela music of Luis Milan may have encouraged this development of an expressive, rather than a purely functional, dance music. Certainly the connections between French and English culture were a contributory factor, for Dowland himself had a brilliant continental reputation, and at one time stayed at the court of Henri IV; while it was common for French musicians to visit England, some of them, such as Jacques Gaultier the elder, for considerable periods. Possibly the dolorous nature of Dowland's temperament encouraged a comparable gloom on the part of the French composers; possibly an elegiac quality native to the Frenchmen was reinforced by the development of the lute with eleven strings instead of the traditional nine, for the additional strings gave increased opportunity for a grave solemnity of harmony and for richness of part-writing. In any case, outside influences and material circumstances did no more than intensify a development which was native to French culture.

The English lutenists were highly developed art composers who were still related to a folk culture; there was with them no sharp division between esoteric and popular elements. The French lutenists, on the other hand, soon began to lose contact with their popular origins, becoming an autonomous school associated with the *précieux* movement in society. In the first generation of lute composers—the adventurous Bocquet, the virtuoso Vincent, the fragrant Mézangeau,

Jacques and Ennemond Gaultier, Etienne Richard and Germain Pinel—there was something of the freshness and spontaneity of the English composers, if not their comprehensive power. But the second generation of lutenists—the great Denis Gaultier, Jacques Gallot, and Charles Mouton—were artists of high sophistication, the leading musical representatives of the *ruelles* and salons. Like the *air de cour* writers and the other mid-century exponents of *préciosité*, they strove, in their ornamentation, their stylized refinement, even their methods of fingering their instrument, to become a musical Elect, preserving their music from popular contagion. They even invented a semi-private language for the fanciful and cryptogrammatic titles of their pieces; the tradition survives in Couperin's work. At the same time, the stylization did not imply any emotional frigidity. The pictures in the beautiful contemporary edition of Denis Gaultier's *La Rhétorique des Dieux*, that describe the relation of the various modes (the sixteenth-century terminology is somewhat incongruously adhered to) to different passions, are a further indication of the interest in subtle states of feeling which this society cultivated. Charmé even added quasi-psychological descriptive comments to some of Gaultier's pieces.

There is nothing in the lute music of this hyper-civilized society as passionately lugubrious as the wonderful chromatic fancies of Dowland; but the tone of the pieces, though always restrained, is elegiac, tenderly melancholy or dreamily noble, comparable with that of the *airs de cour*, only less enervating. Passages of ripe chromatic harmony such as this:

are fairly frequent in the work of Mouton, while the dissonant suspensions, sequential sevenths, and false relations of this passage are typical of the work of Jacques Gallot:

This composer is also enterprising in the matter of tonality, having some powerfully gloomy pieces in F sharp minor, a key known to the lutenists as 'le ton de la chèvre'. The pieces of the greatest of the lutenists, Denis Gaultier, show a similar union of a polyphonic inheritance with an interest in the sensuous implications of harmony; but it is significant that it is he who most puts the stress on the moulding of his line and the balance of his clauses. The lovely *Tombeau* or funeral oration for the uncle of the famous Ninon de l'Enclos illustrates this clearly; note how the soprano line leads up—intensified by the chromatic progression of the bass—to the climax of a modulation into E minor, only to resolve into a cadence in C:

from which point the lines and harmonies subside to their source. All Gaultier's pieces have this instinct for dignity and proportion. Not only the grand *tombeaux* and sarabandes, but also the subtle-rhythmed courantes, are pervasively melancholy. Even the canaris, gigues, and galliards are more wistfully fanciful than joyous.

But Gaultier's expression of the aristocratic values of his community is revealed most remarkably in the cantabile character of his line. His rhythms have not the rather insensitive symmetry of some eighteenth-century music; but he does sometimes achieve a measured gravity of line, involving clearly defined modulation, which almost suggests Italian bel canto, or a fresher, more delicate Handel:

That is one aspect of Gaultier, which we shall see echoed in Chambonnières, and later in Couperin himself. A more adequate notion of

192

his genius will be given if we quote, before leaving him, the end of the *Tombeau* which he wrote for himself:

Here we may call attention to the noble span of the line; the caressing suspensions; the occasional tense diminished interval; the resonant spacing of the parts, derived from lute technique; and the sombre repetition of the Bs, and of the grave minor triad, in the last bar.

The most distinctive feature of lute technique—clearly revealed in most of the foregoing examples—is what one might call simulated polyphony. The broken arpeggio technique is used to create an illusion of part-writing which both preserves the sense of movement in the composition (despite the short sustaining power of the instrument), and at the same time establishes a solid harmony. The skill called for in interpreting the polyphony latent in the lute tablature was what principally gave its highly virtuoso character to lute technique. Only very sensitive and resourceful players were capable of an adequate 'realization'.

Further evidence of this virtuosity both of technique and feeling is found in the ornamentation which was often not indicated in the

193

text. This ornamentation was adapted to the lute from the embellishments of the *air de cour*, and Jehann Basset's *L'art de toucher le luth* of 1636 indicates that in employing ornaments the lutenists were inspired by similar motives as were the composers of *airs de cour;* 'de là vient que le jeu de nos devanciers n'avoit point les mignardises et les gentillesses qui embellissent le nostre par tant de diversitez'. The ornaments, which were an integral part of both line and harmony, included all kinds of slide or portamento effects, the sudden damping of strings, the *ver cassé* or vibrato, and various kinds of *tremblement*— for instance a rapid tremolo on a single string or an alternation of two notes coupled with a sighing diminuendo. The intimacy and subtlety of these ornaments came from the direct contact between the string and the human agency of the finger; Segovia gives an idea of this, on the more emotional guitar, in his recording of a most beautiful dance suite of the German lutenist and contemporary of Bach, S. L. Weiss. Couperin's attempt to obtain expression in keyboard music was largely a search for a substitute for this intimate relationship between the finger and the sounding medium. The esoteric culture of the court of Charles I perhaps suggests that the English lutenists might have developed in a similar, more stylized and formal manner had not the tradition been interrupted by the Civil War.

Of the forms which the French lutenists adopted, the prelude was closest to the improvisatory style of the lute air. Written in unmeasured notation, to be interpreted by the performer, it was a more organized development of the preliminary flourishes in arpeggios and other obvious instrumental techniques which the player might improvise to a song. In a more measured form, the technique survives in both Louis and François Couperin, particularly in the pieces explicitly called Prelude, and in the most famous of all examples, the first prelude of Bach's Forty-Eight. The dances themselves, pavane (and later allemande), courante, sarabande, and gigue, preserve the features of the ballet dances, but, as with the bigger galliards and pavanes of the Tudor virginalists, the original character of the dance may sometimes be submerged in the melodic and figurative developments. This is not often the case, however, with the slighter dances, such as bourrées, canaris, and branles.

All these forms, and many of the techniques implicit in the nature of the lute, were taken over by the first composers for clavecin, who often wrote in a more or less identical manner for the lute or keyboard instrument. To them the clavecin was a kind of mechanized lute, and spread chord formations, plucked string effects, and overlapping canonic entries were all elements of lute technique which survived, or were modified, in the technique of the keyboard instrument; indeed simulated polyphony survived even though a naturally polyphonic instrument made deceit unnecessary. Almost from the start, however, the clavecinists strove to develop the formal aspects of the convention—as hinted at by Denis Gaultier—at the expense of the improvisatory elements. They belonged more to the new age of the mid-baroque. Possibly the best way to demonstrate this is by way of a comparison between the work of Chambonnères and that of his pupil, Louis Couperin.

Like Gaultier, Chambonnères was a product of *précieux* society, a leading musical representative of the Hôtel de Rambouillet, and later court clavecinist to Louis XIV. In most ways it is legitimate to regard his work as an extension of that of the lutenists, who were emulated as much for social as for musical reasons, the lute being the traditional instrument of nobility. His finest pieces derive from the polyphonic elements of the lute idiom. The three big G minor pavanes, with their contrapuntal entries, false relations, and rhythmic flexibility, can even be connected with the more massive polyphony of the religious choral and organ schools:

We can here see Chambonnières exploiting the traditions of the
sixteenth century, together with luxuriant ornamentation, and with
a richness of harmony encouraged by the spacing of the lute parts.
The warm sound of the tenth and of the dominant seventh is especially attractive to him: he will dwell on the chords, revelling in
their sensuous appeal:

These pieces, like the lute *tombeaux*, often attain a surprising grandeur
and power.

Then there is a range of pieces analogous to the delicately proportioned sarabande of Gaultier which we have already quoted. Within
their sophisticated symmetry, these pieces have a conscious naïveté
which seems to entail a civilized reincarnation of the fragrance of
French folk song; or we may relate it perhaps to French art song in
the Middle Ages, to the troubadours' mating of innocence with
sophistication. At the same time, the suave progression of the harmonies, with the sonorous spacing and fragile ornamentation, are the
product of a courtly society:

196

We have already observed a development of this manner in some of Couperin's work, other than his keyboard music. In the following passage, the effect of the rising sharp seventh, succeeded by the flat seventh in the descent, is particularly reminiscent of the Couperin of the organ *Messe des Convents*:

An even subtler case is this little sarabande in F, which combines its diatonically innocent air with inner parts in which ornamentally

197

resolved suspensions create tender augmented and diminished intervals and other dissonances at the points marked; note also, in the
first section, the slightly disturbing effect of the modulation to D
minor, before the conventional resolution in the dominant:

A further anticipation of Couperin's early work is found in the
warm, quietly flowing gigue in G (No. 55 in the Senart edition).

Some of Chambonnières's quick pieces, such as the delightful
Gigue bruscambille—built on an irregular rising scale passage in imitation—are also successful; and a few pieces, such as the B flat galliard
with its *double* in clattering semiquavers, have an unexpectedly
manly vigour. In general, however, his best movements are those
which are in direct contact with the polyphonists, or with the lutenists, or with both. They tend, like Gaultier's work, to the elegiac and
contemplative, without reaching, perhaps, the sombre refinement of
198

Gaultier's best music. When Chambonnières attempts to build his pieces not on latently polyphonic principles, nor on the simple dominant-tonic basis of the G major sarabande, but on a more developed scheme of tonal relationships, the result is not very convincing. The larger allemandes, though interesting for their flexible part-writing, have not the balance between polyphonic vitality and harmonic architecture which marks the mature alle-mandes of Couperin and Bach. From this point of view, this nor-mally impeccable artist suggests a development which he did not live to fulfil. The rather gauche allemande, *La Loureuse*, may be referred to as an illustration.

Comparatively, Chambonnières's pupil, Louis Couperin, is a much more vigorous personality: the Abbé Le Gaulois said that his playing was 'estimé par les personnes sçavantes à cause qu'elle est pleine d'accords et enrichie de belles dissonances, de dessins et d'imitations'. His pieces show a sturdy contrapuntal technique and an aggressive use of dissonance alien to the refined discretion of his master—witness this opening of a D minor sarabande:

More interesting, however, is the increasingly mature command of tonal organization which he manifests. He writes grandly expressive sarabandes which, even more than the 'exquisite' sarabandes of Chambonnières, provide some anticipation of Handel; and his con-trol of incidental modulation, within the tonic-dominant-tonic or minor-relative major-minor framework, gives no impression of the tentative or experimental. The E minor sarabande, No. 65 in the Lyrebird edition, is an imposing example, and we may mention the very Handelian D major (No. 60), and the canonic sarabande in D minor (No. 47). The polyphonic-homophonic compromise sug-gested by this last-mentioned sarabande is especially impressive, since

199

the canonic entry starts on the last beat of the sarabande rhythm, so that the counterpoint consistently negates the bar measure. The most significant of the allemandes also preserve the linear independence of Chambonnières and the lutenists while achieving a satisfying tonal order; in this respect they anticipate the finest allemandes of Bach and Couperin le Grand. We may instance the slow rhapsodic allemande in D No. 58, the E minor No. 61, and the gentle G major No. 82, which recalls the silvery sound of the baroque organ.

Even the pieces of Louis Couperin which incline to the old polyphonic methods show this more vigorously organized quality. The famous *Tombeau de M. de Blancrocher* is in the tradition of the resplendently decorated *tombeaux* of the lutenists, but it intensifies the conventional improvisatory effects and dissonances to a pitch of dramatic passion that is almost operatic; consider the odd grinding noise of the unresolved sevenths at the end of this passage:

A comparable piece is the big pavane in F sharp minor—a key which crops up intermittently in the clavecin music, being a survival from the lutenists' *ton de la chèvre*. This pavane is again founded on lute technique; its chromatic alterations give it a remarkable pathos. The classical stability of its proportions, together with the sensuous, melodically derived augmented intervals of the incidental har-

monies, might even be compared with the elegiac late nocturnes of
Fauré:

Another piece looking back to the false relations and polyphony of
the lutenists is the G minor allemande, No. 92:

Less successful is the curious G minor fantasia which begins contrapuntally in the manner of the organ fancy, and then develops by widely skipping arpeggio figurations, without any attempt to return to the fugal principles of the opening. The new age of the dance and the theatre has here routed the old world of the church. In this case one feels that there is no organic growth from the one to the other.

This is probably an organ piece, related to the work of a man such as Nicolas le Bègue. The lively sense of the keyboard which it displays is more convincingly demonstrated in the *Duo*, perhaps the finest of Louis Couperin's more animated movements, notable for the variety of its linear patterns, and for the surprising richness and piquancy of the harmony produced by the movement of the two parts:

But the most impressive of Louis Couperin's pieces, as well as the most 'modern' in effect, are those using the transitional technique of chaconne or passacaglia, which we have already discussed with reference to Lully. Louis Couperin's chaconnes proceed with relentless power, and are usually dark in colour and dissonant in texture; consider the spiky clash in the first bar of No. 55:

Here again Couperin introduces a bold modification in the chaconne-rondeau technique, since he occasionally allows the modulations of the couplets to be continued into the repetitions of the theme, thereby making a compromise between the traditional static technique and the new sense of tonal relationship. The G minor chaconne, No. 122, is also remarkable for its dramatic use of diminished seventh chords.

Among the Passacailles, the G minor No. 95 is characterized by a rhythmic freedom in line and ornamentation which reminds one of operatic recitative. This is a fine piece, but still finer are Louis Couperin's two masterpieces, the C major passacaille No. 27, and the passacaille in G minor and major, No. 99. The C major is a gravely massive piece which uses ornamentation, dotted rhythms, and scale passages to build up a cumulative power almost comparable with the chaconne of Couperin le Grand's C minor violin suite, or with the grand choral chaconnes in Lully's last operas. It ends in evocative solemnity with a repetition of the *grand couplet* in the minor instead of the major, a reversal of the normal procedure such as one occasionally finds in Purcell. The great G minor passacaille No. 99 is Louis Couperin's biggest piece in every sense. It is built over a falling scale bass, and employs every device afterwards used by Couperin le Grand to build up an overwhelming climax—dissonant suspensions, more animated movement, flowing scale passages in parallel and contrary motion. There is a wonderful modulation into the major, incorporating richly spaced suspensions, and a chromatically modified version of the bass which is balanced by soaring diatonic scale figures:

etc.

The final couplet keeps the chromatic bass but returns sombrely to the minor.

Two other pupils of Chambonnières should be mentioned among Couperin's predecessors—Jean Henri d'Anglebert and Gaspard le Roux. D'Anglebert represents perhaps the culmination of the mid-baroque period that preceded Couperin le Grand. He transfers to the clavecin idiom much of the contrapuntal power and harmonic luxuriance which we observed in his organ fugues, a quotation from which was given in chapter five. His clavecin work has a remarkable grandeur, whether it be in a brilliantly expansive piece such as the long variations on La Folia, a grave, austerely wrought movement such as the G minor allemande, or a spaciously serene piece such as the D major chaconne, which has a Claude-like quietude fully worthy of comparison with the rondeau from the *Impériale* suite of François Couperin himself.

Le Roux's *Pièces pour Clavecin*, although not published till 1705, were written considerably earlier. With d'Anglebert he is the last representative of the *grand goût* of the mid-century, and his music has much of the valedictory nobility of Denis Gaultier. But if he is less of a modernist than Louis Couperin, he is a more mature and developed artist than Chambonnières; his work is remarkable for the lyrical contour of its melody, and for the richness of its balanced sequential writing, as we may see from this passage from a courante:

We may mention also, from the Amsterdam edition of 1706, the beautiful suite in F sharp minor, which may be compared with Louis Couperin's movements in the same *ton de la chèvre*; the D minor chaconne which deserves to keep company with the grandest pieces in this contemporary form; and the long sarabande with variations in G minor. This last sarabande is really an elaborate chaconne, and although less remarkable musically than the other pieces mentioned is interesting for its unexpectedly progressive treatment of keyboard technique. Its use of arpeggio and scale figurations almost suggests the Handel of the harpsichord passacaglias. An appendix to the Amsterdam volume includes a second clavecin part for five of the pieces. Both this fact and the quality of the music argue strongly in favour of a modern edition; the pieces would make a fascinating contribution to two-piano literature.

When Couperin le Grand started to write clavecin music he had the music of Chambonnières, Louis Couperin, d'Anglebert, and le Roux to work from. Behind them was the school of lutenist composers; and behind them in turn were, as we have seen, generations of French musical tradition, from folk song and troubadours, to the polyphony and harmonized dance music of the sixteenth century. Interacting with these traditional French elements were Italian influences: the implicit presence of the operatic aria and occasionally of the dramatic harmonic formulae with which the continuo accompanies recitative; the influence of Italian dance music and the popular culture of the *commedia dell'Arte*, linking up with the French popular culture; and the influence of Corelli and his conception of the tonal formalization of dance movements. In the work of all Chambonnières's successors, one can observe these French and Italian elements slowly merging into one another, whether it be at the level of the finest work of Louis Couperin or of d'Anglebert or at the level of the unpretentious dances of Nicolas le Bègue. The fusion is consummated in the clavecin music, as in the concerted music, of Couperin le Grand. In the first book of his clavecin pieces we are most conscious of the constituent materials, French and Italian, as such; in the fourth they are so completely assimilated into an idiom of classical maturity that we are conscious of the perfect proportions of the whole building, rather than of the richness of detail that goes to make it up.

Some dance movements of the lute suite Couperin takes over as they stand, though he presents them in a more lucidly diatonic form. The gigue and sarabande survive in their Italianized version; the pavane is replaced by the allemande, as it was tending to be in the work of Chambonnières and Louis Couperin. These dance rhythms are all absorbed into the binary principles of the baroque sonata, with first section ending in the dominant or relative major, the complementary second section returning to the tonic (the dances and their structure will be discussed in detail in the next chapter). All the pieces which are not basically dance movements of this type are rondeaux or chaconne-rondeaux—an extension of the old technique of dance tune with couplets, whereby the symmetrical theme is stated, followed by a short episode of allied but distinct material possibly involving a simple modulation, followed by a restatement of the tune in its original form always without modulation, followed by another episode, and so on, *ad libitum*. Both techniques were, as we have seen, in the first place functional, arising out of the practical exigencies of the dance; and both, especially the rondeau, may seem to be extremely limited. But Couperin le Grand—like Bach and Scarlatti, and like Louis Couperin before him—shows how the limitation may be used to convey an intensity of experience such as can be achieved only in the full maturity of a civilization. We may compare Corneille's, Racine's and Pope's use of the alexandrine and heroic couplet.

Although the plan of Couperin's movements is harmonically dictated he still, like Bach and Scarlatti, occupies a transitional position between polyphony and homophony, in so far as his music normally entails a dialogue between melody and bass; the latter nearly always has melodic significance. Implied polyphony exists alongside the ripest development of tonal harmony; the lucid harmonic scheme both moulds, and is moulded by, the dialogue of the parts. Like Bach, Couperin borrows vitality and subtlety from the polyphonic tradition, and from the homophonic a classical objectivity. Not only the violin sonata which we have already discussed, but also the gigue of the keyboard suite had long manifested this harmonic-contrapuntal fusion, since its clear harmonic basis was combined with fugal treatment 'inverted' in the second half of the structure, the inversion of the themes corresponding with the inversion of the sequence of keys. But the melodic-harmonic fusion is much subtler than this in Bach's and Couperin's conception of keyboard technique, reaching its most profound expression in their more baroque movements (such as the allemandes of Bach's E minor and D major partitas, or a piece of Couperin such as *Les Langueurs Tendres*). Here the symmetrical harmonic periods are no more than implicit beneath the continuous, unmetrical flow of ornamental lyricism. This is the consummation of a technique which we have already observed in a tentative form in some movements of the organ masses.

Couperin's first book of clavecin pieces was published in 1713, though many of the pieces had been written much earlier. If the 'Bachian fusion' is least evident in this volume, one can perhaps find here the various types of piece which Couperin is subsequently to develop, in their most accessible form. Firstly there are, particularly in the second *ordre*, a number of simple undeveloped dances, more or less the same as those which were actually danced to in the ballets. These are often charming and are interesting as one of the roots from which Couperin's art grew, but are not otherwise remarkable. Secondly there are, closely related to these dances, slightly more sophisticated dance pieces in which the influence of Corelli's tonal plan is more perceptible; *La Milordine, La Pateline,* and *La Florentine* are obvious examples. These are straightforward movements in Italian binary style, though with a gallic delicacy in the texture. Then, thirdly, there is a class of pastoral pieces which are ostensibly French in manner, related to the *brunette* tradition and the ballet. Some of these are charmingly personal in flavour; the idiom of a piece such as *La Fleurie ou la Tendre Nanette*, though more harmonic, resembles the chansons of a Guillaume de Costeley in its combination of sophisticated ornament with a melodic and harmonic naïveté which has the spiritual innocence of folk song. Others (*La Tendre Fanchon, La Bandoline, La Flore*) link this innocence of melody with a technique of figurative sequences built on seventh chords, thereby creating a delicate voluptuousness which we have seen to be one of the most typical features of Couperin's sensibility:

This is the kind of technique, reconciling a mannered 'social' artificiality with a latently personal emotion, in which it is possible to trace some analogy with the painting of Watteau. Beneath the apparently passive acceptance of the courtly convention there is an intense apprehension of the loneliness of the individual consciousness.

A somewhat different aspect of the Watteau-like manner is shown in the fourth group of pieces—those exploiting the arpeggio figurations of lute technique. *Les Idées Heureuses* has a tranquil flow of arpeggio figuration which, by means of tied notes and suspensions, creates a quasi-polyphonic effect. Both the melodic interest and the harmonic subtlety of the piece profit from this treatment. The movement also includes a touching passage built over a descending chromatic bass in a manner much favoured later by Couperin himself, and by Bach. *La Garnier* is another beautiful piece in the lute tradition, exploiting the resonance of the clavecin's overtones in a

way that might almost be called impressionistic. This too is a style
that Couperin develops in later work.

The fifth group of pieces comprises those influenced by the more
powerful aspects of lute technique—bigger movements in the tradition of the *tombeau*. The finest examples are the allemande and sarabande, *L'Auguste* and *La Majestueuse* in the G minor *ordre*, and the
comparable movements, *La Ténébreuse* and *La Lugubre*, from the
ordre in C minor. These are magnificent pieces, using massed broken
chords, passionate ornamentation, lute-like percussive effects and
harmonic acridities, and revealing a closeness of texture which
rivals the graver suite movements of Bach. Such a passage as this
from *La Ténébreuse*, almost as much as the larger contrapuntal movements in the late violin sonatas, at once reveals the absurdity of the
account of Couperin—at one time current—as a hot-house composer:

The courantes, too, have a rhythmic and contrapuntal virility that makes them more comparable with Bach than with any other exponent of the late baroque.

The last group of pieces includes the most mature movements in the first volume—those which already illustrate what we have called the Bachian compromise. The allemande *La Logiviere* is a splendid example, reconciling its architectural structure and latent dance rhythm with a continuous stream of baroque melody, powerful dissonances in the inner parts, and some characteristically 'impressionistic' drone effects. *La Laborieuse* is a similar piece, with strange, melodically derived modulations; and another remarkable movement is *Les Regrets*, in which the pathos is attained by means of suspensions continuously hovering over a bass which proceeds with measured gravity. But the finest piece in the book is the C minor chaconne *La Favorite*, which defies precedent by being in duple time instead of triple.[19] This is a work which, even by Bach's standard, one may call great. There is nothing outside Bach which has such massive dignity of workmanship, and yet it is quite unlike Bach, and could have been written by no one but Couperin. This piece demonstrates superbly how Couperin's technique depends on a dialogue between soprano melody and bass, for the bass line is throughout of a wonderfully cantabile character, always balancing the sombre articulation of the main melody:

[19] 'Autrefois, il y avait des chaconnes à deux tems et à trois; mais on n'en fait plus qu'à trois.' (Rousseau's *Dictionnaire*.)

With the B minor *Passacaille*, the piece is also perhaps the most impressive instance of Couperin's ability to extort a monumental power from the very rigidity of the chaconne-rondeau convention. Its disciplining of intense passion is again both a personal achievement and an achievement of civilization.

From the second volume onwards, each *ordre* begins to acquire a definite character of its own. Since we have now dealt in general terms with the main classes into which Couperin's pieces fall, it will be simplest if henceforward we deal with each *ordre* as we come to it in sequence. The second volume appeared in 1716–1717, and the first *ordre* in it (the sixth of the whole series) is tender and delicate in mood. It contains one of Couperin's most beautiful works from the linear point of view—*Les Langueurs Tendres*, a piece we have already mentioned as an example of the reconciling of a highly ornamented, rhythmically fluid line with a latently regular pulse and harmonic development. The ornamentation, inherited from the *air de cour*, smooths all angles off the line, gives it a caressing flexibility which suggests some kinship with the ordered plasticity of Racine's rhythm. Here the ornamentation is not, like much of Handel's ornamentation, something applied to a symmetrical harmonically conceived melody, but a part of the melodic contour, a means of achieving nuance and gradation:

While the method is the same as that of Bach in, say, the theme and some of the slow movements of the Goldberg variations, Couperin's flavour, his radiance, is unique. It may be partly attributable to the covert relation of his line to the French language, which certainly influenced the line of the *air de cour*. Such a relationship need not manifest itself as patently as in the case of Lully's recitative.

A simpler, more homophonic piece in the same mood is *Les Bergeries*. This is melodically of great distinction, wistfully sophisticated like Watteau and yet not altogether remote from French folksong. The second couplet of the rondeau makes an impressionistic

use of the bagpipe drone effect, an evocative, summer-like noise on
the harpsichord, which cannot be translated into pianistic terms:

Nothing could more effectively illustrate how Couperin's melodic
grace and economy of texture can invest the stock ingredients of the
brunette tradition with a personal and subtle poetry. This ordre also
includes another evocation of the countryside, the gay rondeau *Les
Moissonneurs*; a very famous piece in lute figuration, with chains of
resonant suspensions, *Les Baricades Mistérieuses*; and a number of
witty pieces written with characteristic precision in two parts, of
which both the subtlest and the funniest is *Le Moucheron*, an 'Italian'
gigue in which the line exasperatingly dances round itself.

The next *ordre*, the seventh, is in G, and is also mainly pastoral in
mood. It is on the whole less distinguished than the previous (B flat)
ordre, but contains some interesting harpsichord writing in syncopation in the first part of *Les Petits Ages*. *La Ménetou* is a lovely piece
combining baroque line with 'impressionistic' suspensions; *Les
Délices* is especially rich in sonorous sequential writing:

In contrast, the eighth *ordre*, in B minor, is almost uniformly
serious, even tragic, in style; and while as a whole the second book
cannot compare with the fourth in maturity, a good case can be

made out for the eighth as the greatest individual *ordre*. It opens with a magnificent allemande, *La Raphaéle*, which in complexity of rhythm and harmony and in architectural power, can be justly compared to the analogous movements in Bach. A quotation will indicate its intensity, the dissonances over a pedal point, the lute-like suspensions, the disciplined chromaticisms:

Equally majestic is the sarabande, *L'Unique*, with its dramatically percussive harmonies and violent changes of rhythm. The two courantes are among the most tightly wrought of all Couperin's dance movements, while the allemande, *L'Ausoniéne*, though simpler in texture, has dignified Bachian sequences and suspensions over a regular metrical pulse.

But the climax of the *ordre*—unquestionably the greatest single piece in Couperin's clavecin music and one of the greatest keyboard pieces ever written—is the terrific *Passacaille*. The tragic effect of this movement is attributable to the tension between the audacious fluidity of the harmonies, and the rigid repetition not merely of the bass, but of the whole opening period at the remorselessly regular intervals demanded by the chaconne-rondeau convention:

213

Each couplet adds to the intensity—even the quiet episodes such as the third, with its sparse texture and drooping, weeping suspensions contrasting with the chromatic sonority of the harmonization of the theme—until a shattering climax is reached in the seventh couplet, with its great spread discords, and anguished suspensions percussively exploiting the whole range of the instrument:

Although the passion increases cumulatively, the unaltered repetition of the opening clause gives the music a timeless, implacably fateful quality. It is astonishing that the composer of this terrifying music could ever have been regarded as exclusively amiable and elegant; we may compare the nineteenth-century legend of the 'tender' Racine. Certainly there is no music which has a more profoundly Racinian quality than this *Passacaille*, in which the rigidity of a social and technical convention (having reference to accepted standards in social intercourse), only just succeeds in holding in check a passion so violent that it threatens to engulf both the personality and the civilization of which that personality is a part. Just as we are conscious of Racine's alexandrine holding in control the wayward passion of *Phèdre's* rhythms and metaphors, so we are aware of the severe chaconne-rondeau form damming the flood of Couperin's chromaticism and dissonance. Rather oddly, after the *Passacaille* this B minor *ordre* is rounded off with an amiable Corellian gigue, *La Morinéte*; as though Couperin wished to reassert the validity of social elegance after his incursion into the merciless psychological and spiritual terrors that surround our waking lives.

The ninth *ordre* in A is again gentle, Watteau-like in tone. It contains one supremely lovely, and quite well-known piece, the rondeau *Le Bavolet Flotant*. This is a melody of the simple *brunete* type; and the two-part texture is airy and luminous. There is also a subtle movement, *Les Charmes*, using suave, overlapping lute figurations, and introducing a radiant change from minor to major in the second section. *La Séduisante* and *La Rafraîchissante* make effective use of sequences and of the sonorous registers of the keyboard, and the *ordre* opens with a fine polyphonic allemande for two clavecins, which provides evidence of what one might call the interior density of Couperin's style. As with Bach, the expressive quality of the harmonies is here largely the result of the flexibility of the lines within a clearly ordered harmonic framework. The *Passacaille* represents an extreme manifestation of this.

The next *ordre*, the tenth, in D, is musically less interesting, though it is interesting historically because it contains some fairly developed examples of descriptive music—an aspect of Couperin's work to which the conventional account devotes a disproportionate attention. The first three pieces are battle pictures, cleverly exploiting the metallic and percussive features of the harpsichord; on the piano they are apt to sound perfunctory. The second of them, *Allégresse des Vainqueurs*, is also a fine piece of music, expressing an extreme degree of joyful buoyancy by the simplest of means—an engaging 6 : 8 lilt, with melodic sequences phrased across the bar, and making brilliant play with extended trills:

La Mézangére, in the minor, is a more concentrated movement, using lute technique with the dotted rhythm of the Lullian overture. *Les Bagatelles* is an effective piece for two keyboards, depending more on the metallically glinting sonority of the crossed parts, than on melodic appeal. The other pieces are of slighter interest.

The eleventh *ordre*, in C, is notable mainly for another biggish descriptive work, this time of considerable musical value. *Les Fastes de la Grande et Ancienne Mxnxstrxndxsx* demonstrates to a remarkable degree the influence on Couperin of popular music; we find here not merely a general relationship to folk-song such as we have often referred to before, but the direct presence of the 'low' music of the towns. Couperin's love for and understanding of popular music—bagpipes, fiddlers, street-songs, rarefied in the economy of his technique—suggests that although he was, like Racine, an artist who worked for an aristocracy, he none the less embraced an unexpectedly comprehensive range of experience. There is about some of these pieces a quality almost comparable with the painting of Chardin—a tender sympathy for the things of everyday life, together with a technical delight in problems of balance and form, whereby these things are objectified, released from the temporal and local. The subtle precision of Couperin's and Chardin's technique gives to things that are mundane a quality that seems eternal, and by inference divine.

Thus the popular element in Couperin's work is reconcilable with its more serious aspects, just as Lully's aristocratic tunes were whistled by errand boys, and found their way into folk-song. Couperin's wit belongs without incongruity to the salon, the fair, the street, the village green, and the cathedral. If less obviously than an Englishman of Jonson's time, Couperin still worked before head and heart, laughter and tears, were divorced, and one can listen

216

to a frivolously impudent piece such as *Les Jongleurs et les Sauteurs* from this *ordre* immediately after, say, the noble chaconne *La Favorite*, without experiencing any emotional jolt; there is clearly the same sensibility behind the clarity of the texture. We are not therefore surprised that this work in five *actes* should include, side by side with comic drum-and-fife pieces like those about drunkards, bears, and monkeys, a grave, stately movement such as *Les Invalides*; and should also in one movement use a popular technique—a wailing, monotonous air of *Les Viéleux et les Gueux*, over a plodding *bourdon*—to produce an effect not merely lugubrious, but unexpectedly pathetic:

This piece, as well as the brisk musette-like movements in the popular vein, needs the nasal tone of the harpsichord if its poetry is to be realized adequately.

The last *ordre* in the second book (No. 12 in E), is comparatively slight. It includes a charmingly suave courante, a most polite *La Coribante*, and a delightful piece, *L'Atalante*, in running semiquavers, over a quaver pulse.

Five years were to elapse before the appearance of Couperin's third book. But in the same year as the second volume he published his theoretical work, *L'art de toucher le Clavecin*, and incorporated in it, for illustrative purposes, a series of eight preludes and one allemande. The allemande is a solidly made two-part invention with a good deal of canonic imitation, but is not especially interesting. The preludes, however, contain pieces which must rank among the finest examples in Couperin's work of the 'Bachian compromise' between harmonic proportion and melodic independence.

Couperin explains that though he has 'measured' them for the convenience of performers, these pieces are preludes and therefore, in

217

accordance with the lutenist tradition, should be played with the utmost freedom:

> Quoy que ces Préludes soint écrits mesurés, il y a cependant un goût d'usage qu'il faut suivre. Je m'explique: Prélude est une composition libre, où l'imagination se livre à tout ce qui se présente à elle. Mais comme il est assez rare de trouver des génies capables de produire dans l'instant, il faut que ceux qui auront recours à ces Préludes réglés les jouent d'une manière aisée, sans trop s'attacher à la précision des mouvements, à moins que je ne l'aye marqué exprès par le mot *Mesuré*. Ainsi, on peut hasarder de dire que dans beaucoup de choses la Musique (par comparison à la Poéie) a sa prose, et ses vers.

The connection with the lutenists is explicit in the first prelude in C, since this depends almost entirely on spread chord formations in suspension (cf. Bach's C major prelude). The second prelude, in D minor, uses a similar technique, only with a more independent and rhapsodic line. The conventional dotted rhythm appears more or less consistently, and some of the sweeping scale passages suggest the influence of Italian recitative effects similar to those found in the *tombeaux* of the lutenists and violists; dissonant appoggiaturas are frequent:

The third prelude, in G minor, is a courante, lucid in its part-writing. No. 4, in F, returns to the suspensions and decorative

arabesques of lute technique, and may be compared with Louis
Couperin's *Tombeau de M. Blancrocher*. No. 5, in A, is one of the
finest pieces in which a metrical beat is dissolved in a supple, delicately ornamented line. The B minor, No. 6, is a two-part invention
again notable for the way in which the bar-metre disappears in the
ellipses of the counterpoint:

Like the fifth, the seventh prelude, in B flat, has a highly ornamented baroque melody in which the convolutions of the line
create some peculiar harmonic effects:

and the last prelude, in E minor, is an elegant piece with a typical undertone of wistfulness, using beautifully wrought figurations in sequence.[20]

Couperin intended his preludes to be used as 'loosening-up' exercises before any group of his pieces in the appropriate key; they were not conceived with reference to any particular book, or *ordre*. It was in 1722 that the third volume of clavecin pieces appeared, and this time it opens with an *ordre* which is among the peak points of Couperin's keyboard music. It is in B minor again, a key which seems to have had a significance for Couperin analogous to Mozart's G minor; and it starts with a tender movement, *Les Lis Naissans*, in melodically grouped arpeggios. This is followed by a rondeau, *Les Roseaux*, which ranks with *Les Bergeries* and *Le Bavolet Flotant* as one of the loveliest of his works in a simple melodic, homophonically accompanied style. The balanced rise and fall of the opening clause is subtly underlined by the harmonies; here once more we can see how a poise which in one sense is a virtue of Society, may in another sense become a moral and spiritual quality:

[20] Here we may mention also the *Sicilienne* published as an appendix to the Oiseau Lyre edition of the first volume of clavecin pieces. This was first published anonymously by Ballard in his collection of *Pièces Choisies . . . de différents Auteurs* (1707.) It seems to have been popular, for it appears in several MSS. all anonymous with the exception of one inscribed *Sicilienne de M. Couprin*. The question of the authorship is not of much importance. It is an amiable, undistinguished little product of the *brunete* tradition with Italian influence, such as might have been written by Couperin in his youth or by any minor clavecin composer of the period.

But most of the *ordre* is taken up by the big chaconne *Les Folies Françoises ou les Dominos*. This is a series of variations on a ground bass, on a principle analogous to that of Bach's Goldberg Variations, without the strict contrapuntal movements. Though the *Folies* are, of course, on a much smaller scale than Bach's work, their emotional range is wide, extending from the melting harmonies of the variation called *La Langueur*, to the powerful internal chromaticisms of *La Jalousie taciturne*; from the simplicity of *La Fidélité* to the vigorous dotted rhythm of *L'Ardeur* and the ponderous tread of *Les Vieux Galans*; from the rhythmic whimsicalities of *La Coquéterie* to the whirling figuration of *L'Esperance* and *La Frénésie*. The work is a microcosm of Couperin's art, its tragic passion, its witty urbanity, its sensous charm. Whereas the earlier B minor suite had been rounded off with a piece of inconsequential gaiety, Couperin adds as an epilogue to this *ordre* a short movement, *L'Ame en peine*, which, apart from *La Passacaille*, is perhaps his most impassioned utterance. It is composed of almost continuously dissonant, drooping suspensions, including a high proportion of strained augmented intervals:

Although short, it produces an impression of grandeur and tragedy; iust as *Les Folies Françoises*, though its duration in time is not long, seems—through the variety of its mood and the architectural precision of its structure—to be a work of imposing dimensions.

The next *ordre*, No. 14 in D, is mostly of the pastoral type. It opens with one of Couperin's most exquisite pieces of decorated melodic writing, *Le Rossignol en amour*, in which the line can be related to his baroque method of treating the human voice in parts of the *Leçons des Tenèbres*, and still more in the *Brunete* of 1711. *Les Fauvétes Plaintives* is plaintive indeed, with its tremulous treble registration, its chromaticism, and its tender appoggiaturas in dotted rhythm. *Le Carillon de Cithére*, again 'scored' in the high registers of the instrument, is among the most beautiful of all bell pieces; and *Le Petit Rien* is a nimble two-part invention.

From the fifteenth *ordre* onwards, the level of the movements remains almost uniformly high. This A minor *ordre* begins with a noble allemande, *La Régente*, combining irregular baroque lines with great richness of texture and harmony; this use of the chord of the ninth is representative:

The lullaby that follows, *Le Dodo*, is a tender and civilized re-creation of a popular nursery song—a simple melody phrased across the bar, accompanied by a rocking figure. Again a most touching effect is achieved by the simple contrast between major and minor in the complementary sections. The two *Musétes* are in the popular drum-and-fife style, with short, excitingly irregular periods over the drone, and some clattering trills. *La Douce* is a sophisticated-naïve piece in the folk-song manner, and *Les Vergers Fleuris* perhaps the most remarkable of all Couperin's impressionistic pieces, creating an effect of heat and summer haze through a line which seems to be gradually dissolving into its suave ornamentation, and through the use of protracted suspensions which seem only to resolve on to other suspensions, over a sustained drone:

Here again the sensuousness of the harmony and ornamentation is disciplined by the symmetrical form in a way which recalls Watteau's structural disciplining of his idealized version of the hues of nature.

In the sixteenth *ordre*, the finest piece is *La Distraite*, which preserves a civilized symmetry beneath its 'distraught' scale passages. *L'Himen-Amour* uses widely skipping leaps and arpeggio formations; *Les Vestales* is a charming rondeau with a folk-song-like melody. Both the seventeenth and the eighteenth *ordre* contain magnificent pieces of a Bach-like polyphonic texture (*La Superbe* and *La Vernéville*), brilliant movements in harpsichord figuration of a quasi-descriptive order (*Les Petits Moulins à Vent, Les Timbres, Le Tic-Toc-Choc*), and a fine piece (*Le Gaillard-Boîteux*) 'dans le goût burlesque'. But more outstanding still is the nineteenth *ordre* in D minor, which begins with one of the very finest pieces in the popular manner, *Les Calotins et les Calotines*, includes a piece, *Les Culbutes Ixcxbxnxs*, in which irregularly grouped clauses and abrupt leaps are combined in sequences to produce at times a quasi-polytonal effect:

and has penultimately a lilting movement over a gently chromatic bass (*La Muse Plantine*) which simultaneously demonstrates Couperin's sensuousness and his classical detachment:

Another eight years elapsed before, in 1730, Couperin published his fourth book of clavecin pieces. Though it contains no piece on the scale of *La Passacaille*, it must on the whole be regarded as the culmination of his achievement in keyboard music. It is also one of his last works, for he died in 1733, and owing to ill-health composed nothing during the last few years of his life. In his preface, Couperin explains that the pieces in the fourth book had mostly been finished some three years previously; this would place them more or less contemporary with the great suites for viols.

The volume opens unpretentiously with an *ordre* which is pervasively witty in tone. *La Princesse Marie, Les Chérubins,* and *Les Tambourins* all use very short phrases, in unexpectedly irregular groupings, often based on a syncopation of the phrase rhythm against the bar rhythm. The suaver movements, *La Crouilli* and *La Douce Janneton*, are also habitually phrased across the bar, the falling sevenths of the last named being typical of Couperin's late work. The next *ordre*, the twenty-first, in E minor, is mainly grave and serious. *La Reine des Cœurs* has a proud nobility, conveyed through balanced sequential sevenths, in sarabande rhythm:

La Couperin, a large-scale allemande, is one of the most magnificent of all Couperin's Bach-like pieces, with superbly devised keyboard polyphony in three parts:

Lute figurations and internal chromaticisms give to *La Harpée* and *La Petite Pince-sans-rire* a surprising harmonic piquancy.

The twenty-second *ordre* in D is the climax of Couperin's urbane wit. Almost all the pieces have some elegantly comic feature; *L'Anguille* in particular is a brilliant two-part invention, in which the abrupt harmonies and reiterative figuration convey as appropriately as musically the eel's writhings.

A *galant et magnifique* opening to the twenty-third *ordre* is provided by *L'Audacieuse*, a piece consistently in the dotted rhythm of the Lullian overture. *Les Tricoteuses* is a descriptive piece suggested by the metallic rustle of the harpsichord in quick semiquaver movement; it makes an impressionistic, homophonic use of the chord of the diminished seventh. Still more extraordinary harmonically is the next piece, *L'Arlequine*, which, in the tradition of the *commedia*, has some exciting percussive effects, and some startlingly modern progressions of seventh and ninth chords:

etc.

The passage is a fine example of Couperin's ability to attain to great sonorous richness with the minimum of means; it is this kind of effect which made so deep an appeal to Debussy, and still more to Ravel, since they found in its emotional quality something that was not irrelevant to their position in the modern world. This quality is extremely subtle. A little swaying figure, oscillating between the fifth and sixth, opens the piece with an air of wide-eyed diatonic innocence which is belied by the artificial symmetry of the clauses,

'Dans le Goût burlesque':
Watteau, Portrait of Gilles

by the witty major and minor seconds, and by the melancholy of the sequential harmonies. As a whole, the piece is balanced between a bumpkin simplicity and a sophisticated hyper-sensitivity, in a manner that almost justifies a comparison with Watteau's wonderful painting of Gilles. Both Watteau and Couperin seem, in works such as these, to be attempting to transmute a personal loneliness or distress into the world of the *commedia*, precisely because the theatre can idealize the crudities and indignities of everyday life into 'something rich and strange'. It is the tenderness of the feeling—the sympathy with the outcast—that is so remarkable in Watteau's pictorial, and Couperin's musical, representation of the Fool. We may relevantly recall that at the time they created these works both Watteau and Couperin were sick men.

In *Les Satires*, another movement *dans le goût burlesque* in this *ordre*, we may find similar qualities. The tenderness is here less evident; but the weird dissonances, the percussively treated diminished seventh chords, are never crudely obtrusive. They give a sudden ironic twist to an apparently innocuous phrase:

here again the Harlequin resolves his spiritual gaucherie into a world of exquisite artifice.

The twenty-fourth *ordre*, in A, is distinguished by one of the longest and noblest of Couperin's clavecin pieces, the *passacaille*, *L'Amphibie*. This is not in the chaconne-rondeau convention of the more intense B minor *Passacaille*, but is a series of variations on a ground bass which is itself treated very freely. It is the only movement in Couperin's keyboard works that can be compared with the big chaconnes from the two-violin suites, and it uses similar technical methods to build up an increasing momentum. Lute-like suspensions, virile dotted rhythms, flowing triplet figures are all employed

227

in a technique which covers the whole range of the keyboard. As in the violin suites, the bass itself shares in the growing excitement by acquiring more animation and by introducing chromaticisms. The piece concludes with a massive statement of the theme in its original form. *Les Vieux Seigneurs* is a sarabande, also in the old *grand goût*. It is complemented by a piece called *Les Jeunes Seigneurs, cy-devant les Petits Maîtres*, in a perky 2 : 4 with semi-quaver figuration phrased across the beat; again, a witty use is made of diminished seventh effects. Couperin possibly intends some satirical reference to the new, exquisite style of the *divertissement* in the manner of Mouret—compared with the old-style Lullian majesty of *Les Vieux Seigneurs*. In *Les Guirlandes* we come to one of the finest pieces using lute arpeggios in a sonorously impressionistic manner. Played on a big, resonant harpsichord, this piece rivals *Les Vergers Fleuris* in its richly atmospheric effect.

The twenty-fifth *ordre* is possibly the most technically experimental of all. The first piece, *La Visionnaire*, is a Lullian overture in miniature, with a slow, powerful introduction which mingles the intense recitative-like line and surging portamentos of the violists with very dramatic harmonies, in a manner that recalls the sarabande of Bach's E minor partita:

The quick section, though in two parts throughout, produces an energetic effect through the vigour and complexity of its rhythms.

228

The next piece, *La Mistérieuse*, is centred in C major, in contrast to the overture's E flat; its mysteriousness seems to consist mainly in its abstruse transitions of key. A passage such as this dissolves the sense of tonality almost as remarkably as does Bach's B minor fugue from Book I of the Forty-Eight;

But Couperin never relinquishes his tonal sense as completely as does Bach in the twenty-fifth of the Goldberg Variations; he remains too much a part of a civilized aristocracy. *Les Ombres Errantes* depends mainly on the insistent syncopation of its phrasing, and on 'weeping' internal suspensions which create a fluid chromaticism in the inner parts. Despite the emotional harmony, the impression is throughout one of dignified refinement. As in so much of Bach, the figuration is consistent from start to finish; the expressive quality arises out of the subtleties of phrasing.

The twenty-sixth *ordre*, in F sharp minor, is possibly—with the B minor *ordre* from Book II—the finest. If it has no movement of such overwhelming intensity as the B minor *Passacaille*, it has perhaps greater variety than the earlier suite, and has such consummate lucidity and economy in its technique that it is a joy to look at, as well as to play and listen to. This is immediately apparent in the opening allemande-like movement, *La Convalescente*, with its beautiful supensions over a chromatic bass:

its rich harmonic sequences:

and its almost Chopin-like sensuous coda which, in its context, attains to a spiritual poise beyond Chopin's febrile imagination.

Equally lovely is the rondeau, *L'Epineuse*, in which tied notes and suspensions combine with melodic figuration to produce an effect as of part-writing. The third couplet uses a simple lulling rhythm across the bar-line, recalling the earlier *Dodo*; and the fourth couplet introduces one of those radiant transitions to the major which give intimation of how Couperin's civilized deportment is not merely a social virtue, but is, as it were, a spiritual illumination. In this passage, the texture luminously 'glows'; and the gentle yearning of the rising melodic figure is counterpoised by the symmetrical grouping of the clauses:

The last piece in this *ordre*, *La Pantomime*, is a superb example of Couperin's *commedia dell'Arte* style, using percussive guitar-like effects and brusque dissonances of minor and major ninth with an irresistibly witty vivacity:

The twenty-seventh and last *ordre*, in B minor again, is in the same mood as the F sharp minor, and is hardly less beautiful. The allemande, *L'Exquise*, has the same serenity and plasticity of part-writing as *La Convalescente*—a keyboard technique comparable with that of Bach's most mature works, though more delicate in texture. *Les Pavots* evokes an impression of heat and languor through broken chords and appoggiaturas in an even crochet rhythm in the high register of the instrument. A very French *Les Chinois* is remarkable for its rhythmic surprises; and the last piece, *Saillie*,[21] has a Bach-like technique of neat imitative writing which on the last page dissolves into quintessential Couperin—a simple repeated figure involving a falling fourth. The peculiarly disembodied feeling which this figure, in conjunction with the level flowing movement, gives to the music is enhanced by the fact that the figure does not occur in the first half of the binary architecture (which ends in the dominant and starts off again in the relative major). In its softly floating repetitiveness the figure has an eternal quality that is at once elegant and wistful; we may note too the touching Neapolitan sixth effect of the flattened C in the last few bars:

[21] The Saillie or Pas Echappé was a step used in a dance called La Babette, according to P. Rameau's *Le Maître à danser* of 1725. The literal meaning of the word is to 'start' or to burst out.

THE CLAVECIN WORKS

Despite its ostensible limitations compared with, say, the *Art o, Fugue*, the Mass in B minor, the Jupiter Symphony, the Hammerklavier sonata, or Byrd's five-part Mass, Couperin's fourth book of clavecin pieces seems to me to be among the most remarkable feats of creative craftsmanship in the history of music. If we have understood the significance of its lucidity aright, we shall have no difficulty in appreciating how the exquisite Couperin could on the whole have more than any other composer has in common with Bach. Nor shall we have any difficulty in understanding how the composer of a funny piece about monkeys, or a charming piece like *Le Bavolet Flotant*, could also create, in *La Passacaille* and the finest of the church works, music in which a tremendous tragic passion, revealed in a tautness of linear and harmonic structure, should hide beneath the surface elegance; in which Couperin's habitual preoccupation with social values and 'states of mind' receives what it is hardly excessive to call a spiritual re-creation.

Like Bach, Couperin preserves a delicate balance, perhaps peculiar to his epoch, between the claims of the individual personality, of society, and of God. Though the Phèdre-like vehemence of *La Passacaille* may endanger his formal lucidity, though the melancholy that lurks in the eyes of Watteau's harlequins is perceptible beneath even his most witty moods, Couperin never forgets that he is the *honnête homme*, living by a code of values which, if they are more than personal, are, in the conventionally accepted sense of the term, more than social too. And in his greatest work he seems to indicate—as does Racine in *Athalie*, and as does Bach, who lived much more directly in contact with a religious community, through the whole of his career—that in the long run such values are meaningless unless one accepts the notion of an absolute, or God.

Chapter Ten

The Concerts Royaux and Suites for Viols

Le goût Italien et le goût François ont partagé depuis longtemps (en France) le République de la Musique; à mon égard,
j'ay toujours estimé les choses qui le méritoient sans acception
d'Auteurs, ni de Nation; et les premières Sonades Italiennes
qui parurent à Paris il y a plus de trente années ne firent aucun
tort dans mon esprit, ny aux ouvrages de monsieur de Lulli,
ny à ceux de mes Ancêtres.

FRANÇOIS COUPERIN, *Les Goûts Réünis*, 1724

COUPERIN'S 'CONCERTS' WERE published in two volumes in 1722
and 1725. The first volume of four suites was entitled *Concerts
Royaux*; the second collection of ten *concerts*, with the addition of
the two *Apothéose* sonatas, was given the generic title of *Les Goûts
Réünis*. The suites were written for the court, after the last of the
church works, the *Leçons des Tenèbres*; their composition therefore
dates from 1714 onwards. Composed to soften and sweeten the
King's melancholy, they are conceived in a style more French than
Italian. They are not concertos in the Italian sense of the word but
simply concerted music in dance form scored for an ensemble group.
None the less the music throughout, as well as the titles in the later
volume, indicates how deeply Couperin's French idiom is impregnated with Italianism.

No particular medium is specified for the pieces. They were
usually printed on two staves, as though for clavecin, and in this
medium are mostly effective. But Couperin remarks in his preface
that 'ils conviennent non seulement au clavecin, mais aussi au
Violon, au hautbois, à la viole, et au basson'; and it seems clear that
it was on some such combination of instruments that the works were
performed at court. Couperin says that they were originally played

234

by Duval, Philidor, Alarius, and Dubois, with himself at the clavecin. Duval was a celebrated violinist, Alarius a violist, and Philidor
and Dubois were virtuosos on the oboe and bassoon. The ideal
arrangement would thus seem to be for two stringed instruments,
two wind instruments, and continuo, the strings and wind playing
either together or alternately. The choice of instruments should
depend on the expressive qualities of the movement in question.
Contemporary opinion associated particular instruments with specific passions, as we may see from this passage in Avison's *Essay of
Musical Expression* (1752):

> We should also minutely observe the different qualities of the instruments
> themselves: for, as vocal Music requires one kind of Expression, and instru-
> mental another, so different instruments have also different expression
> peculiar to them.
> Thus the Hautboy will best express the Cantabile or singing style, and
> may be used in all movements whatever under this denomination, especially
> those movements which tend to the Gay and Chearful.
> In compositions for the German flute is required the same method of
> proceeding by conjunct degrees or such other natural intervals, as, with the
> nature of its tone, will best express the Languishing, or Melancholy style.

In general oboes and bassoons are suitable for merry movements
such as rigaudons and bourrées, perhaps because of the instruments'
rustic associations; flutes are appropriate to tender and melancholy
movements such as the sarabandes. Violins, in Couperin's *concerts*,
are essentially lyrical and noble, though less pathetic than the flutes.
A more specifically instrumental character is discernible in the later
volume, in which Couperin expressly states that some of the pieces
are to be played on unaccompanied viols.

Almost all the *concerts* are in the form of dance suites; and like the
suites of the lutenists and clavecinists, they adapt their movements
from the dances of the ballet and theatre. The only movement which
is an exception to this is the Prelude, which is usually related to the
grave opening of the Italian sonata de chiesa. It is always a more
formal piece than the improvisatory prelude of the lutenists.

Many of the dance forms have already been briefly described in
other contexts in this book; since, however, Couperin's *concerts* are
his apotheosis of the contemporary dance, this seems an appropriate
place to attempt some more systematic catalogue. We must remember that, deriving as they do from the theatre, the opera, and

the ballet, these dances have all an expressive intention. All the theorists insisted that 'la première et la plus essentielle beauté d'un air de ballet est la convenance, c'est à dire le juste rapport que l'air doit avoir avec la chose représenté' (Noverre); that 'chaque caractère et chaque passion ont leur mouvement particulier; mais cela depend plus du goût que des règles'. (Rameau.) Moreover, although taste may have been more important than rules, this does not mean that rules were non-existent. The relationships between different passions and different physical movements were as rigidly classified as were the possible relationships between passions and pictorial formulae in the painting of Lebrun. 'La danse est aujourd'hui divisée en plusieurs caractères . . . les gens de métier en comptent jusqu'à seize, et chacun de ces caractères a sur le théâtre, des pas, des attitudes et des figures qui lui sont propres'. Of course, there was not any 'psychological' intention in the dances; they did not deal in individual passions. But they had a general relation to types of experience and types of people. They were musical and terpsichorean Humours, and as such were carefully graded and differentiated.

The first dance in the suites, the allemande, had gradually displaced the pavane which, some authorities suggest, had been metamorphosed into the slow section of the French overture. Couperin uses two types of allemande. One, which he called *allemande légère*, is in four time, light and flowing, but unhurried; this is probably a survival of the popular allemande which was a sung dance. The other type of allemande, of a more grave character, is an instrumental sophistication of the original dance, and is of all the dance forms except the chaconne, the most musically developed. Rousseau says that it 'se bat gravement à 4 tems', and Mace describes it as 'heavie . . . fitly representing the nature of the People whose Name it carryeth, so that no Extraordinary Motions are used in dancing it'. The titles of Couperin's most typical pieces in allemande form make clear that he associated the dance with a certain seriousness and dignity, though the pace should never be sluggish. Even his *allemandes légères* incline, as we have seen, to contrapuntal treatment. Both kinds are regarded as highly wrought instrumental compositions, bearing out Mattheson's comment that between allemandes danced and allemandes played there is as much difference as there is between Earth and Heaven.

236

The differences between the two types of courante, French and Italian, have been discussed previously. Originally a very quick dance, as its name suggests, it must, by Couperin's day, have become considerably slower. A crochet pulse is essential if the cross rhythms and other metrical complications are to be intelligible. Rousseau describes the dance as being 'en trois tems graves', while D'Alembert, in 1766, even goes as far as to call it 'une sarabande fort lente'. Both writers, however, remark that the courante 'n'est plus en usage'. Most contemporary indications of tempo give the courante and the sarabande the same speed (see Appendix D). On the whole, however, the evidence indicates that played, as opposed to danced, sarabandes were slower and more noble than courantes; despite their rhythmic complexity courantes preserved something of the quality referred to by Mace when he described them as being 'commonly of two strains, and full of Sprightfulness, and Vigour, Lively, Brisk, and Chearful'. Quantz says that courantes should be played with vigour and majesty, at a speed of approximately a crochet for one beat of the pulse. Some such combination of stateliness with energy seems an appropriate speed for courantes, and Quantz's suggested pace seems reasonable for Couperin's courantes in the French manner, in which the animation depends so much on cross accents between 6 : 4 and 3 : 2. The smoother 3 : 4 Italian courantes may be taken slightly faster, though even in these movements Couperin is apt to spring disconcerting rhythmic surprises on the performer. According to P. Rameau's *Maître à danser* of 1725 even the danced courante was, by that date, a very solemn dance with a nobler style and a grander manner than the others. The subtlety of its danced rhythm depended on the fact that only two steps were danced for each three beats of the music, the first of the steps taking up two parts in three of the measure. (Feuillet's *L'Art de décrire la danse*, 1700.)

The sarabande was one of the oldest of the ballet dances, having been introduced into France from Spain in 1588. Transplanted into England in the seventeenth century, it became a rapid and skittish dance, as we may see from the sarabandes of the Elizabethan virginalists. During the seventeenth century it progressively slowed down, culminating in the powerfully pathetic sarabandes of Couperin, Bach, and Handel. The mature form of it is characterized by a slight stress on the second beat of a slow triple rhythm, and Brossard defines it as 'n'étant à la bien prendre qu'un menuet, dont le mouvement est grave, lent, sérieux etc.' Grassineau adds that it differs from the courante in ending on the up beat instead of the down. Lacombe also described the sarabande as 'une espéce de menuet lente'. Rémond de St Mard remarked in 1741 that the sarabande, 'toujours mélancolique, respire une tendresse serieuse et délicate', and this elegiac languishing mode must for long have been typical of the sarabandes of the ballet. Couperin frequently composed sarabandes of this type, sometimes specifying them as *sarabande tendre*. But, as we have observed, he also writes sarabandes in a *grave* style, which although melancholy, are anything but relaxed in effect. Even more than the lutenists, Couperin reserves the *grave* sarabande for many of his most passionate utterances.

Rivalling the sarabande in grandeur is the chaconne, which also came from Spain and was widespread throughout the seventeenth century. This dance too was in triple time, with a slight stress on the second beat, though it was less ponderous in movement than the sarabande. Its formal structure over a repeated bass makes it perhaps the most important of all the dances from a musical point of view; for it offers opportunities for musical development on a more extensive scale than the other dances. Originally chaconne basses had taken the form of the descending tetrachord major, minor or chromatic. By Couperin's time the range of possible basses was more extensive; nor was it necessary for the bass to be preserved unaltered through the whole composition. For Couperin, the bass may be a linear ground; or it may be merely an ostinato harmonic progression, as it is in the gigantic chaconne of Bach's Goldberg Variations. D'Alembert adequately defines the chaconne as 'une longue pièce de musique à trois tems, dont le mouvement est modéré et la mesure bien marquée. Autrefois la basse de la chaconne était une basse contrainte de 4 en 4 mesures, c'est à dire qui revenoit toujours la même de 4 en 4 mesures; aujourd'hui on ne s'astreint plus à cet usage. La chaconne commence pour ordinaire non en frappant, mais au second tems'.

The growth of the music over the regular bass called for considerable skill on the composer's part if a satisfactory sense of climax was to be obtained; we have repeatedly noticed that this was a challenge to which François Couperin, like Lully and Louis Couperin before him, responded with enthusiasm. Couperin writes two types of chaconne, corresponding with his two types of allemande and sarabande. The *chaconne grave* is in 3 : 2 or 3 : 4 and is derived from the ceremonial chaconnes of the operatic finales. The *chaconne légère* is normally in 3 : 8, more moderate in movement and slighter in texture, though still rather serious in temper. Chaconnes are most commonly in the minor mode, but often have a series of variations or couplets in the major in the middle of the composition. In the biggest pieces this may paradoxically suggest the effect of a ternary structure, despite the essentially monistic nature of chaconne technique.

The passacaille may be taken as identical with the chaconne. Quantz maintains that its tempo is slightly faster than that of the chaconne, Rousseau and D'Alembert say that it is 'plus lente et plus tendre'. Some authorities suggest that the chaconne has the syncopated sarabande rhythm whereas the passacaille has a smooth three beats in a bar. Modern musicologists have attempted to establish a distinction between the passacaglia as a composition on a linear ground and the chaconne as a movement built on a harmonic ostinato. The exceptions are so numerous and the evidence so conflicting that it would probably be equally easy to make out a case for the opposite view. The above remarks apply to real chaconnes and passacaglias not to the hybrid chaconne-rondeau, which will be referred to later.

The gavotte is a dance in 2 : 2 time, beginning on the second beat. Its movement was moderate, and its mood usually that of 'une gaieté vive et douce'. It was, however, susceptible of somewhat varied interpretations. Rousseau says that it is 'ordinairement gracieux, souvent gai, quelquefois aussi tendre et lent', and Lacombe defines it as 'quelquefois gai, quelquefois grave'. In general—like Couperin, and his civilization—it avoids extremes. If gay, it is never rumbustious; if sad, it is never oppressively so: or in the words of D'Alembert it is 'tantôt lent, tantôt gay; mais jamais extrèmement vif, ni excessivement lent'. Perhaps its dominant characteristic is an amiable wistfulness.

Also in 2 : 2 or 2 : 4, but beginning on the last quarter of the bar, is the rigaudon, 'composé de deux reprises, chacune de 4, de 8, de 12 etc. mesures' (D'Alembert). This dance was especially popular during Couperin's time, and was very merry, with a popular flavour. It is robust and simple in rhythm, having an open-air jauntiness. The tambourin (used by Couperin only once under this title), and the bourrée are similar to the rigaudon, except that the tambourin, with a drone bass, is still more rustic in flavour, while the bourrée often has a syncopation on the first half of the bar. Another dance in 2 : 2 of a popular and rustic type is the contredanse, the name of which is a corruption of the English country-dance; we may see in this further evidence of the self-conscious interest of a sophisticated society in the naïve and 'primitive': 'les choses les plus simples sont celles dont on se lasse le moins', as Rousseau said. Contredanses are symmetrical in melody and rhythm and were employed in the joyous finales of operas. Despite their popular virility, they are not in any way wild, as are the tambourins. They begin on the second beat of the 2 : 2 rhythm, and may thus be regarded as a racier, less civilized version of the gavotte.

Three related types of quick, triple-rhythmed dance are the loure, gigue, and canaris. The loure is usually in 6 : 4, sometimes in 6 : 8, and is always lilted, in a dotted rhythm, with a slight 'push' on the short note. Its movement is flowing, but dignified and graceful. The gigue, which came from England, is 'vive et un peu folle', in the words of Rémond de St Mard. Some gigues, in 12 : 8 or 9 : 8, are in equally flowing quavers, after the Italian manner; others, in the French style, are in a skittish dotted rhythm; this type of gigue 'n'est proprement qu'une loure très vive' (D'Alembert). The gigue was extremely fashionable in Couperin's day. The French form of it is indistinguishable from the canaris, a farouche dance performed in the ballets by pseudo-Canary Islanders, and other exotics. The same rhythms are found at a more moderate tempo in the sicilienne and forlane. Not all Couperin's siciliennes are in the conventional dotted rhythm; some are in level quavers, like a slower Italian gigue. Couperin's one lovely example of the forlane is in the dotted rhythm. Rousseau, in his *Dictionnaire*, says that the forlane 'se bat gaiement, et la danse est aussi fort gaie. On l'appelle forlane parce qu'elle a pris naissance dans le Frioul, dont les habitants s'appellent Forlans'. D'Alembert says that it has 'un mouvement modéré, moyen entre la loure et la gigue'. The dance flourished especially during the Regency.

240

Like the sarabande, the minuet seems progressively to have slowed down in tempo. In Couperin's time it was written in 3 : 4 or 3 : 8, and had 'une élégante et noble simplicité; le mouvement en est plus modéré que vite, et l'on peut dire que le moins gai de tous les genres de danse usités dans nos bals est le minuet. C'est autre chose sur le théâtre'. (Rousseau.) Couperin's minuets would seem to be closer to those of the theatre than to those of the ballroom. They are graceful, but should flow along quite speedily. The passepied is similar, and still faster. 'Une espace de minuet fort vif', it is usually in 3 : 8, beating one a bar. Unlike the minuet, it begins on the third quaver, not the first, and introduces frequent syncopations. Both are sophisticated dances, with regional origins.

The musette is much favoured by Couperin, and has been admirably described by Rousseau: 'Sorte d'air convenable à l'instrument de ce nom, dont la mesure est à deux ou trois temps, le caractère naïf et doux, le mouvement un peu lent, portant une basse pour l'ordinaire en tenue ou point d'orgue, telle que la peut faire une musette, et qu'on appelle à cause de cela basse de musette. Sur ces airs onforme des danses d'un caractère convenable, et qui portent aussi le nom de musettes'. Here the dance is derived from the music, instead of—as is more usual—the music from the dance.

In addition to these specific dance forms, Couperin also uses, as do the opera and ballet composers, the term *air* to describe dance pieces of a variously characteristic nature. The term no doubt comes from the 'air de symphonie par lequel débute un ballet'; Couperin always qualifies it adjectivally—*air tendre*, *air gracieux*, *air grave*, and so on.

All these dances are treated either in some type of binary form, or in rondeau. If in binary form, the second section, after the modulation to the dominant or relative, may start off with the original theme in the new key, reflecting the material of the first section in the same order; or it may start off with subsidiary material, returning to the original ideas towards the end; or it may include no thematic repetition at all, achieving unity rather by the balance of keys and the grouping of figuration. The second sections, incorporating the modulations, tend to be longer than the first. Most of the more serious binary pieces depend on the growth of linear figuration and harmonic pattern, rather than on the easily recognizable tune. When Couperin writes simple dance *tunes*, he tends to treat them *en ron-*

241

deau; they are then self-enclosed periods in one section, interspersed with contrasting episodes. Gavotte, minuet, forlane, rigaudon, passepied—all the lighter, more tuneful dances are thus treated *en rondeau*; and the connection of the rondeau with the round suggests a popular origin for this sophisticated technique. Significantly, the more complicated dances, allemandes, sarabandes, and courantes, are never 'rondeau-ed'. The one exception to this is the chaconne; but although the chaconne-rondeau has ceased to be a chaconne, it remains distinct, in its majestic power, from all the more customary, frivolous types of rondeau. Something of the remorselessness of the chaconne's repetitions is transferred into the more lyrical repetitions of the rondeau.

Two or more of the smaller dances are sometimes linked together —gavottes and bourrées in major and minor, for instance, or any of the rustic dances in the minor with a musette in the major. In these interlinked pieces the musette with drone is a prototype of the trio section of what later became the sonata scherzo. As in the classical scherzo, the first dance of the pair is often repeated after the second, making a primitive ternary or 'sandwich' form; this, however, did not become obligatory till some time after Couperin's day.

The first four *concerts*, Couperin says, are arranged *par tons*, beginning in G, and proceeding up the cycle of fifths to the key of the dominant—to D, A, and E. Like most of the Preludes, that to the G major *concert* is influenced by Italian models. Though an elegant piece, light in texture, it has a modulation to A minor, incorporating some abstruse dissonances and a cadential false relation, in a style which is familiar to us from the grander preludes to the violin sonatas:

The allemande is of the *léger* type, in the usual binary structure, with neat imitative writing but without much polyphonic complexity. Towards the end of the second section a gently rocking figure suggests an undercurrent of wistfulness:

The sarabande, in the minor, is a simple, noble piece with drooping sevenths in sequence. The remaining movements, gavotte, gigue, and minuet, are slight. The gigue has some amusing repeated scale figures, and the minuet uses floating scale passages in contrary motion.

The second *concert* is in D. The prelude is gracefully pathetic, with soft appoggiaturas and ornamented suspended sevenths over a chromatic bass. The *allemande fuguée* is again of the *léger* variety but, as its title implies, gives a quite elaborate contrapuntal development to this perky theme:

In the second half the theme is very freely inverted. The *air tendre* is in the minor, in the style of the *air de cour*, with portamentos and intermittent canonic entries:

The *air contrefuguée* is a counterpart of the allemande, with a similar jaunty subject. Its second section has some wittily unexpected harmonies, similar to those in the Harlequin clavecin pieces:

For the last movement of the *concert* we have an extremely beautiful rondeau in the *Echo* convention, comparable in mood with the rondeau of the *Impériale* sonata in the same key. Symmetrical clauses, a tranquil rhythm, and a 'luminous' diatonicism produce a Claude-like effect of pastoral serenity:

244

A couplet in the minor develops a richer harmony. The later statements of the theme are ornamented in the *brunete* fashion.

A more serious style and more extended developments are observable in the third *concert*, in A. The prelude, with its *contre-partie* for
viol, violin, flute, or oboe, has a Bachian polyphonic texture; the
sense of metre disappears in the interlappings of the lines:

Though lighter in character, the allemande uses a similar technique,
and has a typical passage of 'aspiring' chromatic sequences. The
courante, in the minor, is more complicated, both rhythmically and
harmonically. Although ostensibly a quick piece, it uses diminished
intervals with a Purcellian pathos.

With the *sarabande grave*, we come to a movement which looks far
beyond the normal confines of entertainment music; which stands
with the greatest sarabandes in the clavecin *ordres* and violin sonatas.
Again it has an additional *contre-partie*, and the intensity of its polyphony is reinforced by elaborate ornamentation, often producing
incidental dissonances, and by considerable rhythmic variety. These
points are illustrated in the following quotation; note the stress on

the chord of the augmented fifth, on the accented second beat of the sarabande rhythm:

In the second half, the dissonances are even more abstruse, and the piece has a monumental power worthy of comparison with the greatest dance movements of Bach:

Founded on a little figure in rising thirds, the gavotte is unpretentious, but still somewhat melancholy in tone—'quelquefois gai, quelquefois grave'. The musette, in two sections, one in the major and one in the minor, is a 6 : 8 pastoral over a *bourdon*, elegant,

246

but still with a flavour of folk-song. Its coda is especially beautiful, floating in a summer haze between the major and minor third:

We may compare such an effect as this with the tremulous haze into which, in the background of many of Watteau's *fêtes champêtres*, two lovers are strolling.

This large-scale suite ends with a chaconne of the *léger* type. While this is not a piece of the monumental order of Couperin's *chaconnes graves*, it is of considerable dimensions, and fine polyphonic workmanship. In the chaconne-rondeau convention, it makes repeated use of dynamic contrasts of *fort* and *doux*. The mood again is of pastoral wistfulness. A couplet in the major, with a drone accompaniment, has a 'glow' comparable with the preceding musette; the main theme, in the minor, is given a tersely linear treatment.

The fourth *Concert Royal*, in E minor, maintains the high level of the third; indeed it is possibly the finest of the group. The prelude is a noble piece of polyphonic writing which invites comparison with the prelude of the Corelli *Apothéose*. The ornamented lines are superbly moulded, over a bass which is as much melodic as harmonic in significance. Though a slighter movement, the allemande contains some fascinating imitative treatment of the little rising scale figure with which it opens. The *courante française* changes the tonality to the major, and rhythmically and harmonically is even more complicated than the A minor courante. Much of the part-writing depends on opposition between 3 : 2 and 6 : 4 rhythms, occurring simultaneously in different lines; passages of elliptical harmony, created by the movement of the parts, are frequent:

The *courante à l'italienne* returns to the minor and is rhythmically more straightforward. On the other hand, it is possibly the biggest of Couperin's courantes, the second section being developed at more than usual length, with relatively complex modulations. Here the part-writing is fluid, and the harmonies rich. At times there are acute dissonances, and ripe sequential writing:

The trills at the seventeenth, at the end of this passage, are further developed in a longish coda. As a whole, the piece is remarkable for its cantabile lyricism and sonorous harmony.

The sarabande, in the major, has an independent *contre-partie*, and is in Couperin's *très tendrement*, serenely diatonic vein. The second section involves a pathetic modulation to the minor of the dominant, proceeding by way of a flattened seventh in the bass:

The melodies have a Chambonnières-like fragrance, but are developed with greater architectural control. Also in the major, the rigaudon is a perky dance in binary form with a pseudo-contrapuntal treatment of a little rising fourth motive, which is inverted in the second half. After the entry, there is little pretence of counterpoint. The last movement, *Forlane*, is in rondeau, and is one of

249

Couperin's most personal conceptions. The tranquilly gay tune again suggests an exquisitely civilized re-creation of a folk-dance:

In the couplets the warm harmonies suffuse the music with a mellow Watteau-like sunshine. The last couplet, in the minor, achieves a touching unexpectedness by the simplest of means—a melody lilting between the interval of a second and a fourth, with a drone accompaniment rocking on the interval of a sixth:

The E minor is the last of the *Concerts Royaux* collection. No. 5, the first suite in the volume which Couperin called *Les Goûts Réünis*, is in F major, and is slight in texture and character. Its prelude is marked *gracieusement*, instead of the customary *grave*; it is a charming piece in 3 : 8, with falling scale figures neatly imitated in two parts. The *allemande légère* is also freely contrapuntal in technique, with a theme leaping up a fifth, and then a sixth, to a tied note. The motive is often imitated in stretto, thereby creating some elliptical phrases across the bar-line:

Majestically in the minor, the *sarabande grave* has not the passionate and personal tone of the A minor sarabande; but its phrases have a Handelian grandeur, especially in the final clause, when the line mounts by way of a trill to A flat, and then subsides. Also in the minor, the gavotte is a wistful piece in quaver movement, *coulamment*. The *Muséte dans le Goût de Carillon* is a lovely bell piece with the flavour of a *vaudeville*. It would sound well on a small baroque organ.

The prelude of the sixth *concert* in B flat is constructed almost entirely out of a tied crochet, followed by a semiquaver figure, usually treated as a resolution of the suspension. The allemande, *à 4 tems légers*, is quite a big movement, contrapuntally developed. Delicately dancing, it tosses a little scale figure to and fro between the parts:

Marked *noblement*, the *sarabande mesurée* lives up to its pretensions, though it is among the more simply euphonious, and less passionate, of Couperin's sarabandes. Subtle effects of cross-rhythm are obtained by the concurrence of an appoggiatura-ornamented main melody, with a triplet figure in the bass:

In the next piece the Devil makes an amiable appearance. This mephisto, though fiery, is as well-mannered as the devils in Lully's operas. Electrically shooting scale passages, and the discreet introduction of that *diabolus in musica*, the tritone, do not substantially modify this *Air du Diable*'s urbanity:

Its mood and technique may be related to the harlequin and pantomime pieces for clavecin; there is a devil-may-care jauntiness, rather than a dæmonic quality, about the persistent leaping sixths. The last movement of this B flat suite is a sicilienne, a smooth 12 : 8 pastoral with a few dissonant canonic entries.

With the seventh *concert*, we return to a more serious tone. The prelude is both *grave* and *gracieuse*. Its lines are beautifully rounded, and repeated entries in stretto give to the level movement a subdued melancholy:

The allemande is gay, its perky theme being treated in unusually sustained canon. Bachian harmonic sequences occur in the piece's extensive development:

The sarabande returns to the mood of the prelude; the theme, again imitatively treated, incorporates a rising minor sixth which droops back expressively to the fifth. A relaxed melancholy, derived from the lutenists, is suggested by the chromatic harmony, and by the drooping phrases, sometimes ornamented with appoggiaturas, sometimes built on arpeggio figures:

The *Fuguéte* has this interesting, rather spiky subject:

Despite its title, it is an extensively developed movement, in a compromise between fugal technique and harmonic binary form; and despite its feathery texture, it shows a Bach-like contrapuntal solidity. After the first section has ended in D, the second half starts off in B flat—the relative major of the original G minor—with a modified version of the theme inverted. The development of the scale passage and the leaping figure create an exciting animation; on the last page a telling climax is reached by stretching the scale passage through an eleventh. The gavotte also uses a rising scale figure, and contains much canonic writing, while the graceful sicilienne has some tritonal progressions in the bass.

This last piece is Italianate in style. The next *concert*, with the sub-title *Dans le Gout Théatral*, is ostensibly French, a miniature Lullian opera in instrumental form, without the recitative. The overture has the familiar ceremonial opening in dotted rhythm, followed by a quick fugal section in triple rhythm. Here the nature of the theme and the texture recalls the French Couperin of the organ masses. The piece rises to a sonorous climax with the appearance of the theme in thirds:

In the coda, there is a characteristic false relation. The *Grande Ritournelle* is a stately curtain tune; the opening illustrates the measured dignity, and the powerfully dissonant texture obtained by the use of passing notes and appoggiaturas:

A section in four time leads into a Lullian aria in 3 : 2, of a type which had originally been modelled on Carissimi. This piece is imposing, but not among the most interesting of Couperin's movements in this style.

The heroic manner is continued in a French air in 2 : 2, with chromatic progressions and much gallic ornamentation. The *air tendre* is a sweetly melancholy *brunete*; the *air léger*, in the major, another *brunete* in Couperin's vein of limpid diatonicism. A naïve-sophisticated spirit pervades, too, the *Loure* and the next *air tendre*, in which an appealing use is made of repeated detached minims. The *sarabande grave et tendre* is more *tendre* than *grave*, halfway between the manner of Chambonnières and of Handel. The groupings of the phrases, in their level rhythm, are of some subtlety; note how in this passage the rising scale of the third and fourth bars counteracts the falling sequences of the scale figure of the first two bars:

The poised serenity of the clauses places this among the loveliest of Couperin's spacious, Claude-like movements. Then follow two *airs de cour*, the second of which has some charming echo effects in false relation. An *air de Bacchantes*, in the conventional 6 : 4 of the operatic bacchanal, brings the work to a rousing conclusion.

In contrast to the *Concert dans le Gout Théatral*, the next *concert*, No. 9 in E, has an Italian title, *Ritratto dell' Amore*. None the less, though a more Corellian technique is noticeable in the fugal movements, the work is still French in feeling; indeed, the pieces have French sub-titles, like the clavecin *ordres*. The French and Italian styles are now equally, and unselfconsciously, a part of Couperin' sensibility. As a whole, this suite is both one of the most representative, and the most beautiful, of the *concerts*.

The first movement, *Le Charme*, is more *gracieuse* than *grave*, though it is marked both. Its pellucid polyphony often creates an impressionistic sonority:

L'Enjouement is an *allemande légère* in fugal binary form, with the theme inverted in the second half. Suspensions, syncopations, and stretti suggest a delicate impudence. *Les Grâces* is a *courante françoise*, and one of the most complex of this type in rhythm, ornamentation and harmony. It is a revealing instance of the way in which Couperin's harmonic surprises are often the result of linear independence:

Le Je ne sçais quoi is based on a cheeky triadic figure which is later wittily treated in stretto:

In the same mood is *La Vivacité*, but the canonic passages are here more consistently developed, exciting use being made of scale passages travelling both ways. In the minor key, the sarabande, *La*

Noble Fierté, opens with a magnificent phrase, involving a falling tenth, which fully lives up to the piece's title:

Gravement

In the second section a long *falling* scale passage in *rising* sequences builds up a climax of a paradoxically passionate sobriety. The minor key is retained for the next piece, *La Douceur*, one of Couperin's intimate linear movements in a quiet 3 : 8. The ornamented flow of the lines and the use of sequences produce some piquant harmonies and modulations:

L'Et Cætera is a rustic 6 : 8 movement, with a rising third and falling scale passage in canon. The second part, in the minor, is atmospheric, a repeated phrase droningly revolving on itself.

Of equally fine quality is the next *concert*, No. 10 in A minor. The prelude is one of the most concentrated examples of Couperin's polyphony, in which the lines create the intense harmony—note, for instance, the Neapolitan sixth effect in the penultimate bar:

The 4 : 8 *air tendre* is also meditative in tone; and here too the economical part-writing leads to some acute dissonances. *Plaintes*, the next movement, is for two viols and string bass without continuo. The viols play mainly in dotted rhythm, in thirds and sixths, while the bass reiterates a pedal note; the effect is sensuously rich:

A change to the minor is made for the second part, which is more linear and austere. The last movement, *La Tromba*, is a jaunty binary piece built on a 6 : 8 trumpet arpeggio; at the end, some imitations in stretto are irresistibly comic:

A somewhat sombre temper characterizes most of the eleventh *concert*, in C minor. A longish 3 : 2 prelude in consistent dotted rhythm has power and dignity. The allemande, marked *fièrement*, is in fugal binary form, with an angular, instrumental subject such as one frequently meets with in Bach's work:

The second allemande, *plus léger*, is smoother, containing a higher proportion of conjunct motion; the theme is freely inverted after the double bar. Both the courantes, one in the major and one in the minor, are of the French type. The first is particularly free in its rhythmic ellipses between soprano and bass, combined with much ornamentation. In the second courante trills are used in animated ascending sequences.

The *Sarabande*, *très grave et très marqué*, is one of the most notable of Couperin's pieces in the *tombeau* convention. The lines use energetic dotted rhythms and a plethora of tremblements, mordents, and portamentos; these elements, however, serve to reinforce phrases—usually built on spread chord formations—which are at once violent

259

and monumental. The tonal sequences and harmonies are exceptionally bold, even including a cadential chord of the thirteenth:

The *gigue lourée* is a fascinating piece of contrapuntal writing, phrased, like so much of Bach, across the bar lines, with frequent dissonant appoggiaturas. Such appoggiaturas play an important part, too, in the line of the concluding rondeau. This is a dialogue between melody and bass, a quiet 3 : 8 built mainly from semiquavers grouped in pairs. While having no outstanding feature, it is one of those movements, *léger et galant*, to which one must be able to respond if one is fully to appreciate Couperin's savour.

The next two *concerts* are for two viols, mostly unaccompanied. They belong to the great French tradition of viol music, which we shall refer to in greater detail later. Although not musically among the most interesting of the *concerts*, the economy of their part-writing is a delight throughout. The prelude to the A major suite is in a *pointé* 3 : 2, and, as so often occurs in the prelude of the da chiesa sonata, it repeatedly employs trills, with turns, on the second beat of the sarabande rhythm, sometimes in ascending sequences. *Badinage* is a quick contrapuntal movement, with a brilliant conclusion in thirds. It is separated from the final air by a short slow recitative section, again on the analogy of the sonata da chiesa. This

260

is marked *patétiquement*, and is a very emotional piece with whirling portamentos and grinding appoggiaturas:

The air is suave, in regular semiquavers, moving mainly by step.

If the twelfth *concert* had affinities with the Italian sonata, the thirteenth is again unambiguously in French suite form. The prelude, on a little arpeggio figure, is consistently canonic. The air, *agréablement* in the minor, uses an imitative technique in 6 : 8, with interestingly irregular phrase grouping—the first section contains eleven bars, and is answered by a section of fifteen. Calm and warm in its diatonicism, the sarabande returns to the major. Finally the *chaconne légère* is based on a brief rising scale figure and leaping fourth, with a rather odd ambiguity between major and minor third. The figure is later presented in a modified form inverted, and developed in free fugue.

The fourteenth and last *concert* in D is a fine one. The *grave* prelude is powerful in its harmonies, both those contained in the continuo, and those produced by the lines' complex ornamentation:

Here the French dotted rhythm is used within an Italianate movement; while the climax has a Bach-like combination of discipline with emotion. The same architectural logic is found in the allemande's development of an arpeggio-founded figure; Bachian sequences and syncopated phrase-groupings show a fine mastery of instrumental technique. A nobly drooping figure characterizes the theme of the sarabande; note how the falling interval contracts in the first four repetitions, and expands in the following three:

In the second half, the interval is stretched to a sweeping seventh, conveying a sense of emotional liberation.

The last movement, modestly called *Fuguéte*, is a fully developed contrapuntal piece. The 6 : 8 theme, again phrased across the bar, is closely wrought, with syncopations and sequential chromaticisms:

A second subject in semiquavers, founded on arpeggio figuration, is later introduced and cunningly combined with the first theme. As a whole, the piece is a splendid example of classical counterpoint and a fitting conclusion to the whole series.

We have now finished our survey of Couperin's concerted music; but there is one more work—or rather a group of two works—which may conveniently be dealt with at this point, since it is conceived in the same form of the French suite, and since its date is contemporary with the last *concerts*. The suites for two viols were Couperin's last published work, apart from the fourth book of clavecin pieces. The title-page of this publication, which was rediscovered by Bouvet early in the twentieth century, runs 'Pièces de viole, avec la Basse Chiffrée, par M. F. C. Paris, Boyvin, 1728'. The identification of this M. F. C. with Couperin is open to no doubt. It is supported not only by stylistic considerations and by the fact that the suites contain many signs and phrase markings which were used by no other composer, but also by the *privilège du roi* which accompanies the publication, and by Couperin's own catalogue of 1730, which mentions some suites for viols appearing, in his *œuvre*, between *Les Nations* and the fourth book of clavecin pieces. The date 1725, given in the catalogue of the *Mercure de France* in 1729, is supported by no other contemporary document, and is presumably false.

These two suites, coming at the end of Couperin's life, are also the end of a great tradition. The midsummer of the French solo viol music lasted from about 1660 to Couperin's death. If it seems odd that the full flowering of this music should occur at a time when the viol was being superseded by the violin, we must remember that there was still a tendency for the most sophisticated members of this hyper-cultivated society to regard the violin as a rather low and undignified instrument. Hubert le Blanc's *Défense de la Basse Viole* repeatedly points out that the veiled tone and the nature of the bowing of the viol gave it a superior subtlety in the conveyance of emotional nuance; while Rousseau, speaking of the 'Pièces d'Harmonie réglées sur la viole' says:

La tendresse de son Jeu venoit de ces beaux coups d'archet qu'il animoit, & qu'il adoucissoit avec tant d'adresse et si à propos, qu'il

263

charmoit tous ceux qui l'entendoient, & c'est ce qui a commencé à donner la perfection à la Viole & à la faire estimer preferablement à tous les autres instruments.

(*Traité de la Viole*, 1687.)[22]

By Couperin's time, as we have seen, the violin had occasioned a fashionable furore, and Couperin made his own impressive contribution to its literature. But it is possible that, even in his day, in the innermost circle of the Elect, the old instrument was still more fashionable than Fashion.

During the *grand siècle*, as the violin had replaced the viol as the stock instrument for dance and other occasional musics, the older instrument had begun to develop a virtuoso tradition. Like the lute, it had become an instrument of the *ruelles* and salons. Maugars and the other early violists had been in the main occasional composers, as were the early lutenists; Marin Marais and Forqueray and the other composers of the solo viol's heyday were, like the later lutenists, the product of an intellectual and emotional esotericism. We may compare them with the English violists of the court of Charles I and the Interregnum, such as William Lawes, Jenkins, and Simpson. Though the English composers remained more conscious of their polyphonic ancestry, it may have been merely the Civil War that prevented them from developing the virtuoso solo aspects of their tradition—as represented by Simpson's *Divisions*—into a classical Augustan homophony.

The nature of this virtuoso music was in part conditioned by the physical nature of the viol, a six-stringed instrument with a flat back and a flat bridge, which made chord playing relatively easy. The tuning, like that of the lute, was in fourths, with a third between the third and fourth strings—D, G, C, E, A, D; Marin Marais used a viol which had a seventh string, the low A in the bass. In the preface to his *Pièces de Viole* of 1685, de Machy explains that the viol may be used simply as a melody instrument, accompanied by continuo, or

---

[22] Cf. also, Mersenne: 'car le Violon a trop de rudesse, d'autant que l'on est constraint à le monter de trop grosses cordes pour esclater dans les suiets, auxquels il est naturellement propre.' (*Harmonie Universelle*, 1636.)

Pierre Trichet, in his Traité on viol playing, praises the instrument for its 'mignards tremblements' and the 'coups mourants de l'archet'.

it may be used as a bass for one's own singing; but its most characteristic activity is as a solo instrument playing both melody and harmony. It is possible, he points out, to make a pleasing sound by playing a tune with one hand on the clavecin, but nobody would call that real clavecin playing. Similarly, the viol can play a single melody very agreeably if need be, but the instrument fully reveals itself only when it is played solo, its melodies being harmonized with rich chords and arpeggio devices, often involving big leaps. It is this manner of treating the solo viol which was adapted to the violin by German composers such as Biber, Baltzar, and J. S. Bach. If one objects that in this style it is impossible to play cantabile, and with an expressive use of ornaments, the answer is that everything depends on the skill of the player. It is true, too, that the range of tonalities in which one can play fluently in the harmonized style is limited—D, G, A, and E minor are the keys most convenient to the tuning, in which sextuple stopping is easily practicable on the D major triad. Composers trained in the old linear traditions would not, however, find this lack of tonal variety cramping.

The French violists have left fewer works for unaccompanied viols than their English predecessors. But it is clear in most of their works for one or two viols and continuo that they habitually thought of the viol as a solo harmonizing instrument. The richness of the chords and the mellowness of the tone enhance the elegiac quality of their lyricism. Thus the feeling, as well as the technique and tuning, is close to the tradition of the lutenists; most strikingly of all, the viol composers resemble the lutenists in the way they reconcile their ripe harmonic technique with an extreme delicacy and sophistication of ornament. The basis of this ornamentation and of certain rhythmic conventions is identical with that of the lute music of the court. *Ports de voix, tremblements, pincés,* and *batteries* abound, while the technique of the stringed instrument encourages the use of exaggerated portamento effects. In some of the later viol composers, even so fine a one as de Caix d'Hervelois, the ornamentation is apt to get out of hand; the hyper-sophistication of the music seems somewhat precious, just as the degenerated vocal tradition relapses into an excessive finickiness. In the work of the masters of the medium, however, notably Marais and Forqueray, the subtleties of ornamentation

265

intensify the grand pathos of the lyrical line; and Marin Marais, Lully's pupil and Couperin's almost exact contemporary, must be accounted an artist of Racinian power in his music's fusion of dignity, subtlety, and lyrical ardour. His variations on *La Folia* are, for instance, more nobly distinguished than Corelli's famous set. Forqueray's work is scarcely inferior in grandeur, while being harmonically even more audacious.

Not even Marais or Forqueray, however, achieved a work of such ripe beauty as Couperin's two suites which, like so many aspects of the work of Bach, are the last word, and the most significant, in a particular language. They may not have the nervous virility of the B minor *Passacaille*, or the subtle energy of the Corelli *Apothéose* or *L'Impériale* sonata, Couperin's finest contributions to the more modern violin medium; but on the whole they are possibly Couperin's greatest instrumental work.

The suites are written for two viols, one of them figured. In the original editions there is some confusion between singular and plural on the title-page, for the works are variously described as 'Pièces de violes' and as 'Suites de viole'. This confusion has led to some speculation about the manner in which Couperin intended them to be performed. The most probable explanation is that Couperin had in mind two alternatives. The pieces could either be played by two viols unaccompanied; or the first viol part, which is of a highly virtuoso character, could be played by a soloist, while the second part was played as a bass in conjunction with a harpsichord continuo. The prevalence of multiple stopping and the extraordinary richness of the texture suggests that Couperin regarded the unaccompanied version as aesthetically the more satisfying. As unaccompanied pieces they would be completely in accordance with the viol tradition.

The E minor suite has a Handelian grandeur together with a personal harmonic complexity. In the *grave* prelude, the solo or virtuoso viol part is characterized by its sweeping phrases, swirling portamentos, and passionate ornamentation. The harmony, enriched by the double and triple stopping of the solo-part, has tremendous resonance—for instance this use of the chord of the ninth:

The allemande is as complicated, linearly and rhythmically, as the most abstruse examples of Bach; the leaps and phrase groupings of the solo part produce a quasi-polyphonic effect almost comparable with that of Bach's suites and sonatas for a solo stringed instrument:

The sonorous chord of the ninth is again in evidence. Similar effects are obtained through big leaps in the energetic courante, which also has powerful chromatic progressions in double stopping:

VIOLES

The sarabande is one of Couperin's noblest movements, again very rich in harmony, making a majestically strenuous use of the French dotted rhythm. The gavotte and gigue are somewhat less remarkable, but have a tautness of line and harmony which is unexpected in these dances. The gavotte flows in a quiet quaver movement, with melancholy, drooping appoggiaturas.

The final *Passacaille* is in the major, and for the first time lets the sun into this majestically gloomy work. The diatonic radiance of the lines and harmonies is familiar to us from some movements in the violin sonatas and clavecin pieces; in the viol *Passacaille* it acquires a dynamic drive which we do not normally associate with Couperin. As the couplets evolve trills and turns, bouncy dotted rhythms and flowing scale passages, the music becomes a joyous carillon. The minor couplets enhance the passion with sonorous double stoppings and sequential sevenths:

and the return to the major, *Gay*, brings the work to a virtuoso conclusion in a blaze of baroque ornamentation, repeated notes and arpeggios.

This glowing resonance is the dominant feature of the whole of the A major suite. The prelude has not the E minor's ordered dolour, but a ceremonial splendour. Long curving lines polyphonically treated, luxuriant ornamentation, ripe sequences, double stoppings, and flexible, strong rhythms combine with a dignified exuberance. The *Fuguéte* is in fact a fully developed polyphonic movement of over six pages, going through a wide range of keys, with exciting syncopations and a lucidly flowing texture.

The *Pompe Funébre* is the most magnificent of all pieces in the *tombeau* tradition. It has a Racinian gravity and power; one can appreciate its background more adequately if one relates it to the rhetoric of the funeral orations of Bossuet or to the wonderful *Pompe Funébre* scene in Lully's *Alceste*:

Troupe de femmes affligées, troupes d'hommes désolés, qui portent des fleurs et tous les ornamens qui ont servi à parer Alceste. Un transport de douleur saisit les troupes affligées; une partie déchire ses habits, l'autre arrache les cheveux, et chacun brise au pied de l'image d'Alceste les ornamens qu'il porte à la main.

Within the majestic lines of the simple binary structure, the details of ornamentation and harmony are exceptionally rich; there is a still greater profusion of double stoppings and chromatic harmonies—notice in this passage the chord of the ninth once more, the abrupt transition to the G major triad, and the repeated trills and turns (see next page).

After this tragic funeral fresco, the work ends with a typical Couperin *jeu d'esprit*, with the enigmatic title of *La Chemise blanche*. This has a virtuoso first viol part in a chattering moto perpetuo. The second section, in the major, though still impudent, recovers enough of the gallantry of the earlier movements to make the piece a convincing epilogue to the whole work.

The suites for viols, and a few movements in the *concerts*, stand among the very greatest of Couperin's achievements. Normally, however, it is not for profundity or tragic passion that we go to these pieces; we find in them rather the most beautiful and civilized occasional music in European history. To them the definition of

269

Descartes—'la fin de la musique est de nous charmer et d'évoquer en nous de diverses sentiments'—is peculiarly appropriate, and we remember that Couperin himself said, 'J'aime mieux ce qui me touche que ce qui me surprend'. This is music of 'les charmes de la vie', as witty and exquisite as the conversation of the young ladies

and gentlemen in the paintings of Watteau.[23] But, like the paintings of Watteau, it repeatedly gives one a glimpse of unsuspected horizons, and it is in no way inconsistent with the most profound aspects of Couperin's work. There is no music that demonstrates more clearly how narrow, in a civilized society, is the line between art and entertainment; we may learn from it how the music of the casual glance, the fortuitous conversation, may imperceptibly merge into one of the noblest manifestations of European culture. It is apposite that we should end our survey of Couperin's work with music that has such direct social validity, that so intimately reminds us of those values and standards from an examination of which this book began. No aspect of Couperin's work reveals more lucidly that those values and standards depended, not on the denial of the life of the individual member of society, but on a profound appreciation of the issues involved in his relation to the community. These works are not, with the exceptions already mentioned, the greatest of Couperin's creations; but they are perhaps the most essential for an understanding of his work's nature and significance.

[23] Cf. M. de Grenailles, *L'honneste Garçon ou l'art de bien élever la noblesse*, 1642: 'Quant à l'adresse aux honnestes exercices, il faut qu'un jeune homme sache chanter et danser autant qu'il en faut, cela veut dire qu'il prenne ces divertissements pour les ornamens de la vie commune plustôt que pour des occupations continues.'

Chapter Eleven

Chronology, Influence, and Conclusions

IN THIS BOOK we have devoted separate chapters to each genre of Couperin's work and have made little attempt to discuss the evolution of his music chronologically. This method seemed, on the whole, the least unsatisfactory, particularly since Couperin is not the kind of composer whose work undergoes any startling transformations or changes of front. But of course his music does develop. Innately lucid of mind, he writes with a progressively increasing precision; and the greatest precision entails the greatest subtlety.

The organ masses (1690) present us with most of the essential materials—the symmetrical diatonic melodies, related both to folksong and to the sophisticated *air de cour*; the baroque ornamentation of this melody, tending to dissolve the rigidity of the metre; the transparent texture of a polyphonic technique inherited from the seventeenth-century organists; the Purcell-like harmonic flexibility; the formal proportions derived from the theatre music of Lully. The early violin sonatas (1692–95) bring a more lyrical and operatic type of melody; a compromise between the soloists' polyphony and the homophony of the continuo; and a growing sense of harmonic order learned from Corelli in particular. Certain recognizable Couperin traits begin to appear—a fondness for rich spacing and harmonies, especially ninth chords, disciplined by the economy of texture; a peculiar melting effect produced by hushed suspensions in dotted rhythm; a partiality for the 'touching' effect of the sharp seventh in the ascent, followed by the flat seventh descending; many abstruse dissonances created by appoggiaturas and other ornaments derived from the *air de cour*; and a favourite modulation to the minor of the dominant.

The period of the church music and the early clavecin pieces (1697 to 1715) blends these French and Italian elements in forms adapted from the church music of Carissimi, Charpentier, and Lully. During the period of *Les Goûts Réünis* (1715 to 1730), the *Concerts Royaux*, the later clavecin pieces, and the last violin sonatas make use of all these elements, but tend to encourage the French elements at the expense of the Italian. Certain dissonances, spread chord effects, dotted rhythms and portamentos suggested by the lutenists and violists, help Couperin to achieve some of his grandest creations, particularly in sarabande form. And although he is beginning to relinquish his seventeenth-century-like compromise between polyphony and homophony in favour of a balanced harmonic architecture, it is during this period that we become most clearly aware that his technique is founded on a dialogue between soprano and bass. Here, too, we find his most contrapuntally taut and powerful work, that which most invites comparison with the lucid complexity of Bach. We may refer especially to some of the allemandes, and to *L'Apothéose de Corelli* and *L'Impériale*, music in which, as in Bach's work, vertical harmonies are given subtlety and virility through the independence of the parts that make them up, while at the same time the contour of the lines is conditioned by a clearly defined scheme of tonal order. Finally, in the precision of workmanship in his last compositions, such as the fourth book of clavecin pieces and the suites for viols, all suspicion of influences, French or Italian, has vanished. He has created an idiom which we can regard both as a triumph of the declining civilization in which he lived, and as perhaps the most central expression of the French tradition.

In 1733, the year in which Couperin died, Rameau, who had been Couperin's neighbour in the rue des Bons Enfants, produced his first opera. The association of the French musical tradition with the theatre was re-established; it was to continue, more or less unbroken, down to our own day. This renewed association was a further growth of the less autocratic culture we have already noticed in Couperin, and it is ironic that the emergence of a more 'popular' culture should—as the level of taste declined—eventually lead a sensitive spirit, such as Claude Debussy, to the Ivory Tower. Couperin's work, however, attains the perfect equilibrium between an aristocracy of form and an intimate emotion; he could have occurred only at that precise moment in French history. In the work of a Lebrun, the formal gesture defeats the artist's integrity; in the

273

work of a Boucher, emotional indulgence reduces the art to (very charming) sensory tittilation, without—in the widest sense—any moral implications. But in Watteau we find emotional intimacy together with a formal control which reflects a moral and spiritual order. Couperin's relationship to most of his disciples seems to me exactly to parallel that of Watteau to Boucher.

With the great exceptions of Rameau and Leclair, and to a lesser degree Mondonville and Clérambault, Couperin's disciples are musical Bouchers. They write to please; and please they do, for one could scarcely imagine a more deliciously sensuous entertainment music than the *Conversations Galantes et Amusantes* of Dandrieu, Dornel, Du Phly, and Daquin in clavecin music, of Guillemain, Mouret, Blavet, Corrette, and Boismortier in concerted music for strings and wind instruments. Their work implies an instinct for social elegance; their indulgence of their emotions never prevents them from raising their hats and making their bow in the appropriate places. But they have forgotten *why* they raise their hats. The gesture is automatic; they act from habit, having lost their guiding sense of a moral order.

The best of Couperin's minor disciples, Dandrieu and Dagincour, are thus, despite great sensibility and charm, derivative in a bad sense; and they are essentially miniaturists, which Couperin, *essentially*, was not. Even Rameau, Couperin's peer in the French classical tradition, does not achieve in his keyboard music the close texture of Couperin's finest work. His is more harmonic, less linear in lay-out, more virtuoso and theatrical in treatment. It is more brilliant, and more immediately emotional than Couperin's work; but it is not therefore more profound. Perhaps Rameau's very finest pieces, such as the superb A minor allemande and in a quieter vein *Les Tendres Plaintes*, are an exception to this, having much of Couperin's sombre dignity. But they are less characteristic of his work than an audaciously imaginative, 'colouristic' piece like *Le Rappel des Oiseaux*; a grand Handelian piece like the *Gavotte* with variations or the A major *Sarabande*; or an expansive virtuoso piece such as *Les Tourbillons*, *Les Cyclopes*, with its non-melodic Alberti bass, *La Dauphine*, *La Triomphante*, or the exciting rondeau *Les Niais de Sologne*. All these, in the Handelian fashion, are based more on arpeggio formations than on scale-wise motion:

Couperin, like Bach, on the whole favours conjunct motion rather than arpeggio figures.

Rameau, unlike Couperin, looks forwards rather than backwards. There are passages in his clavecin works—which were all written early in his career, before he began to take himself seriously as an operatic composer—which already give intimation of eighteenth-century sonata style. *La Poule* is a genuine harpsichord piece in the classical baroque tradition; yet towards the end, just before the coda, there is a passage, harping on the chord of the dominant seventh, which has in miniature the structural and harmonic effect of the cadenza to the Mozartian concerto:

There is nothing comparable with this in Couperin. Similarly one of the most remarkable of Rameau's pieces, *L'Enharmonique*, is deliberately a study in tonal relationships. It has a diminished seventh cadence which is not produced by linear movement, but which is harmonic in its own right, marking a rhetorical or dramatic point in the structure, as do the cadences in the eighteenth-century sonata:

Rameau's delightful *Pièces de clavecin en concert*, cast in the three-movement Italian form of allegro-andante-allegro, illustrate this progressive 'modernism' even more clearly. Their keyboard part is not a continuo part like that of Couperin's trio sonatas, nor a piece of polyphonic writing like that of Bach's sonatas. The keyboard is treated as a virtuoso solo instrument, in a way that suggests Haydn and Mozart's treatment of the combination of piano with strings. The relation of the string writing to the new bourgeois rococo style becomes patent in the version for string sextet which some disciple made after Rameau had deserted chamber music for the theatre.

Perhaps the most illuminating instance of the decadence of the French clavecin school is provided by the four volumes of pieces by Du Phly, engraved by Mlle Vandôme and published by Boyvin in 1755 and subsequently. A few of Du Phly's pieces have still a little of Couperin's spirit; we may mention a charming rondeau on page 10 of the first book, and the first half of the *Gavotte tendrement* called *La De Villeneuve*. But the second half of this piece is explicitly harmonic rather than linear in effect, and in general Du Phly tends to build his movements on simple chordal progressions rather than on line. Movements such as *La Cozamajor, La Larare, La Victoire*, exploit arpeggio and scale figuration in the virtuoso manner of Rameau, though with a vague improvisatory flourish instead of Rameau's intense brilliance. Perhaps the most extreme example of this technique is the very long, and dull, chaconne in F, which has extensive passages of unambiguous Alberti bass—a device which Couperin, as a linear composer, justly regarded with suspicion.

Most of the pieces in the fourth book, which seems to be of somewhat later date than the others, have a 'tune' at the top, with many sequential repetitions, accompanied by Alberti basses; *La De Guign* and *La Du Drummond* are typical examples. The third volume includes pieces in concert with violin; even the first volume ends with a piece in C, marked *légèrement*, which is built out of more than usually footling scale passages and arpeggios rounded off, after a double bar, with a reiterated Handelian full close—a musical method of saying The End which is almost comic in its naïveté.

It is clear that Couperin stood for something which, by Du Phly's time, already belonged to a past world. Apart from Rameau, only the great Leclair came close to Couperin's elegiac aristocracy, and even he developed a more symphonic and harmonic style. Although like Rameau he favoured a monothematic as much as a bithematic technique, in his work too the suite is superseded by the Italian concerto and the classical triptych of allegro-andante-allegro. Couperin stood for something from which the French tradition was turning away. His influence survived in France for barely twenty-five years after his death. By 1771 Grimm was able to say: 'il y a deux choses auxquelles les François seront obligés de renoncer tôt ou tard, leur musique et leurs jardins'. The noble architectural symmetry of the classical tradition had perished.[24]

Couperin had an enthusiastic Belgian disciple in J. H. Fiocco. Some of his pieces make a genuine attempt to reproduce both

[24] An interesting gloss on the inability of the Handelians to appreciate Couperin's linear idiom is provided by Dr Burney's comments on his ornamentation: 'The great Couperin . . . was not only an admirable organist but, in the style of the times, an excellent composer for keyed instruments. His instructions for fingering, in his *L'Art de Toucher le Clavecin*, are still good; tho' his pieces are so crowded and deformed by beats, trills and shakes, that no plain note was ever left to enable the hearer of them to judge whether the tone of the instrument on which they were played was good or bad.' (*A General History of Music*.)

Couperin's complexity of line (*L'Inconstante* or the dotted rhythmed allemande from the D minor suite), and his serene naïveté (*La Légère*, the two gavottes from the D minor suite). *Les Promenades de Bierbéeck ou de Buerbéeck* is a very close imitation of one of Couperin's gentle flowing 3 : 8 movements with consistent semiquaver figuration. The pieces are not however very distinguished, and are all disfigured by clumsy passages of parallel octaves which betray Fiocco's inability to maintain a consistently linear style. Even in these his most Couperin-like pieces he seems in danger of falling into the easy homophonic *style galant* of a Du Phly; in pieces such as *La Fringante* or *L'Anglaise* he quite explicitly writes straightforward arpeggiated movements in the Italianate Handelian style. Most of the other Belgian clavecinists, such as Boutmy and Gheyn, also use the Italian technique. Such relations as they have with Couperin are only superficial.

In England and Italy the music of Lully had exerted a most powerful influence, but the influence died with the culture that produced it, if we except the reminiscences of Lully in Handel's English work. Only in Germany was the French spirit deeply entrenched.

Because of the time lag occasioned by the Thirty Years' War Germany was culturally somewhat behind the times, so that the French vogue in Germany came to its height after *la gloire* had decayed. Communications between France, Belgium, and southern Germany were stimulated by the Bavarian alliance, and French culture became the accepted criterion of taste. In the last decade of the seventeenth century German composers were as eager to emulate Lully as were their aristocratic patrons to emulate Lully's master the Roi Soleil. French musicians such as Buffardin frequently visited Germany, castles were built in Germany on the model of Versailles, and a movement that had started in the Catholic south soon spread to Prussia and the north. Frederick the Great was to entertain Voltaire, and to speak French more graciously than German.

Even before Lully's triumph composers such as Rosenmüller and Bleyer had been influenced by the French ballet. By the end of the seventeenth century many German composers had gone to Paris to study the French methods under Lully himself. Possibly J. J. Froberger was a professional copyist in French employment; he wrote clavecin works—including a highly impressive piece modelled on

278

Louis Couperin's *Tombeau de M Blancrocher*—which derive from the lute-like French keyboard style. Erlebach and Mayr were for a time among Lully's pupils, writing quantities of dance suites in the French manner; while in 1682 J. S. Kusser published in Stuttgart his *Composition de musique suivant la méthode française, contenant six Ouvertures de Théâtre accompagnées de plusieurs Airs*. A little later appeared Johann Casper Fischer's *Le Journal de Printemps consistant en Airs et Balets à 5 parties et les Trompettes à plaisir*, entrancingly fresh occasional music modelled on the *Musique pour le Souper du Roi* of La Lande and others. The first volume of Fischer's clavecin music was published in 1696. Most of the little dances are a more muscular version of those of Chambonnières, though some of the big chaconnes, notably the G major, are worthy of Lully himself.[25]

The most notable of all Lully's German pupils and disciples was, however, Georg Muffat, whose *Florilegia* suites were published in 1695. Muffat, who came from Passau, had at one time played in Lully's orchestra. In his preface to the *Florilegia*, he maintained that of Lully's work he had 'fait autre fois à Paris pendant six ans un assez grand Estude . . . à mon retour de France je fus peut-estre le premier qui en apportay quelque idée assez agréable aux musiciens *de bon goût*, en Alsace'. (My italics.) He can hardly have been justified in claiming to be the first German composer to use the French style, but it is true that he offers an example 'd'une mélodie naturelle, d'un chant facile et coulant, fort éloigné d'artifices superflus, des diminutions extravagantes', and that for solidity of part-writing and richness of harmony his example could hardly be improved upon. Each suite has a title referring to some human quality (Gratitudio, Impatientia, Constanzia, etc.), and the titles of the individual pieces that make up the suites are in French. Some are dances—allemandes, bourrées, sarabandes, canaris, ballets, airs, passepieds, and so on; others are of a descriptive nature—*Les Gendarmes, Balet pour les Amazones*, even *Gavotte de Marly*. Each suite is prefaced by a full-scale Lullian overture, complete with double dotted rhythm, the familiar crochet tied to a semiquaver figuration ♩♫♫ , and

[25] The most interesting pieces in the collection are not, however, in the French style, but in the German development of Italian toccata technique which Bach was to use with wonderful effect in such things as the Chromatic Fantasia. Some of Fischer's preludes, for instance the D major, are remarkably bold experiments in harmonic progression.

a triple-rhythmed fugal section often with a rousing conclusion in parallel thirds. These overtures, and the other big movements such as the passacailles, are exceptionally fine, with all Lully's sonorous grandeur and, in addition, a certain Germanic sobriety. One may mention, in particular, the G minor overture, and the *Passacaille* in A minor. Like Couperin, Muffat was later much influenced by Corelli as well as Lully, and published a series of Italianate concerti grossi.

By the time Couperin had become a musical celebrity, the taste for things French was thus well-established in Germany, and it is not surprising that he too became a dominating force in German music, particularly keyboard music. Fux and Telemann copied not only Couperin's titles, but also his airy texture, and the more percussive features of his style. Telemann was especially francophile; 'les airs françois', he said, 'ont replacé chez nous la vogue qu'avaient les cantates italiennes. J'ai connu des Allemands, des Anglais, des Russes, des Polonais, et même des Juifs, qui savaient par cœur des passages entières de *Bellérophon* et d'*Atys* de Lully'. He was fortunate enough to have his quartets for flute and strings played by such distinguished performers as Blavet,[26] Guignon, Forqueray, and Edouard, while in 1728 a Psalm and cantata of his composition were performed with considerable success at a Concert Spiritual. He published a work called *Musique de table, partagée en trois Productions, dont chacune contient l'Ouverture avec la suite à 7 instruments.* The dances include such typically French forms as the forlane, passepied, loure, chaconne, musette, and rondeau, and the titles suggest a complete Watteau décor, with Réjouissance, Allégresse, Badinerie, Flatterie, and even Bergerie, Harlequinade, and La Douceur. Telemann's treatment of the style is, however, more unambiguously homophonic than Couperin's; for his sympathies, as J. S. Bach realized, were associated more with the new kind of symphonic music than with the old linear style of the classical baroque.

[26] Blavet admired Telemann's work greatly, and, as Lionel de Laurencie has pointed out, his own music betrays Telemann's influence, both in some of its ornamentation and in certain pedal effects—for instance, the tonic pedal for the flute in the Prelude to Blavet's *Nouveaux Quatuours* of 1738. In general, the German composers had a slight reciprocal influence on their French hosts. It is noticeable as late as 1768, in Corrette's *Cinquante Pièces ou Canons lyriques à deux, trois, ou quatre voix*, which are modelled on Telemann's canons. In 1746 an article on *La Corruption du Goût dans la Musique Française*, published in the Mémoires de Trévoux, mentions Telemann among other baleful foreign corruptions, such as Vivaldi, Locatelli, and Handel.

A more significant mingling of French and German styles is provided by the most distinguished of Couperin's German disciples,
Georg Muffat's son Gottlieb, and Johann Mattheson, who in his
Kernmelodische Wissenschaft of 1736 recommended the French style
to young composers, because 'Frankreich ist und bleibt die rechte
Tanzschule'. This verdict on the 'claire et facile' melody of the
French, as opposed to Italian complexity, was endorsed by the
theoretician Quantz, after he had spent several months in Paris in
the late seventeen twenties. Like that of Telemann the musical
thought of Muffat and Mattheson is more consistently homophonic
than Couperin's, and their texture is thicker; but they discover a
common denominator between the French and German styles, and
one may regard them, perhaps, as a cross between Couperin and
Handel. Mattheson's allemandes are often quite involved, in the
manner of Couperin and Bach—for instance that from the C minor
suite:

His more customary manner is represented by the Air with doubles
in arpeggio accompaniment, from the same suite, or by the melancholy sarabande with variations from the F minor suite, Handelian
in technique, but more austere in feeling:

Muffat, on the other hand, with his south German Catholic background, has all Handel's Italianate flamboyance, and writes movements, such as the big prelude and fugue of the B flat suite, in a rhetorical toccata style which Couperin never attempted:

Some of his finest pieces are chordally accompanied airs in Handelian style, rather more abstruse harmonically—for instance the B flat
282

minor sarabande from the same suite, with its poignant Neapolitan sixths:

and throughout Muffat thinks more 'chordally' than Couperin. He has, however, some fine linear pieces which resemble Bach if not Couperin (the G major, E minor and D minor sarabandes, and the allemandes in D major and D minor); and something of the authentic Couperin spirit still survives in the sprightly courantes, with their contrapuntal entries; in the cross rhythms of the B flat Hornpipe; in the audacious portamentos of *La Hardiesse*; in the grandly rigid rhythm of the G major chaconne; and especially in the flowing lilt and dissolving harmonies of the G major gigue. Here too the technique depends on harmonic progression rather than linear movement; Couperin does not use the Neapolitan sixth effect in this explicitly chordal form:

But the grace of the movement, with the undercurrent of wistfulness, recalls Couperin, Watteau, and the world of the *fête champêtre*, and Muffat must have been one of the last composers to understand, intuitively, what the *fête champêtre* had stood for in spiritual terms. Some of Muffat's suites—for instance, the C major and D minor—have an orthodox Lullian overture instead of the toccata prelude. He is a highly impressive keyboard composer whose work ought to be more widely known.

Some of Handel's dances were published in Paris in 1734 by Antoine Bretonne, and were frequently played during the following decade. Reciprocally, both Handel and Bach studied Couperin's work. Although Couperin's influence on Handel, who is temperamentally closer to Lully, can have been merely superficial, we have repeatedly mentioned that Bach found in Couperin a spirit with whom he could sympathize. His own ventures into the French style, in keyboard and orchestral suites, have little of Couperin's *galant* finesse, but bring to his linear draughtsmanship an austerely powerful German contrapuntal science. We have frequently discussed the general similarities between Bach's technique, and Couperin's.

Even in the work of Bach's sons, the influence of Couperin is still discernible, though the use which they make of him differs from their father's. J. S. Bach found in Couperin a composer whose technique was basically linear, like his own; Carl Philipp Emanuel, in his many pieces with French titles,[27] such as *La Caroline*, adapts the

---

[33] Many of C. P. E. Bach's pieces with French titles appeared in Marpurg's *Raccolta delle più nuove composizioni di clavicembalo* (Leipzig, 1756–57), and thus belong to the middle years of C. P. E. Bach's career. The titles include such characteristic formulae as *L'Auguste*, *La Bergins*, *La Lott*, *La Glein*, *La Prinzette*, *La Complaisante*, *La Capricieuse*, *L'Irrésolue*, *La Journalière*, *La Xenophon*, *Les Langueurs Tendres*. Some of the pieces are reasonably convincing imitations of Couperin; we may mention *L'Irrésolue* and *La Journalière*, especially the latter, with its habitually syncopated phrasing and its characteristic breaks in rhythm. In all, there are twenty-four of these 'French' pieces. On Marpurg, see below.

binary structure, the airy texture, the staccato arpeggio figuration and the sequential passage-work typical of Couperin's lighter movements (see opposite).

But the form is now harmonically and metrically dictated, in a way which suggests Haydn and the early symphony; witness the pause followed by a Neapolitan sixth in the coda, a device which, depending on harmonic and dynamic *contrast*, is essentially dramatic and symphonic, rather than a product of linear movement:

A passage such as this seems to invite orchestral treatment.

Similarly, some of Wilhelm Friedemann Bach's 'French' sara-bandes revealingly illustrate the transformation of the sarabande into the slow movement of the eighteenth-century symphony; and although G. M. Monn has a movement with the authentic-sounding *grand-siècle* title of *La Personne Galante*, it is hardly possible to see any affinity between his music and Couperin, beyond a few skipping staccato figures based on triads. His work, composed about the middle of the century, depends on the tonal principles of the diatonic sonata, and from it to the Mannheim symphonists is but a step. It is no accident that the elder Stamitz first achieved fame, in the seventeen fifties, before a middle-class audience in France, as *chef d'orchestre* to the enterprising Le Riche de la Pouplinière; and that the symphonic works of the younger Stamitz and the other Mannheimers were first published in Paris. The age of classical aristocracy, of the late baroque, is outmoded by the age of the rococo. If we take Johann Stamitz and C. P. E. Bach as representative of the two main strands of the new period, we may say that in Stamitz we find the deliberate cultivation of a bold popular style, designed to have a commercial appeal to a relatively wide audience; while in C. P. E. Bach's later work we find a romantic individualism, a preoccupation with *sensibilité*, expressed not only in the almost lushly harmonic nature of the slow movements, but even in his dedication of his volumes to '*Kenner und Liebhaber*'. Since 1750, these two elements, the popular and the personal, have drifted gradually further apart.

Probably the latest examples of Couperin's influence in Germany are to be found in the keyboard work of Graupner, Krebs, Kirnberger, and Marpurg. Graupner has a rather beautiful *Sommeil* movement; Krebs, a duller composer, has a piece called *Harlequinade* which is, however, already more Mozartian than Couperinesque in style and feeling. Some pieces of Kirnberger, such as *Les Complimenteurs* and *Les Carillons*, have more of the authentic manner, and his D major chaconne is interesting as a transition between the *galanterie* of Lully and Couperin, and the new, Mozartian *galant* convention. But most striking is the *Clavierstücke* collection of Marpurg, published in Berlin in 1762. Into this volume Marpurg has transcribed Couperin's *Le Réveil Matin*, and pieces by other clavecinists such as Clérambault, and has added pieces of his own which not only have characteristic titles (*La Badine*, *Les Fifres*, etc.), but which are closer to the linear style of Couperin than are most of the Germanic versions of his idiom mentioned in this chapter. The pieces are not, however, much more than pastiche. The Couperin tradition is no longer a living reality; it has been engulfed by the symphony, as was the tradition of Bach.

And so, as the Viennese symphony prospered, Couperin was forgotten, both in Germany and in his own country. The revival of interest in him has more or less coincided with the revival of interest in Bach; and his position in French musical history is comparable with that of Bach in the history of *European* music. Just as Bach sums up the evolution of European music down to his time, and suggests potentialities which have only recently been investigated; so Couperin, in his less comprehensive way, has the whole of French musical history implicit in him, and hints at later developments in Fauré, Debussy, and Ravel. The two latter played a considerable part in the re-establishment of Couperin and their attempt, in their later work, to reinstate the French classical tradition in place of their earlier 'nervous' introspection is significant—particularly in view of their preoccupation with the world of Watteau and the Harlequin. But still more important is the comparison with Fauré, because Fauré's technique, as has been pointed out, has a similar combination of harmonic subtlety in the inner parts with solid line drawing between melody and bass. Fauré, too, is a guardian of civilization and tradition. His civilization, however, has a less direct relation to a real world than Couperin's; it is an idealization, in an art form, of his response to the French tradition. For this reason, perhaps, his enharmonic fluctuations give to his urbanity a certain precariousness. He cannot aspire to that proud serenity and mastery of stylization which was natural to Couperin because he lived in a society which believed in itself, was confident of its values.

Couperin's civilization, as we have previously suggested, was both real and ideal at the same time. It was real in the sense that it existed outside his music in the world in which he lived; it was ideal in the sense that, in his music, he presented the values of his society in a form distilled of all merely topical and local dross. We have no real parallel to this in English music. In some ways the civilized quality of Couperin's music is, in its finest moments, not incomparable with the urbanity of Ben Jonson. That magnificent poem, *To the World, A Farewell for a Gentlewoman, Virtuous and Noble*, mates courtly elegance with earthy vigour, urbanely balanced movement with tragic passion, in a manner similar to that which we have noticed in Couperin's greatest achievements. The exquisiteness of the courtly lyrical poets, the spirituality of the seventeenth-century devotional poets, and the immediate vitality of the dramatists and the Donne tradition meet in Jonson's work; Couperin, too, shows that urbanity, wit, and courtly grace may exist together with a deeply serious, even religious, attitude to life. And if we feel that in Couperin there is more exquisiteness and less earthy vigour, that should not lead us to underestimate the vigour that is certainly there. Nor is it at all surprising, making allowances for the difference in date and environment, that Couperin should have many temperamental affinities

287

with Jonson. During the latter part of Jonson's life, English Caroline culture was developing in a manner closely parallel to French culture. Had it not been for the Civil War, it is at least feasible that Dryden or some other successor to Jonson might have been as convincing in his heroic work as he was in his critical and satirical; that we might have produced something closer to Racine than in fact we did. In that case, it is possible that the masque might have developed into the mature opera; and that Purcell, as successor to Jenkins and William Lawes, might have been, not a greater genius, but a composer more aristocratically elegant, more precise, more Couperinlike. By the time England had evolved her Augustan civilization she seemed for the most part to have lost an awareness of tragic issues. Apart from a few passages in Pope, our Augustan age has nothing comparable with the greatest things in Couperin and Racine.

Couperin is not, of course, a composer whose outlook on life is fundamentally religious, even mystical, as is Bach; nor has he Bach's comprehensiveness. In some obvious respects, Alessandro Scarlatti, La Lande, Handel, and Rameau are all classical baroque composers on a grander scale than Couperin. None of them, however, comes as close to Bach as does Couperin in his finest work; none of them has anything as aristocratically noble as *La Favorite*, as spiritual as the *Leçons des Ténèbres*, as tightly wrought as *L'Apothéose de Corelli* or *L'Impériale*, as tragic as *La Passacaille*, as civilized as *La Convalescente*. No doubt Rameau is the key figure with reference to the future of French musical culture, since his passionately disciplined theatrical art looks forward to the next supremely great figure in the French tradition, Berlioz. Yet Couperin himself is not as remote from Berlioz as one might superficially imagine; and, unlike Rameau, he also looks back, beyond Lully, to the sixteenth century and even the Middle Ages. It is hardly too fanciful to suggest that Couperin is a central link between Lassus, the richest and most multifarious of the sixteenth-century masters, and Berlioz, the man who, despite his much vaunted romanticism, is the greatest aristocratic master of linear draughtsmanship in the nineteenth century.

And then, by way of Fauré, Couperin establishes a link with the modern world. Perhaps the nature of this connection is indicated if one remarks, in conclusion, that the relation of the classicist Valéry to Racine resembles the relation of Fauré's last works to Couperin.

Part III

Theory and Practice

De tous les dons naturels le Goût est celui qui se sent le mieux et qui s'explique le moins; il ne seroit pas ce qu'il est, si l'on pouvait le définir; car il juge des objets sur lesquels le jugement n'a plus de prise, et sert, si j'ose parler ainsi, de lunettes à la raison. . . .

Chaque homme a un Goût particulier. . . . Mais il y a aussi un Goût général sur lequel tous les gens bien organisés s'accordent; et c'est celui-ci seulement auquel on peut donner absolument le nom de Goût.

ROUSSEAU'S Dictionnaire

Une Musique doit être naturelle, expressive, harmonieuse. . . . J'apelle à la lettre *naturel* ce qui est composé de tons qui s'offrent naturellement, ce qui n'est point composé de tons recherchez, extraordinaires. . . . J'apelle *Expressif* un Air dont les tons conviennent parfaitement aux paroles, et une Symphonie qui exprime parfaitement ce qu'elle veut exprimer. J'apelle *harmonieux, mélodieux, agréable*, ce qui contente, ce qui remplit, ce qui chatouille les oreilles.

BONNET, Histoire de la Musique, 1725

Ce bel Art tout divin par ses douces merveilles,
Ne se contente pas de charmer les oreilles,
N'y d'aller jusqu'au cœur par ses expressions
Emouvoir à son gré toutes les passions:
Il va, passant plus loin, par sa beauté suprême,
Au plus haut de l'esprit charmer la raison même.

PERRAULT, Le Siècle de Louis le Grand

Chapter Twelve

Couperin's Theoretical Work

THE THEORETICAL WRITINGS of Couperin comprise a small treatise called *Règles pour l'Accompagnement*; a larger work entitled *L'Art de toucher le Clavecin*; and miscellaneous passages in the prefaces to his published compositions.

The first of these, the *Règles pour l'Accompagnement*, is an early work, probably dating from the last years of the seventeenth century. It is a straightforward account of the methods of treating discord current in Couperin's day, and is interesting mainly because it indicates Couperin's familiarity with the most advanced Italian techniques. We may observe that Couperin here, early in his career, gives theoretical backing to the abstruse dissonances of eleventh and thirteenth, such as we have called attention to in our discussion of his music.

The important treatise on clavecin playing was published in 1717, at the same time as the second book of clavecin pieces, and was re-issued shortly afterwards. In the preface to the second book of clavecin works Couperin explains that he had written his didactic book because it was 'absolument indispensible pour exécuter mes pièces dans le Goût qui leur convient'. It is not a systematically planned work, but rather a series of random reflections which Couperin puts down as they occur to him. Here it will perhaps be best not to attempt to summarize the contents in the order in which they appear. Instead, we will arrange Couperin's opinions under a series of headings, supplementing what he says in *L'Art de toucher le Clavecin* with such comments from the Prefaces as seem relevant.

A. Hints on Teaching Methods

Couperin begins by explaining his intention in writing his *Méthode*. Playing the clavecin, he says, is not merely a matter of digital facility; it is a question of learning how to interpret, with sympathy and taste:

La Méthode que je donne icy est unique. . . . J'y traite sur toutes choses (par principes démonstrés) du beau Toucher du clavecin. . . . Je ne dois point craindre que les gens éclairés s'y meprennent; je dois seulement exhorter les autres à la docilité. Au moins les dois-je assurer tous, que ces principes sont absolument nécessaires pour parvenir à bien exécuter mes Pièces.

He then goes on to discuss the most suitable age to start learning the instrument:

L'âge propre à commencer les Enfans, est de six à sept ans; non pas que cela doive exclure les personnes avancées; mais naturellement, pour mouler et former des mains à l'exercice du Clavecin, le plus tôt est le mieux.

The player should be seated so that his elbows are approximately level with the keyboard, and his feet resting gently on the floor. In the case of small children whose legs are too short, it is wise to give their feet some support, so that they may be securely balanced. The body should be seated about nine inches from the keyboard.

Little movement of the body is called for in playing the clavecin, and the beating of time with the head or feet should be avoided. 'A l'égard des grimaces du visage, on peut s'en corriger soy-même en mettant un miroir sur le pupitre de l'épinette.' In general one's posture should be attentive but easy. Couperin remarks that, in the early stages, children should not be allowed to play the clavecin except in the presence of their teacher or some other responsible person, because left to themselves they can 'déranger en un instant ce que j'ai soigneusement posé en trois quarts d'heure'. He also offers the sensible advice that it is profitable for children to learn several pieces by ear and memory before studying notation. Thus they can early acquire some command of musical expression without being troubled by the mechanics of music. A very typical touch occurs in a passage wherein Couperin advocates humility on the part of the teacher:

Il serait bon que les parents, ou ceux qui ont l'inspection générale sur les enfans, eussent moins d'impatience, et plus de confiance en celui qui enseigne (sûrs d'avoir fait un bon choix en sa personne) et que l'habile Maître, de son côté, eût moins de condescendance.

He further insists that a spinet or single manual harpsichord is sufficient for children, and that it should always be 'emplumé très faible-ment', so that little muscular force is needed to press down the keys. Only thus can suppleness and independence of the fingers be developed; and these qualities are more important than strength. *Douceur de toucher* depends on keeping the fingers as close to the keys as possible: 'La souplesse des nerfs contribue beaucoup plus au bien jouer, que la force'. This point leads to our second heading:

B. Remarks on the Nature and Technique of the Instrument

Les sons du clavecin étant décidés, chacun en particulier, et par conséquent ne pouvant être enflés ni diminués, il a paru presque insoutenable jusqu'au present qu'on pût donner de l'âme à cet instrument; cependant, par les recherches dont j'ai appuyé le peu de naturel que le ciel m'a donné, je vais tâcher de faire comprendre par quelles raisons j'ai su acquerir le bonheur de toucher les personnes de goût.

Il faut surtout se rendre très délicat au clavier et avoir toujours un instrument bien emplumé. Je comprens cependant qu'il y a des gens à qui cela peut être indifférent, parce qu'ils jouent également mal sur quelque instrument que soit.

These quotations indicate how Couperin regarded the clavecin as an instrument capable of conveying great emotional sensibility; the technique of fingering and ornamentation which he describes later is the means whereby this sensitivity is realized. The French style is essentially a clavecin style, the Italian a violin and sonata style. 'Les personnes médiocrement habiles' prefer the Italian manner because it is more obvious, less dependent on subtleties of phrasing and ornamentation. But the clavecin 'a ses propriétés, comme le violon a les siennes. Si le clavecin n'enfle point ses sons, si les battements redoublés sur une même note ne lui conviennent pas estremement, il a d'autres avantages, qui sont la précision, la néteté, le brillant, et l'étendue'.

With this passage from *L'Art de toucher* we may correlate two passages from the preface to the first book:

L'usage m'a fait connoître que les mains vigoureuses et capables d'exécuter ce qu'il y a de plus rapide et de plus léger ne sont pas toujours celles qui réussissent le mieux dans les pièces tendres et du sentiment; et j'avoueray de bonne foy que j'ayme mieux ce qui me touche que ce qui me surprend;

and

Le clavecin est parfait quant à son étendue et brillant par luy-même; mais,

293

comme on ne peut enfler ny diminuer ses sons, je sçauray toujours gré à
ceux qui, par un art infini soutenu par le goût, pourront arriver à rendre cet
instrument susceptible d'expression; c'est à quoy mes ancêtres se sont
appliquées, indépendamment de la belle composition de leurs pièces; j'ay
tâché de perfectionner leurs découvertes; leurs ouvrages sont encore du
goût de ceux qui l'ont exquis.

Couperin concludes this part of his treatise with some advice which
we have seen to be admirably demonstrated in his own practice:

Pour conclure sur le toucher du clavecin en général, mon sentiment est de
ne point s'éloigner du caractère qui y convient. Les passages, les batteries
à portée de la main, les choses entées et syncopés, doivent être préférées à
celles qui sont pleines de tenues, ou de notes trop graves. Il faut conserver
une liaison parfaite dans ce qu'on exécute; que tous les agrémens soient bien
précis; que ceux qui sont composés de batemens soient faits bien également,
et par une gradation imperceptible. Prendre bien garde à ne point altérer
le mouvement dans les pièces réglées; et à ne point rester sur les notes dont
la valeur soit pincé. Enfin former son jeu sur le bon goût d'aujourd'hui qui
est sans comparaison plus pur que l'Ancien.

This last sentence is sociologically interesting, with reference to the
values of Couperin's society and eighteenth-century notions of
Progress and Perfectability. The rest of the quotation provides a
transition from Couperin's consideration of the nature and technique of his instrument, to the first of the means whereby the instrument is rendered 'susceptible d'expression'.

C. Comments on Tempo and Rhythm

Couperin's comments on rhythm and movement are of great
importance, being one of the sources for our knowledge of the
rhythmic conventions of the early eighteenth century. He explains
that the French style has been underestimated in other countries—he
is thinking, mainly, of Italy—because our pieces are not played as
they are notated, whereas 'les Italiens écrivent leur musique dans les
vrayes valeurs qu'ils l'ont pensée'. Since our pieces have a descriptive intent, they are played freely; we use words, such as *tendrement*
or *vivement*, to indicate the mood of the piece, and it would be helpful if these words could be translated for the benefit of foreigners.
Moreover, we differentiate *mesure* from *mouvement*, whereas the
Italian sonatas 'ne sont guères susceptible de cette cadence'. 'Mesure
definit la qualité et l'égalité des temps, et Cadence est proprement
294

l'esprit et l'Ame qu'il y faut joindre.' 'La cadence et le Goût peuvent s'y conserver indépendamment du plus ou du moins de lenteur.' Here the term *cadence* seems to mean lilt and subtlety of movement; we may compare the definition in Rousseau's *Dictionnaire*:

Cadence est une qualité de la bonne Musique, qui donne à ceux qui l'exécutent ou qui l'écoutent, un sentiment vif de la mesure, ensuite qu'ils la marquent et la sentent tomber à propos, sans qu'ils y pensent et comme par instinct. . . . 'Cette chaconne manque de Cadence.'

This use of the term should not be confused with its significance in the *air de cour*, where it means a trill preceded by an appoggiatura, usually occurring in a cadential phrase.

But although the French pieces are free in movement, there is nothing haphazard about them. Even the *tendre* pieces should not be played too slowly, owing to the short sustaining power of the instrument. *Mesure* (metre) must always be respected; *esprit* must be obtained through *goût* and *cadence*. The correct interpretation of these irregularities of movement is one of the most difficult of all the problems involved in early eighteenth-century music.

Dolmetsch's discussion of the conventional alterations of rhythm seems to me the least satisfactory part of his invaluable book, because he does not explain the complicated conditions which regulated the employment of these effects. These conditions are, however, described in detail in E. Borrel's article on 'Les notes inégales dans l'ancienne musique française', published in the *Revue de Musicologie* of November 1931. Borrel's case is based entirely on contemporary documents, so by supplementing Couperin's own very ambiguous pronouncements on the subject with the testimony of the other seventeenth- and eighteenth-century authorities quoted by Borrel, we may hope to obtain some coherent notion of the correct interpretation of Couperin's rhythms.

The tradition of *notes inégales* goes back, in French music, as far as the early years of the sixteenth century, but the first important and detailed statement on the subject is that of Loulié in 1696. According to him, in any time, but especially in triple rhythms, there are three possible ways of playing notes of half-beat value. Firstly the notes may be all played equally. This method is called *Détacher*, and is used in all passages which proceed by *degrez interrompus* (i.e. by disjunct motion). In passages moving by conjunct motion, when a *détacher* effect is intended, it is customary to place dots over the notes; these dots do not indicate staccato, but merely the rather more weighty effect which even playing gives to the notes, in contrast with the habitually flexible treatment.

Secondly, the first note of each pair may be played slightly longer than the second. This effect is known as *Lourer*, and is used in passages which proceed by conjunct motion. Thirdly, in passages in which the first note of a pair has a dot affixed to it, the first note should be *very much* elongated; this effect is called *Pointer* or *Piquer*. The terms *pointer, piquer, marteler, passer* and *lourer* later became more or less synonymous; where dots are included in the written score a more exaggerated effect is of course intended. The whole of the passage from Loulié described above is so important that it is perhaps worth quoting in his own words:

Dans quelque Mesure que ce soit, particulièrement dans la Mesure à trois tems, les demi-tems s'exécutent de deux manières différentes, quoy que marquez de la même manière.

(1) On les fait quelquefois égaux.
Cette manière s'apelle détacher les Notes, on s'en sert dans les chants dont les sons se suivent par degrez interrompus, *et dans toute sorte de Musique étrangère où l'on ne pointe jamais, qu'il ne soit marqué.* [My italics.]

(2) On fait quelquesfois les premières demytems un peu plus longs.
Cette manière s'apelle *Lourer.* On s'en sert dans les chants dont les sons se suivent par degrez non interrompus.

(3) Il y a une troisième manière, où l'on fait le premier demi-tems beaucoup plus long que le deuxième mais le premier demi-tems doit avoir un point.
On apelle cette 3 manière Piquer ou Pointer.

In 1702, St-Lambert explains that these inequalities of rhythm are introduced 'parce que cette inégalité leur donne plus de grâce'. All the authorities insist that the purpose of the rhythmic alterations is to add subtlety and nuance, and point out that the correct application of them depends ultimately on *le bon goût*. St-Lambert goes on,'Quand on doit inégaliser les notes, c'est au goût à déterminer si elles doivent être peu ou beaucoup inégales; il y a des pièces où il sied bien de les faire fort inégales, et d'autres où elles veulent l'être moins; le goût juge de cela comme du mouvement'. Later, in 1775, Engramelle remarks that it is left to the performer to decide in what proportions

296

the long and short notes shall be played: 'Il est bien des endroits où les inégalités des notes varient dans le même air; quelques petits essais feront recontrer le bon et le meilleur ou pour l'égalité ou pour l'inégalité; l'on verra qu'un peu plus ou un peu moins d'inégalité dans les notes change considérablement le genre d'expression d'un air'. Choquel says that the inequality of rhythm 'lie le chant et le rend plus coulant'. Emy de l'Ilette suggests that 'inégalités' serve to 'donner de l'élégance à l'exécution de la musique', adding that they should be used only in the melodic parts ('parties chantantes'), not in 'l'accompagnement'.

The fundamental rule in the interpretation of unequal notes is stated by Monteclair: 'En quelque mesure que ce soit, les notes dont il faut quatre pour remplir un temps sont toujours inégales, la première un peu plus longue que la seconde'. Duval makes the same point in saying, 'On fait inégales toutes les notes de moindre valeur que celles qui sont indiquées par le chiffre inférieur'; except that in 2 : 4 only semiquavers and demi-semiquavers are played unequally; in 3 : 2 only crochets, quavers and subdivisions of quavers; in 3 : 4, 6 : 4, 9 : 4 and 12 : 4 only quavers and subdivisions of quavers; in 3 : 8, 6 : 8, 9 : 8 and 12 : 8 only semiquavers and demi-semi-quavers. Some theorists maintain that 'les notes inférieures aux notes inégales sont aussi inégales'; others maintain that when notes of smaller value than the unequal notes, as indicated by the time signature, occur in profusion, they are played unequal, while what would have been the unequal notes become equal. For instance, Corrette says, 'A 3 on fait les croches inégales, mais on les joue quelquefois égales, quand il y a des doubles croches, ce qu'on peut voir dans la passacaille d'Armide de M. de Lully et dans la chaconne des *Indes Galantes* de M. Rameau.'

All these devices refer mainly to notes grouped in fours or sixes. When quavers, semiquavers, and sometimes crochets are phrased in twos, with a slur over them and a dot above the second note, a different kind of inequality is implied. In this case, the second note is played slightly longer than the first; a modern interpretation of this notation would probably be directly contrary to eighteenth-century practice. This effect, which Couperin terms *couler*, occurs most frequently in passages involving 'drooping' pairs of quavers. A very slight rest is made after the second quaver.

We may summarize Borrel's conclusions as follows:

(1) There are two kinds of *notes inégales* in use in French music of the period. The most common concerns groups of four or six notes, in which the first note of each pair is elongated; the contrary effect is occasionally found in quavers slurred in pairs.

(2) The following notes are treated in the unequal manner:

In 3 : 1 time	minims.
In 3 : 2 time	'white' crochets and quavers.
In 2, 3, 3 : 4, 6 : 4, 9 : 4, 12 : 4 and ₵ time	quavers.

If the sign ₵ represents two slow beats the quavers are unequal; if it represents four quick beats the quavers are equal and semiquavers unequal.

In 2 : 4, 3 : 8, 4 : 8, 6 : 8, 9 : 8, 12 : 8 and C time	semiquavers.

Some authorities say that semiquavers, but not quavers, are played unequally in allemandes; others say that in allemandes all the notes are equal. Couperin seems to favour this second theory, since he often tells the performer to use the *pointé* effect in an allemande, implying that without this direction it would normally be played equally.

In 3 : 16, 4 : 16, 6 : 16, 9 : 16 and 12 : 16 time	demi-semiquavers.

(3) Notes that would normally be played unequally, in accordance with the rules outlined above, are played equally in the following circumstances:

(*a*) When they are interspersed with notes of shorter value. (As we have seen, however, this exception is not upheld by all theorists, some of whom maintain that in such cases, *all* the smaller valued notes are unequal.)

298

(b) When the lines move by disjunct motion; (and especially, therefore, in arpeggio figuration).

(c) When the words *Notes égales*, *Détachez*, or *Martelées* are written on the score, or when the tempo is marked *Mouvement décidé* or *marqué*.

(d) When there are dots or short lines above the notes which would otherwise be unequal.

(e) When the notes which would otherwise be unequal are interrupted by numerous rests.

(f) When they involve syncopations.

(g) When they involve repetitions of the same note.

(h) When they occur in accompanying parts.

(i) When they occur in the music of other countries. For instance, quavers are played equally in the 3 : 4 sarabande of the Italians, whereas they are unequal in the French sarabande.

(j) In very quick tempi, when the even method of playing semi-quavers, with a slight stress on the first of each group of four, is the only practicable method.

(k) When there is a slur over a group of four, six, or eight notes.

The last two points are not mentioned by the French writers, but occur in Quantz. It seems clear that the *lourer* effect cannot have been employed in very rapid passages.

(4) In passages in which dotted notes occur, the dot is always elongated, the short note played with a snap. In passages in which a dotted note is followed by a group of very rapid notes, the value of the dot is variable. The quick notes should take exactly as long as is indicated by the number of 'tails' affixed to them, the dot being stretched out, or contracted, in order to regularize the measure. In the following rhythm ♪ ♫♫ ♪ , the demi-semiquavers are played very quickly and brightly, never slurred.

(5) Triplet figures are always played equally.

(6) In recitative in duple or triple time, quavers which would normally be unequal are often sung equally; while in four-time recitative quavers which would normally be equal are often unequal. No rules can be established with reference to recitative, for here the rhythmic inequalities are dependent on 'l'expression de la Parole et le goût du Chant'.

(7) The proportionate lengths of the long and short notes in unequal groups depend on the character of the music. The correct interpretation can be achieved only through *le bon goût*, which D'Alembert's *Encyclopédie* of 1757 defines as 'Le talent de démêler dans les ouvrages de l'art ce qui doit plaire aux âmes sensibles, et ce qui doit les blesser'.

In view of the complexity of these regulations, it will perhaps be helpful if we analyse one of Couperin's works from the point of view of the *notes inégales*. Let us take the very representative chaconne *Les Folies Françoises*. This is in 3 : 4 time, so the norm of 'inégalité' is the quaver. In the first couplet, the quavers in bar fourteen are thus to be played with the first one of each pair slightly elongated; in bars three and eleven, on the other hand, the quavers are slurred in pairs, so here the *second* note of the pair is slightly longer than the first. The irregularities should not be strongly marked, since the character of the movement is quiet and dignified.

In the second couplet, bars seven and eight, the quavers are played equally, because they have a slur over them. In the third couplet, in dotted rhythm, the semiquavers after the dot should be very short and sharp, preceded by a brief rest. The fourth couplet, in 9 : 8, is consistently in quavers, and thus is played equally throughout. The fifth couplet is in 3 : 2, in a *pointé* rhythm with 'white' quavers. Here again the dots should be very elongated, and the white semiquavers very short; but in this case they should be smooth and suave, not sharp and precise.

In the sixth couplet the quavers in the left hand follow the usual convention, the first of each pair being slightly longer than the second; but the quaver appoggiaturas in bar fourteen are played with the second note slightly longer than the first (or possibly equally) while the quavers in the left hand are still played in the irregular fashion. The seventh couplet has the time signature of 1 : 2, divided into four 'white' quavers. Quavers in two time would normally be played unequally; but Couperin counteracts this by writing the word *Également* on the score. Here, then, there are four regular quavers a bar.

The eighth couplet, called *La Coquéterie*, has a coquettish medley of time signatures. In the 6 : 8 and 3 : 8 bars, the triplets and the groups of two semiquavers should be equal; in the 2 : 4 bars the scale passages in semiquavers should probably be unequal, unless the movement is taken fast.

The ninth couplet, marked *gravement*, is in *pointé* rhythm. The quavers with dots over them, in the left hand, are played evenly, and detached, rather heavily. Again, the dotted quavers are extremely elongated, the semiquavers very short and brisk. The tenth couplet is in 3 : 8, but the semiquavers are played equally because they proceed by disjunct motion, in arpeggio formation. In the eleventh couplet the 'white' quavers (of crochet value) are irregular; in the twelfth and last couplet, in 3 : 4, the semiquavers are equal because the speed is *très vite*, the quavers are equal because they have *détaché* dots above them. In *L'Ame en peine*, the wonderful little piece which follows *Les Folies Françoises*, the quavers and semiquavers are slightly shortened, except when, as in bar seventeen, they occur in suspensions. A rhythmic interpretation of all Couperin's pieces can be worked out on similar lines. In all difficult cases—and there are many passages in which the interpretation is ambiguous—the performer must rely, as did the eighteenth-century executant, on his own discretion and *bon goût*.

In practice the irregular notes do not occur as frequently as one might expect; for instance in the last *ordre* of all, the B minor from Book 4, there are almost no *notes inégales*. In *L'Exquise* the semiquavers are equal because the piece is an allemande; *Les Pavots*, in 2 time, has no groups of four quavers, only quavers slurred in pairs; the semiquavers in *Les Chinois* are marked *Viste* and therefore move equally, the only unequal notes being a few quavers slurred in pairs and an occasional double-dotted note; while in *Saillie* the scale-wise semiquavers are probably too rapid to be played unequally.

In this discussion we have mentioned only those conventional alterations of rhythm which involve problems of interpretation. Other alterations of rhythm are purely notational, for instance the combination of triplets with dotted figures, the semiquaver coinciding with the third quaver of the triplet.

C. Comments on Ornamentation

As with rhythm, so with ornamentation; this too, as has already been pointed out with reference to Couperin's music and that of his predecessors, is an intrinsic part of the subtlety of both line and harmony. The most important ornament is undoubtedly the *port de voix*, or appoggiatura. Couperin's explanations of the *port de voix* (for he adopts the terminology of the lutenists and the *air de cour* composers) are very inaccurate:

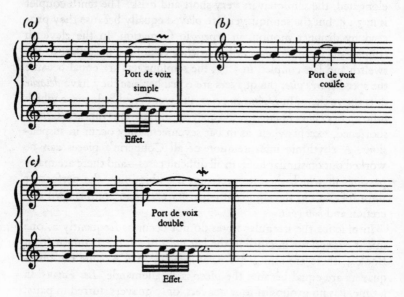

Here the pure form of the *port de voix* is the second cited. As Dolmetsch points out, what Couperin calls the *port de voix simple* is really the *port de voix pincé* (i.e. with a mordent); and in the *port de voix double* it is not the appoggiatura, but the mordent, which is doubled. Couperin makes the important point that in all the *ports de voix* the ornamental notes must be struck *with* the harmony note; and that the length of the ornamental notes must be proportionate to the value of the note to which they are attached. As Dolmetsch remarks, however, he does not tell us what this proportion is. According to C. P. E. Bach, the *port de voix* takes half the value of the harmony note in duple times, two-thirds in triple times. It is always slurred to, and played slightly louder than, the note of resolution. The ornamental notes must never anticipate the beat, because then the effect of discord is ruined; on the other hand, harmonic considerations frequently lead to modifications in the normal treatment of the appoggiatura. These are not dealt with by Couperin, but are covered by Dolmetsch, on the evidence of other contemporary authorities. Again, in difficult cases the player must make his own decisions, in accordance with *le bon goût*; he will usually find some special case, cited in Dannreuther or Dolmetsch, which is relevant to any problem Couperin's work may offer. (See Appendix E, Section II.)

Couperin's treatment of the mordent or *pincé* is more straightforward. These tables from the 1713 book of clavecin pieces, and from the *méthode* of 1717, offer no difficulty, except possibly that the use of a note of full value for the final resolution of the ornament might erroneously suggest that the mordent anticipates the beat:

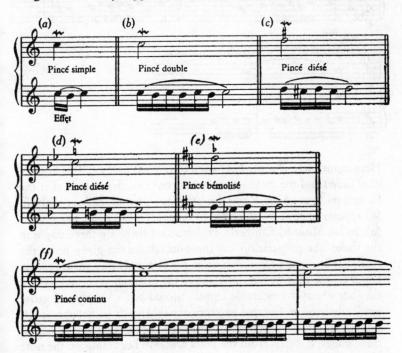

Mordents on long notes should be more extended (*doublé*) than those on short notes. The *pincé continu* is a shake on the note *below* the main note. *Pincés* always end with the note which they decorate.

Couperin gives the following table of *tremblements*, or *cadences* (not to be confused with the rhythmic device referred to above), in the 1713 preface:

Here again there is some confusion over terminology. The *tremblement ouvert* and the *tremblement fermé* seem to differ only in that the former resolves upwards and the latter downwards; and the shake in (*d*) appears to be as much prepared (*appuyé*) as the shake in example (*a*). In his *Méthode*, Couperin explains that there are three stages in the shake: the preparation on the note above the given note; the shake itself; and the resolution on to the essential note. Shakes *always* begin on the tone or semitone above the essential note, and, where they are of any considerable length, should begin slowly and grow gradually quicker. In rapid passages, the shake—or half-shake, as it is sometimes called in such circumstances—has no time to establish its three stages; it differs from the *pincé double* in beginning on the note above the essential note, instead of on the note below it.

Most of the long shakes end with a turn; this Couperin indicates by the following sign: ∾. He does not devote much attention to the turn itself, giving only these two examples in the *Méthode*:

304

Sometimes he places the turn sign after the essential note; in that case, it is played after the principal note has been sounded. Usually it takes half the principal note's value in duple time, a third in triple time.

Couperin gives two examples of the slide:

Here again his notation suggests that the ornament anticipates the beat; but his verbal description is unambiguous. What Couperin calls the *Accent* is distinct from the accent of Bach, which is an appoggiatura. Couperin's ornament is derived from lute technique, being originally the stopping of an auxiliary note on the lute without actually plucking it. The effect is similar to the use of sympathetic vibrations in modern piano music, and would be more adequately described by Rousseau's term *L'Aspiration*, were it not that Couperin uses the term *Aspiration* for a completely different ornament. The effect, whatever one calls it, cannot really be translated into terms of the harpsichord; the player approximates to it by playing the auxiliary note, usually a tone above and in dotted rhythm, as faintly and vaguely as possible:

This is identical with one variety of Bach's *Nachschlag*.[28]

Two examples of *batteries*, or upward and downward arpeggios, are given in Couperin's 1713 collection:

Here too the first note of the arpeggio should come on the beat. These arpeggios are much employed in pieces influenced by lute technique. The dash over a note does not indicate a real staccato, but a more emphatic, *détaché* treatment.

Some very beautiful effects of rubato may be obtained through the use of what Couperin calls the *aspiration* and the *suspension*. These terms should not be confused with the *aspiration* of Rousseau and other authorities previously referred to, nor, of course, with the normal harmonic suspension. Couperin notates them thus:

and describes them in these words:

Quant à l'effet sensible de l'aspiration, il faut détacher la note sur laquelle

[28] In many respects Bach's ornamentation seems to derive from that of Couperin. His *Trillo* is the same as Couperin's *tremblement détaché*; his *Mordant* is Couperin's *pincé simple*; his *Cadence* Couperin's *double*; his *Accent steigend* Couperin's *port de voix*; and his *Accent und Mordant* Couperin's *port de voix simple*. There is no evidence that Bach was acquainted with Couperin's *L'Art de toucher le Clavecin*. But of course he knew Couperin's clavecin music, and copied out *Les Bergeries* in Anna Magdalena's *Noten-buch*. He acquired a fairly extensive knowledge of French music at Celle, about 1700; it was probably at this time that he copied out Nicolas de Grigny's fine *Livre d'Orgue*, and two clavecin suites of Dieupart, with their table of ornaments as appendix. He may also have known the keyboard music of Gaspard le Roux, since Pirro tells us that pieces by this composer are found in a notebook of Bach's pupil, Krebs.

elle est posée, moins vivement dans les choses tendres et lentes que dans celles qui sont légères, et rapides.

A l'égard de le suspension, elle n'est guères usitée que dans les morceaux tendres et lents. Le silence qui précède la note sur laquelle elle est marquée doit être réglé par le goût de la personne qui l'exécute.

Employed with taste and feeling, by 'personnes susceptibles de sentiment', these ornaments can greatly enhance the music's expressiveness. But it is important that the slight catch in the breath of the ornaments should not disrupt the flow of the lines. Once more, their purpose is to impart nuance and sensitivity, without harming the architectural proportions. Couperin adds that effects of *aspiration* and *suspension* may be effectively combined with the *tremblement*, though only, one imagines, in rather slow pieces. He also claims to be the first to use these ornaments. He may have been the first to develop them extensively in keyboard music, but similar devices must have been in common use among the lutenists.

As *suspensions* and *aspirations* may be combined with *tremblements*, so most of Couperin's ornaments are compound ones. He seems to have considered it accepted procedure that the *port de voix* should be rounded off by a mordent; and that the *tremblement* should be prepared by an appoggiatura. He makes no reference to the acciaccatura, which is less congenial to his idiom than to the more percussive style of Scarlatti. Couperin's most important pronouncement on the general significance of the ornamentation in his music occurs in the preface to his third book of clavecin pieces, when he protests against performers who have not taken the ornaments seriously enough:

Je suis toujours surpris, après les soins qui je me suis donnés pour marquer les agréments qui conviennent à mes pieces, d'entendre les personnes qui les ont apprises sans s'y assujettir. C'est une négligence qui n'est pas pardonnable, d'autant qu'il n'est point arbitraire d'y mettre tels agréments qu'on veut. Je déclare que mes pièces doivent être exécutées comme je les ai marquées et qu'elles ne feront jamais impression sur les personnes qui ont le goût vrai, tant qu'on n'observera pas à la lettre tout ce que j'ai marqué, sans augmentation ni diminution.

Here again we have the insistence on the connection between ornamentation and sensibility; and the suggestion that the ultimate judge must always be, in the self-assured phrase of the period, 'le goût vrai'.

D. Comments on Fingering and Phrasing

In the *Méthode* Couperin gives copious examples of his methods of fingering which, he claims, constitute a new system. They do not, perhaps, seem very new to us, being closer to the methods of the sixteenth and seventeenth centuries than to modern technique. But though they concentrate on the second, third, and fourth fingers and share the old music's distrust of the thumb, they anticipate the modern method of playing parallel thirds smoothly and they establish the principle of finger-substitution to secure a legato. Moreover, we must remember, as Dolmetsch has demonstrated, that the fingering and phrasing of the old music were always inter-dependent. It may be more difficult to play Couperin with his own than with a modern fingering; but the performer who uses Couperin's fingering can be sure that he will be phrasing the music correctly. Much the same is true of the keyboard work of Bach, whose system of fingering was directly based on Couperin's. For both composers, fingering was not a means of scampering about the keyboard with maximum facility; it was a means of revealing, as fully as possible, the musical sense of a composition. These two, among many possible, examples will make this clear without further comment:

etc. (Les Silvains)

(L'Amazone)

The general nature of Couperin's phrasing is indicated in his own copious and accurate marking. Not only slurs, across the beat and with the beat:

but dashes, a more exaggerated effect, both across the beat and with the beat:

and commas:

and a combination of all three:

are used to make the groupings unmistakable. It is patent from all the examples which Couperin gives that the continuous legato of nineteenth-century music, or even of the Viennese classics, is alien to Couperin's music as it is to Bach's. The life of the phrasing depends on the clear articulation of short clauses phrased, on principles analogous to string bowing, as much across the beat as with it; and

309

some of the most subtle effects arise from the combination of contrasting phrasings in different parts. (See Appendix E.)

What one might not gather from the phrase marks, but is clear from the fingering, is that even unimportant passages of figuration should be phrased according to the same general principles. The fingering of *Le Moucheron* provides an admirable instance:

(La Moucheron)

while the fingering of the thirds in *La Passacaille* suggests that they should be phrased in pairs, across the beat:

(La Passacaille)

It is for the light which it throws on such minute points of phrasing that Couperin's fingering should be studied by all conscientious performers of his keyboard music today.

The comma, which Couperin introduces into his later work, can perhaps best be regarded not as an authentic phrase mark, but as a rhythmic device analogous to the *aspiration* and *suspension*; Couperin's comment on it is as follows:

On trouvera un signe nouveau dont voicy la figure[,]. C'est pour marquer la terminaison des chants ou de nos Pièces harmoniques, et pour faire comprendre qu'il faut un peu séparer la fin d'un chant avant de passer à celui qui le suit, cela est presque imperceptible en général, quoy qu'on n'observant pas ce petit silence, les personnes de goût sentent qu'il manque quelque chose à l'exécution, en un mot, c'est la différence de ceux qui lisent de suite, avec ceux qui s'arrêtent aux points et aux virgules; ces silences se doivent faire sentir sans altérer la mesure.

E. Comments on Continuo Playing

Couperin advocates that one should not take up continuo playing until one has become reasonably proficient as a solo performer. The reasons he gives are both intellectual and physical. On the one side, the expressive realization and performance of the bass line calls for a high degree of skill and taste; on the other side, the right hand's playing of regular sequences of chords, as opposed to the melodic style of solo clavecin music, might have a stiffening effect on inexperienced fingers, 'la main droite n'étant occupée qu'à faire des accords'. This remark would seem to indicate that Couperin, in his realization of the continuo parts, followed a widespread convention, playing the bass line as written, in a very cantabile style, with the left hand, and filling in the chords with the right. Such a treatment would be consistent with the melodic-harmonic compromise we have frequently noted in his music, and with his tendency to base his composition on a dialogue between soprano and bass.

There are a considerable number of contemporary treatises which provide evidence as to the interpretation of the figured bass in French baroque music. The two most important are perhaps the *Traité de l'accompagnement* of St-Lambert published in 1707 and that of Boyvin published in 1715. The following comments are based largely on these two works.

Originally, when the harmony was comparatively simple, the basses were unfigured and the chords employed did not extend beyond diatonic triads on the bass note and, in certain circumstances, first inversions. Figures became necessary as harmony grew more complicated. In Couperin's day all the diatonic concords, chords of the seventh and ninth, and various dissonant suspensions were indicated by the figures. The sharp sign denoted a major or augmented interval, the flat denoted a minor or diminished interval, and the natural sign was used for a major interval that could otherwise be minor, or to indicate the return of an interval to its initial form. Used without a figure the sharp sign meant the major third or triad, the flat sign the minor.

Normally one chord is played on the continuo for each note of the bass, but where the bass line moves by conjunct degrees, or when the bass is rapid, one chord on the clavecin may serve for two or more

311

notes on the bass line as played by the viol. These exceptions to the rule are described in detail by St-Lambert, thus:

(1) Quand les notes de Basse sont par degrez successifs on n'est pas obligé de les accompagner toutes; on peut n'accompagner que de deux notes l'une alternativement.

(2) Quand les notes marchent par degrez interrompus, il faut aussi les accompagner toutes, *excepté lorsqu'un même accord peut servir à plusieurs notes*. (My italics.)

(3) Quand la mesure est à trois temps et que l'air se joue vite, on peut se contenter d'accompagner seulement la première note de chaque mesure; pourvu que les notes marchent par degrez successifs.

(4) Quand la mesure est si pressée que l'Accompagnateur n'a pas la commodité de jouer toutes les notes, il peut se contenter de jouer et d'accompagner seulement la première note de chaque mesure, laissant au basses de Viole ou de Violon à jouer toutes les notes.

On the other hand, 'quand les basses sont peu chargées de notes ... il peut y ajouter d'autres notes pour figurer d'avantage, pourvu qu'il connoisse que cela ne fera point de tort à l'Air. . . . Car l'Accompagnement est fait pour seconder la voix et non pas pour l'étouffer et la défigurer par un mauvais carillon. . . . Quiconque joue en Concert doit jouer pour l'honneur et la perfection du Concert et non pas pour son honneur particulier'. Long-held pedal notes especially provide opportunities for the player to decorate the bass with chords not indicated in the figures, though of course he must take care not to ruin the harmony.

The usual convention in France was for the left hand to play the bass line alone while the right hand filled out the chords in three or sometimes four parts:

La méthode la plus ordinaire et la plus commode est de faire tous les accompagnements de la main droite. Elle fait communément trois parties, quelquefois aussi jusqu'à quatre, parce qu'on double quelque consonance, ou parfois aussi la seconde, suivant que la main se trouve disposée. Ainsi la main gauche ne joue simplement que la Basse, sinon qu'elle fait l'Octave quand la main droite tient un accord parfait. (Boyvin.)

On joue la Basse de la main gauche, et à chaque note de Basse que l'on touche, on en ajoute trois autres de la main droite, faisant ainsi un accord sur chaque note. (St-Lambert.)

If the voice to be accompanied is very slight, or if the texture of the music is thin, the notes of the right hand chord may be reduced to two. On the other hand, in powerful passages, for instance in choral or symphonic music, the left hand may double the right with three or four part chords also, subject to certain restrictions:

La main gauche peut aussi doubler les Sixtes et les Tierces mineures qui se trouvent sur les diézes, sur les Mi, les Si en montant, et autres, ce qui fait beaucoup d'effet dans un grand Concert. (Boyvin.)

On peut doubler de la main gauche quelqu'une des Parties que fait la main droite; on peut même doubler toutes, si les voix sont très-fortes. (St-Lambert.)

Dissonances should not be doubled, however, except the second.

Dissonance was encouraged in the continuo part, since 'une musique sans dissonance est une soupe sans sel, un ragoût sans épices, une compagnie sans femmes'. The dissonances of the continuo were treated, moreover, with surprising freedom:

Quoyque l'usage ordinare demande que la Dissonance soit précédée d'une Consonance, on ne laisse pas de se dispenser quelquefois de cette Régle, et on en fait qui ne sont pas précédées; cela se connoit par le bon usage et le bon goût. (Boyvin.)

Eugène Borrel has demonstrated that it was customary to introduce dissonances into the continuo part even when they were not indicated by the figures. St-Lambert remarks

on peut en jouer quelquefois une quatrième [note] dans les accords prescrits par les Régles ordinaires, soit pour adoucir la dureté d'une dissonance ou au contraire pour la rendre plus piquante.

and according to this principle some remarkable effects were obtained. Not only were sevenths and ninths added where appropriate, but the texture was often surprisingly enriched with added seconds, sixths and sevenths. These were not necessarily resolved in the normal way, though they were dissolved into the flow of the chords by ties and retardations.

As a general principle it was considered advisable to preserve continuity between the chords by tying notes common to two successive harmonies:

Quand on passe d'un accord à un autre, on doit examiner si quelques-unes des notes de l'accord dont on sort ne pourront point servir à l'accord où l'on entre; et quand cela se peut il ne faut pas changer ces notes. (St-Lambert.)

La main droite doit toujours prendre ses accords au lieu le plus proche où ils se trouvent, et ne les aller jamais chercher loin d'elle. (St-Lambert.)

Normally the two hands should not move far apart, and should play in the middle of the keyboard, except for some special effect of sonority when they may move together to the top or bottom register:

La Partie supérieure de l'accompagnement ne doit jamais monter plus haut que le Mi de la dernière Octave du Clavier, ou tout au plus jusqu'au Fa, en passant, excepté que la Basse devient Haut Contre; car alors on monte tout fort haut. (St-Lambert.)

An excellent example of this exception is provided by the *Adolescentulus sum* of Couperin's *Quatre Versets d'un Motet*.

So long as a full and satisfactory harmony was obtained, the theorists did not severely enforce, in continuo playing, the usual rules governing consecutives. As a general principle of course 'les mains doivent toujours faire mouvement contraire'; but

Quoique deux Octaves et deux Quintes de suite par mouvement semblable soient ce qu'il y a de plus rigoureusement deffendu en Musique, on n'en fait pas grands scrupules dans l'accompagnement,

especially 'quand on accompagne dans un grand chœur de Musique où le bruit des autres Instruments couvre tellement le Clavecin'. The progression from the diminished to the perfect fifth was even regarded as admirable.

The accepted ornaments, especially trills and the Chute, were frequently employed in continuo parts, often adding their share to the dissonance:

On peut soit sur l'orgue, soit sur le Clavecin, faire de temps en temps quelques tremblemens, ou quelqu'autre agrément, soit dans la Basse ou dans les Parties, selon qu'on juge que les passages le demandent. On fait toujours un tremblement sur la note qui porte un accord double quand cette note est d'une valeur un peu considérable. On en fait un sur la penultième d'une Cadence Parfaite. (St-Lambert.)

In accompanying recitative, and sometimes in instrumental passages in a relatively free movement and at moderate pace, the chords should be split or arpeggiated at varying speeds and with varying degrees of violence, according to the nature of the passions the music is expressing. But

Les harpégemens ne sont convenables que dans le Récitatif, où il n'y a proprement point de mesure: car dans les Airs de mouvement il faut frapper les accords tout à la fois avec la Basse: Excepté que quand toutes les notes de la Basse sont Noires, et que la mesure est à 3 tems, on sépare les notes de chaque accord de telle manière qu'on en réserve toujours une pour la faire parler entre 2 tems. Cela forme une espece de battement qui sied tout à fait bien.

And

Sur l'orgue on ne rebat point les accords et l'on n'use guère d'harpége-mens: on lie au contraire beaucoup les sons en coulant les mains adroite-ment. On double rarement les Parties. (St-Lambert.)

The general conclusion one must come to is that the contemporary realization of the continuo was closer than one might have imagined to the interpretation which a sensitive musician of today would be likely to give, if left to his own devices. This is especially the case in the matter of the added seconds, sixths, and so on.

This free homophonic realization of the continuo should be regarded as the norm in Couperin's work. But there is evidence that Bach played continuo parts in a highly polyphonic style, and there is even a tradition that Handel's realizations involved counterpoint. St-Lambert's treatise suggests that the French were not averse to contrapuntal realizations in certain circumstances:

Quand on accompagne une voix seule qui chante quelqu'Air de Mouve-ment, dans lequel il y a plusieurs imitations de chants, tels que sont les Airs Italiens, on peut imiter sur son clavecin le Sujet et les Fugues de l'air, faisant entrer les Parties l'une après l'autre. Mais cela demande une science consom-mée et il faut être du premier ordre pour y réussir.

Since Couperin, though not a polyphonist of Bach's kind, is in some ways the most Bach-like of late baroque composers, some such contrapuntal passages would seem to be appropriate to his continuo parts, on certain occasions, in his more linear compositions; the last page of the 2me Leçon des Ténèbres is an obvious example. Such passages should be regarded, however, as exceptional, and the texture should never be allowed to grow crowded. Here as elsewhere the final arbiter is le bon goût: 'Le discernement délicat d'un accom-pagnateur habile pourroit peut-être lui en permettre encore d'autres dont il n'est pas aisé de parler, puisqu'elles ne dépendraient que de son bon goût; car on sait que le bon goût détermine souvent à des choses dont on ne peut donner d'autre raison que le goût même'.

All the theorists insist that the difficult task in continuo playing is not to realize the bass according to the rules—in the matter of correctness considerable latitude may be allowed; the difficulty is rather to interpret the bass in a manner which is exactly suited to the spirit—gay, fierce, doleful or languishing—of the music. If the player introduces ornaments or dissonances on his own initiative they must be appropriate to the feeling. He must alter his clavecin or organ registration according to the sentiments expressed and according to the nature—the power or the frailty—of the resources which he is accompanying. Always he must remember that he does not play for himself alone but for 'l'honneur et la perfection du Concert'. Geminiani makes the same point in his treatise on thorough-bass:

A good Accompanyer ought to possess the Faculty of playing all sorts of Basses in different manners, so as to be able, on proper Occasions, to enliven the Composition and delight the Singer and Player. But he is to exercise this Faculty with Judgment, Taste, and Discretion, agreeable to the Stile of the Composition, and the Manner and Intention of the Performer. If the Accompanyer thinks of nothing but satisfying his own Whims and Caprice, he may perhaps be said to play well, but will certainly be said to accompany ill.

Couperin himself regarded sensitive continuo playing as of hardly less importance than solo playing; though amour-propre may make solo playing seem more rewarding!

S'il était permis d'opter entre l'accompagnement et les pièces pour porter l'un ou l'autre à l'accompagnement, je sens que l'amour-propre me ferait préférer les pièces à l'accompagnement. Je conviens que rien n'est plus amusant pour soi-même et ne nous lie plus avec les autres que d'être bon accompagnateur. Mais quelle injustice! L'accompagnement du clavecin dans ces occasions n'est considéré comme les fondemens d'un édifice, qui cependant soutiennent tout et dont on ne parle jamais.

F. Comments on Aims and Intentions

A famous passage from *L'Art de toucher le Clavecin* merits some discussion here:

J'ai toujours eu un objet, en composant ces pièces; des occasions différentes me l'ont fourni: ainsi les titres répondent aux idées que j'ai eues. On me dispensera d'en rendre compte. Cependant, comme, parmi ces titres, il y en a qui semblent me flatter, il est bon d'avertir que les pièces qui les portent sont des espaces de portraits qu'on a trouvés quelquefois assez rassemblants sous mes doigts, et que la plupart de ces titres avantageux sont plûtot donnés aux aimables originaux que j'ai voulu représenter qu'aux copies que j'en ai tirées.

The pieces with 'titres avantageux' are, of course, those called *La Majestueuse*, *L'Auguste*, etc., and possibly those called La Belle this or the other.

It has been found surprising that so classical and 'objective' a composer as Couperin should thus confess to an expressive intention; and it has sometimes been remarked that his 'portraits', as such, are not very successful, since they mostly sound alike. This type of remark is not normally meant as a pejorative reflection on Couperin's *music*; but it does perhaps suggest an inability to comprehend what Couperin, and French classical civilization, have to offer. Couperin's stylization is, as we have seen, the reflection of the world in which he lived and worked; he could not, and would not have wished to, modify it. But, as we have also seen, the essence of that civilization was that it permitted great subtlety and variety of emotional experience within its stylization; and the variety—psychological as well as musical—is there in Couperin's portraits when one has learned to listen to them. The point is not one of much practical importance, since one cannot estimate Couperin's psychological acumen, as revealed in his portraits, without personal acquaintance with the people whom he is portraying. It is probable, however, that the appropriateness of the portrait was clear enough to Couperin's contemporaries. In any case, we must remember the words of Rousseau:

L'art du musicien ne consiste point à peindre immédiatement les objets, mais à mettre l'âme dans une disposition semblable à celle où la mettrait leur presence.

And the idea of the musical portrait links up with the preoccupation of the period with psychology and 'character'.

Far from Couperin's practice being in any way exceptional, all the theorists of the classical age insist on music's expressive purpose. Lecerf de la Viéville even said that 'la science de la musique de l'Eglise, plus que de la profane, n'est autre chose que la façon d'émouvoir vraiment et à propos'; while in the succeeding generation the theory of imitation became one of the basic tenets of the Encyclopaedists:

Toute musique qui ne peint rien n'est que du bruit. (D'Alembert.)
La musique qui ne peint rien est insipide. (Marmontel.)
Il falloit donner aux sentiments humains plus d'expression et plus d'accent par les formes de la musique. (Perrin.)

L'expression de la pensée, du sentiment, des passions, doit être le vrai but de la musique. (Rameau.)

So deeply engrained was the pictorial and expressive habit in the minds of musicians that pure instrumental music met with considerable opposition in some quarters, simply on the grounds of its purity. 'Toute cette musique purement instrumentale,' says D'Alembert, 'sans dessein, sans objet, ne parle ni à l'esprit ni à l'âme et mérite qu'on lui demande avec Fontenelle "Sonate, que me veux-tu?" Il faut avouer qu'en general on ne sent toute l'expression de la musique que lorsqu'elle est liée à des paroles et à des danses.' Though one may think it odd that music such as Couperin's sonatas should ever have been considered *sans dessein* or *sans objet* one can see that D'Alembert's objection, however naïve, derives from an instinct that was healthy enough—from a belief that music ought to have a direct relation to a social function.

This preference for the opera, for music which was dependent on something outside itself, reached its culmination in the writings of Rousseau. The only eighteenth-century theorists who opposed the imitative view were the Chevalier de Castallux and Gui de Chabanon, who both maintained that music was not imitative but creative; therefore a purely instrumental music might be as significant as operatic music. Though music might not crudely imitate natural phenomena, however, it was in a deeper sense an imitation of human emotion. Both writers stressed the theory of communication.

In England a similar attitude is found in Charles Avison's *Essay of Musical Expression* of 1752. He maintained that 'the composer is culpable who, for the sake of a low and trifling imitation, deserts the beauties of Expression':

And, as dissonance and Shocking sounds cannot be called Musical Expression, so neither do I think, can mere imitation of several other things be entitled to this name, which, however, among the generality of mankind, hath often obtained it. Thus the gradual rising or falling of the notes in a long succession, is often used to denote ascent or descent; broken intervals to denote an interrupted motion; a number of quick divisions to describe swiftness or flying; sounds resembling laughter, to describe laughter; with a number of other contrivances of a parallel kind, which it is needless here to mention. Now all these I should chuse rather to style Imitation than Expression; because it seems to me, that their tendency is rather to fix the Hearer's attention on the similitude between the sounds and the things

318

which they describe, and thereby to excite a reflex act of the understanding, than to affect the Heart and raise the passions of the Soul.

On the other hand Avison follows the Encyclopædists in believing that 'the finest instrumental music may be considered as an imitation of the vocal'. Only Diderot seems to have had any appreciation of the individual techniques—as opposed to 'affections'—of instruments, and of the importance which was to be attributed to those qualities in the music of the future.

Couperin seems to have been unimpressed by the contemporary insistence on the supremacy of music which is closely related to literature. Even in the field of vocal music his work to Latin words (which as Brijon points out in his *Réflexions sur la Musique* of 1763 were often unintelligible to the audience) is both more extensive and more interesting than his work to French words; while many of his most psychologically expressive portraits dispense with words altogether. Since Couperin's position as one of the greatest masters of his time seems to have been unquestioned, it would appear that the pronouncements of the theorists on the subject of instrumental music were not taken too seriously.

Not all Couperin's portraits are of persons; some are of scenes and places (*Les Moissonneurs, Les Vergers Fleuris*). The descriptions are stylized but are, and are meant to be, atmospheric and evocative. While some of the titles are no doubt purely fanciful or wilfully enigmatic, far more have a realistic intent than one might superficially imagine. If they seem artificial it is because the world which Couperin imitates is itself so close to art, for it entailed, to a degree which is seldom found in communities, both emotion and discipline, both complexity and order.

The significance of Expression in baroque music has, I think, sometimes been misunderstood. The nature of Bach's musical symbolism of religious truths as described by Schweitzer and Pirro, and of Couperin's musical symbolism of character and place, is basically similar. In both cases there is no question of our being able to draw, as it were, a graph of the pictorial, descriptive and expressive implications which lurk beneath what may appear to be a piece of absolute instrumental music. The point is simply that certain extramusical concepts served to release in Bach's and Couperin's mind an appropriate musical response. The analogical habit was hardly a conscious intellectual process for them, however naïve the interpretations of the theorists may have become. Bach embodied the conception of Christ on the Cross in tone as naturally as a painter would express it in visual symbols; similarly with Couperin's musical presentation of the pathos of Harlequin. And there is nothing odd about this; both Bach and Couperin are, in this respect as in many others, the end of a tradition. It is almost possible to say that up to their day the dependence of music on extra-musical elements —and in particular the intimate relation between music and literature—was accepted without question. It is only because we have been brought up in a culture which takes for granted a divorce between music and literature and the other arts that we can find anything at all peculiar in their method. The divorce is a matter of some general aesthetic significance which does not work to our advantage.

All through baroque music the expressive elements really amount to a kind of musical (not literary or pictorial) stylization. Whereas the nineteenth-century composer tended to think of his work as self-expression, the attitude of the baroque composer is not less passionate but more objective. His selfhood is revealed through the expression and description of something outside himself; consider the significance of the Emblematic habit all through the seventeenth century. The Crucifixus of the B minor Mass is one of the most heart-rending pieces of music ever written; but Bach thought of it primarily as Christ's suffering, which happened also to be his own, and that of the people who listened to it. Similarly, in its smaller way, the pathos of Couperin's Harlequin is primarily Harlequin's suffering, which is also Couperin's, and which corresponds to a deeply rooted melancholy in his society. Both Couperin and Bach invented a musical myth apposite to the myths by the light of which people live. There is no egoism in their music. If Bach composed for 'the glory of God and the instruction of my neighbour' Couperin did much the same, though he would not have put it in quite those terms. He would have said he wrote for the entertainment of *les honnêtes gens*; but this would have implied both that his music was a communal activity, and that it was an act of praise to an Absolute, because he knew what *honnêteté* was.

Descartes, who so neatly summarized the consciousness of the *grand siècle*, had regarded music primarily as the creation of intellectual order. This is why he tended to suggest that simple music was *ipso facto* 'better' than complicated music; why he preferred homophony to polyphony; and why he tried to develop a rationalistic system of harmony which tabulated the emotional effects of chords as rigidly as Lebrun tabulated the pictorial counterparts of different passions. Lully was the realization of Descartes's musical theory, as he was of Boileau's aesthetic, despite the latter's strong disapproval of the opera. But his was a creative, not a text-book, realization; and he showed that the search for order and symmetry entailed a humane attitude to the problems which people have to face in living together. In Couperin's subtler style there is the same search for clarity and order, without Lully's (and Descartes's) tendency to simplify the issues. Couperin's clarity is both more hardly won and more richly satisfying. His 'philosophy of music' cannot be separated from the music itself.

Chapter Thirteen

Couperin's Resources and his use of them

(with Notes on the Modern Performance of his Work)

IN THIS SECTION I propose first to attempt a brief summary of the conditions governing music-making in Couperin's day; and then to offer some more detailed and specific comments on his use of the media which were available to him.

A composer brought up in Couperin's environment would have had no need to complain of a lack of opportunity to express himself. Whatever the direction of his talents, there was plenty of demand for his work. The choices open to him may be grouped as follows:

(1) Opera and ballet.
(2) Musique de Chasse.
(3) Musique des Soupers.
(4) Musique des soirées et des bals.
(5) Chamber music for the concerts du dimanche.
(6) Church music for the Chapelle Royale.

The following orchestras and bands took part in these various activities:

Les Vingt-quatre Violons du Roi.
Les Petits Violons (directed by Lully and used especially for ballet music and dances).
Les Menus Plaisirs du Roi.
La Musique de la Reine.
La Musique de la Chambre du Roi (for ballets, balls, fêtes and les Soupers).
Les Corps des Violons du Cabinet.
La Musique de la Chapelle Royale.
Les Bandes de la Grande et de la Petite Écurie (for festivities, military reviews, hunting expeditions, open-air fêtes, etc.).

The ballets and even the operas sometimes took place in the open air, in specially constructed settings; the architect Vigarani, for instance, designed a 'parc' for the performance of *La Princesse d'Elide* in 1664. For these performances many of the different instrumental groups combined together. For the *Fêtes nautiques* which were staged on the Grand Canal as many as a hundred players were often employed; here the violins, viols, lutes, theorbes, guitars and clavecins of the various bands of the Chambre and Chapelle performed with the flutes, fifes, oboes, trumpets, horns and drums of the bands of the Ecuries. La Lande in particular excelled at writing grand music for these festivities.

From 1669, the operas were repeated before the public in Paris, at a theatre established by Perrin with the King's authority. Lully took over the public performance of all opera in 1672, establishing an opera house in the rue de Vaugirard. Later, operas were produced in the Salle des Tuileries.

Most of Couperin's church music was written for performance in the Chapelle Royale. Originally built in 1682, the Chapel was reconstructed in 1710 according to plans of Robert de Cotte and Mansart. In its revised form it was not only an extremely beautiful and harmoniously proportioned religious establishment, but a magnificently equipped concert hall. The four-manual organ was placed above the altar, and was flanked by terraces which accommodated the choristers, orchestra and conductor. The choir normally numbered twenty-four and the orchestra nineteen; but on festive occasions there were sometimes ninety or more performers. In Couperin's time the full complement of singers and players comprised ten sopranos, twenty-four altos, twenty tenors, twenty-three baritones, eleven basses, six violins, three continuo instruments, three bass viols, two flutes, two serpents and three bassoons.

High Mass was celebrated every day. Three motets were included; a lengthy movement lasting from the beginning of the ceremony to the Elevation (about a quarter of an hour); a short piece sung by a few picked voices during the Elevation; and the *Domine salvum fac regem* for full choir and orchestra as a conclusion. The motets were usually scored for soloists, chorus, strings and organ, with occasionally some obbligato wind instruments. The choral and string writing was commonly in five parts.

323

Two choirs, working in alternation, were maintained; only thus, one presumes, was it possible for the singers to keep pace with the very extensive repertory of new works. It was probably for this reason that four organist-directors of the Chapel were appointed simultaneously, working in rotation for periods of three months each a year. The royal performances of church music were repeated publicly at Notre-Dame de Versailles, St Germain l'Auxerrois, and the big Parisian churches, St Jean en Grève, St Louis des Jésuites, St Paul and St Jacques de la Boucherie.

Public concerts, in the modern sense of the term, were not a conspicuous feature of musical activity in the early part of the seventeenth century. But Louis XIV's Concerts du dimanche were regularly organized professional performances; and they set a fashion which rapidly increased during the latter part of Couperin's life. Mme de Montespan organized music-making at Clagny where, according to Mme de Sévigné, 'il y a concert tous les jours'; Mme de Maintenon put on regular concerts to enliven the King's *tristesse*.

In 1725 Philidor founded the institution of the Concerts Spirituels at the Salle des Suisses aux Tuileries. These were public concerts of church music, at which Italian as well as French works were frequently played. During the eighteenth century the increasingly powerful rich bourgeoisie emulated the aristocracy by encouraging and financing concerts of chamber and orchestral music. The artistic activities of Crozat (patron of Watteau) and of Le Riche de la Pouplinière, friend and patron of Rameau and later of Stamitz, were no less celebrated than those of the Duchesse du Maine, whose salon preserved the old aristocratic dignity and haughty refinement.

Of Couperin's own works the organ masses were written before he received any official court appointment, as part of his duties at St Gervais. His later motets and *elevations* were mostly composed for the Chapelle Royale. His concerted music for instruments, in the form of sonatas, suites, and *concerts royaux*, was written for the King's concerts du dimanche. The solo harpsichord music was partly intended for these entertainments, partly for the use of his pupils and, perhaps, for private performance to the King and nobility. It will be observed that Couperin restricted himself to the more intimate forms of music-making current in his day. This, as we have suggested previously, was a matter of temperament, and does not imply any restriction on the range and nobility of his art.

After this brief survey of the various fields in which Couperin might have worked, we will now examine his treatment of the media in which he chose to express himself.

A. Organ Music

Couperin's organ at St Gervais is one of the most magnificent of all baroque instruments. It was mostly built in the early part of the seventeenth century, probably by Pierre Pescheur and Pierre Thierry; additions and improvements throughout the century were mainly the work of later members of the Thierry family, and important modifications were made in 1768 by the great organ builder F. H. Clicquot. This, however, was after Couperin's day; the instrument he used must have been substantially the same as that played by his uncle Louis.

During the nineteenth century, the dust of the years and various acts of God took their toll, and the organ was repeatedly threatened with complete destruction and 'restoration'. The threats came to nothing, however, and the organ fell into a state of slow decay. It suffered severely from bombardment in the 1914 war, but what appeared to be tragedy turned out to be the organ's salvation. Something, after the bombardment, had to be done; the plight of the organ could no longer be quietly ignored. Inspection proved that the damage was not as fundamental as had been feared; and a commission, consisting of Charles Widor, Félix Raugel, Maurice Emmanuel, A. de Vallombrosé, Joseph Bonnet and Paul Brunold, was appointed to decide how the organ might best be reconstructed. Between 1921 and 1923, the reconstruction was carried out with an integrity and sympathy which would certainly have been lacking, had reconstruction been attempted in the palmy days of the nineteenth century. After the reconstruction the instrument was still, in essentials, Couperin's instrument. Since Couperin left detailed indications of registration and we could still play the music on the organ to which the registration refers, we had here invaluable evidence as to colour and balance in Couperin's work. Unfortunately, during the second World War the organ once more fell into decay.

The specification of the organ is given in detail in Brunold's book on the subject. Since this book is not generally accessible, we may quote the specification here, because it may be of help to modern organists who wish to play Couperin's masses in particular, and baroque organ music in general. The terms are translated into their English equivalent, where there is no possible ambiguity.

1st Manual: Choir, the pipes enclosed in a 'petit buffet', a miniature replica of the great organ, placed behind the organists' back. (See Plate VIII.)

> 51 notes, from C to A.
>
> Diapason 8. The basses in wood. 15 pipes. 18th c.
>
> Flute 8. 16 in wood, 8 in metal. Restored 1612.
>
> Principal 4. 14 pipes, Alexandre Thierry, 1676, and 18th c.
>
> Doublette 2. Pierre Thierry, 1659.
>
> Nazard 2⅔. Pierre Thierry, 1659.
>
> Tierce 1⅗. Pierre Thierry, 1659.
>
> Plein Jeu, 5 ranks. Restored, 1843.
>
> Trumpet 8. F. H. Clicquot, 1768.
>
> Clairon 4. F. H. Clicquot, 1768.
>
> Cromhorne 8. F. H. Clicquot, 1768.
>
> Basson-Clarinette. F. H. Clicquot, 1768; restored, 1812.

2nd Manual: Great Organ, 51 notes.

> Diapason 16. Pescheur or Thierry, restored by Clicquot and Dallery.
>
> Diapason 8. Pescheur or Thierry.
>
> Bourdon 16. Wood and lead. Pierre Thierry, 1659.
>
> Bourdon 8. Wood and lead. Pierre Thierry, 1659.
>
> Flute 8. Pescheur, 1628.
>
> Principal 4. Pierre Thierry, 1659.
>
> Doublette 2. Pierre Thierry, 1659.
>
> Nazard 2⅔. Pierre Pescheur, 1628.
>
> Quarte de Nazard. Pierre Pescheur, 1628.
>
> Tierce 1⅗. Pierre Pescheur, 1628.
>
> Plein Jeu, 6 ranks. Restored, 1843.
>
> Grand Cornet, 5 ranks. Pierre Thierry, 1649.
>
> 1st Trumpet 8. Pierre Thierry, 1649.

326

2nd Trumpet 8. Dallery, 1812.
Clairon 4. Pierre Pescheur, 1628; restored, Clicquot, 1768.
Voix Humaine. Pierre Pescheur, 1628.

3rd Manual: Bombard, 51 notes.
Bombard 16. Clicquot, 1768.

4th Manual: Swell. 32 notes, G to A.
Oboe 8. Clicquot, 1768.
Cornet, 5 ranks. Alexandre Thierry, 1676.

5th Manual: Echo. 27 notes, C to A.
Flute 8. Built from the ancient Cornet d'echo, Pierre Thierry, 1659.
Trumpet 8. François Thierry, 1714 (originally placed in the Choir).

Pedal: 28 notes, A to C.
Flute 16. Pierre Thierry, 1649; Alexandre Thierry, 1676.
Flute 8. The painted pipes from the organ of St Catherine's, the rest by Pierre Thierry, 1649.
Flute 4. Pierre Thierry, 1649.
Bombard 16. Clicquot, 1768.
Trumpet 8. François Thierry, 1714; rebuilt by Clicquot, 1768.
Clairon 4. François Thierry, 1714; rebuilt by Clicquot, 1768.

For the benefit of those not versed in organ technicalities, we may add that the Cromhorne, like the German Krumhorn, is a rather nasal clarinet, the clairon a trumpet, and the bourdon a stopped diapason. The Plein Jeu is a mixture without thirds or fundamental; the cornet is also a mixture playing a chord without the fundamental. The Nazard, Quinte, and Tierce are mutations, playing the twelfth, fifteenth, and seventeenth respectively. A few stops seem to have disappeared; we know, for instance, that there was a *jeu de viole* in Louis Couperin's time. The first three manuals can be coupled. The Bombard is always coupled with the Great.

Both in the range of its keyboards and the number of its stops the St Gervais organ is, by contemporary standards, a very large one. It is not, however, for its size that it is remarkable, but for the purity and subtlety of its tone.[29] As with all baroque organs, the purity depends on the extremely low wind pressure; (if volume is wanted, the purity must be sacrificed); the subtlety depends on the high proportion of mixtures and mutations. The round, sweet tone of the Cromhorne and Basson-Hautbois of the Choir, the lucent glow of the Echo flute and trumpet, have a purity which seems made for Couperin's music, as his music was made for them; but the harmonics of the mixtures and mutations add a cleanly metallic edge to the tone, giving the lines a glinting animation. The doubling of the line by the harmonics two octaves or a twelfth up sometimes creates an extraordinary sound, as of rustling tin-foil. Most remarkable of all is the use of the tierce. Here the major third is added, transposed up two octaves; the effect is especially piquant in minor tonalities owing to the persistent clash of the minor thirds of the notated music, with the major thirds of the distant harmonics. The minor section of the Fourth Couplet of the Gloria of the *Messe Solemnelle* may be examined from this point of view; in the major section, the added seventeenth and octaves produce a much richer effect than the notation suggests, without in any way harming the clarity of texture. This last point is important, because mixtures and mutations are used, of course, on modern as well as on baroque organs. But whereas on the baroque organ the mixtures and mutations give edge and point to the tone, on the modern organ they merely increase the natural tone's crudity and confusion.

It need hardly be said that the turgidity of the modern organ is quite inappropriate to Couperin's music. The big Offertory of the first Mass can stand a considerable volume, so long as the edges are not blurred. For the *Messe des Convents* a delicate, fluting sonority is

[29] Dr. Burney gives the following description of the St Gervais organ as reconstructed by Clicquot in 1768, after visiting the church in the course of his travels. The M. Couperin referred to here is Armand-Louis, nephew of François le Grand:

'The organ of St Gervais, which seems to be a very good one, is almost new; it was made by the same builder, M. Clicquot, as that of St Roche. The pedals have three octaves in compass; the tone of the loud organ is rich, full, and pleasing, when the movement is slow; but in quick passages, such is the reverberation in these large buildings, every thing is indistinct and confused. Great latitude is allowed to the performer in these interludes; nothing is too light or too grave, all styles are admitted and though M. Couperin has the true organ touch, smooth and connected, yet he often tried, and not unsuccessfully, mere harpsichord passages, sharply articulated, and the notes detached and separated.'

indicated, but mixtures should provide a certain acidity, which prevents the sound from degenerating to the vaguely pastoral.

A word should be added on the loft and casing of the St Gervais organ. The buffet was a creation of the great years of the Roi Soleil. The case of the great organ was substantially rebuilt in the reign of Louis XV, but preserves the nobility and dignity of the classical age. One can see in its discreetly ornamented proportions something of the balanced gravity which one finds in such a piece of Couperin as *La Favorite*. The two sides of the instrument 'answer' one another as serenely as the soprano and bass parts answer one another in Couperin's wonderful chaconne. The proportions of the organ are as harmoniously resolved as the sounds it produces.

Couperin was organist of St Gervais all his working life. From 1693 he was also one of the organists of the Chapelle Royale. When he took over this post, the great organ at Versailles had not been built. It was not started until 1702, and was not finished until 1736, three years after Couperin's death. Thus during the early years of Couperin's duties at Versailles, the services did not include any dialogues between organist and choir, in the conventional manner of the parish service, as indicated in the structure of the organ masses. The service was mainly choral, and the organ, a small positive placed near the singers, was employed merely to accompany the voices. This is suggested by all the church music which Couperin wrote during this period of his career—up to 1715. In the *Leçons des Tenèbres*, for instance, the bass line should preferably be played by a stringed instrument, while the organ quietly fills in the harmonies; clearly it must not be allowed to disturb the balance between solo voices and string bass. In Couperin's vocal church music, the organ is essentially an accompanying instrument. Where solo instrumental parts are needed, they are played by violins, viols, flutes, or oboes, in the manner of the Carissimi or Bach cantatas.

Although incomplete, the new organ was inaugurated at Versailles in 1710. Couperin may have played the instrument at the ceremony, and it seems probable that he must have used it frequently during the remaining years of his court appointment. There is no evidence of this in his music, however. None of his motets and elevations calls for a large instrument; on the contrary, as we have seen, they suggest a positive. Couperin did not favour a grandiose style

329

in church music, or in anything else. Lully and La Lande, who cultivated the massive and imposing in church music, had obtained their effects through the use of a large orchestra. So the early organ masses remain Couperin's only developed compositions for the instrument; and in connection with them, it is the organ of St Gervais, rather than that of the Chapelle Royale, that we must think of.

B. Vocal Church Music

In performing Couperin's vocal church music, the main difficulty is to find singers with the requisite flexibility, and the appropriate timbre—anything approaching an Italian luxuriance is unsuitable. The soprano parts written for Marguerite-Louise Couperin are especially high, and need great purity of tone. A further difficulty is provided by the counter-tenor parts, since Couperin writes with considerable virtuosity through the whole range of the counter-tenor compass. The parts tends to be too agile, as well as too high, for the normal tenor, while the substitution of a woman's voice upsets the balance of the parts. The problem of the counter-tenor is not, however, peculiar to Couperin's music. It crops up repeatedly in baroque vocal music, and can be satisfactorily solved only by the building up of a new tradition of counter-tenor singing. The true counter-tenor is a natural tenor with an exceptionally high tessitura; neither the male alto nor the bass or baritone voice singing in falsetto can provide an adequate substitute for its limpid yet virile tone. Mr John Hough, in a paper on the counter-tenor given to the Musical Association, points out that Purcell used his counter-tenors against the high trumpets in the orchestra, while he usually associated the altos with flutes. Roughly speaking, the counter-tenor's range is a third higher than the ordinary tenor; Couperin writes long passages of fioriture ranging between D and high B. His counter-tenor parts seem mostly to have been intended for an exceptional singer called Du Four.

The chorus in Couperin's church music does not involve any special difficulties. On the rare occasions when it is used it should be small—not more than two or three singers to a part.

Couperin's recitative and arioso, which become important only in the *Leçons des Ténèbres*, should be sung very flexibly, but without

The Organ of St Gervais

The Organ of the Chapelle Royale

losing the sense of the measure. In this respect, the recitative of motets and cantatas differed from that of the opera 'qui tend à se rapprocher de la parole'. None the less, it is essential that 'la mesure qu'on y remarque ne s'observe pas à la rigueur' (Lacassagne, 1766). Since Couperin's arioso is much more lyrical and cantabile in character than the usual operatic recitative, it may introduce a rich ornamentation. This was deprecated in French operatic recitative on the grounds that it destroyed the speech-like naturalness of the musical line.

The peculiar recitative which occurs before the final chorus of the *Motet de Ste Suzanne*, accompanied by bass line only, without harmony, should probably be sung more freely than Couperin's habitual, fully accompanied arioso. 'Le ₵ servant pour les récitatifs, son mouvement est arbitraire et ce sont les paroles qui le déterminent.' (Choquel.) The conventional account of operatic recitative is probably applicable to this case: 'Les accompagnateurs sçavants ne suivent point de mesure dans le récitatif; il faut que l'oreille s'attache à la voix pour la suivre et fournir l'harmonie au chant qu'elle débite tantôt légèrement tantôt lentement, de sorte que les croches deviennent quelquefois blanches et quelquefois les blanches deviennent croches par la célérité, selon l'entouziasme et l'expression plus ou moins outrée des personnes qui chantent.' Here the rules concerning *les notes inégales* do not apply, the time values being determined by the words.

The beautiful French H.M.V. records of the third *Leçon des Tenèbres* employ soprano voices for the vocalises, two tenors for the arioso, and trumpet, harpsichord and string continuo in addition to the organ. The result is impressive, and should not be quibbled over, for Couperin, like Bach and all late baroque composers, was not fastidious about the medium in which his works were performed. None the less, the original medium, in which both vocalises and ariosos are sung by two soprano soloists, while the continuo is played on organ and string bass, is perhaps more satisfactory, and preserves the purity of line and sonority which should characterize all Couperin's work. The composer's own words suggest that the string bass is desirable but not essential: 'Si l'on peut joindre une basse de Viole ou de Violon à l'accompagnement de l'Orgue ou du clavessin, cela fera bien.' This passage also reveals that the continuo part, even in church music, may be played on the harpsichord instead of on the organ.

In those of Couperin's motets and elevations which have independent obbligato parts, the instruments used should vary according to the character of the music. Couperin often specifies viols, oboes, or flutes. Where no instrument is mentioned, violins should normally be used, on the analogy of the Carissimi cantata. The conductor, however, should use his own discretion, paying deference to the contemporary association of specific instruments with specific passions. For instance, obbligato flutes would clearly sound well in some movements of the *Ste Suzanne* motet, and might alternate with the violins, both instruments playing together in the most brilliant movements.

Usually, a soloist is sufficient to play each obbligato part; but they may be doubled where the acoustic conditions of the church or concert hall seem to require it.

C. Violin Sonatas and Suites

These do not offer any serious problems to modern performers in respect of the resources employed. Two violins, harpsichord, and string bass is the ideal combination. *La Sultane* alone calls for an additional independent cello or gamba. With harpsichord, the three string parts form a perfect balance. If a piano has to be used, the medium is bound to be rather heavily weighted in the bass, but even in these circumstances it is inadvisable to omit the cello. It is important that the listener should be aware of the string bass line as the foundation of the soloists' polyphony; the completely different tone colour of the piano cannot be an adequate substitute. The da chiesa sonatas may be performed with a discreet organ continuo, instead of harpsichord or piano. Again the string bass should on no account be omitted.

Close attention should be paid to the phrasing of the solo parts, remembering that according to contemporary practice all rhythmically strong notes should be taken on the down bow, whatever their position in the measure. The articulation should allow plenty of 'air' in the phrasing. (See Appendix E.) Players should remember that to Couperin and his contemporaries vibrato was a special effect, a grace comparable with the *tremblement* or trill.

332

Couperin explains that other instruments may be substituted for the violins and the works may even be played on two keyboards:

cela engage à avoir deux exemplaires, au lieu d'un; et deux clavecins aussi, mais, je trouve d'ailleurs qu'il est souvent plus aisé de rassembler ces deux instruments, que quatre personnes faisant leur profession de la musique. Deux épinettes à l'unisson (à un plus grand effet prés) peuvent servir de même. . . . L'exécution n'en paroistra pas moins agréable.

The works are certainly effective in this form, and as domestic music-making will afford much enjoyment to twentieth-century players, as they did to Couperin and his family and pupils. But they are conceived—with the possible exception of the theatrical *Apothéose de Lully*—as string music, and it is in this form that they should be presented for concert performance.

D. Clavecin Music

For his clavecin music, Couperin calls for a full-sized two-manual harpsichord with two sets of strings and pedal couplings. Apart from the Bach of the Goldberg variations, no composer has shown so comprehensive a mastery of harpsichord technique; the variety of his methods of treating the instrument has already been commented on in our discussion of the music. Some pieces, such as *La Passacaille* or *La Lugubre*, need tremendous sonorous resources, and can be adequately 'realized' only on a very large instrument. Normally, however, Couperin's pieces do not call for great volume; it is precision and delicacy that are necessary, as Couperin remarks in the typically ironic passage from *L'Art de toucher le Clavecin* which we have already quoted. ('Il faut surtout se rendre très délicat en claviers . . . .')

But this certainly does not mean that the instrument ought ever to sound tepid. Even the percussive Harlequin pieces and the fragilely ornamented linear movements need an instrument capable of giving them a varied registration similar to that of the baroque organ. The instrument need not be large, but it must have resonance; and it must be capable of distinguishing between effects of line and effects of ornamental filigree. In particular, the pieces with bell and drone devices require an instrument rich in overtones. The relation of Couperin's harpsichord to the grand piano resembles the relation of

333

the baroque organ to the modern. An instrument with two sets of strings is essential for the adequate performance of the *mains croisées* pieces on two keyboards; only on such an instrument can complete equality between the parts be obtained.

Couperin has himself summed up the potentialities of the harpsichord in several passages already quoted in the section on his theoretical work (see page 293). The sumptuous instrument used by Wanda Landowska in her recordings is a hyper-sophistication of the resources available to Couperin. His harpsichord probably had one four-foot and two eight-foot stops, certainly no sixteen-foot; and it is reasonably certain that he would have considered the din of the sixteen-foot stop quite intolerable. None the less I do not sympathize with the purist's disapproval of Mme Landowska's performances, and I would even say that—given the different conditions involved in the fact that she usually plays in a large concert-hall—the effect of her performances is right in principle. Certainly the varied 'orchestral' registration of the fully developed clavecin is essential for all Couperin's representative music. Only the unpretentious little dance pieces—such as occur most prolifically in the first book—are completely successful on the épinette (the French one-manual equivalent of the virginals).

Couperin understood his instrument so well that his pieces do not sound very convincing on the piano, when once one has heard them on a good harpsichord; he 'translates' to the modern instrument even less successfully than Scarlatti. The latter's rhythmic and percussive pieces lose much of their wit and guitar-like piquancy on the piano, but can be made to sound effectively pianistic. Some of Couperin's hazily droning, resonant pieces, such as *Les Vergers Fleuris* or *La Garnier*, are next to impossible to bring off on the piano. With the big sonorous movements such as *La Passacaille* the only course is one which is to be adopted only in extremities— namely, to attempt to make the piano sound as much like a harpsichord as possible. Some instruments lend themselves to this more easily than others. The most successful pieces of Couperin, pianistically speaking, are the various bell movements, which can sound very beautiful. In any case, it is better to play Couperin on the piano than not to play him at all.

Just as some of Couperin's concerted works can alternatively be played on the harpsichord, so some of his harpsichord pieces can be played on other instruments. The linear nature of his keyboard writing lends itself well to translation into terms of wind instruments. The crossed hands pieces on two keyboards, and the musettes and other popular dances, sound exquisite on flute, oboe, and bassoon; Couperin adds a note, explaining that 'Elles sont propres à deux flutes, ou Hautbois, ainsy que pour deux Violons, deux Violes, et autres instrumens à l'unisson'. He also suggests that '*Le Rossignol* réussit sur la flute Traversière on ne peut pas mieux, quand il est bien joué'. His condition is interesting, for this lovely piece demands the utmost subtlety of phrasing and nuance if it is not to sound *précieux* to an almost finical degree. *La Julliet* 'se peut jouer sur différens instrumens. Mais encore sur deux clavecins ou Epinettes; scavoir, le sujet avec la basse, sur l'un; et la même Basse avec la contre-partie, sur l'autre. Ainsi des autres pièces qui pouront se trouver en trio'.

E. *The Concerts and Suites for Viols*

Something has already been said in Part II about the medium of the *concerts royaux* and the suites for viols. (See page 266.) For modern performance of the *concerts*, almost any balanced group of instruments can be used. The original compromise between strings and woodwind is still the ideal. But they are effective on strings alone, and may sound very beautiful on groups of woodwind—flutes, oboes, bassoons—thus offering a valuable addition to the scanty repertory for wind instruments. Harpsichord continuo should be included where possible, unless there is any specific indication to the contrary; but it is better to play the suites without continuo if only a piano is available, since the modern instrument dangerously disturbs the balance of tone, and does not dissolve into the strings and woodwind in the self-effacing manner of the plucked-string instrument. The pieces are written so as to make complete harmonic sense, even if only the two outer parts are played.

The modern performance of the suites for viols offers peculiar difficulties. Players of the viol are not plentiful nowadays, and players with sufficient virtuosity to tackle the first viol part of these suites are almost non-existent. There is no objection on æsthetic grounds to playing the works on modern instruments, but unfortunately there are technical objections, since the music arises so naturally out of the technique and tuning of the viol that many of the double and triple stoppings are unplayable on modern instruments. Some of the emotional impact of the work comes from the manner in which the music is written 'through' the technique of the viol. If one modifies the lines slightly to make them performable on modern instruments one sacrifices the feeling of oneness between music and instrument; if one rewrites them 'through' the technique of the modern instruments, one is straying too far from Couperin.

Yet the suites are such magnificent music that one would like to hear them widely performed today. Bouvet's published version for cello and piano is adequate but inevitably out of character. A more satisfactory version might be made for viola and cello unaccompanied. The multiple stopping would have to be modified in some places, and the effect might occasionally be rather gauche. None the less I think such a version would give a more authentic impression of the nature and quality of the music than could any arrangement for cello and piano.

In general Couperin, like Bach, is primarily a linear composer, a draughtsman who is interested in tone-colour only as a means of making his linear structure clear. This does not alter the fact that there is a specific and sensuously beautiful tone colour which is, as it were, implicit in his texture. As with Bach, when the tone-colours appropriate to a particular group of lines have been decided on, they should normally be adhered to throughout the movement. Frequent dynamic gradations are unnecessary; sharp, architectural oppositions of *forte* and *piano* may be used, though not to excess. The words *fort* and *doux* are the only dynamic indications which Couperin permits himself, and they occur infrequently. Moreover although Couperin's expressive intentions are suggested by the adjectival and adverbial indications of mood and tempo which he gives, these indications do not imply a romantic theory of interpretation. If the music is sensitively phrased, the lines create their own 'expression'. The general nature of Couperin's phrasing has been discussed in the previous chapter.

Chapter Fourteen

Editions of Works by Couperin

A. ORGAN MASSES

Pieces d'Orgue consistantes en deux messes, 1690. (MS. copies with engraved title page.)

FIRST PUBLISHED, ASCRIBED to François Couperin the elder, in the fifth volume of Guilmant's *Archives des Maîtres de l'orgue*, with pre face by André Pirro.

Republished in Lyrebird edition of the works of Couperin le Grand.

B. VIOLIN SONATAS AND SUITES

La Purcelle, La Visionnaire, L'Astree, La Steinquerque. No contemporary edition under these titles.

Modern reprints published by Senart, edited by Peyrot and Rebufat. This edition is very inaccurate; for instance, appoggiaturas and other dissonant ornamental notes are frequently omitted, thus emasculating the harmony.

Les Nations; engraved by Couperin, 1726. Includes *L'Impériale*, and all of the above sonatas under different titles, with a suite of dance movements added to each sonata. Modern edition published by Durand, edited by Julien Tiersot. This is a scholarly edition with the ornaments transcribed into modern notation. The transcription is sensitively done, though the use of a dotted crochet followed by a quaver for the *coulé* effect perhaps suggests an inappropriate rigidity. The continuo of the sonatas is simply realized, the right hand playing chords in a manner that is probably in accordance with Couperin's practice. (See page 312.) In the continuo part of the suites Tiersot adopts the unconvincing method of doubling the solo parts more or less consistently.

La Sultane, La Superbe. No contemporary edition.

337

L'Apothéose de Corelli. Engraved by Couperin, 1724.

L'Apothéose de Lulli. Engraved by Couperin, 1725.

Modern edition of the *Apothéoses* published by Durand, edited by G. Marty. This edition, unlike Peyrot and Rebufat, respects eighteenth-century convention. The continuo parts are somewhat unimaginative.

All these sonatas and suites republished in the Lyrebird edition, with continuo realized by Jean Gallon. These continuo parts make no attempt to emulate contemporary practice; they are almost certainly of greater polyphonic elaboration than Couperin's were. But they are musicianly and perhaps may be said to conform to the spirit, if not the letter, of Couperin's work.

C. SECULAR VOCAL MUSIC

Air serieux, *Qu'on on ne me dise plus*, published by Ballard in Collection of Airs, 1697.

Pastourelle, 1697.

Air Serieux, Les Solitaires, Muséte, Brunete, Vaudeville, Les Pélerines, published in Receuils d'airs serieux et à boire, 1711–12.

Air Gracieux, published in La Collection Ch. Bouvet (Demets).

All these and other secular pieces in MS. republished in Lyrebird edition, with bass realized by Jean Gallon. A simple homophonic treatment of the continuo is the only one possible for these songs. Gallon's version is completely satisfactory.

D. VOCAL CHURCH MUSIC

Versets de Motets, published by Ballard, 1703, 1704, 1705.

Leçons des Ténèbres, engraved by Couperin, 1714. The other church works in MS., mostly Bib. de Versailles, and MS. du Cons. de Paris. The Elevation, *O Misterium Ineffabile*, republished by Durand.

All the church works published in Lyrebird edition, with continuo realized by Paul Brunold. This continuo part is simple and convincing. It is mostly homophonic; canonic entries are effectively and legitimately used in certain places—for instance the end of the *Jerusalem convertere* aria of the second *Leçon des Tenèbres*.

Troisième Leçon de Tenèbres, Desoff Choir Series, ed. by P. Boepple. Music Press Inc., New York, and Oxford U.P., London.

E. CLAVECIN MUSIC

Four books of clavecin ordres, engraved by Couperin, 1713, 1716, 1722, and 1730. This edition is one of the most beautiful examples of early eighteenth-century engraving, exquisitely proportioned and remarkably free from serious errors.

Selections from Couperin's clavecin pieces have appeared in numerous modern editions, the most important of which are

Trésor des pianistes (Farrenc),

Les Clavecinistes (Amédée Mereaux),

Les Clavecinistes Français (Diémer).

Early Keyboard Music, Vol. II (Oesterle).

Some of these are inaccurate.

The complete series has been republished by Durand, edited by Louis Diémer (also inaccurate), and by Augener, edited by Brahms and Chrysander (1887). This last named is founded on the original edition, with Couperin's five clefs transposed into the modern treble and bass, but with the ornaments and phrase markings preserved intact. Much of the handsome appearance of the original edition survives, and Brahms-Chrysander is an excellent, practical working edition for students and performers, with relatively few, unimportant errors. The Lyrebird volumes correct some, but not all, of these errors.

F. CONCERTS ROYAUX

Engraved by Couperin, 1722. Transcribed for two violins and continuo by G. Marty, published Durand (a not very satisfactory version). Republished in Lyrebird edition with continuo by Jean Gallon. (Solo parts usually written on two staves, as for clavecin; sometimes on three staves, with contre-partie.)

Les Goûts Réunis, ou nouveaux concerts. Engraved by Couperin, 1724. Modern edition, transcribed by Paul Dukas, published by Durand. Republished in Lyrebird edition in same manner as the Concerts Royaux, with continuo realized by Jean Gallon.

Pièces de Violes. Engraved by Couperin, 1728, transcribed by Charles Bouvet for cello and piano and published by Durand.

Republished in Lyrebird edition with continuo by Jean Gallon.

G. THEORETICAL WORKS

Règles pour l'accompagnement, 1696, MS. Published in Lyrebird edition.

L'Art de toucher le Clavecin. Published by Couperin, 1715. Second edition, 1716. Republished in Lyrebird edition.

As a whole, the Lyrebird edition (1933) is a monumental feat of scholarship. Like the Brahms-Chrysander edition of the clavecin pieces, it endeavours to keep as close to Couperin's original text as is consistent with the production of an edition that shall be fully intelligible to modern readers. Thus Couperin's varied clefs are abandoned, but his ornamentation and phrasing are preserved. Certain peculiarities of rhythmic notation are also adhered to; for instance the use of semiquaver triplets where a modern composer would write quaver triplets, and the elastic treatment of the dot in passages involving very rapid notes, for instance (𝅘𝅥𝅭 𝅘𝅥𝅯𝅘𝅥𝅯𝅘𝅥𝅯). This convention, described in the last chapter, is sensible, for it is both simple and easily intelligible.

The Lyrebird edition is the work of Paul Brunold, Amédée Gastoué, and André Schaeffner under the general direction of Maurice Cauchie. It is essentially a library edition. Some of the more important or charming works that have been recorded are published in sheet music form, but even these are a students' rather than a performers' edition since, except in the case of *La Sultane*, no parts are as yet provided. It is to be hoped that a practical performing edition of a representative selection of works will follow without delay, for the magnificent Lyrebird set should not remain a museum piece but should be a signal for the active renaissance of Couperin's music. Since this music is so intimately in tune with the outlook and feeling of many young musicians today, there is no need to fear that a scholarly practical edition would not meet with a satisfactory response.

Appendix A

THE AUTHORSHIP OF THE ORGAN MASSES

THE EVIDENCE PRO and contra in the case for Couperin le Grand's author-ship of the organ masses is given in detail in an appendix to Julien Tiersot's *Les Couperins*, and in the preface to the Lyrebird edition of the works. On the contemporary engraved title-pages to the manuscript copies, the masses are described as being by 'François Couperin, Sieur de Crouilly, organiste de St Gervais'. The one-time conventional ascription of the works to the first François Couperin depended on two assumptions: one, that he was the Couperin who bore the title of Sieur de Crouilly; the other, that he was organist of St Gervais in 1690, when the masses were prepared for publication.

The researches of Pirro, Bouvet, Tessier, and of M. Tiersot himself have proved that the title of Sieur de Crouilly was one to which none of the Couperins had any legitimate right. There is no evidence at all that the elder François ever used it, and the identification of him with the Couperin of the organ masses dates from no earlier than the nineteenth century. There is no direct evidence that the younger François used the title either, though there is a contemporary document referring to 'Marie Guérin, veuve de Charles Couperin, sieur de Crouilly', and it would have been natural enough if François had taken over the title from his father. If it be asked why François never used the title subsequently, the obvious answer is that a few years later, probably in 1696, he acquired a legitimate title from Louis, and so was able to sign himself 'le comte Couperin'. Significantly, the old title re-appears in the name of one of his last clavecin pieces, *La Crouilli ou La Couperinette*, possibly a portrait of his daughter, or an evocation of his child-hood, or both.

As for the second and more important point, there is again no evidence that the elder François was ever organist of St Gervais. A passage from the contemporary chronicler Titon du Tillet suggests that the second François, young as he was, had the post reserved for him for a while, until he was old enough to succeed to his father:

François Couperin avait des dispositions si grandes qu'en peu de temps il devint excellent organiste et fut mis en possession de l'orgue qu'avait eu son père.

341

That the post was so reserved for the young François is put beyond doubt by a document recently discovered by Paul Brunold, and published in his book on the organ of St Gervais. This proves irrefutably that La Lande was appointed deputy organist, during the interim period, in addition to his two other Parisian churches. The relevant portion of this document is worth quoting:

Convention Messieurs les Marguilliers St Gervais pour l'orgue . . . lesquels mettant en consideration les longs services que le feu Charles Couperin et auparavant luy, feu son frère, ont rendus en qualité d'organistes de ladite Eglise, et desirant conserver à François Couperin son fils cette place jusqu'à ce qu'il ait atteint l'âge de dix-huit ans et qu'il soit en estat de rendre luy même son service en ladite année et ladite qualité Lesquels Sieurs Marguilliers ont choisy et retenu Michel de La Lande organiste demeurt rue Bailleul, Lequel par ces fins et souz les conditions cy aprez, s'est obligé et s'oblige par ces présentes envers lesdites SSr Marguilliers de jouer de ladite orgue dans tous les cours desdites années et jusqu'au dit tems. . . . Ceque ledit La Lande a accepté.

The document goes on to refer to a pension given to Couperin and his mother during the period of La Lande's tenure, and establishes the fact that occupation of the St Gervais organist's house was a legalized privilege of the Couperins at this time, even though La Lande was organist.

There is reasonably definite evidence that Couperin took over the duties of St Gervais in his eighteenth year. This was in 1685. It is certain that Couperin le Grand was organist in 1690, when he applied for a *privilège du Roi* to publish his organ masses. This document gives Couperin de Crouilly's address as 'rue de Monceau, proche l'Eglise'; furthermore the recently discovered Carpentras manuscript also gives the rue de Monceau address. We have seen that the younger François had been living here with his mother ever since his father's death, and we know that the elder François can never have been official organist at St Gervais, nor have lived in the traditional home of the St Gervais organists, since the document concerning La Lande's temporary appointment leaves no period of tenure unaccounted for. A small point of interest is that La Lande, in a written tribute to the excellence of the organ masses and their suitability for publication, omits the title of Sieur de Crouilly altogether. Taking it all round, it seems to me that there is no positive evidence whatever to support the attribution of the masses to the elder François. It cannot be more than a hypothesis, and a singularly perverse one, for all the known facts point to François the Great.

Presumably the hypothesis was made only because the music of the masses seemed too mature to be the work of a young man. But on artistic grounds, as we have seen, the masses provide just the evidence we need to complete our account of Couperin's evolution. One would not expect music of such fine quality to come from the pen of an obscure musician who seems to have written nothing else, and never to have been referred to by his contemporaries as a creative artist.[30] On the other hand, the masses are just the kind of music one would expect to be written by a young composer of genius, *coming at the end of a great and long tradition*. It is just possible to believe that someone else might have written the chromatic elevation of the *Messe Solemnelle*, since this technique occasionally leads other composers to create a rather Couperin-like texture and harmony. But it is not possible to believe that any other composer could have written the *Qui tollis* from the *Messe des Convents*; and we have observed how Couperin did not discard, but substantially modified, this idiom as he grew older.

Both on factual and on artistic grounds one can thus have no hesitation in regarding the Masses as the first work of Couperin le Grand; and one by no means unworthy of his later accomplishment.

---

[30] Titon du Tillet says of him: 'Le second des trois frères Couperin s'appeloit François; il n'avoit pas les mesmes talens que ses deux frères de jouer de l'orgue et du Clavecin, mais il avoit celui de montrer les Pièces de clavecin *de ses deux frères* avec une netteté et une facilité très grande. C'étoit un petit homme qui aimoit fort le bon vin.'

Appendix B

THE ORGANISTS OF ST GERVAIS

Antoine de Roy, 1545–1546.
Simon Bismant, ?–1599.
Robert du Buisson, 1599–1629.
Du Buisson fils, 1629–1655.
Louis Couperin, 1655–1661.
Charles Couperin, 1661–1679.
Michel de La Lande, 1679–1685.
François Couperin, 1685–1733.
Nicolas Couperin (son of François Couperin the elder), 1733–1748.
Armand-Louis Couperin (son of Nicolas Couperin), 1748–1789.
Pierre-Louis Couperin (son of Armand-Louis Couperin), 1789.
Gervais-François Couperin (younger son of Armand-Louis Couperin), 1789–1826.

Appendix C ˑ

LORD FITZWILLIAM AND THE FRENCH CLAVECIN COMPOSERS

IN WRITING THIS book I have consulted the copies of the original editions of Couperin's *L'Art de Toucher le Clavecin* and of the first two books of clavecin pieces which are in the library of the Fitzwilliam Museum, Cambridge. Classical French music is fairly well represented in Lord Fitzwilliam's collection: he bought the magnificent contemporary editions of La Lande's motets and of many operas of Lully and Rameau; while of the French clavecin school he acquired, in addition to the Couperin, volumes of Marchand, Dieupart, Du Phly, and the Amsterdam edition of Gaspard le Roux. His library also includes a volume of clavecin pieces by Froberger published during his sojourn in France; and there are manuscript pieces of Du Phly and Nivers in Fitzwilliam's exercise books. Most of the volumes bear Fitzwilliam's signature on the title-page, together with the date on which he bought them during his continental travels. They were mostly acquired between 1766 and 1772.

I have already briefly discussed the musical significance of the four Du Phly volumes, which are bound together, in the chapter on Couperin's influence. They have, however, an additional historical interest in that Du Phly appears, from the evidence of an exercise book in the library, to have been Fitzwilliam's composition and harpsichord teacher. The volumes were presented to Fitzwilliam *de la part de l'auteur*; and on the fly-leaf of the first book are written some comments on fingering in what appears to be Fitzwilliam's hand, signed by Du Phly. It is interesting to compare these remarks with Couperin's comments on fingering in the *Art de Toucher le Clavecin*. Both writers stress the importance of an easy and natural finger action, of *douceur de toucher*, and of a good legato; and both advocate the principle of finger substitution. We may note that even in 1755—or later if the inscription postdates publication—Du Phly still shows the traditional distrust of the thumb and fifth finger. I quote the inscription in full:

Du Doigter

La Perfection du Doigter consiste en général dans un mouvement doux, léger et régulier.

Le mouvement des doigts se pend à leur racine: c'est à dire à la jointure qui les attache à la main.

Il faut que les doigts soient courbés naturellement, et que chaque doigt ait un mouvement propre et indépendant des autres doigts. Il faut que les doigts tombent sur les touches et non qu'ils les frappent: et de plus qu'ils coulent de l'une à l'autre en se succedant: c'est à dire, qu'il ne faut quitter une touche qu'apres en avoir pris une autre. Ceci regarde particulièrement le jeu françois.

Pour continuer un roulement, il faut s'accoutumer à passer le pouce par-dessous tel doigt que ce soit, et à passer tel autre doigt par-dessus le pouce. Cette manière est excellente surtout quand il se rencontre des dièses et des bémols: alors faites en sorte que le pouce se trouve sur la touche qui précède le dièse ou le bémol, ou placez-le immédiatement après. Par ce moyen vous vous procurerez autant de doigt de suite que vous aurez de notes à faire.

Eviter, autant qu'il se pourra, de toucher du pouce ou du cinquième doigt une touche blanche, surtout dans les roulemens de vitesse.

Souvent on exécute un même roulement avec les deux mains dont les doigts se succèdent consécutivement. Dans ces roulemens les mains passent l'une sur l'autre. Mais il faut observer que le son de la première touche sur laquelle passe une des mains soit aussi lié au son précédent que s'ils étaient touchés de la même main.

Dans le genre de musique harmonieux et lié, il est bon de s'accoutumer à substituer un doigt à la place d'un autre sans relever la touche. Cette manière donne des facilités pour l'exécution et prolonge la durée des sons.

Here the passages about legato in *le jeu françois* and about finger substitution in *le genre harmonieux et lié* would seem to be derived directly or indirectly from Couperin.

In view of Fitzwilliam's enthusiasm for French clavecin music it seemed worth while investigating whether the French composers, and Couperin in particular, left any imprint on his own amateur efforts at composition. But the earliest examples of his work I was able to find date from 1781; and while he copies out in the back of the volume a piece of Du Phly (*La Victoire*) and a dance of Rameau, along with pieces by Purcell, Handel and D. Scarlatti, his own style is by that date unambiguously Handelian. The only French element is an occasional hint of the styles of the Lullian overture and march, both of which he could have found in the music of Handel himself. One imagines that any pieces Fitzwilliam may have written in the seventeen sixties would have been more in the harmonic manner of Du Phly than in the linear style of Couperin. The rapid dominance of the Handelian fashion over Fitzwilliam's work suggests how completely the anglicized Handel routed the French—and for that matter the native English—tradition. As Handelian exercises, Fitzwilliam's pieces are competent and agreeable.

346

Appendix D

ON THE TEMPO OF THE EIGHTEENTH-CENTURY DANCE MOVEMENTS

THE CONTEMPORARY STATEMENT of tempi which is most closely relevant to Couperin's work is that of Michel d'Affilard, who based his primitive metronomic system on the earlier work of Sauveur. The tables which he published in 1705 may be summed up as follows:

¢	Marche	♩ = 120
C		♩ = 72
2	Gavotte	
	Rigaudon	
	Bourrée	♩ = 120
	Air gaye	
	Pavane	♩ = 90
3	Sarabande en rondeau	♩ = 88
	Passacaille	♩ = 106
	Chaconne	♩ = 156
	Menuet	♩. = 70
3 : 2	Sarabande	♩ = 72
	Air tendre	♩ = 80
	Air grave	♩ = 48
	Courante	♩ = 90
3 : 8	Passepied	♩. = 84
	Gigue	♩. = 116
	Air léger	♩. = 116
6 : 4	Sarabande	♩ = 133
	Marche	♩ = 150
	Air grave	♩ = 120
6 : 8	Canaris	♩. = 106
	Menuet	♩. = 75
	Gigue	♩. = 100

M. Eugène Borrel has interestingly compared these metronome marks with

347

those of later theorists. On the whole their statements show a remarkable uniformity:

		AFFILARD 1705	LACHAPELLE	ONZEMBRY 1732	CHOQUEL 1762
Bourrée	♩	120	120	112–120	..
Chaconne	♩	156	120	156	..
Gavotte	♩	120	152	96	126
Gigue	♩.	116–120	120	112	120
Menuet	♩.	72–76	..	78	80
Passepied	♩.	84	..	100	92
Rigaudon	♩	120	152	116	126
Sarabande	♩	66–72–84	63	78	..
or	♩				

All the above figures are correlated with Maelzel's metronome.

Quantz, in his *Versuch einer Anweisung die Flöte traviere zu spielen* of 1752, estimates tempi by the simple method of pulse-beats. His account of the French dance movements is as follows:

Entrée, Loure and Courante (played pompously, the bow being lifted for each crochet): one pulsation for each crochet.
Sarabande: same tempo as above, but played more smoothly.
Chaconne: one pulsation for two crochets, played pompously.
Passacaille: slightly quicker than the chaconne.
Musette: one pulsation for each crochet in 3 : 4 time, or each quaver in 3 : 8.
Furie: one pulsation for two crochets.
Bourrée and Rigaudon: one pulsation for a bar.
Gavotte: slightly slower than rigaudon.
Gigue and canaris: one pulsation for every bar.
Menuet (played with rather heavy, but short bowing): one pulsation for two crochets.
Passepied: slightly quicker than Menuet.
Tambourin: slightly quicker than the Bourrée.
Marche (alla breve): two pulsations to a bar.

According to Schering, one of Quantz's pulse-beats equals about 80 on Maelzel's metronome. This gives the following table, which may be compared with those of the French theorists cited above:

Entrée, Loure, Courante, Sarabande	♩ = 80
Chaconne	♩ = 160
Passacaille	♩ = 180
Musette	♩ = 80
Furie, Bourrée, Rigaudon	♩ = 160

Gavotte		♩ = 120
Gigue, Canaris		♩ = 160
Menuet		♩ = 160
Passepied, Tambourin	♩ or ♪	= 180
Marche		♩ = 80

Georg Muffat, in his *Observations sur la manière de jouer les airs de balets à la françoise selon la méthode de feu Monsieur de Lully*, has some illuminating comments on the general significance of tempo indications in the classical age. According to him the sign C indicates four slowish beats in a bar—a largo or adagio movement, certainly not faster than andante, since if the speed quickens one would beat two in a bar and use a different time signature.

The sign 2 indicates two slowish beats in a bar, or sometimes four quick ones. It is used for a quiet allegro or flowing andante, but does not suggest a precipitate movement. Sometimes, in overtures, it may have a somewhat maestoso character: but an overture in 2 time is faster than one marked ₡.

The sign ₡ indicates two quickish beats in a bar. Muffat implies that it is quicker than 2 time, though not all the theorists agree with him. No hard and fast rule can be decided on; composers seem to use the two signs indiscriminately in gavottes, bourrées and rigaudons, for instance, and the precise speed of each piece will depend on its character. Muffat's view of the two time signatures seems, however, to be supported by works in which the two signatures occur within the same movement, as they often do in overtures. Here the change from 2 to ₡ seems to imply a change to a faster tempo.

The sign 3 : 2 indicates 'un mouvement fort lent'. Its character is largo and maestoso rather than adagio.

The sign 3 : 4 covers considerable variety of tempi. It is always less slow than 3 : 2, but still 'un peu grave' in sarabandes and airs; 'plus gaye' in rondeaux; and gayer still in courantes, minuets and the fugue sections of overtures. In gigues and canaris it is very quick indeed. This account applies directly to Couperin's earlier work; in his later pieces he often employs the 3 : 4 sign in a *sarabande grave*, where Lully would have used 3 : 2.

Appendix E

GEORG MUFFAT ON BOWING, PHRASING, AND ORNAMENTATION IN FRENCH INSTRUMENTAL MUSIC

GEORG MUFFAT'S *Premières Observations sur la manière de jouer les Airs de Balet à la Françoise selon la Méthode de feu M. de Lully* gives a detailed and revealing account of Lully's techniques of performance. Couperin's *Concerts Royaux* are directly in the Lully tradition; so Muffat's comments on bowing may be taken as relevant to the performance of Couperin's concerted music also.

I

The rules about bowing may be summarized as follows:

1. The first note of each bar, when it falls on the beat, is taken on the down bow, *whatever its length*. This is the fundamental rule, on which most of the others depend. It is what principally distinguishes the French technique from the Italian, adding a more accentual emphasis to the dance movement.

2. In *Tems Imparfait* (binary time), of all the notes that divide the bar into equal parts the odd numbers are taken on the down bow, the even numbers on the up. The rule applies in triple time to notes of lesser value than the lower note of the time signature (i.e. to crochets, quavers and semiquavers in 3 : 2 time). This rule is not modified by the substitution of rests for notes.

3. In *Tems Parfait* (triple time), when the tempo is slow, the first beat is taken on the down bow, the second on the up and the third on the down. The first beat of the next bar follows on the down bow again, in accordance with rule 1. But at faster tempi the second and third beats of each bar are elided on the up bow, in order to secure 'plus de facilité'.

4. In 6 : 8, 9 : 8 and 12 : 8 time (or 6 : 4, 9 : 4 and 12 : 4) the bar is divided into two, three or four groups of three notes, each group being treated in accordance with rule 3. If there is a rest on the first beat, the second note of the group is taken on the down bow, the third on the up.

APPENDIX E

5. Several successive notes, each of which lasts a complete bar, are all taken on the down bow. In 6 : 8 or 12 : 8 successive dotted crochets are taken on alternate down and up bows. Dotted crochets in 9 : 8 follow the first part of rule 3.

6. Equal notes syncopated are taken on alternate down and up bows.

7. When notes of unequal value occur in the same bar, groups of notes of the same value are taken on alternate down and up bows. In fast tempi a crochet followed by two quavers may adopt the principle of the second part of rule 3; the crochet is then taken on the down bow, the two quavers being elided on the up. Rests count as notes of the same value.

8. In groups of three notes in dotted (siciliano) rhythm, the short note is taken on the up beat, the two longer notes on the down.

9. Single notes interspersed with rests are taken on alternate down and up bows.

10. A short note before the strong beat is always taken on the up bow. Any note following a syncopated note is elided on the up bow.

To the above rules, there are the following exceptions:

1. In courantes, owing to the animation of the movement, the first note of the second group of three may, 'par manière de licence', be taken on the up bow, providing that the first beat of the bar is always on the down.

2. In gigues and canaris the speed is often too quick for rules 4, 8 and 10 to be practicable. In these circumstances each note may be taken on alternate down and up bows. The same licence is allowed in bourrées.

3. Two short notes following a long one (for instance two semiquavers after a dotted crochet) are usually slurred on the up bow.

Muffat finally gives an example of a passage bowed according to the French and Italian conventions. This illustrates clearly the dependence of the French rules on the association of the opening beat of each bar with the down bow; and the more crisply defined rhythm achieved by the French method. The French technique is dominated by physical movement, the Italian by lyrical grace. The Lullian principles of bowing should probably be observed in the performance of Couperin's string parts, though not too rigidly. One should remember that Lully's technique was evolved in music intended for the dance; Couperin's chamber music is in dance forms but is not meant to be danced to. Probably a mixture of French and Italian technique is appropriate to Couperin's more lyrical movements.

II

The following is the list of ornaments which Muffat gives:

1. *Pincés, simples et doubles*. His explanation of these is the same as Couperin's.

2. *Tremblements, simples et doubles*. His explanation of these is broadly the same as Couperin's.

3. *Ports de voix* and *Préoccupations* (anticipatory notes).

   In notating the *Port de voix* Muffat writes the dissonant note as a semiquaver, the resolution as a dotted quaver. Couperin's notation is, as we have seen, ambiguous; but almost all the authorities, from Chambonnières and d'Anglebert in the seventeenth century to C. P. E. Bach in the eighteenth, give the dissonance and its resolution an *equal* value. Boyvin is the only authority who unambiguously supports Muffat; so it may be doubted whether Muffat has accurately transcribed Lully's practice in this matter.

4. *Coulements*—in various subdivisions:

   (*a*) *Coulement simple*. This is the same as Couperin's *coulé*. In dance music it links two successive notes in conjunct motion, slurring them on the same bow.

   (*b*) *Le Tournoyant*. A *coulement* sliding through a wider interval than the *coulement simple*, all the linking notes being slurred on the same bow.

   (*c*) *L'Exclamation*. A *coulement* introduced in the interval of a rising third. The *Exclamation accessive* places the ornamental notes, slurred on one bow, before the beat; the *Exclamation superlative* places them after the beat.

   (*d*) *L'Involution*. This is the same as Couperin's *double* or turn.

   (*e*) *Le Pétillement*. This is the same as the *Tournoyant*, only in this case the ornamental notes are played 'distinctement, en les faisait craqueter sous un même trait d'archelet'.

   (*f*) *La Tirade*. A *coulement* is which the linking notes cover a complete octave, and are all bowed *separately*. Thus this is 'la plus vive' of all the varieties of *coulement*.

5. *Le Détachement*. This is the same as Couperin's *Détaché* effect.

6. *Les Diminutions*. The ornamental splitting up of long notes, in accordance with the seventeenth-century principle of division.

Lully uses only one sign, a cross, to indicate the position of an ornament, without explaining which ornament is appropriate. Muffat's account of the circumstances in which the different ornaments are to be introduced is thus important. We may summarize his remarks as follows:

1. *Pincés* may be introduced on any note that requires stress, even on two consecutive notes, so long as the speed is moderate.

2. *Tremblements* should rarely be used on the opening note of a piece or phrase, except on the major third, and on sharpened notes.

3. In rising scale passages a *port de voix*, either simple or with a mordent, may serve as an approach to the strong beat. When the tempo is slow, the *port de voix* may be combined with the *préoccupation* and the *tremblement*. Trills (*tremblements*) should not be used on the strong beat without preparation except on the third, the leading note, and sharpened notes.

4. In descending scale passages *tremblements* may be more freely introduced, especially on dotted notes.

5. In upward leaps *ports de voix* and *coulements* may be introduced, alone or in combination with *tremblements*. The *Tirade* should be introduced rarely, for a special effect of vehemence. The *Exclamation* can effectively be used in rising thirds, 'pour adoucir le jeu'. *Tremblements* should seldom be approached by a leap, except on the third and sharpened notes.

6. In downward leaps *tremblements* should never be used except after a fall of a third or a tritone, or a fall on to a sharpened note. Falling intervals may be decorated with the *préoccupation*, the *coulement*, the *pétillement*, occasionally with the *tirade*, and most effectively of all with the *coulement* rounded off by a *tremblement* on the last note of the descent.

7. In cadences *tremblements* should be used on the final note only after a fall from the third or the second to the tonic or, combined with the *préoccupation* or anticipatory note, on the major third (i.e. the ornamental resolution of the fourth).

Muffat gives a series of examples of cadential formulae and of diminutions or divisions, and concludes this part of the treatise with some remarks on the use of the *détachement* to give rhythmic animation.

Couperin uses much more precise signs for his ornaments than does Lully; it would seem that his ornamentation is broadly in accord with Lully's principles as described by Muffat. In his violin sonatas and church music he uses the cross, not in the indiscriminate manner of Lully, but to indicate *pincés* and *tremblements*; which of the two is intended depends on the context. He writes out in small notes the appoggiaturas (*ports de voix*) and the various types of *coulement* and *diminution*. Though he does not use Muffat's terminology, most of Muffat's ornaments can be found, written out, in Couperin's work. In his later music—the clavecin pieces, the *concerts*, and the last sonatas—he writes out the appoggiaturas and *coulements* and uses for the *pincés*, *tremblements* and *doubles* the specific signs which we have described in our account of his theoretical work.

In order to illustrate the correlation between Muffat's rules and Couperin's practice we may perhaps comment on the ornaments in some of the passages from the *Leçons des Ténèbres* which we have quoted previously. For instance, on page 178 the *port de voix* on the last syllable of the word 'incipit' probably follows Muffat in being short (about a semiquaver in length), for in that form it is most satisfactory harmonically. But the *port de voix* on the word 'prophetae' probably takes half the value of the main note. The crosses in this quotation all indicate *tremblements*, beginning with the 'prepared' note above. The wriggle at the end of 'prophetae' is a written-out *coulement* of the *tournoyant* type, followed by (in Muffat's terminology) an *Involution* or turn, also written out. On page 179 both the *ports de voix* probably have half the value of the main note. On page 180 the cross represents a mordent, which intensifies the phrase. On page 181 the first cross (on the last syllable of 'convertere') indicates a *pincé*; the *port de voix* on the last syllable of 'Dominum' takes half the value of the main note; and the cross on 'tuum' represents a *tremblement* possibly preceded by a *préoccupation*. On page 185 the first *port de voix* on 'dolor' is probably long rather than short; the second is almost certainly a quaver. The wriggles on the word 'sicut' are examples of the *Exclamation accessive*, written out.

Muffat's account does not greatly help us to solve the most difficult problem of Couperin's ornamentation. This is the problem of the precise length of the appoggiaturas which, in his engraved scores, he has marked so carefully. In the many passages similar to that quoted on page 211 from *Les Langueurs Tendres* the appoggiaturas—*ports de voix*—obviously have half the value of the main note, or perhaps slightly less than half, the notes being slurred in pairs. On the other hand the *ports de voix* followed by *pincés* in the passage quoted on page 220 would seem, from the rest that appears in the third bar, to have the value of one quaver; whereas according to C. P. E. Bach and most of the authorities except Muffat they should have two-thirds of the value of the main note. Similarly on page 221, in the quotation from *L'Ame en peine*, the appoggiaturas should have the value of a crochet, if one follows Bach; but their dissonance is much more poignant if they are played as quavers, on a principle analogous to Muffat's. On page

228 the *ports de voix* all seem to require half the value of the main note if the power and intensity of the music is to be adequately expressed.

The lack of unanimity among the theorists would seem to suggest that the precise interpretation was as much a matter of taste as of rule. Where there is doubt one must choose the interpretation that *sounds* right, as we have tried to do in the above examples.

Appendix F

NOTES ON THE TITLES OF
COUPERIN'S CLAVECIN PIECES

Almost all the titles of Couperin's clavecin pieces, and of those of other composers of the classical age, are in the feminine. Some writers have therefore assumed that the pieces are all addressed to women. But such a title as *La Harpée* (*Pièce dans le gôut de la harpe*), where the word 'harpée' is clearly an invented adjective agreeing with the omitted noun 'Pièce', suggests that a similar construction may be implicit in some of the movements where the titles are obviously based on people's names. It is much more probable that Couperin dedicated a piece to the great viol player and composer Forqueray, or to the renowned organist who was also his friend, Gabriel Garnier, than that he dedicated the pieces to their respective wives, however charming. The implied title of the first of these pieces would thus be *La pièce* (or *la Muse*) *Forqueray, ou la pièce* (or *la Muse*) *superbe*.

FIRST BOOK
ORDRE I

L'Auguste, La Majestueuse. These pieces may be portraits of women, but it is more likely that the construction is *La Pièce* (or *La Sarabande*) *Majestueuse*, and that they are tributes to Louis.

La Milordine. This title makes no sense in the feminine, for the French use the feminine version, 'Milady'. This therefore is *La Pièce* (or *Gigue*) *Milordine*, the word Milordine being an invented adjective. It is a playful picture of the young English lord, probably on his Continental travels. Its treatment of the Corellian gigue form is fairly typical of English classical style.

Les Abeilles. This is one of the pieces that were first printed by Ballard in 1707.

La Pastorelle. There is a vocal version of this piece, dated August 1711.

Gavotte la Bourbonnoise. Probably a portrait of a girl from this province of central France, though possibly a dance with this particular local colour. The word also means a flower rather like a campion.

Les Plaisirs de St Germain en Laye. The palace at St Germain en Laye was celebrated for its gardens and for the *fêtes champêtres* held there.

ORDRE II

La Laborieuse. The word means industrious, assiduous, rather than laborious.

L'Antonine. Almost certainly an invented adjective on the name Anton, so the character portrayed is masculine.

356

APPENDIX F

La Charoloise. Le Charolais is a district in central Burgundy.

La Diane. As a noun this word means the reveille, and the piece and its sequel are both based on trumpet fanfares. But it is probably a pun on a woman's name also.

La Florentine. First published by Ballard 1707.

La Garnier. As previously suggested, this is probably a portrait of Gabriel Garnier the organist, a close friend of Couperin. Garnier, Couperin, Nivers and Buterne were joint organists of the Chapelle Royale.

ORDRE III

Les Pélerines. There is a vocal version of this piece, dated 1712. The pilgrims start on their march very merrily; the middle section in the minor is called *La Caristade* (alms-giving); the third returns to the major for *Le Rémerciement.*

Les Laurentines. Possibly an order of nuns? 'Laurentine' is a flower (the bugle), and also material embroidered with flowers.

L'Espagnolette. Probably a little Spanish girl; though the word means window-latch.

Les Matelotes Provençales. Note that they are feminine sailors—a musical-comedy touch suggested by the ballet divertissement.

La Lutine. A female spright or goblin. Or it might possibly mean *La Pièce* (or *Muse*) *Lutine*.

ORDRE IV

La Marche des Gris-Vêtus. The Gris Vêtus were a famous regiment, with a distinctive grey uniform.

Les Baccanales. A somewhat ironically compressed version of the bacchanalian revels of the classical opera.

La Pateline. Patelin was a figure in a fifteenth-century French farce. He was characterized by an excessively suave, crafty charm. This may be his female counterpart or it may be a '*pièce pateline*'.

Le Réveil-Matin. One of Couperin's programmatic pieces. This alarm-clock must be played at a fairly brisk speed if it is to sound convincingly alarming.

ORDRE V

La Logivière. A name?

La Badine. First published by Ballard 1707. Probably a girl, coquettish and tricksy.

La Bandoline. Possibly a woman from Bandol, near Toulon. Bandoline was a hair-dressing, but this hardly seems relevant.

La Villers. Christophe-Alexandre Pajot, to whom the book is dedicated, or his wife, Anne de Mailly.

Les Agréments. Graces, ornaments, in both the technical and the social sense.

357

SECOND BOOK

ORDRE VI

Le Gazouillement. One of the bird pieces. A twittering, warbling.

La Bersan. André Bauyn, seigneur de Bersan, or his daughter.

Les Baricades Mistérieuses. 'Baricade' had its modern sense, at least after 1648. This would seem to be a technical joke, the continuous suspensions being a mysterious barricade to the basic harmony.

La Commére. The gossip.

ORDRE VII

La Ménetou. A little monastery, or possibly church. But Tessier thinks it is somebody's name.

Les Petites Ages. The three sections of this piece are called *La Muse Naïssante*, *L'Enfantine*, and *L'Adolescente*. It is clear that in this case the words 'enfantine' and 'adolescente' are adjectives to the implicit word Muse, the sex of the child being indeterminate.

La Chazé. A name?

ORDRE VIII

L'Ausoniéne. An archaic, poetical name for an Italian (after Ausonius).

La Morinéte. Daughter of Jean-Baptiste Morin (1677–1745), a composer.

ORDRE IX

La Princesse de Sens. There was no Princess of Sens; it merely means she was a very fine, princess-like creature.

Le Bavolet-Flottant. A *bavolet* was a peasant's cap or bonnet.

Le Petit-deuil ou les trois Veuves. 'Petit-deuil' is half-mourning; though it is not clear why there are *three* widows.

ORDRE X

La Mézangère. Almost certainly a fabricated adjective from Mézangeau, the lute player and composer. The piece is in lute style. It is just possible that some pun on '*mésange*' (tomtit) is intended.

La Noitéle. Jean de Turmenies, seigneur de Noitèle, or his wife (the daughter of a rich banker).

La Fringante. Frisky, nimble, agile (girl or piece).

ORDRE XI

La Castelane. Has this something to do with a castle-keeper's daughter, or an inhabitant of Provence or the Basses-Alpes?

L'Etincelante ou la Bontemps. 'Bontemps' means diversion, pleasure, frolic; here it is used in the feminine with reference to Charlotte de Vasseur, who married Louis-Nicolas Bontemps, first valet de chambre to the king, in 1693. The character of the piece is probably more influenced by the meaning of the word than by the temperament of the woman.

APPENDIX F

Les Fastes de la Grande et Ancienne Ménestrandise. The *Ménestrandise* was a musicians' guild or trade union, founded in 1321. The leader was called the *roi de ménétriers.* The *ménestrandise* was formally sanctioned by Louis in 1659, and tried to establish authority over all composers, organists and clavecinists, as well as the lower ranks of professional musicians. Only accredited members of the *Ménestrandise* were supposed to be licensed to perform. In 1693 a group of composers, including Couperin, made a protest to the King. The same trouble broke out again in 1707; and on both occasions the *Ménestrandise* was defeated. Couperin's group of satirical pieces is a part of the propaganda war against the 'closed shop'; he presents the *ménétriers* as low characters, on a level with acrobats, strolling players, bears and monkeys, cripples and beggars.

ORDRE XII

La Vauvré. Presumably a name.

La Boulonoise. An inhabitant of the area of the Pas de Calais.

THIRD BOOK

ORDRE XIII

Les Folies Françaises. This chaconne is a procession of carnival characters representing different human passions, each sporting a different (and symbolically) coloured 'domino' or costume. The theme represents Virginity, with a domino *'couleur d'invisible'*; the next six couplets personify *La Pudeur (couleur de rose), L'Ardeur (incarnat), L'Esperance (vert), La Fidélité (bleu), La Persévérance (gris de lin),* and *La Langueur (violet).* The eighth couplet represents *La Coquéterie, sous différens Dominos*; and the ninth, ancient gallants and the wives of superannuated treasurers, *'sous les Dominos pourpres et feuilles mortes'.* The tenth couplet introduces some benevolent cuckoos, having a yellow domino appropriate to the traditional joke about cuckoos. They are followed suitably enough by *La Jalousie Taciturne,* with a domino *gris de maure*; and by *La Frénésie ou le Désespoir,* with a domino black as hell. It is almost certainly intentional that the *Folies Françaises* are followed by

L'Ame en Peine, the soul in purgatory. All these verbal jokes do not, of course, affect the power and pathos—as well as the wit—of the music.

ORDRE XIV

Le Rossignol en amour. La Linote éfarouchée. Les Fauvétes Plaintives. Le Rossignol Vainqueur. This group of bird pieces is quite subtly descriptive, with liquid flourishes for the nightingale and plaintive tweets for the warblers. The linnet does not sound particularly scared, perhaps, though his reiterated rising third suggests a mild agitation.

La Julliet. A girl's name? If so, a somewhat unexpected spelling.

Le Carillon de Cithére. Bells in Cytherea, a Watteauesque paradise.

ORDRE XV

La Régente ou la Minerve. Minerva, of course; but there was no Regent when this piece was written. '*Régente*' may be an adjective—i.e. '*La Muse Régente ou la Minerve*'.

Le Dodo ou l'amour au berceau. A traditional French nursery song; and the word Dodo is equivalent to our by-by. The little boy who is being lulled to sleep is presumably Cupid.

L'Evaporée. Probably a girl. It means something between vapid and giddy, in the colloquial sense.

Musétes de Choisi et de Taverni. Presumably Choisy-en-Brie. There is also a Taverny in the Couperin country.

La Princesse de Chabevil ou la Muse de Monaco. This princess was the fifth daughter of the Prince of Monaco, a patron of Couperin. There is extant a letter from the Prince thanking Couperin for the piece.

ORDRE XVI

La Conti ou les Grâces incomparables. Louise-Elisabeth de Bourbon, who married de Conti in 1713.

Le Drôle de Corps. A bizarre creature, a grotesque. Perhaps related to the burlesque.

La Létiville. A name?

La Forqueray ou la Superbe. Antoine Forqueray (1671–1745), *maître de musique* to the Duc d'Orléans, and one of the greatest viol players and composers of his day.

Les Timbres. Probably little bells.

Les petites Chrémières de Bagnolet. These little milkmaids have quite a rustic flavour, though they are elegantly stylized, *à la* Boucher. Bagnolet is a few miles from Paris.

ORDRE XVIII

La Vernéville. La Vernevilléte. Presumably a woman, and her daughter.

Le Turbulent. Here is one of the rare titles in the masculine. It constitutes a bit of evidence for those who believe that the feminine gender denotes the female sex; but not enough, I think, to discount the contrary shreds of evidence we have referred to.

Le Tic-toc-choc ou les Maillotins. ' *Maillotins*' may be a diminutive of '*mail*', and mean little hammers—a rather vague way of referring to the 'works' of the clock and the clattering hammers of the clavecin. But '*maillot*' means swaddling-bands. It seems rather far-fetched to think that the implied collocation is that tick-tocks are things that infants enjoy playing with.

Le Gaillard boiteux. This merry fellow limps in a witty dotted triplet rhythm, with the quaint time signature of 2 : 6.

APPENDIX F
ORDRE XIX

Les Calotins et les Calotines ou la piéce à Tretous. The calotins were members of a secret society (*la calotte*), composed of bright young things mostly coming from the military class. They wore as their insignia a '*calotte de plomb et des grelots*', and the purpose of their burlesque regiment was to protest against the growing melancholy of the court. They wrote satirical verses and performed burlesque plays. They were founded in 1702. Later, after Couperin's day, they were transformed into a serious military society which established an elaborate and sophistical code of honour and instituted courts to try defections therefrom.

'*Tretous*' ought to be a superlative of '*tous*'. It seems curious to describe a piece about a secret society as a piece for everybody, unless it is an ironic joke, in the same way as we make witticisms about Freemasons. Couperin might well go in for that kind of humour. On the other hand, '*tretous*' is probably a variant of '*trétaus*'. This would make it a piece on trestles; and the burlesque plays were often acted on some such improvised stage.

Les Culbutes Jacobines. The Jacobins are the religious order, though we do not know to which particular Parisian community Couperin refers. Nor do we know whether their 'somersaults' are literal or intellectual.

La Muse-Plantine. Perhaps Plantin is a person's name. If not, it would appear to be an adjective fabricated from 'plant'; though why a growing plant should be so melancholy is difficult to imagine. This is one of the most enigmatic of the titles.

FOURTH BOOK
ORDRE XX

La Princesse Marie. Marie Leszczynska, fiancée of Louis XV; hence the sequel '*dans le goût Polonois*'.

La Bouffone. This may be a female buffoon, or it may be a piece in the *bouffon* style.

La Crouilly ou la Couperinette. This is usually said to be a portrait of Couperin's daughter but it seems to me more likely to be Couperin's memories of himself when young; for his connexion with Crouilly must have been closer than his daughter's.

La Sézile. Nicolas Sézile was treasurer of the Offrandes et Aumônes du Roi. This may be he or his wife, Angélique Beaudet.

ORDRE XXI

La Couperin. This has been variously described as a portrait of Couperin's daughter Marguerite-Antoinette, of his wife, and of Couperin himself. One can take one's choice; the grave and closely wrought texture of the piece is certainly worthy of François.

La Petite Pince-sans-rire. Probably a woman, with a rather malicious turn of humour.

ORDRE XXII

Le Point du jour. Daybreak, or possibly the district with that name paradoxically in the west of Paris.

Le Croc-en-jambe. The trip-up.

Les tours de passe-passe. Legerdemain (rabbits out of hats, etc.).

ORDRE XXIII

Les Gondoles de Délos. Mythical gondolas in a Watteauesque fairyland.

ORDRE XXIV

Les vieux Seigneurs. Les jeunes Seigneurs ci-devant les petits-maîtres. Pieces contrasting the old *grand goût* of the Lullian opera with the new divertissement.

Les dars-homicides. Fatal darts—presumably Cupid's.

Les brimborions. Gewgaws, trifles.

La Belle Javotte, autre fois l'Infante. We do not know who this belle is, nor whether it is she who was formerly an Infanta, or the piece which first appeared under a different title.

L'Amphibie. I can suggest no explanation for this. If the title is facetious it seems odd when applied to the longest and one of the most grandly noble pieces in the ordres.

ORDRE XXV

La Monflambert. Anne Darboulin, who married Monflambert, the King's wine merchant, in 1726. Almost certainly the wife this time, for this is a very feminine piece.

Les Ombres Errantes. Wandering shades; ghosts, very sad and languishing.

ORDRE XXVI

L'Epineuse. Probably the spinet-player (feminine); applied to this suavely gentle piece it can hardly refer to anything prickly or thorny.

ORDRE XXVII

Les Chinois. An example of eighteenth-century *chinoiserie.*

Saillie. The word means a leap, a sudden start, a gushing out; or figuratively a witticism. The Saillie was also a step used in a dance called La Babette. A shaft of wit seems the most likely meaning here; the music is not characterized by any strongly marked leaps and bounds.

Appendix G

BIOGRAPHICAL NOTES ON THE PRINCIPAL PERSONS MENTIONED IN THE TEXT

ANGLEBERT, Jean-Henri d' (1630–1691). Composer of clavecin and organ music. Successor to Chambonnières as official clavecinist of the Chambre du Roi.

AULNOY, Mme d' (died 1730). Novelist and writer of fairy tales.

BACH, Carl Philipp Emanuel (1714–1788). } Discussed in relation to
BACH, Wilhelm Friedemann (1710–1784). } French classical
BACH, Johann Sebastian (1685–1750). } tradition.

BACILLY, Bénigne de (1625–1690). Priest and teacher of singing. *Remarques curieuses sur l'art de bien chanter*, published 1668.

BALBASTRE, Claude (1727–1799). Composer and organist of St-Roch and Notre Dame. Clavecin teacher of Marie-Antoinette.

BALLARD. French family of music printers. Founded by Guillaume le Bé in 1540, the firm flourished until the latter years of the eighteenth century.

BENSERADE, Isaac de (1612–1691). Friend of Mazarin and Richelieu: devised ballets.

BERLIOZ, Louis-Hector (1803–1869). Discussed in relation to the classical tradition.

BOËSSET, Antoine (1587–1643). Composer of *ballets de cour* and *airs de cour*. Court musician to Louis XIII.

BOILEAU, Nicolas (1636–1711). Representative of the classical ideal. Continued the work of Malherbe. *Art Poétique*, published 1674.

BOISMORTIER, Joseph Bodin de (1691–1765). Composer of opera-ballets and of concerted music, especially for wind instruments.

BOSSUET, Jacques-Bénigne (1627–1704). Bishop of Meaux and member of the Academy. An authoritarian, famous for his sermons, especially funeral orations.

BOUCHER, François (1703–1770). Painter and decorator of the Regency and of the age of Louis XV.

BOURDALOUE, Louis (1632–1704). Jesuit father, celebrated as a preacher.

BULL, John (1563–1628). English composer, mainly of keyboard music. Organist of Antwerp Cathedral from 1613 until his death.

BUSSY, Roger de Rabutin, comte de (1618–1693). Kinsman and correspondent of Mme de Sévigné.

Buterne, Jean (1650–1727). Organist and composer. Pupil of Henri Du Mont. Organist of Chapelle Royale, 1678.

Caix d'Hervelois, Louis de (1670–1760). Gamba player and composer. In the service of the Duc d'Orléans.

Cambert, Robert (1628–1677). Composer of ballets, motets and *airs à boire*. Member of Académie Royale, 1671. Settled in London 1672, where he remained until his death.

Campra, André (1660–1744). Composer of ballets, divertissements and church music. Organist of Toulon Cathedral and later of St Louis des Jésuites and Notre Dame de Paris.

Caproli, Carlo (1615–1685). Italian opera composer called to Paris by Mazarin. Maître de la Musique du Cabinet du Roi, from January to June, 1654.

Carissimi, Giacomo (1605–1674). Italian composer of church music, adapting operatic techniques to the oratorio. Worked in Rome, but exerted a great influence on French church music.

Caurroy, François Eustache de (1549–1609). Composer of motets, instrumental fantasias, and *airs de cour*.

Cavalli, Pierre-Francesco Caletti-Bruni (1602–1676). Pupil of Monteverdi and choir master of St Mark's, Venice. Composer of operas. *Serse* and *L'Ercole Amante* were produced in Paris in 1660 and 1662.

Cesti, Marc' Antonio (1623–1669). Pupil of Carissimi, composer of operas.

Chambonnières, Jacques Champion de (1602–1672). Composer of clavecin music. Of noble birth, he followed his father and grandfather as official organist and clavecinist of the Chambre du Roi. Taught most of the composers of the French clavecin school.

Champagne, Philippe de (1602–1674). Painter. Friend of Poussin and associate of Port-Royal.

Champmeslé, Marie Desmares (1644–1698). Tragic actress, famous for her portrayals of the heroines of Racine.

Chardin, Jean-Baptiste-Siméon (1699–1779). Painter (of bourgeois origin) of scenes from middle-class life; still influenced by the spirit of the classical tradition.

Charpentier, Marc-Antoine (1634–1704). French composer, mainly of church music, who studied in Italy under Carissimi.

Claude Gelée, le Lorrain (1600–1682). Painter; with Poussin the greatest exponent of the classical tradition. Studied in Rome.

Clérambault, Louis-Nicolas (1676–1749). Composer of clavecin music, organ music, and sacred and secular cantatas. Pupil of J. B. Moreau; organist of St Sulpice.

CLIQUOT, François-Henri (1728–1791). Famous organ builder.

CORELLI, Arcangelo (1653–1713). Italian violinist and composer whose work had great influence in France.

CORNEILLE, Pierre (1606–1684). Creator of the classical ideal in tragedy.

CORNEILLE, Thomas (1625–1709). Younger brother of Pierre. Collaborated with Lully.

COSTELEY, Guillaume de (1531–1606). Composer, especially of chansons for several voices.

COTTE, Robert de (1656–1735). Architect and decorator; designed the organ case and decorations of the Chapelle Royale at Versailles.

COUPERIN, Louis (1626–1661). Composer for clavecin and organ. Organist of St Gervais and of the Chapelle Royale. Wrote some ballet music.

COUPERIN, François the elder (1631–1701). Brother of Louis. Music teacher and organist.

COUPERIN, Charles (1638–1679). Brother of above. Organist and composer. Succeeded Louis as organist of St Gervais, 1661.

COUPERIN, François le Grand (1668–1733). Son of Charles.

COUPERIN, Marguerite-Louise (1676 or 1679–1728). Daughter of François Couperin the elder. Member of the Musique du Roi. Many of the soprano parts in François Couperin le Grand's motets were written for her. She was also a fine clavecin player.

COUPERIN, Marie-Anne (1677–?). Sister of Marguerite-Louis. Entered a convent where she played the organ.

COUPERIN, Nicolas (1680–1748). Brother of above. Organist to the Comte de Toulouse. Succeeded François le Grand as organist of St Gervais.

COUPERIN, Marie-Madeleine (1690–1742). Daughter of François le Grand. Became a nun, and was organist of the Abbey of Maubuisson, having taken the name of Cécile.

COUPERIN, Marguerite-Antoinette (1705–1778?). Daughter of François le Grand. Became celebrated as a clavecinist and succeeded to some of her father's court appointments. She taught the daughters of Louis XV.

COUPERIN, Armand-Louis (1727–1789). Son of Nicolas. Composer of organ music, clavecin music, sonatas and motets. Organist of St Gervais, and successively of six other Parisian churches, culminating in Notre Dame. Was also an expert on organ building.

COUPERIN, Pierre-Louis (1755–1789). Son of Armand-Louis. Organist of the Chapelle Royale, St Gervais, Notre Dame, St Jean-en-Grève, and St Merry. Composer of motets.

COUPERIN, Gervais-François (1759–1826). Son of Pierre-Louis. Composer of symphonies, sonatas and religious music.

COUPERIN, Nicolas-Louis (1760–18?). Son of Gervais-François.

COUPERIN, Céleste (1793–1860). Daughter of Gervais-François. Last member of the Couperin dynasty. Lived at Beauvais with her mother until 1830, when she moved to Belleville near Paris and gained a living by giving piano and singing lessons.

COUSSER, Johann-Siegmund (1660–1727). German composer, especially of operas. Studied with Lully, 1674–1682. Director of the Hamburg opera, 1694.

D'AQUIN, Louis-Claude (1694–1772). Composer of clavecin and organ music. Organist of the Chapelle Royale in 1739, and of Notre Dame de Paris.

DEBUSSY, Achille-Claude (1862–1918). Discussed in relation to the classical tradition.

DESCARTES, Réné (1590–1650). Philosopher and mathematician, educated at the Jesuit College of La Flèche. His works, especially the *Traité des Passions de l'âme*, profoundly influenced every aspect of the culture of the *grand siècle*, including musical theory.

DESTOUCHES, André-Cardinal (1672–1749). Amateur composer of operas and divertissements. A pupil of Campra, he succeeded La Lande as Surintendent de la Musique de Chambre in 1718, and was Inspecteur Général of the Opera from 1713–1728.

DORNEL, Antoine (1685–1765). Organist and composer of concerted music and cantatas.

DOWLAND, John (1563–1626). English or Irish lutenist and composer. Visited France in 1580, and became court musician to Christian IV of Denmark in 1598. Settled in London finally in 1606.

DU MAGE, Pierre (?–?). Seventeenth to eighteenth-century organist and organ composer. Organist of collegiate church of St Quentin, 1703–1713.

DU MONT, Henri de Thier (1610–1684). Organist of St Paul, Paris, 1640, and of the Chapelle Royale, 1663. Important composer of church music, including masses on plainsong themes, a Magnificat, and Cantica sacra for solo voices and continuo. (Published Ballard, 1652 and 1662.)

DU PHLY (1718–1788). Clavecin player and composer.

ERLEBACH, Philipp-Heinrich (1657–1714). German composer who studied in Paris the methods of Lully.

FAURÉ, Gabriel-Urbain (1845–1924). French composer, discussed in relation to the classical tradition.

FÉNELON, François de Salignac de la Mothe- (1651–1715). Priest, Archbishop of Cambrai, tutor to the duc de Bourgogne, author of the *Traité de l'éducation des filles* and *Traité de l'existence de Dieu*. One of the most profoundly religious minds of his time.

FISCHER, Johann Kaspar Ferdinand (1650–1746). Composer of organ, clavecin and concerted music; studied the work of Lully. *Le Journal du Printemps*, 1696.

FONTENELLE, Bernard de Bouvier de (1612–1691). Critic and theorist engaged in the war of the Ancients and Moderns. Collaborated with his uncle Thomas Corneille in ballet and opera.

FORQUERAY, Antoine (1671–1745). Gamba player and composer.

FRANCISQUE, Antoine (1570–1605). Lutenist and composer, *Le Trésor d'Orfée*, published 1596.

FRENEUSE, Lecerf de la Viéville de (1674–1707). Francophile musical theorist. Author of *Comparaison de la musique française et de la musique italienne*.

FRESCOBALDI, Girolamo (1583–1643). Italian organist and composer. Organist of St Peter's, Rome, from 1608.

GALLOT, Jacques (Gallot le vieux), (16?–1685). Lutenist and composer.

GALLOT, Jacques (Gallot le jeune), (*c.* 1640–1700 or later). Lutenist and composer, son of above.

GAULTIER, Ennemond (1575–1651). Lutenist and composer, teacher of Marie de Médicis and Richelieu.

GAULTIER, Jacques (?–?). Lutenist and composer, son of above. Fled to London, 1617, and was attached to the English court until 1647.

GAULTIER, Denis (d. 1672). Nephew or cousin of Ennemond Gaultier. The greatest of the lute school.

GARNIER, Gabriel. Succeeded Le Bègue as organist of the Chapelle Royale in 1702. Friend of Couperin le Grand.

GIBBONS, Orlando (1583–1625). English composer; discussed as writer of organ music.

GIGAULT, Nicolas (1625–1707). Organist and organ composer, one of the teachers of Lully. Organist of St Martin and St Nicolas des Champs.

GRIGNY, Nicolas de (1671–1703). Pupil of Le Bègue, organist of the Abbey of St Denis, and later of Rheims Cathedral. Composer of organ music, mostly of a liturgical nature.

GUÉDRON, Pierre (1565–1625). Composer of ballets and *airs de cour*. Maître de la Musique de la Reine and Surintendant de la Musique du Roi, 1609.

HANDEL, Georg Friedrich (1685–1759). Discussed in relation to French classical tradition.

JENKINS, John (1592–1678). English composer, lutenist, and string player. Composer of fantasias for strings and some church music and songs.

JONSON, Ben (1573–1637). English poet, dramatist, and masque writer. Discussed in relation to the French classical tradition.

JOSQUIN des Prés (1445–1521). Flemish composer of religious and secular music.

JULLIEN, Gilles. Late seventeenth-century organist and composer. Organist of Chartres Cathedral; *Livre d'orgue*, published 1690.

LA BARRE, Pierre Chabanceau de (1592–1656). Composer of ballets and *airs de cour*. Organist of the Chapelle Royale.

LA BRUYÈRE, Jean de (1645–1696). Writer of *Les Caractères*. Of bourgeois origin, he became tutor to the family of the Condés, and a friend of Bossuet.

LA FAYETTE, Marie de (1634–1693). Novelist, author of *La Princesse des Clèves*. Friend of La Rochefoucauld.

LA FONTAINE, Jean de (1621–1695). Author of Contes and Fables. Elected to Academy, 1683.

LA LANDE, Michel Richard de (1657–1726). Leading composer of church music in the time of Louis XIV. Also wrote ballets, and divertissements. Organist of St Gervais, St Louis, St Jean-en-Grève, and of the Petit Couvent St Antoine. Maître de la Musique de la Chambre et de la Chapelle.

LAMBERT, Michel (1610–1696). Composer of *airs de cour* and operas. A pupil of de Nyert, he was famous as a teacher of singing. Became Maître de la Musique de Chambre, 1661.

LA POUPLINIÈRE, Alexandre-Jean-Joseph le Riche de (1693–1762). Farmer-general of taxes who acquired an immense fortune and became a patron of music. Supported Rameau, Stamitz and others.

LA ROCHEFOUCAULD, François duc de (1613–1680). Grand seigneur and honnête homme. Writer of *Maximes*. Influenced by Port-Royal, though not himself a Jansenist.

LAWES, William (1602–1645). English composer of Charles I's court. Wrote music for viols, masques, church music, etc.

LE BÈGUE, Nicolas (1630–1702). Composer of organ and clavecin music. Pupil of Chambonnières, organist of St Merry and of the Chapelle Royale, 1678.

LE BLANC, Hubert. Author of treatise defending the viols against the encroachments of the violin family.

LEBRUN, Charles (1619–1690). Official court painter. Founded l'Académie Royale de Peinture, 1648, Académie de France à Rome, 1666.

LE CAMUS, Sebastien (1610?–1677). Composer of *airs de cour*, etc. Maître de la Musique du Roi, 1640.

LECLAIR, Jean-Marie (1697–1764). Composer of operas, violin sonatas, and concertos, etc. One of the greatest figures at the end of the classical tradition. Served as instrumentalist in the Musique du Roi and at the Court of Don Felipe at Chambery. Visited Holland to meet Locatelli.

LEJEUNE, Claude (1523–1600). Franco-Flemish composer of polyphonic music and of *musique mesurée*.

LE NÔTRE, André (1613–1700). Designer of the gardens at Versailles and elsewhere.

LE ROUX, Gaspard (1660–1710). Clavecinist and composer of clavecin music, motets and *airs sérieux*.

LE ROY, Adrien (?–1589). Lutenist, theorist, composer and music publisher. Associated with Ballard. Published books on lute playing.

L'HERMITE, Tristan (1601–1655). Lyrical poet and writer of tragedies.

LOUIS XIII (1601–1643). Enthusiastic amateur singer and composer.

LOUIS XIV (reigned 1663–1715).

LOUIS XV (reigned 1715–1774).

LULLY, Jean-Baptiste de (1632–1687). Leading composer of opera and ballet for Louis XIV. Started his career as dancer and violinist in the ballet. Of Florentine origin, he became a strenuous opponent of Italian influence in French music.

MAINTENON, Mme de (1635–1719). Married to Scarron and governess of the children of Mme de Montespan; it is probable that she secretly married Louis XIV. Wrote works of instruction for the school of St Cyr which she directed; and much valuable correspondence.

MALEBRANCHE, Nicolas (1638–1715). Disciple of Descartes. A priest, he identified Reason with the Word of God.

MALHERBE, François de (1555–1628). Poet and theorist; link between Ronsard and the Pléïade, and the classicism of Boileau. Secretary to the duc d'Angoulême.

MANSART, Jules-Hardouin (1645–1708). Official architect to Louis XIV.

MARAIS, Marin (1656–1728). The greatest of the classical composers for the viol; also wrote operas of remarkable interest. Pupil of Lully and chef d'orchestre of the opera (1695).

MARCHAND, Louis (1669–1732). Organist and composer of organ music, greatly celebrated as a virtuoso. Organist of many churches and ultimately of the Chapelle Royale, 1706.

MARPURG, Friedrich Wilhelm (1718–1795). German composer and writer of theoretical works.

MATTHESON, Johann (1681–1764). German composer and theorist.

MAUDUIT, Jacques (1557–1627). Lutenist and member of the Académie de Baïf. Composer of religious music, *chansonnettes mesurées* and ballets for Louis XIII.

MAUGARS, André (1580–1645). Violist, politician, and English interpreter to Louis XIII. Musician to Cardinal de Richelieu. Author of a *Réponse faite sur le sentiment de la musique d'Italie*, 1639.

MAZARIN (Guilio Mazarini) (1602–1661). Cardinal, minister of state and patron of music. Introduced many Italian musicians into France, in his enthusiasm for the Italian opera.

MÉZANGEAU, René (15?–1639). Lutenist and composer.

MIGNARD, Nicolas (1610–1695). Official court painter, especially of portraits.

MERSENNE, Marin (1588–1648). A Minorite friar, ordained in 1613. Taught philosophy at Nevers, and studied mathematics and music at Paris, with Descartes and the elder Pascal. Wrote important theoretical treatises on music. Corresponded about musical theory with Titelouze and others.

MOLIÈRE (pseudonym), Jean-Baptiste Poquelin (1622–1673). The greatest comic dramatist of the classical age. Collaborated with Lully in opera-ballet.

MONDONVILLE, Jean-Joseph-Cassanea de (1711–1772). Composer of operas, opera-ballets, and concerted music especially for violin, on which instrument he was a virtuoso. Wrote works for the Concerts Spirituels from 1737–1770, Surintendant de la Chapelle Royale, 1744. Represented the French national school in the Guerre des Bouffons.

MONTEVERDI, Claudio (1567–1643). Discussed in relation to French tradition.

MOREAU, Jean-Baptiste (1656–1733). Composer, especially of religious music to plays and poems of Racine. Maître de Chapelle at Langres and Dijon.

MOURET, Jean-Joseph (1682–1738). Composer mainly of ballets, orchestral suites, and divertissements for the Italian comedies. Succeeded Philidor as director of the Concerts Spirituels, 1728.

MOUTON, Charles (*c*. 1626–*c*. 1710). Pupil of Denis Gaultier, the last of the great lutenist school.

MOZART, Wolfgang Amadeus (1756–1791). Discussed in relation to French tradition.

MUFFAT, Georg (1645–1704). Alsatian composer who studied with Lully in Paris, 1665. Organist of Strasbourg Cathedral and later music director at Passau.

MUFFAT, Gottlieb Theophil (1690–1770). Son of above. Composer mainly of organ and harpsichord music.

NIVERS, Guillaume-Gabriel (1617–1714). Organist and composer. Organist of St Sulpice and of the Chapelle Royale, 1678.

NOVERRE, Jean (1727–1810). Ballet dancer and dance theorist.

NYERT, Pierre de (1597–?). Rich amateur musician and teacher of singing. Disciple of the Italians.

PASCAL, Blaise (1623–1662). Mathematician, scientist, writer, and Christian apologist. Later associated with Port-Royal.

PERRAULT, Charles (1628–1703). Author of the *Parallèles des Anciens et des Modernes*, and of fairy tales.

PERRIN, Pierre (1620–1675). Poet and founder of the Académie Royale de Musique.

PESCHEUR, Pierre. One of the builders of the organ of St Gervais.

PHILIDOR, André (1647–1730). Composer and windplayer for the Ecurie Royale and Librarian of the King's Music.

PINEL, Germain (?–1664). Lutenist and lute composer. Collaborated in ballets de cour.

POUSSIN, Nicolas (1594–1665). Greatest painter of the classical age. Studied and worked in Rome.

PURCELL, Henry (1659–1695). Discussed in relation to the French tradition.

QUINAULT, Philippe (1635–1688). Poet and librettist to Lully.

RACINE, Jean (1639–1699). Greatest of the classical writers of tragedy. Associated with Port-Royal.

RAISON, André (?–1719). Organist and organ composer. Celebrated as a virtuoso.

RAMBOUILLET, Catherine, marquise de (1588–1665). Woman of society; established salon in the rue St Thomas du Louvre.

RAMEAU, Jean-Philippe (1683–1764). The last great musical representative of the classical age. Composer of operas, ballets, harpsichord music, concerted music and theoretical treatise on harmony. His operatic work dates from the latter part of his life.

REBEL, Jean-Féry (1666–1747). Violinist, clavecinist and composer of ballets and concerted music. Pupil of Lully.

RIGAUD, Hyacinthe (1659–1743). Court and society painter, especially of portraits.

ROBERDAY, François (c. 1620–c. 1690). Organist and composer of organ music. Teacher of Lully.

ROSENMÜLLER, Johann (1619–1684). German composer of motets, cantatas and sonatas. Worked for some time in Venice.

ROSSI, Luigi Aloysius Rubens (1598–1653). Italian opera composer, called to France by Mazarin. His *Orfeo* was performed at the court in 1647.

ROUSSEAU, Jean-Jacques (1712–1778). Referred to as author of *Dissertation sur la musique moderne* and *Dictionnaire de la musique*, 1767.

SAINT-EVREMOND, Charles de St-Denis, sieur de (1613–1703). Critic, letter-writer and man of society. Settled in London, 1661.

SAINT-AMANT, Marc-Antoine de Gérard de (1594–1661). Tavern poet and member of the Academy. Wrote sophisticated lyrics, grotesques, and *caprices.*

SAINT SIMON, Louis, duc de (1675–1755). Member of a noble family, courtier at Versailles. Wrote his famous memoirs of the age of Louis XIV many years after the events described.

SCARLATTI, Alessandro (1660–1725). Italian opera composer.

SCARLATTI, Domenico (1685–1757). Son of above. Composer of harpsichord music and operas. Celebrated as harpsichordist.

SCARRON, Paul (1610–1660). Writer of nouvelles and burlesques.

SCHÜTZ, Heinrich (1585–1672). German composer mainly of church music.

SCUDÉRY, Madeleine de (1607–1701). Novelist; her salon was more bourgeois, and more precious in tone than the Hôtel de Rambouillet.

SÉVIGNÉ, Marquise de (1626–1696). Celebrated as letter writer. Sympathized with the Jansenists.

SIMPSON, Christopher (?–1669). English gamba player and composer for his instrument. Wrote theoretical works on the *Principles of Practical Musick* and on gamba playing.

SOREL, Charles (1602–1674). Author of *Histoire comique de Françion,* a picaresque novel, with real contemporary characters disguised among the personae.

STAMITZ, Johann Wenzel Anton (1717–1757). Composer and director of the famous symphony orchestra for the Elector of Mannheim. Visited Paris at the invitation of Le Riche de la Pouplinière.

STAMITZ, Karl (1746–1801). Bohemian composer. Pupil of his father, (above) trained in the Mannheim orchestra. Visited Paris in 1770.

SWEELINCK, Jan Pieterszoon (1562–1621). Dutch composer, organist and harpsichordist.

THIBAUT DE COURVILLE, Joachim (late sixteenth century). Founded with Antoine de Baïf the Académie de poésie et de musique, 1570. Composed *airs de cour.*

THIERRY Family. Seventeenth-century organ builders who worked on the organ at St Gervais.

THOMELIN, Jacques (1640–1693). Organist and composer, principal composition teacher to François Couperin. Organist of the Chapelle Royale, 1678. Previously had been organist of St German des Prés and St Jacques de la Boucherie.

TILLET, Evrard Titon du (1677–1762). Amateur of the arts. Author of *Parnasse François,* 1732 (containing memoirs of the Couperins).

TITELOUZE, Jean (1563–1633). Founder and perhaps the greatest representative of the classical French organ school. All his music is liturgical. Organist of Rouen Cathedral.

URFÉ, Honoré d' (1567 or 8–1625). Author of the pastoral romance *L'Astrée*, known as 'le bréviaire des courtisans' (cf. St François de Sales's *Introduction à la vie dévote*, which was called 'le bréviaire des gens de bien').

VAUGELAS, Charles Favre, baron de (1585–1650). Authority on the language of polite society. *Remarques sur la langue française*, 1647.

VAUVENARGUES, Luc de Clapiers, marquis de (1715–1747). Author of *Introduction à la connoissance de l'Esprit humain*. 'Un cœur stoique et tendre'—halfway between La Rochefoucauld and Pascal.

VOITURE, Vincent (1598–1648). Son of a wine dealer. Wit and writer of society verse for the salons.

WATTEAU, Antoine (1684–1721). The greatest painter among Couperin's immediate contemporaries. Worked in Paris, painting especially the *fête champêtre* and scenes from the Italian comedy.

Catalogue Raisonné

ABBREVIATIONS

THE Key is shown thus:
  (A) = A major.
  (a) = A minor.
Volumes of the Oiseau Lyre edition are shown thus
  OL 1.

  b.-c.—basso-continuo.
  S. —soprano.
  A. —alto.
  T. —tenor.
  B. —bass.
In the case of the harpsichord music, the numbers of book and/or *ordre* are quoted thus:
  II, 12—Livre II, Ordre 12.

(a) WORKS

Series 1. Theoretical works. OL I.
  Règle pour l'accompagnement. MS.., c. 1698.
  L'Art de toucher le clavecin, 1716 and 1717.
  (Contains 1 allemande and 8 preludes for harpsichord.)

Series 2. Harpsichord music. OL II–V.
  Premier livre de clavecin, 1713.
  Ordre No. 1 (g).
  „ „ 2 (d).
  „ „ 3 (c).
  „ „ 4 (F).
  „ „ 5 (A).
  (*L'Art de toucher le clavecin*) 1 allemande and 8 preludes, 1716.
  Second livre de clavecin, 1717.
  Ordre No. 6 (B♭).
  „ „ 6 (G).
  „ „ 8 (b).
  „ „ 9 (A).
  „ „ 10 (D).
  „ „ 11 (c).
  „ „ 12 (E).

Troisiéme livre de clavecin, 1722.
  Ordre No. 13 (b).
    „   „ 14 (D).
    „   „ 15 (a).
    „   „ 16 (G).
    „   „ 17 (e).
    „   „ 18 (f).
    „   „ 19 (d).
Quatriéme livre de clavecin, 1730.
  Ordre No. 20 (G).
    „   „ 21 (e).
    „   „ 22 (D).
    „   „ 23 (F).
    „   „ 24 (A).
    „   „ 25 (E♭ and C).
    „   „ 26 (f♯).
    „   „ 27 (b).

Series 3. Organ music. OL VI.

  Pièces d'orgue consistantes en deux messes, 1690.
    Mass No. 1 'Pour les paroisses'.
      „   No. 2 'Pour les convents'. [*sic*]

Series 4. Instrumental chamber music. OL VII–X.

  Pièces de violes. 2 'viols' and b.-c. OL X.
    Suite No. 1 (e).
      „   No. 2 (A).
    Trio-sonatas, etc.
    La Pucelle. (e) *c.* 1692. Published as *La Françoise* in Ordre No. 1
      of *Les Nations*, 1726. OL IX.
    La Steinquerque. (B♭) *c.* 1692. MS. OL X.
    La Visionnaire. (c) *c.* 1693. Published as *L'Espagnole* in Ordre
      No. 2 of *Les Nations*, 1726. OL. IX.
    L'Astree. (g) *c.* 1693. Published as *La Piemontoise* in Ordre
      No. 4 of *Les Nations*, 1726. OL IX.
    La Superbe. (A) *c.* 1693. MS. OL X.
    L'Impériale. (d) *c.* 1710–15. Published in Ordre No. 3 of *Les
      Nations*, 1726. OL IX.
    Le Parnasse ou l'Apothéose de Corelli. (b) 1725. OL X.
    Apothéose de Lulli. (g) 1725. OL X.

FRANÇOIS COUPERIN

Les Nations: Sonades et Suites de Simphonies en Trio. 1726.
OL IX.

Ordre No. 1 (e) *La Françoise*, and suite of 8 dances.
„ „ 2 (c) *L'Espagnole*, and suite of 10 dances.
„ „ 3 (d) *L'Impériale*, and suite of 9 dances.
„ „ 4 (g) *La Piemontoise*, and suite of 6 dances.

Concerts.

Concerts Royaux. Composed *c.* 1714–15, published 1722. Varying
instrumentation. OL VII.

Concert No. 1 (G).
„ „ 2 (D).
„ „ 3 (A).
„ „ 4 (e).

Les Goûts-Réünis ou Nouveaux Concerts. Published 1724. OL VIII.

Concert No 5 (F).
„ „ 6 (Bb).
„ „ 7 (g).
„ „ 8 (G) 'Dans le Goût Théatral'.
„ „ 9 (E) 'Ritratto dell' Amore'.
„ „ 10 (a).
„ „ 11 (c).
„ „ 12 (A) 'A deux violes ou autres instrumens à
l'unisson'.
„ „ 13 (G) 'A deux instrumens à l'unisson'.
„ „ 14 (d).

Sonade en quatuor, La Sultane (d) for 2 violins, 2 'basses de violes'
and b.-c. *c.* 1695. MS. OL X.

Series 5. Secular Vocal Music. OL XI.

(1) Solo songs.

Doux liens de mon cœur. Air serieux. (A) S. + b.-c. *c.* 1701.
Qu'on ne me dise. Air serieux. (e) T. + b.-c. 1697.
Zephire, modere en ces lieux. (Brunete.) Air serieux. (G)
S. + b.-c. 1711.

(2) Duets.

A l'ombre d'un ormeau. (Musette.) Air serieux. (F) S.A. +
b.-c. 1711.
Epitaphe d'un paresseux: Jean s'en alla comme il étoit venu.
(d) S.B. + b.-c. 1706.
La Pastorelle: Il faut aimer. Air serieux. (G). T.B. + b.-c.
1711.

376

Les Pellerines: Au temple d l'Amour. Air serieux. (C) S.B. +
b.-c.

Les Solitaires: Dans l'Isle de Cythere. Air serieux. (g) A.B. +
b.-c. 1711.

(3) Trios.

A moy! Tout est perdu! Canon for S.S.S. (C.)

La femme entre deux draps. Canon for S.S.S. (d.)

Trois Vestales champetres et trois Poliçons: Quel bruit soudain. Trio en dialogue. (G) S.S.A. c. 1710.

Vaudeville: Faisons du temps. Air serieux. (G) A.A.B. + b.-c.
1712.

Series 6. Sacred Vocal Music. OL XI–XII.

(1) 'Dialogue.'

Dialogus inter Deum et hominem: Accedo ad te mi Jesu.
(g) A.B. + b.-c. N.D. OL XII.

(2) 'Elevations.'

Audite omnes et expanescite. (c) A., 'Symphonie' (2 Vns.) +
b.-c. N.D. OL XII.

O amor, O gaudium. (A) A.T.B. + b.-c. N.D. OL XII.

O Jesu amantissime. (c) A.T. + b.-c. N.D. OL XII.

O misterium ineffabile. (A) S.B. + b.-c. N.D. OL XII.

Quid retribuam tibi Domine. (e) A. + b.-c. N.D. OL XII.

Venite exultemus Domino. (e) S.S. + b.-c. N.D. OL XII.

(3) Leçons de Tenèbres.

No. 1 Incipit Lamentatio Jeremiae Prophetae. (D) S. + b.-c.
c. 1714–15. OL XII.

No. 2. Et egressus est a filia. (D) S. + b.-c. c. 1714–15.
OL XII.

No. 3. Manum suam misit hostis. (D) S.S. + b.-c. c. 1714–15.
OL XII.

(4) Magnificat. (d) S.S. + b.-c. N.D. OL XII.

(5) Motets, etc.

Converte nos, Deus. Sept versets du Motet de Psaume lxxxv,
Benedixisti Domini. (g) S.S.S.A.B.B., Chorus and Orch.
+ b.-c. 1704. OL XI.

Festiva laetis cantibus. Motet de St. Anne. (B♭) S.T.B. N.D.
OL XII.

Jucunda vox Ecclesiae. Motet de St. Augustin. (A) S.S.B. +
b.-c. N.D. OL XII.

Laetentur coeli. Motet de St. Barthélemy. (C) S.S. + b.-c.
N.D. OL XII.

Laudate Pueri Dominum. Motet de Psaume cxiii. (a) S.S. 'Symphonie,' (?2 Vns.) + b.-c. 1697. OL XI.

O Domine quia refugium. Motet (on Psalm xc). (c) B.B.B. + b.-c. N.D. OL XII.

Qui dat nivem. Verset du Motet 'de l'année dernière'. (e) S. 2 Fl Str. + b.-c. 1702. OL XI.

Qui Regis Israel. Sept versets du Motet de Psaume lxxx. (c) S.A.A.B.B. 'Symphonie' (2Fl 2Ob.Str.) + b.-c. 1705. OL XI.

Tabescere me fecit. Quatre versets du Motet de Psaume cxix, Mirabilia testimonia tua. (e) S.S., Chorus, 'Symphonie' (2 Vns.) + b.-c. 1703. OL XI.

Veni, veni, sponsa Christi. Motet de St. Suzanne. (D) S.A.B., Chorus, 'Symphonie' (à 3). c. 1698. OL XI.

Victoria Christo resurgenti. Motet pour le jour de Pâques. (A) S.S. + b.-c. N.D. OL XII.

(b) TITLE INDEX OF HARPSICHORD MUSIC

Les Amours badins. *See* La Divine Babiche, ou les Amours badins.

L'Amphibie, Mouvement de Passacaille (A) IV, 24.

Les Amusemens, Rondeaux (G and g) II, 7.

L'Angélique (a and A) I, 5.

L'Anguille (d) IV, 22.

L'Antonine (D), I, 2.

L'Ardeur. *See* Les Folies Françoises, Pt. 3.

L'Arlequine (F) IV, 23.

L'Artiste (D) III, 19.

L'Atalante (e) II, 12.

L'Atendrissante (f) III, 18.

L'Audacieuse (F) IV, 23.

L'Auguste, Allemande (g) I, 1.

L'Ausoniéne, Allemande (b) II, 8.

La Babet (d and D) I, 2.

Les Baccanales I, 4.

    Pt. 1. Enjouemens Bachiques (F).

    Pt. 2. Tendresses Bachiques (f).

    Pt. 3. Fureurs Bachiques (f and F).

La Badine (A) I, 5.

Les Bagatelles (D) II, 10.

La Bandoline (a) I, 5.

Les Baricades Mistérieuses (B♭) II, 6.

La Basque (g) II, 7.

Le Bavolet-flotant (A) II, 9.

La Belle Javotte autre fois l'Infante (a) IV, 24.

Les Bergeries (B♭) II, 6.

La Bersan (B♭) II, 6.

Les Blondes. *See* Les Nonètes, Pt. 1.

La Bondissante (e) IV, 21.

La Bontems. *See* L'Etincelante ou La Bontems.

La Boufonne (G) IV, 20.

La Boulonoise (e) II, 12.

La Bourbonnoise, Gavotte (G) I, 1.

Les Brinborions (A-a-a-A) IV, 24.

Bruit de Guerre. *See* La Triomphante.

Les Brunes. *See* Les Nonètes, Pt. 2.

Les Calotines (D and d) III, 19.

Les Calotins, et les Calotines, ou la Piéce à tretous (d) III, 19.

Canaries and Double (d) I, 2.

Le Carillon de Cithére (D) III, 14.

Enjouemens Bachiques. *See* Les Baccanales, Pt. 1.

L'Epineuse (f♯) IV, 26.

L'Espagnolète (c) I, 3.

L'Esperance. *See* Les Folies Françoises, Pt. 4.

L'Etincelante ou La Bontems (c) II, 11.

L'Evaporée (A) III, 15.

L'Exquise, Allemande (b) IV, 27.

Fanfare (D). *See* La Triomphante, Pt. 3.

Fanfare pour la Suitte de la Diane (D) I, 2.

Les Fastes de la grande et ancienne Mxnxstrxndxsx (Pts. 1–5 in C and c) II, 11.

Les Fauvétes Plaintives (d) III, 14.

La Favorite, Chaconne à deux tems (c) I, 3.

La Fidélité. *See* Les Folies Françoises, Pt. 5.

La Fileuse (E) II, 12.

La Fine Madelon (G) IV, 20.

La Flateuse (d) I, 2.

La Fleurie ou la tendre Nanette (G) I, 1.

La Flore (a) I, 5.

La Florentine (d) I, 2.

Les Folies Françoises ou les Dominos (b) III, 13.

1. La Virginité.
2. La Pudeur.
3. L'Ardeur.
4. L'Esperance.
5. La Fidélité.
6. La Persévérance.
7. La Langueur.
8. La Coquéterie.
9. Les Vieux Galans et les Trésorieres suranées.
10. Les Coucous Bénévoles.
11. La Jalousie taciturne.
12. La Frénésie, ou le Désespoir.

La Forqueray. *See* La Superbe, ou La Forqueray.

La Frénésie, ou le Désespoir. *See* Les Folies Françoises, Pt. 12.

La Fringante (D and d) II, 10.

Fureurs Bachiques. *See* Les Baccanales, Pt. 3.

La Gabriéle (D) II, 10.

Le Gaillard-Boiteux (F) III, 18.

La Galante (E) II, 12.

La Garnier (D) I, 2.

Gavotte, la Bourbonnoise (G) I, 1.

Gavotte (b) II, 8.

,, (c) I, 3.

,, (f♯) IV, 26.

,, (g) I, 1.

Le Gazouillement (B♭) II, 6.

Gigue la Milordine (g) I, 1.
Gigue (A) I, 5.
     „   (b) II, 8.
Les Gondoles de Délos (F) IV, 23.
Les Graces incomparables, or La Conti (G) III, 16.
Les Graces Natureles (C and c) II, 11.
Gris-Vêtus. *See* La Marche des Gris-Vêtus.
Les Guirlandes (A and a) IV, 24.
La Harpée (e) IV, 21.
L'Himen-Amour (g and G) III, 16.
Les Idées Heureuses (d) I, 2.
L'Infante. *See* La Belle Javotte autre fois l'Infante.
L'Ingénue (D and d) III, 19.
L'Insinuante (a) II, 9.
L'Intîme, Courante (e) II, 12.
La Jalousie taciturne. *See* Les Folies Françoises, Pt. 11.
Les Jeunes Seigneurs, cy-devant les petits Maîtres (a and A) IV, 24.
La Julliet (d) III, 14
Les Juméles (E and e) II, 12.
La Laborieuse, Allemande (d) I, 2.
La Langueur. *See* Les Folies Françoises, Pt. 7.
Les Langueurs-Tendres (Bb) II, 6.
Les Laurentines (C and c) I, 3.
La Létiville (G) III, 16.
La Linote éfarouchée (D) III, 14.
Les Lis naissans (b) III, 13.
La Logiviére (A) I, 5.
La Lugubre, Sarabande (c) I, 3.
La Lutine (c) I, 3.
Les Maillotins. *See* Le Tic-Toc-Choc, ou les Maillotins.
La Majestueuse, Sarabande (g) I, 1.
La Manon (G) I, 1.
La Marche. *See* Les Pélerines,.Pt. 1.
La Marche des Gris-Vêtus (F) I, 4.
Les Matelotes Provençales (c) I, 3.
La Ménetou (G) II, 7.
Menuet (A) II, 9.
     „   (c) I, 3.
     „   (d) I, 2.
     „   (D and d) IV, 22.
     „   (g) I, 1.

La Mézangére (d) II, 10.
La Milordine, Gigue (g) I, 1.
La Mimi (d) I, 2.
La Minerve. *See* La Régente ou La Minerve.
Le Mistérieuse (C) IV, 25.
Les Moissonneurs (B♭) II, 6.
La Monflambert (c) IV, 25.
La Morinete (b) II, 8.
Le Moucheron (B♭), II, 6.
La Muse de Monaco. *See* La Princesse de Chabeuil, ou La Muse de Monaco.
La Muse Naissante. *See* Les Petites Ages, Pt. 1.
La Muse-Plantine (d) III, 19.
La Muse Victorieuse (C) IV, 25.
Muséte de Choisi (A and a) III, 15.
Muséte de Taverni (A and a) III, 15.
La Nanète (g) I, 1.
La Nointéle (d and D) II, 10.
Les Nonètes, I, 1.
   Pt. 1. Les Blondes (g).
   Pt. 2. Les Brunes (G).

L'Olimpique (A) II, 9.
Les Ombres Errantes (c) IV, 25.
Les Ondes (A) I, 5.
La Pantomime (f♯) IV, 26.
Les Papillons (d) I, 2.
La Passacaille (b) II, 8.
Passacaille L'Amphibie (A) IV, 24.
Passepied (d and D) I, 2.
La Pastorelle (G) I, 1.
La Pateline (F) I, 4.
Les Pavots (b) IV, 27.
Les Pellerines (c) I, 3.
   Pt. 1. La Marche.
   Pt. 2. La Caristade.
   Pt. 3. Le Remerciement.

La Persévérance. *See* Les Folies Françoises, Pt. 6.
Le Petit-deuil, ou Les trois Veuves (A) II, 9.
Le Petit-Rien (D) III, 14.
La Petite Pince-sans-rire (e) IV, 21.
Les Petites Chrémiéres de Bagnolet (e) III, 17.

FRANÇOIS COUPERIN

Les Petits Ages (G and g) II, 7.
  Pt. 1. Le Muse Naissante.
  Pt. 2. L'Enfantine.
  Pt. 3. L'Adolescente.
  Pt. 4. Les Délices.
Les Petits Maîtres. *See* Les Jeunes Seigneurs.
Les Petits Moulins à Vent (e) III, 17.
La Piéce à tretous. *See* Les Calotins et les Calotines, ou la Piéce à tretous.
Les Plaisirs de St. Germain-en-Laye (g) I, 1.
Le Point du jour, allemande (D) IV, 22.
Preludes, in L'Art de toucher le clavecin.
  No. 1. (C).   No. 5. (A).
  No. 2. (d).   No. 6. (b).
  No. 3. (g).   No. 7. (B♭).
  No. 4. (F).   No. 8. (e).
La Princesse de Chabeuil, ou la Muse de Monaco (A) III, 15.
La Princesse de Sens (a) II, 9.
La Princess Marie, IV, 20.
  Pt. 1. (G).
  Pt. 2. (g).
  Pt. 3. (g) Air dans le goût Polonois.
La Prude, Sarabande (d) I, 2.
La Pudeur. *See* Les Folies Françoises, Pt. 2.
La Rafraîchissante (a and A) II, 9.
La Raphaéle (b) II, 8.
La Régente, ou la Minerve (a) III, 15.
Les Regrets (c) I, 3.
La Reine des Cœurs (e) IV, 21.
Le Remerciement. *See* Les Pélerines, Pt. 3.
Le Réveil-matin (F), I, 4.
Rigaudons (d and D) I, 2.
Rondeau (b) II, 8.
Le Rossignol-en-amour (D) III, 14.
Le Rossignol-vainqueur (D) III, 14.
Les Rozeaux (b) III, 13.
Saillie (b) IV, 27.
Sarabande la Dangereuse (A) I, 5.
Sarabande la Lugubre (c) I, 3.
Sarabande la Majestueuse (g) I, 1.
Sarabande la Prude (d) I, 2.
Sarabande les Sentimens (G) I, 1.

384

Sarabande l'Unique (b) II, 8.
Sarabande les Vieux Seigneurs (a) IV, 23.
Les Satires Chevre-pieds (F) IV, 23.
La Séduisante (A) II, 9.
Les Sentimens, Sarabande (G) I, 1.
La Sezile (G) IV, 20.
Sicilienne (G) Supplement to Livre 1.
Les Silvains, Rondeau (G) I, 1.
Sœur Monique (F) III, 18.
La Sophie (f♯) IV, 26.
La Superbe, ou la Forqueray (e) III, 17.
Les Tambourins (G and g) IV, 20.
La Tendre Fanchon (a) I, 5.
La tendre Nanette. *See* La Fleurie, ou la tendre Nanette.
La Ténébreuse, Allemande (c) I, 3.
La Terpsicore (D) I, 2.
Le Tic-Toc-Choc, ou les Maillotins (F) III, 18.
Les Timbres (e) III, 17.
Les Tours de Passe-passe (D) IV, 22.
Les Tricoteuses (f) IV, 23.
La Triomphante (D) II, 10.
   Pt. 1. Bruit de guerre.
   Pt. 2. Allégresse des Vainqueurs.
   Pt. 3. Fanfare.
Les trois Veuves. *See* Le Petit-deuil ou les trois Veuves.
Le Trophée (D) IV, 22.
Le Turbulent (F) III, 18.
L'Unique, Sarabande (b) II, 8.
La Vauvré (E) II, 12.
Les Vendangeuses (a) I, 5.
Les Vergers fleuris (a and A) III, 15.
La Verneuil, Allemande (f) III, 18.
La Verneuilléte (f) III, 18.
Les Vestales (G and g) III, 16.
Les Vieux Galans, et les Trésorieres suranées. *See* Les Folies Françoises, Pt. 9.
Les Vieux Seigneurs, Sarabande grave (a) IV, 24.
La Villers (a and A) I, 5.
La Visionaire (E♭) IV, 25.
La Virginité. *See* Les Folies Françoises, Pt. 1.
La Voluptueuse (d) I, 2.
La Zénobie (c) II, 11.

FRANÇOIS COUPERIN

(c) ALPHABETICAL INDEX OF SECULAR VOCAL MUSIC

A l'ombre d'un ormeau (Musette) Air serieux. (F) Duet for S.A. + b.-c. 1711.

A moy! Tout est perdu! Canon for S.S.S. (C.)

Au nom charmant. *See* Les Pellerines, Pt. 3, La Caristade.

Au temple de l'Amour. Air Serieux. (C) Duet for S.B.+b.-c. *See* Les Pellerines, Pt. 2. La Marche.

Brunete. *See* Zephire, modere en ces lieux.

La Caristade. *See* Les Pellerines. Pt. 3.

Dans l'Isle de Cythere. (Les Solitaires.) Air Serieux. (g) Duet for A.B. + b.-c. 1711.

Doux liens de mon cœur. Air serieux. (A) S. + b.-c. *c.* 1701.

Epitaphe d'un paresseux. *See* Jean s'en alla comme il étoit venu.

Faisons du temps. (Vaudeville.) Air serieux. (G) Trio for A.A.B. + b.-c. 1712.

La femme entre deux draps. Canon for S.S.S. (d.)

Il faut aimer. (La Pastorelle.) Air serieux. (G) Duet for T.B. *c.* 1711.

Jean s'en alla comme il étoit venu. (Épitaphe d'un paresseux.) (d) Duet for S.B. + b.-c. 1706.

La Marche. *See* Les Pellerines. Pt. 2.

Musette. *See* A l'ombre d'un ormeau.

La Pastorelle. *See* Il faut aimer.

Les Pellerines. (C.) Duet for S.B.+b.-c. 1712.
    Pt. 1. Les Pellerines.
    Pt. 2. La Marche. (Au temple de l'Amour.)
    Pt. 3. La Caristade. (Au nom charmant.)
    Pt. 4. Le Remerciement. (Que désormais.)
    (*See also* Harpsichord Music, Livre I, Ordre No. 3.)

Que désormais. *See* Les Pellerines. Pt. 4. Le Remerciement.

Quel bruit soudain. (Trois Vestales champêtres et trois Poliçons.) Trio en dialogue. (G) S.S.A. *c.* 1710.

Qu'on ne me dise. Air serieux. (e) T. + b.-c. 1697.

Le Remerciement. *See* Les Pellerines. Pt. 4.

Les Solitaires. *See* Dans l'Isle de Cythere.

Trois Vestales champêtres et trois Poliçons. *See* Quel bruit soudain.

Vaudeville. *See* Faisons du temps.

Zephire, modere en ces lieux. (Brunete.) Air serieux. (G) S. + b.-c. 1711.

(d) INDEX OF SACRED VOCAL MUSIC

Accedo ad te mi Jesu. Dialogus inter Deum et hominem. (g) A.B. + b.-c.
N.D. OL XII.

Audite omnes et expavescite. Elevation .(c) A., 'Symphonie' (2 Vns.) +
b.-c. N.D. OL XII.

Benedixisti Domini. Motet on seven verses of Psalm lxxxv. (g) S.S.S.
A.B.B., Chorus, 2 Fl., 2 Ob., Str.+b.-c. 1704. OL XI.

Converte nos, Deus. *See* Benedixisti Domini.

Dialogus inter Deum et hominem. *See* Accedo ad te mi Jesu.

Elevations. *See*
{
O amor, O gaudium.
O Jesu amantissime.
O misterium ineffabile.
Quid retribuam tibi, Domine.
}

Et egressus est a filia. Leçon de Tenèbre, No. 2. (D) S. + b.-c. *c.* 1714–15.
OL XII.

Festiva Laetis cantibus. Motet de St. Anne. (B♭) S.T.B. + b.-c. N.D.
OL XII.

Incipit Lamentatio Jeremiae Prophetae. Leçon de Tenèbre, No. 1. (D)
S. + b.-c. *c.* 1714–15. OL XII.

Jucunda vox Ecclesiae. Motet de St. Augustin. (A) S.S.B. + b.-c. N.D.
OL XII.

Laetentur coeli. Motet de St. Barthélemy. (C) S.S. + b.-c. N.D. OL XII.

Laudate Pueri Dominum. Motet on Psalm cxii. S.S., 'Symphonie' (? 2 Vns.)
+ b.-c. 1697. OL XI.

Leçons de Tenèbres du Mercredi Saint. Nos. 1–3. 1714–15. OL XII.

Magnificat. (d) S.S. + b.-c. N.D. OL XII.

Manum suam misit hostis. Leçon de Tenèbre, No. 3. (D) S.S. + b.-c.
c. 1714–15. OL XII.

Mirabilia testimonia tua. Motet on four verses of Psalm cxix. (e) S.S.,
Chorus, 'Symphonie' (2 Vns.) + b.-c. 1703. OL XI.

Motet de l'année dernière. *See* Qui dat nivem.

Motet de St. Anne. *See* Festiva Laetis cantibus.

Motet de St. Augustin. *See* Jucunda vox Ecclesiae.

Motet de St. Barthélemy. *See* Laetentur cœli.

Motet de St. Suzanne. *See* Veni, veni, sponsa Christi.

Motet pour le jour de Pâques. *See* Victoria! Christo **resurgenti.**

O amor, O gaudium. Elevation. (A) A.T.B. + b.-c. N.D. OL XII.

O Domine quia refugium. Motet. (c) B.B.B. + b.-c. N.D. OL XII.

O Jesu amantissime. Elevation. (c) A.T. + b.-c. N.D. **OL XII.**

O misterium ineffabile. Elevation. (A) S.B. + b.-c. N.D. OL XII.

Quatre versets de Psaume cxix. *See* Mirabilia testimonia tua.

Qui dat nivem. Verset du Motet de l'année dernière. (e) S., 2Fl., Str. + b.-c. 1702. OL XI.

Qui Regis Israel. Motet on seven verses of Psalm lxxx .(c) S.A.A.B.B., 'Symphonie' (2 Fl., 2 Ob., Str.) + b.-c. OL XI.

Quid retribuam tibi, Domine. Elevation. (e) A. + b.-c. N.D. OL XII.

Sept versets de Psaume lxxx. *See* Qui Regis Israel.

Sept versets de Psaume lxxxv. *See* Benedixisti Domini.

Tabescere me fecit. *See* Mirabilia testimonia tua.

Veni, veni, sponsa Christi. Motet de St. Suzanne. (D) S.A.B., Chorus, 'Symphonie' (? 2 Vns.) + b.-c. *c.* 1698. OL XI.

Venite exultemus Domino. Elevation. (e) SS. + b-c. N.D. O.L. IIX

Verset du Motet de l'année dernière. *See* Qui dat nivem.

Versets de Psaume lxxx. *See* Qui Regis Israel.

    „   „   „   lxxxv. *See* Benedixisti Domini.

    „   „   „   cxix. *See* Mirabilia testimonia tua.

Victoria! Christo resurgenti. Motet pour le jour de Pâques. (A) SS. + b.-c. N.D. OL XII.

(e) INDEX OF DESCRIPTIVE OR PICTORIAL TITLES OTHER THAN HARPSICHORD AND VOCAL MUSIC

Air de Baccantes (G) in Concert No. 8 'Dans le goût Théatral'.

Air de Diable (B♭) in Concert No. 6.

L'Apothéose de Corelli. *See* Le Parnasse, ou l'Apothéose de Corelli.

Apothéose de Lulli. Trio-sonata. (g.)

L'Astree—La Piemontoise in Ordre No. 3 of Les Nations.

Badinage (A) in Concert No. 12.

Bruit de Guerre (B♭) in La Steinquerque. (Trio-sonata.)

Le Charme (E) in Concert No. 9.

La Chemise Blanche (a and A) in Pièces de Violes, Suite No. 2.

La Douceur (e) in Concert No. 9.

L'Enjouement (E) in Concert No. 9.

L'Espagnole (c) (Trio-sonata) in Les Nations, Ordre No. 2.

L'Etcœtera ou Menuets (e and E) in Concert No. 9.

La Françoise (e) Trio-sonata in Les Nations, Ordre No. 1.

Le Gout Théatral, Concert dans. *See* Concert No. 8.

Les Graces, Courante Françoise (E) in Concert No. 9.

L'Impériale (d) Trio-sonata in Les Nations, Ordre No. 3.

Le je-ne-scay-quoy (E) in Concert No. 9.

La Noble Fierté, Sarabande (e) in Concert No. 9.

La Paix du Parnasse. Trio-sonata (g) in L'Apothéose de Lulli.

Le Parnasse, ou l'Apothéose de Corelli. Trio-sonata (b).

La Piemontoise (g) Trio-sonata, in Les Nations, Ordre No. 4.

Pompe funébre (A) in Pièces de violes, Suite No. 2.

La Pucelle— La Françoise in Ordre No. 1 of Les Nations.

Ritratto dell'Amore (E). *See* Concert No. 9.

La Steinquerque, Trio-sonata (Bb).

La Sultane, Sonata à 4 (d).

La Tromba (A) in Concert No. 10.

La Visionnaire, Trio-sonata (c) = L'Espagnole in Ordre No. 2 of Les Nations.

La Vivacité (E) in Concert No. 9.

Bibliography

GENERAL

BOUVET, Ch. *Une dynastie de musiciens français; Les Couperins.* 1919.
TESSIER, André. *Couperin* (Les Musiciens Célèbres). 1926.
TIERSOT, Julien. *Les Couperins* (Les Maîtres de la Musique). 1926.

Part I
ORIGINAL TEXTS

BONNET, J. *Histoire de la Musique.* 1725.
BURNEY, Ch. *General History of Music.* 1789.
TILLET, Titon du. *Le Parnasse François.* 1732. (Supplements 1743 and 1755.)

AULNOY, Mme d'. *Contes de Fées.* 1697.
BOILEAU. *Art Poétique.* 1674.
BOSSUET. *Selected sermons.*
BOURDALOUE. *Selected sermons.*
BUSSY, Rabutin. *Mémoires* and correspondence.
CORNEILLE. *Théâtre.*
DESCARTES. *Abrégé de la Musique.* 1618.
    Discours de la Méthode. 1639.
    Traité des Passions de l'Ame. 1649.
FÉNELON. *De l'Education des Filles.* 1687.
    Lettres Spirituelles. 1718.
LA BRUYÈRE. *Caractères.* 1688.
LA FAYETTE, Mme de. *La Princesse de Clèves.* 1678.
LA FONTAINE. *Fables,* 1668–1694, and other works.
LA ROCHEFOUCAULD. *Maximes.* 1665.
MAINTENON, Mme de. *Lettres sur l'éducation des filles.*
    Correspondence générale.
MALHERBE. *Œuvres diverses.*
MOLIÈRE. *Théâtre.*
NOVERRE. *Lettres sur la danse.* 1760.

PASCAL. *Les Provinciales.* 1656.
  Pensées.
PERRAULT, Ch. *Le Siècle de Louis XIV.*
  Parallèles des Anciens et des Modernes. 1688.
  Histoires ou Contes du Temps Passé. 1697.
RACINE. *Théâtre.*
ST-EVREMOND. *Lettre* to the Duke of Buckingham. 1711.
ST SIMON. *Mémoires sur le Siècle de Louis XIV.*
SCARRON, *Jodelet,* 1643, and other works.
SCUDÉRY, Mlle de. *Le Grand Cyrus.* 1653.
  Clélie. 1660.
SÉVIGNÉ, Mme de. Selections from *Lettres.*
SOREL. *Francion.* 1623.
TRISTAN l'Hermite. *Poésies.*
D'URFÉ. *L'Astrée.* 1607.
VAUGELAS. *Remarques sur la langue française.* 1647.
VAUVENARGUES. *Introduction à la connoissance de l'esprit humain, suivi de réflexions et de maximes.* 1747.
LA DESCRIPTION DE VERSAILLES. Paris, 1694.
VOITURE. *Œuvres Diverses.* 1649.
VOLTAIRE. *Histoire du Siècle de Louis XIV.* 1751.

Paintings of Poussin, Claude, Le Brun, Watteau, Philippe de Champagne, Chardin, Boucher, etc.

MERIAN. *Topographica Galliæ.* Vol. I, 1655.

MODERN WORKS

CLARK, G. N. *The Seventeenth Century.* 1929.
McDOUGALL, Dorothy. *Two Royal Domains of France.* 1931.
OGG, David. *Europe in the Seventeenth Century.* 1938.
PRUNIÈRES, Henri. *Lully.* 1910.
  Le Ballet de Cour en France. 1913.
  L'Opéra Italien en France avant Lully. 1913.
ROLLAND, Romain. *Musiciens d'autrefois.* 1908.
TILLEY, Arthur. *From Montaigne to Molière.* 1923.
  The Decline of the Age of Louis XIV. 1929.
TURNELL, Martin. Articles on Molière, Racine, Corneille, *La Princesse de Clèves. The Classical Moment* (1948).
WELSFORD, Enid. *The Court Masque.* 1927.

Parts II and III

(a) CRITICAL AND THEORETICAL

ORIGINAL TEXTS

D'ALEMBERT, J. *Réflexions sur la Musique.* 1773.
  Elémens de la Musique. 1752.
AVISON, C. *An Essay of Musical Expression.* 1752.
BONNET, J. *Histoire Générale de la Musique.* 1715 and 1725.
BOYVIN, J. *Traité Abrégé de l'accompagnement.* 1715.
DE CAHUSAC, L. *La Danse Ancienne et Moderne.* 1754.
BROSSARD, S. *Dictionnaire de Musique.* 1703.
COUPERIN, F. *Œuvres Didactiques* (Oiseau Lyre).
DE CHABANON, M. *Observations sur la musique.* 1779.
DE CHASTELLUX, F. J. *Essai sur l'union de la poésie et de la musique.* 1765.
CORETTE, M. *Le Maître de Clavecin.* 1753.
FEUILLET, R. A. *Choréographie ou l'art de décrire la danse* (English trans.).
  1710.
LACOMBE. *Dictionnaire Portatif des beaux-arts.* 1758.
LE BLANC, H. *Défense de la Basse de viole.* 1740.
LA VIÉVILLE, Lecerf de. *Comparaison de la musique Italienne et de la musique Française.* 1705.
GOUDAR, A. *Le Brigandage de la musique italienne.* 1777.
GRÉTRY, A. *Mémoires.* 1795.
LOULIÉ, E. *Elémens de la musique.* 1696.
MERSENNE, M. *Harmonie Universelle.* 1636.
  Correspondence (Bibliothèque des Archives de Philosophie).
PERRAULT, C. *Parallèles des Anciens et des Modernes.* 1688.
RAGUENET, F. *Parallèles des Italiens et des François.* 1705.
RAMEAU, J. P. *Traité de l'harmonie.* 1722.
RAMEAU, P. *Le Maître à danser.* 1725.
ROUSSEAU, J. J. *Dictionnaire de la Musique.* 1768.
ROUSSEAU, J. *Traité de la Viole.* 1687.
ST LAMBERT, M. de. *Nouveau Traité de l'accompagnement.* 1707.
ST MARD, R. de. *Réflexions sur l'opéra.* 1741.

MODERN WORKS

BORREL, E. *L'Interprétation de la Musique Française de Lully à la Révolution.* 1934.
BUKOFZER, M. *Music of the Baroque Era.* 1948.

BRENNET, M. *Marc-Antoine Charpentier.* 1913.

BRUNOLD, P. *L'Orgue de St Gervais.* 1934.

CHAMPIGNEULLE, B. *L'Age Classique de la Musique Française.* 1946.

CHRYSANDER. Preface to Augener edition of *Clavecin Works of François Couperin.* 1887.

DANNREUTHER, E. *Musical Ornamentation.* 1894.

DOLMETSCH, A. *The Interpretation of the Music of the Seventeenth and Eighteenth Centuries.* 1916.

GÉROLD, T. *Le Chant au XVIIième Siècle.* 1921.

DE LAURENCIE, L. *Les Violinistes Françaises de Lulli à Viotto.* 1922–24.

PINCHERLE, M. *Corelli.* 1933.

PIRRO, A. *Les Clavecinistes.* 1924.

PRUNIÈRES, Henri. *Nouvelle Histoire de la Musique.* Vol. II, 1936.

RAUGEL, Felix. *Les Organistes.* 1933.

SCHWEITZER, A. *J. S. Bach.* 1911.

WESTRUP, J. A. *Purcell.* 1937.

The Prefaces to the Lyrebird Edition. 1933.

(b) MUSIC

D'ANGLEBERT, J. *Keyboard Works* (Société Française de Musicologie).

BACH, C. P. E. *Miscellaneous Keyboard Works.*

BACH, J. C. *Miscellaneous Keyboard Works.*

BACH, J. S. *Miscellaneous Keyboard Works.*

BALLARD. *Collections of Brunettes.*

BLAVET, M. *Flute Sonatas and other Concerted Works* (Rudall Carte).

DE BOISMORTIER, J. D. *Concerted Works* (Edition Nationale).

BOUTMY, L. Pieces in *Les Clavicinistes Flamands* (Elewyck).

CAMPRA, A. *L'Europe Galante.*
    Les Fêtes Vénitiennes, and other works.

CARISSIMI, G. *Cantatas and Sacred Histories* (Schola Cantorum).

DE CHAMBONNIÈRES, J. C. *Keyboard Works* (Senart).

CHARPENTIER, A. *Cantatas and Sacred Histories* (Schola Cantorum).

CLERAMBAULT, L. N. *Concerted Works and Cantatas* (Edition Nationale).
    Organ Works (Archives Guilmant).

CORELLI, A. *Sonatas and Concerti Grossi* (Augener, edited Joachim and Chrysander).

CORRETTE, M. *Concerted Works* (Edition Nationale).

COUPERIN, Louis. *Complete Keyboard Works* (Oiseau Lyre).

BIBLIOGRAPHY

COUPERIN, François. *Complete Works* (Oiseau Lyre).

DAGINCOUR, F. *Pièces pour orgue* (L. Panel, 1934).

DIEUPART, H. *Pièces pour clavecin* (Oiseau Lyre).

DOWLAND, J. *Lute Pieces* (Curwen, ed. Warlock), and *Ayres* (Stainer & Bell).

DUMONT, H. *Motets and Masses* (Schola Cantorum).

DU PHLY. *Pièces de Clavecin*. 4 vols. (Boyvin, 1755).

EXPERT, H. (ed.). *Les Maîtres Musiciens de la Renaissance Française* (Senart).

FIOCCO, J. H. Pieces in *Les Clavecinistes Flamands* (Elewyck).

FISCHER, J. K. F. *Œuvres complètes pour clavecin et orgue* (E. von Werra). *Concerted Works* (Denkmäler der Tonkunst).

FROBERGER, J. *Keyboard Works* (Peters). *Suites de Clavecin* (Amsterdam, ?).

FRESCOBALDI, G. *Musices Organicæ and other Keyboard Works* (Breitkopf and Härtel).

FUX, J. J. *Concentus Musico-instrumentalis* (Denkmäler der Tonkunst).

GAULTIER, Denis (and other lutenists). *La Rhétorique des Dieux* (Société Française de Musicologie).

GIGAULT, N. *Organ Works* (Archives Guilmant).

GRIGNY, N. de. *Organ Works* (Archives Guilmant).

GROVLEZ, G. (ed.). Collections of *Les Clavecinistes* (Chester).

HANDEL, G. Violin sonatas, keyboard suites, etc.

D'HERVELOIS, Le Caix. *Pièces de Violes* (Paris, 1725).

LECLAIR, J. M. *Livres de Sonates* (Boyvin et Leclerc, 1723.)

LA LANDE. M. de *Musique pour les Soupers du Roi* (Oiseau Lyre). *Motets* (Paris, 1729).

LULLY, J. S. *Theatre and Church Music* (Editions de la Revue Musicale).

LE BÈGUE, N. *Organ Works* (Archives Guilmant).

LE ROUX, G. *Pièces de Clavecin* (Amsterdam, 1706).

MONDONVILLE, J. *Pièces de Clavecin en Sonates avec Accompagnement de Violon* (Société Française de Musicologie). *Sonates pour le Violon avec la Basse Continue* (Paris, 1733).

MOURET, J. *Suites pour des Violons, des hautbois et des cors de Chasse* (Renée Viollier, 1729).

MARAIS, Marin. *Pièces de viole* (Paris, 1690–1729, isolated pieces published by Schott).

MARCHAND, L. *Organ Works* (Archives Guilmant). *Pièces de Clavecin* (Etienne Roger).

MARPURG. *Suites for clavier*, 1762 (no modern edition).

MATTHESON, J. *Suites for clavier*, 1714 (no modern edition; some pieces in Schirmer's *Early Keyboard Music*). *Les Maîtres du Chant*, book 4 (Heugel).

MUFFAT, Georg. *Florilegia*, and other concerted works (Denkmäler der Tonkunst).

MUFFAT, Gottlieb. *Harpsichord Works* (Denkmäler der Tonkunst).

PURCELL, H. *Trio Sonatas*, and other works (Oiseau Lyre).

RAISON, A. *Organ Works* (Archives Guilmant).

RAMEAU, J. *Harpsichord Works* (Durand).

RAUGEL, Félix (ed.) *Les Maîtres Françaises de l'Orgue* (Schola Cantorum).

REBEL, F. *Concerted Works* (Edition Nationale).

ROBERDAY, F. *Organ Works* (Archives Guilmant).

ROSSI, L. *Six Cantatas* (Senart).

SCHUTZ, H. *Sacred Histories*, and other works (Ed. Spitta, Breitkopf and Härtel).

TELEMANN, G. P. *Musique de table* (Denkmäler der Tonkunst).

TITELOUZE, J. *Organ Works* (Archives Guilmant).

TORCHI (ed.). *L'Arte Musicale in Italia* (Ricordi).

WARLOCK (ed.). Songs from Bataille's *Airs de différents auteurs*, 1608–18 (O.U.P.).

NOTE: This Bibliography aims at including all the more important works, creative and critical, which have been consulted during the writing of this book. It does not claim to be a comprehensive list of all the works which could legitimately be considered relevant to the subject. I have specified the editions of musical works which I have been able to use; it does not necessarily follow that the specified edition is the best one, though I have tried to use the most authoritative edition where possible.

Index of Persons

General Index

All titles in italics refer to works by Couperin unless otherwise stated.

Académie Baïf de Musique et de Poésie, 64
Académie Royale de Musique, 71
accent (ornament), 136, 305, 306n.
acciaccatura, 307
Acis et Galathée (Lully), 76
air à boire, 138
air champêtre, 138
air de cour, 21, 63–5, 73, 85, 128 *et seq.*, 178–9, 190, 194, 211, 243, 272
air de mouvement, 138
air passioné, 138
air sérieux, 133, 139, 140, 142
air tendre, 110, 112, 140, 241, 243
Alberti bass, 277
Alceste (Lully), 73, 76, 269
allemande, 113, 236
Allégresse des vainqueurs, 215
Amadis (Lully), 73, 74
Les Amans Magnifiques (Lully), 70, 71
L'Ame en peine, 221, 301, 354
A moi, tout est perdu, 144
L'Amour Médecin (Lully), 70, 71
L'Amphibie, 227–8
Ancients and Moderns, quarrel of, 57, 119n.
L'Anguille, 226
L'Apothéose de Corelli, 103, 118–22, 127, 162, 234, 247, 266, 273, 288, 338
L'Apothéose de Lully, 103, 118, 122–5, 162, 234, 333, 338
appoggiatura, 106, 111, 160, 180, 186, 222, 243, 261. See also Port de voix
Ariane abandonée, 21
L'Arlequine, 226
Armide (Lully), 73, 74
L'Art de décrire la danse (Feuillet), 237
Art of Fugue (Bach), 233
L'Art Poétique (Boileau), 56
L'Art de toucher le Clavecin, 23, 217, 291 *et seq.*, 333, 345
L'Art de toucher le luth (Basset), 194
L'Astree (d'Urfé), 49–50, 53, 103, 139
Aspiration (ornament), 305, 306–7, 310
L'Atalante, 217
Athalie (Racine), 39–40, 154, 177, 233
Attaignant collection of 1557, 61
Atys (Lully), 73

L'Audacieuse, 226
Audite omnes, 172
L'Auguste, 26, 209, 317

Bagpipes, 212
ballad opera, 54n.
Ballet d'Alcine (1610), 65
ballet de cour, 65 *et seq.*
ballet mélodramatique, 65, 129
Ballet des Muses (Lully), 70
Ballet de la Nuit (Lully), 69
Ballo delle Ingrate (Monteverdi), 66
La Bandoline, 208
Les Baricades Mistérieuses, 212
batteries, 306
Le Bavolet Flotant, 215, 220, 233
Les Bergeries, 211, 220, 306n.
Binary principle in dance movements, 206, 241
Le Bourgeois Gentilhomme (Lully), 70, 71
bourrée, 240, 242
Bowing in French classical music, 350–1
Brahms-Chrysander edition (of Couperin's clavecin pieces), 339
brunete, 112, 128, 138, 140–1, 158, 186, 207, 215, 245, 254
Brunete, 142, 222
burlesque (literature), 54–5
burlesque (in music), 125, 223, 226–7

Cadence (rubato), 294–5
cadence (ornament), 136
Cadmus et Hermione (Lully), 71
Les Calotins et les Calotines, 223
canaris, 240
Caractères (La Bruyère), 31
Le Carillon de Cithère, 222
Cartesianism, 40, 56–7
catch (English), 140
cavalière, à la, 140
chaconne, 70, 115, 202 (Louis Couperin), 206, 238–9, 242
chaconne à deux tems, 210
chaconne-rondeau, 206
chanson à boire, 128, 139–40, 144
chanson à danser, 138
chant religieux, 137

403

A CATALOGUE OF SELECTED DOVER BOOKS
IN ALL FIELDS OF INTEREST

A CATALOGUE OF SELECTED DOVER BOOKS
IN ALL FIELDS OF INTEREST

WHAT IS SCIENCE?, *N. Campbell*
The role of experiment and measurement, the function of mathematics, the nature of scientific laws, the difference between laws and theories, the limitations of science, and many similarly provocative topics are treated clearly and without technicalities by an eminent scientist. "Still an excellent introduction to scientific philosophy," H. Margenau in *Physics Today*. "A first-rate primer . . . deserves a wide audience," *Scientific American*. 192pp. 5⅜ x 8.
Paperbound $1.25

THE NATURE OF LIGHT AND COLOUR IN THE OPEN AIR, *M. Minnaert*
Why are shadows sometimes blue, sometimes green, or other colors depending on the light and surroundings? What causes mirages? Why do multiple suns and moons appear in the sky? Professor Minnaert explains these unusual phenomena and hundreds of others in simple, easy-to-understand terms based on optical laws and the properties of light and color. No mathematics is required but artists, scientists, students, and everyone fascinated by these "tricks" of nature will find thousands of useful and amazing pieces of information. Hundreds of observational experiments are suggested which require no special equipment. 200 illustrations; 42 photos. xvi + 362pp. 5⅜ x 8.
Paperbound $2.00

THE STRANGE STORY OF THE QUANTUM, AN ACCOUNT FOR THE GENERAL READER OF THE GROWTH OF IDEAS UNDERLYING OUR PRESENT ATOMIC KNOWLEDGE, *B. Hoffmann*
Presents lucidly and expertly, with barest amount of mathematics, the problems and theories which led to modern quantum physics. Dr. Hoffmann begins with the closing years of the 19th century, when certain trifling discrepancies were noticed, and with illuminating analogies and examples takes you through the brilliant concepts of Planck, Einstein, Pauli, Broglie, Bohr, Schroedinger, Heisenberg, Dirac, Sommerfeld, Feynman, etc. This edition includes a new, long postscript carrying the story through 1958. "Of the books attempting an account of the history and contents of our modern atomic physics which have come to my attention, this is the best," H. Margenau, Yale University, in *American Journal of Physics*. 32 tables and line illustrations. Index. 275pp. 5⅜ x 8.
Paperbound $1.75

GREAT IDEAS OF MODERN MATHEMATICS: THEIR NATURE AND USE, *Jagjit Singh*
Reader with only high school math will understand main mathematical ideas of modern physics, astronomy, genetics, psychology, evolution, etc. better than many who use them as tools, but comprehend little of their basic structure. Author uses his wide knowledge of non-mathematical fields in brilliant exposition of differential equations, matrices, group theory, logic, statistics, problems of mathematical foundations, imaginary numbers, vectors, etc. Original publication. 2 appendixes. 2 indexes. 65 ills. 322pp. 5⅜ x 8.
Paperbound $2.00

THE MUSIC OF THE SPHERES: THE MATERIAL UNIVERSE — FROM ATOM TO QUASAR, SIMPLY EXPLAINED, *Guy Murchie*
Vast compendium of fact, modern concept and theory, observed and calculated data, historical background guides intelligent layman through the material universe. Brilliant exposition of earth's construction, explanations for moon's craters, atmospheric components of Venus and Mars (with data from recent fly-by's), sun spots, sequences of star birth and death, neighboring galaxies, contributions of Galileo, Tycho Brahe, Kepler, etc.; and (Vol. 2) construction of the atom (describing newly discovered sigma and xi subatomic particles), theories of sound, color and light, space and time, including relativity theory, quantum theory, wave theory, probability theory, work of Newton, Maxwell, Faraday, Einstein, de Broglie, etc. "Best presentation yet offered to the intelligent general reader," *Saturday Review*. Revised (1967). Index. 319 illustrations by the author. Total of xx + 644pp. 5⅜ x 8½.
Vol. 1 Paperbound $2.00, Vol. 2 Paperbound $2.00,
The set $4.00

FOUR LECTURES ON RELATIVITY AND SPACE, *Charles Proteus Steinmetz*
Lecture series, given by great mathematician and electrical engineer, generally considered one of the best popular-level expositions of special and general relativity theories and related questions. Steinmetz translates complex mathematical reasoning into language accessible to laymen through analogy, example and comparison. Among topics covered are relativity of motion, location, time; of mass; acceleration; 4-dimensional time-space; geometry of the gravitational field; curvature and bending of space; non-Euclidean geometry. Index. 40 illustrations. x + 142pp. 5⅜ x 8½.
Paperbound $1.35

HOW TO KNOW THE WILD FLOWERS, *Mrs. William Starr Dana*
Classic nature book that has introduced thousands to wonders of American wild flowers. Color-season principle of organization is easy to use, even by those with no botanical training, and the genial, refreshing discussions of history, folklore, uses of over 1,000 native and escape flowers, foliage plants are informative as well as fun to read. Over 170 full-page plates, collected from several editions, may be colored in to make permanent records of finds. Revised to conform with 1950 edition of Gray's Manual of Botany. xlii + 438pp. 5⅜ x 8½.
Paperbound $2.00

MANUAL OF THE TREES OF NORTH AMERICA, *Charles Sprague Sargent*
Still unsurpassed as most comprehensive, reliable study of North American tree characteristics, precise locations and distribution. By dean of American dendrologists. Every tree native to U.S., Canada, Alaska; 185 genera, 717 species, described in detail—leaves, flowers, fruit, winterbuds, bark, wood, growth habits, etc. plus discussion of varieties and local variants, immaturity variations. Over 100 keys, including unusual 11-page analytical key to genera, aid in identification. 783 clear illustrations of flowers, fruit, leaves. An unmatched permanent reference work for all nature lovers. Second enlarged (1926) edition. Synopsis of families. Analytical key to genera. Glossary of technical terms. Index. 783 illustrations, 1 map. Total of 982pp. 5⅜ x 8.
Vol. 1 Paperbound $2.25, Vol. 2 Paperbound $2.25,
The set $4.50

IT'S FUN TO MAKE THINGS FROM SCRAP MATERIALS,
Evelyn Glantz Hershoff
What use are empty spools, tin cans, bottle tops? What can be made from rubber bands, clothes pins, paper clips, and buttons? This book provides simply worded instructions and large diagrams showing you how to make cookie cutters, toy trucks, paper turkeys, Halloween masks, telephone sets, aprons, linoleum block- and spatter prints — in all 399 projects! Many are easy enough for young children to figure out for themselves; some challenging enough to entertain adults; all are remarkably ingenious ways to make things from materials that cost pennies or less! Formerly "Scrap Fun for Everyone." Index. 214 illustrations. 373pp. 5⅜ x 8½. Paperbound $1.50

SYMBOLIC LOGIC and THE GAME OF LOGIC, *Lewis Carroll*
"Symbolic Logic" is not concerned with modern symbolic logic, but is instead a collection of over 380 problems posed with charm and imagination, using the syllogism and a fascinating diagrammatic method of drawing conclusions. In "The Game of Logic" Carroll's whimsical imagination devises a logical game played with 2 diagrams and counters (included) to manipulate hundreds of tricky syllogisms. The final section, "Hit or Miss" is a lagniappe of 101 additional puzzles in the delightful Carroll manner. Until this reprint edition, both of these books were rarities costing up to $15 each. Symbolic Logic: Index. xxxi + 199pp. The Game of Logic: 96pp. 2 vols. bound as one. 5⅜ x 8. Paperbound $2.00

MATHEMATICAL PUZZLES OF SAM LOYD, PART I
selected and edited by M. Gardner
Choice puzzles by the greatest American puzzle creator and innovator. Selected from his famous collection, "Cyclopedia of Puzzles," they retain the unique style and historical flavor of the originals. There are posers based on arithmetic, algebra, probability, game theory, route tracing, topology, counter and sliding block, operations research, geometrical dissection. Includes the famous "14-15" puzzle which was a national craze, and his "Horse of a Different Color" which sold millions of copies. 117 of his most ingenious puzzles in all. 120 line drawings and diagrams. Solutions. Selected references. xx + 167pp. 5⅜ x 8. Paperbound $1.00

STRING FIGURES AND HOW TO MAKE THEM, *Caroline Furness Jayne*
107 string figures plus variations selected from the best primitive and modern examples developed by Navajo, Apache, pygmies of Africa, Eskimo, in Europe, Australia, China, etc. The most readily understandable, easy-to-follow book in English on perennially popular recreation. Crystal-clear exposition; step-by-step diagrams. Everyone from kindergarten children to adults looking for unusual diversion will be endlessly amused. Index. Bibliography. Introduction by A. C. Haddon. 17 full-page plates, 960 illustrations. xxiii + 401pp. 5⅜ x 8½. Paperbound $2.00

PAPER FOLDING FOR BEGINNERS, *W. D. Murray and F. J. Rigney*
A delightful introduction to the varied and entertaining Japanese art of origami (paper folding), with a full, crystal-clear text that anticipates every difficulty; over 275 clearly labeled diagrams of all important stages in creation. You get results at each stage, since complex figures are logically developed from simpler ones. 43 different pieces are explained: sailboats, frogs, roosters, etc. 6 photographic plates. 279 diagrams. 95pp. 5⅝ x 8⅜. Paperbound $1.00

PRINCIPLES OF ART HISTORY,
H. Wölfflin
Analyzing such terms as "baroque," "classic," "neoclassic," "primitive,"
"picturesque," and 164 different works by artists like Botticelli, van Cleve,
Dürer, Hobbema, Holbein, Hals, Rembrandt, Titian, Brueghel, Vermeer, and
many others, the author establishes the classifications of art history and style
on a firm, concrete basis. This classic of art criticism shows what really
occurred between the 14th-century primitives and the sophistication of the
18th century in terms of basic attitudes and philosophies. "A remarkable
lesson in the art of seeing," *Sat. Rev. of Literature.* Translated from the 7th
German edition. 150 illustrations. 254pp. 6⅛ x 9¼.   Paperbound $2.00

PRIMITIVE ART,
Franz Boas
This authoritative and exhaustive work by a great American anthropologist
covers the entire gamut of primitive art. Pottery, leatherwork, metal work,
stone work, wood, basketry, are treated in detail. Theories of primitive art,
historical depth in art history, technical virtuosity, unconscious levels of pat-
terning, symbolism, styles, literature, music, dance, etc. A must book for the
interested layman, the anthropologist, artist, handicrafter (hundreds of unusual motifs), and the historian. Over 900 illustrations (50 ceramic vessels,
12 totem poles, etc.). 376pp. 5⅜ x 8.   Paperbound $2.25

THE GENTLEMAN AND CABINET MAKER'S DIRECTOR,
Thomas Chippendale
A reprint of the 1762 catalogue of furniture designs that went on to influence
generations of English and Colonial and Early Republic American furniture
makers. The 200 plates, most of them full-page sized, show Chippendale's
designs for French (Louis XV), Gothic, and Chinese-manner chairs, sofas,
canopy and dome beds, cornices, chamber organs, cabinets, shaving tables,
commodes, picture frames, frets, candle stands, chimney pieces, decorations, etc.
The drawings are all elegant and highly detailed; many include construction
diagrams and elevations. A supplement of 24 photographs shows surviving
pieces of original and Chippendale-style pieces of furniture. Brief biography
of Chippendale by N. I. Bienenstock, editor of *Furniture World.* Reproduced
from the 1762 edition. 200 plates, plus 19 photographic plates. vi + 249pp.
9⅛ x 12¼.   Paperbound $3.50

AMERICAN ANTIQUE FURNITURE: A BOOK FOR AMATEURS,
Edgar G. Miller, Jr.
Standard introduction and practical guide to identification of valuable
American antique furniture. 2115 illustrations, mostly photographs taken by
the author in 148 private homes, are arranged in chronological order in extensive chapters on chairs, sofas, chests, desks, bedsteads, mirrors, tables, clocks,
and other articles. Focus is on furniture accessible to the collector, including
simpler pieces and a larger than usual coverage of Empire style. Introductory
chapters identify structural elements, characteristics of various styles, how to
avoid fakes, etc. "We are frequently asked to name some book on American
furniture that will meet the requirements of the novice collector, the beginning dealer, and . . . the general public. . . . We believe Mr. Miller's two
volumes more completely satisfy this specification than any other work,"
Antiques. Appendix. Index. Total of vi + 1106pp. 7⅞ x 10¾.
                              Two volume set, paperbound $7.50

CATALOGUE OF DOVER BOOKS

THE BAD CHILD'S BOOK OF BEASTS, MORE BEASTS FOR WORSE CHILDREN, and A MORAL ALPHABET, *H. Belloc*
Hardly and anthology of humorous verse has appeared in the last 50 years without at least a couple of these famous nonsense verses. But one must see the entire volumes — with all the delightful original illustrations by Sir Basil Blackwood — to appreciate fully Belloc's charming and witty verses that play so subacidly on the platitudes of life and morals that beset his day — and ours. A great humor classic. Three books in one. Total of 157pp. 5⅜ x 8.
Paperbound $1.00

THE DEVIL'S DICTIONARY, *Ambrose Bierce*
Sardonic and irreverent barbs puncturing the pomposities and absurdities of American politics, business, religion, literature, and arts, by the country's greatest satirist in the classic tradition. Epigrammatic as Shaw, piercing as Swift, American as Mark Twain, Will Rogers, and Fred Allen, Bierce will always remain the favorite of a small coterie of enthusiasts, and of writers and speakers whom he supplies with "some of the most gorgeous witticisms of the English language" (H. L. Mencken). Over 1000 entries in alphabetical order. 144pp. 5⅜ x 8.
Paperbound $1.00

THE COMPLETE NONSENSE OF EDWARD LEAR.
This is the only complete edition of this master of gentle madness available at a popular price. *A Book of Nonsense, Nonsense Songs, More Nonsense Songs and Stories* in their entirety with all the old favorites that have delighted children and adults for years. The Dong With A Luminous Nose, The Jumblies, The Owl and the Pussycat, and hundreds of other bits of wonderful nonsense. 214 limericks, 3 sets of Nonsense Botany, 5 Nonsense Alphabets, 546 drawings by Lear himself, and much more. 320pp. 5⅜ x 8.
Paperbound $1.00

THE WIT AND HUMOR OF OSCAR WILDE, *ed. by Alvin Redman*
Wilde at his most brilliant, in 1000 epigrams exposing weaknesses and hypocrisies of "civilized" society. Divided into 49 categories—sin, wealth, women, America, etc.—to aid writers, speakers. Includes excerpts from his trials, books, plays, criticism. Formerly "The Epigrams of Oscar Wilde." Introduction by Vyvyan Holland, Wilde's only living son. Introductory essay by editor. 260pp. 5⅜ x 8.
Paperbound $1.00

A CHILD'S PRIMER OF NATURAL HISTORY, *Oliver Herford*
Scarcely an anthology of whimsy and humor has appeared in the last 50 years without a contribution from Oliver Herford. Yet the works from which these examples are drawn have been almost impossible to obtain! Here at last are Herford's improbable definitions of a menagerie of familiar and weird animals, each verse illustrated by the author's own drawings. 24 drawings in 2 colors; 24 additional drawings. vii + 95pp. 6½ x 6.
Paperbound $1.00

THE BROWNIES: THEIR BOOK, *Palmer Cox*
The book that made the Brownies a household word. Generations of readers have enjoyed the antics, predicaments and adventures of these jovial sprites, who emerge from the forest at night to play or to come to the aid of a deserving human. Delightful illustrations by the author decorate nearly every page. 24 short verse tales with 266 illustrations. 155pp. 6⅝ x 9¼.
Paperbound $1.50

THE PRINCIPLES OF PSYCHOLOGY,
William James
The full long-course, unabridged, of one of the great classics of Western literature and science. Wonderfully lucid descriptions of human mental activity, the stream of thought, consciousness, time perception, memory, imagination, emotions, reason, abnormal phenomena, and similar topics. Original contributions are integrated with the work of such men as Berkeley, Binet, Mills, Darwin, Hume, Kant, Royce, Schopenhauer, Spinoza, Locke, Descartes, Galton, Wundt, Lotze, Herbart, Fechner, and scores of others. All contrasting interpretations of mental phenomena are examined in detail—introspective analysis, philosophical interpretation, and experimental research. "A classic," *Journal of Consulting Psychology.* "The main lines are as valid as ever," *Psychoanalytical Quarterly.* "Standard reading . . . a classic of interpretation," *Psychiatric Quarterly.* 94 illustrations. 1408pp. 5⅜ x 8.
Vol. 1 Paperbound $2.50, Vol. 2 Paperbound $2.50,
The set $5.00

VISUAL ILLUSIONS: THEIR CAUSES, CHARACTERISTICS AND APPLICATIONS,
M. Luckiesh
"Seeing is deceiving," asserts the author of this introduction to virtually every type of optical illusion known. The text both describes and explains the principles involved in color illusions, figure-ground, distance illusions, etc. 100 photographs, drawings and diagrams prove how easy it is to fool the sense: circles that aren't round, parallel lines that seem to bend, stationary figures that seem to move as you stare at them — illustration after illustration strains our credulity at what we see. Fascinating book from many points of view, from applications for artists, in camouflage, etc. to the psychology of vision. New introduction by William Ittleson, Dept. of Psychology, Queens College. Index. Bibliography. xxi + 252pp. 5⅜ x 8½.   Paperbound $1.50

FADS AND FALLACIES IN THE NAME OF SCIENCE,
Martin Gardner
This is the standard account of various cults, quack systems, and delusions which have masqueraded as science: hollow earth fanatics. Reich and orgone sex energy, dianetics, Atlantis, multiple moons, Forteanism, flying saucers, medical fallacies like iridiagnosis, zone therapy, etc. A new chapter has been added on Bridey Murphy, psionics, and other recent manifestations in this field. This is a fair, reasoned appraisal of eccentric theory which provides excellent inoculation against cleverly masked nonsense. "Should be read by everyone, scientist and non-scientist alike," R. T. Birge, Prof. Emeritus of Physics, Univ. of California; Former President, American Physical Society. Index. x + 365pp. 5⅜ x 8.   Paperbound $1.85

ILLUSIONS AND DELUSIONS OF THE SUPERNATURAL AND THE OCCULT,
D. H. Rawcliffe
Holds up to rational examination hundreds of persistent delusions including crystal gazing, automatic writing, table turning, mediumistic trances, mental healing, stigmata, lycanthropy, live burial, the Indian Rope Trick, spiritualism, dowsing, telepathy, clairvoyance, ghosts, ESP, etc. The author explains and exposes the mental and physical deceptions involved, making this not only an exposé of supernatural phenomena, but a valuable exposition of characteristic types of abnormal psychology. Originally titled "The Psychology of the Occult." 14 illustrations. Index. 551pp. 5⅜ x 8.   Paperbound $2.25

FAIRY TALE COLLECTIONS, *edited by Andrew Lang*
Andrew Lang's fairy tale collections make up the richest shelf-full of traditional children's stories anywhere available. Lang supervised the translation of stories from all over the world—familiar European tales collected by Grimm, animal stories from Negro Africa, myths of primitive Australia, stories from Russia, Hungary, Iceland, Japan, and many other countries. Lang's selection of translations are unusually high; many authorities consider that the most familiar tales find their best versions in these volumes. All collections are richly decorated and illustrated by H. J. Ford and other artists.

THE BLUE FAIRY BOOK. 37 stories. 138 illustrations. ix + 390pp. 5⅜ x 8½.
Paperbound $1.50

THE GREEN FAIRY BOOK. 42 stories. 100 illustrations. xiii + 366pp. 5⅜ x 8½.
Paperbound $1.50

THE BROWN FAIRY BOOK. 32 stories. 50 illustrations, 8 in color. xii + 350pp. 5⅜ x 8½.
Paperbound $1.50

THE BEST TALES OF HOFFMANN, *edited by E. F. Bleiler*
10 stories by E. T. A. Hoffmann, one of the greatest of all writers of fantasy. The tales include "The Golden Flower Pot," "Automata," "A New Year's Eve Adventure," "Nutcracker and the King of Mice," "Sand-Man," and others. Vigorous characterizations of highly eccentric personalities, remarkably imaginative situations, and intensely fast pacing has made these tales popular all over the world for 150 years. Editor's introduction. 7 drawings by Hoffmann. xxxiii + 419pp. 5⅜ x 8½.
Paperbound $2.00

GHOST AND HORROR STORIES OF AMBROSE BIERCE,
edited by E. F. Bleiler
Morbid, eerie, horrifying tales of possessed poets, shabby aristocrats, revived corpses, and haunted malefactors. Widely acknowledged as the best of their kind between Poe and the moderns, reflecting their author's inner torment and bitter view of life. Includes "Damned Thing," "The Middle Toe of the Right Foot," "The Eyes of the Panther," "Visions of the Night," "Moxon's Master," and over a dozen others. Editor's introduction. xxii + 199pp. 5⅜ x 8½.
Paperbound $1.25

THREE GOTHIC NOVELS, *edited by E. F. Bleiler*
Originators of the still popular Gothic novel form, influential in ushering in early 19th-century Romanticism. Horace Walpole's *Castle of Otranto*, William Beckford's *Vathek*, John Polidori's *The Vampyre*, and a *Fragment* by Lord Byron are enjoyable as exciting reading or as documents in the history of English literature. Editor's introduction. xi + 291pp. 5⅜ x 8½.
Paperbound $2.00

BEST GHOST STORIES OF LEFANU, *edited by E. F. Bleiler*
Though admired by such critics as V. S. Pritchett, Charles Dickens and Henry James, ghost stories by the Irish novelist Joseph Sheridan LeFanu have never become as widely known as his detective fiction. About half of the 16 stories in this collection have never before been available in America. Collection includes "Carmilla" (perhaps the best vampire story ever written), "The Haunted Baronet," "The Fortunes of Sir Robert Ardagh," and the classic "Green Tea." Editor's introduction. 7 contemporary illustrations. Portrait of LeFanu. xii + 467pp. 5⅜ x 8.
Paperbound $2.00

CATALOGUE OF DOVER BOOKS

EASY-TO-DO ENTERTAINMENTS AND DIVERSIONS WITH COINS, CARDS, STRING, PAPER AND MATCHES, *R. M. Abraham*
Over 300 tricks, games and puzzles will provide young readers with absorbing fun. Sections on card games; paper-folding; tricks with coins, matches and pieces of string; games for the agile; toy-making from common household objects; mathematical recreations; and 50 miscellaneous pastimes. Anyone in charge of groups of youngsters, including hard-pressed parents, and in need of suggestions on how to keep children sensibly amused and quietly content will find this book indispensable. Clear, simple text, copious number of delightful line drawings and illustrative diagrams. Originally titled "Winter Nights' Entertainments." Introduction by Lord Baden Powell. 329 illustrations. v + 186pp. 5⅜ x 8½. Paperbound $1.00

AN INTRODUCTION TO CHESS MOVES AND TACTICS SIMPLY EXPLAINED, *Leonard Barden*
Beginner's introduction to the royal game. Names, possible moves of the pieces, definitions of essential terms, how games are won, etc. explained in 30-odd pages. With this background you'll be able to sit right down and play. Balance of book teaches strategy — openings, middle game, typical endgame play, and suggestions for improving your game. A sample game is fully analyzed. True middle-level introduction, teaching you all the essentials without oversimplifying or losing you in a maze of detail. 58 figures. 102pp. 5⅜ x 8½. Paperbound $1.00

LASKER'S MANUAL OF CHESS, *Dr. Emanuel Lasker*
Probably the greatest chess player of modern times, Dr. Emanuel Lasker held the world championship 28 years, independent of passing schools or fashions. This unmatched study of the game, chiefly for intermediate to skilled players, analyzes basic methods, combinations, position play, the aesthetics of chess, dozens of different openings, etc., with constant reference to great modern games. Contains a brilliant exposition of Steinitz's important theories. Introduction by Fred Reinfeld. Tables of Lasker's tournament record. 3 indices. 308 diagrams. 1 photograph. xxx + 349pp. 5⅜ x 8. Paperbound $2.25

COMBINATIONS: THE HEART OF CHESS, *Irving Chernev*
Step-by-step from simple combinations to complex, this book, by a well-known chess writer, shows you the intricacies of pins, counter-pins, knight forks, and smothered mates. Other chapters show alternate lines of play to those taken in actual championship games; boomerang combinations; classic examples of brilliant combination play by Nimzovich, Rubinstein, Tarrasch, Botvinnik, Alekhine and Capablanca. Index. 356 diagrams. ix + 245pp. 5⅜ x 8½. Paperbound $1.85

HOW TO SOLVE CHESS PROBLEMS, *K. S. Howard*
Full of practical suggestions for the fan or the beginner — who knows only the moves of the chessmen. Contains preliminary section and 58 two-move, 46 three-move, and 8 four-move problems composed by 27 outstanding American problem creators in the last 30 years. Explanation of all terms and exhaustive index. "Just what is wanted for the student," Brian Harley. 112 problems, solutions. vi + 171pp. 5⅜ x 8. Paperbound $1.35

CATALOGUE OF DOVER BOOKS

SOCIAL THOUGHT FROM LORE TO SCIENCE,
H. E. Barnes and H. Becker
An immense survey of sociological thought and ways of viewing, studying, planning, and reforming society from earliest times to the present. Includes thought on society of preliterate peoples, ancient non-Western cultures, and every great movement in Europe, America, and modern Japan. Analyzes hundreds of great thinkers: Plato, Augustine, Bodin, Vico, Montesquieu, Herder, Comte, Marx, etc. Weighs the contributions of utopians, sophists, fascists and communists; economists, jurists, philosophers, ecclesiastics, and every 19th and 20th century school of scientific sociology, anthropology, and social psychology throughout the world. Combines topical, chronological, and regional approaches, treating the evolution of social thought as a process rather than as a series of mere topics. "Impressive accuracy, competence, and discrimination . . . easily the best single survey," *Nation*. Thoroughly revised, with new material up to 1960. 2 indexes. Over 2200 bibliographical notes. Three volume set. Total of 1586pp. 5⅜ x 8.
Vol. 1 Paperbound $2.75, Vol. 2 Paperbound $2.75, Vol. 3 Paperbound $2.50
The set $8.00

A HISTORY OF HISTORICAL WRITING, *Harry Elmer Barnes*
Virtually the only adequate survey of the whole course of historical writing in a single volume. Surveys developments from the beginnings of historiography in the ancient Near East and the Classical World, up through the Cold War. Covers major historians in detail, shows interrelationship with cultural background, makes clear individual contributions, evaluates and estimates importance; also enormously rich upon minor authors and thinkers who are usually passed over. Packed with scholarship and learning, clear, easily written. Indispensable to every student of history. Revised and enlarged up to 1961. Index and bibliography. xv + 442pp. 5⅜ x 8½. Paperbound $2.50

JOHANN SEBASTIAN BACH, *Philipp Spitta*
The complete and unabridged text of the definitive study of Bach. Written some 70 years ago, it is still unsurpassed for its coverage of nearly all aspects of Bach's life and work. There could hardly be a finer non-technical introduction to Bach's music than the detailed, lucid analyses which Spitta provides for hundreds of individual pieces. 26 solid pages are devoted to the B minor mass, for example, and 30 pages to the glorious St. Matthew Passion. This monumental set also includes a major analysis of the music of the 18th century: Buxtehude, Pachelbel, etc. "Unchallenged as the last word on one of the supreme geniuses of music," John Barkham, *Saturday Review Syndicate*. Total of 1819pp. Heavy cloth binding. 5⅜ x 8.
Two volume set, clothbound $13.50

BEETHOVEN AND HIS NINE SYMPHONIES, *George Grove*
In this modern middle-level classic of musicology Grove not only analyzes all nine of Beethoven's symphonies very thoroughly in terms of their musical structure, but also discusses the circumstances under which they were written, Beethoven's stylistic development, and much other background material. This is an extremely rich book, yet very easily followed; it is highly recommended to anyone seriously interested in music. Over 250 musical passages. Index. viii + 407pp. 5⅜ x 8.
Paperbound $2.00

THREE SCIENCE FICTION NOVELS,
John Taine
Acknowledged by many as the best SF writer of the 1920's, Taine (under the name Eric Temple Bell) was also a Professor of Mathematics of considerable renown. Reprinted here are *The Time Stream*, generally considered Taine's best, *The Greatest Game*, a biological-fiction novel, and *The Purple Sapphire*, involving a supercivilization of the past. Taine's stories tie fantastic narratives to frameworks of original and logical scientific concepts. Speculation is often profound on such questions as the nature of time, concept of entropy, cyclical universes, etc. 4 contemporary illustrations. v + 532pp. 5⅜ x 8⅜.
Paperbound $2.00

SEVEN SCIENCE FICTION NOVELS,
H. G. Wells
Full unabridged texts of 7 science-fiction novels of the master. Ranging from biology, physics, chemistry, astronomy, to sociology and other studies, Mr. Wells extrapolates whole worlds of strange and intriguing character. "One will have to go far to match this for entertainment, excitement, and sheer pleasure . . ."*New York Times.* Contents: The Time Machine, The Island of Dr. Moreau, The First Men in the Moon, The Invisible Man, The War of the Worlds, The Food of the Gods, In The Days of the Comet. 1015pp. 5⅜ x 8.
Clothbound $5.00

28 SCIENCE FICTION STORIES OF H. G. WELLS.
Two full, unabridged novels, *Men Like Gods* and *Star Begotten*, plus 26 short stories by the master science-fiction writer of all time! Stories of space, time, invention, exploration, futuristic adventure. Partial contents: *The Country of the Blind, In the Abyss, The Crystal Egg, The Man Who Could Work Miracles, A Story of Days to Come, The Empire of the Ants, The Magic Shop, The Valley of the Spiders, A Story of the Stone Age, Under the Knife, Sea Raiders*, etc. An indispensable collection for the library of anyone interested in science fiction adventure. 928pp. 5⅜ x 8.
Clothbound $4.50

THREE MARTIAN NOVELS,
Edgar Rice Burroughs
Complete, unabridged reprinting, in one volume, of Thuvia, Maid of Mars; Chessmen of Mars; The Master Mind of Mars. Hours of science-fiction adventure by a modern master storyteller. Reset in large clear type for easy reading. 16 illustrations by J. Allen St. John. vi + 490pp. 5⅜ x 8½.
Paperbound $1.85

AN INTELLECTUAL AND CULTURAL HISTORY OF THE WESTERN WORLD,
Harry Elmer Barnes
Monumental 3-volume survey of intellectual development of Europe from primitive cultures to the present day. Every significant product of human intellect traced through history: art, literature, mathematics, physical sciences, medicine, music, technology, social sciences, religions, jurisprudence, education, etc. Presentation is lucid and specific, analyzing in detail specific discoveries, theories, literary works, and so on. Revised (1965) by recognized scholars in specialized fields under the direction of Prof. Barnes. Revised bibliography. Indexes. 24 illustrations. Total of xxix + 1318pp.
Vol. 1 Paperbound $2.00, Vol. 2 Paperbound $2.00, Vol. 3 Paperbound $2.00,
The set $6.00

HEAR ME TALKIN' TO YA, *edited by Nat Shapiro and Nat Hentoff*
In their own words, Louis Armstrong, King Oliver, Fletcher Henderson, Bunk Johnson, Bix Beiderbecke, Billy Holiday, Fats Waller, Jelly Roll Morton, Duke Ellington, and many others comment on the origins of jazz in New Orleans and its growth in Chicago's South Side, Kansas City's jam sessions, Depression Harlem, and the modernism of the West Coast schools. Taken from taped conversations, letters, magazine articles, other first-hand sources. Editors' introduction. xvi + 429pp. 5⅜ x 8½.   Paperbound $2.00

THE JOURNAL OF HENRY D. THOREAU
A 25-year record by the great American observer and critic, as complete a record of a great man's inner life as is anywhere available. Thoreau's Journals served him as raw material for his formal pieces, as a place where he could develop his ideas, as an outlet for his interests in wild life and plants, in writing as an art, in classics of literature, Walt Whitman and other contemporaries, in politics, slavery, individual's relation to the State, etc. The Journals present a portrait of a remarkable man, and are an observant social history. Unabridged republication of 1906 edition, Bradford Torrey and Francis H. Allen, editors. Illustrations. Total of 1888pp. 8⅜ x 12¼.
Two volume set, clothbound $25.00

A SHAKESPEARIAN GRAMMAR, *E. A. Abbott*
Basic reference to Shakespeare and his contemporaries, explaining through thousands of quotations from Shakespeare, Jonson, Beaumont and Fletcher, North's *Plutarch* and other sources the grammatical usage differing from the modern. First published in 1870 and written by a scholar who spent much of his life isolating principles of Elizabethan language, the book is unlikely ever to be superseded. Indexes. xxiv + 511pp. 5⅜ x 8½.   Paperbound $2.75

FOLK-LORE OF SHAKESPEARE, *T. F. Thistelton Dyer*
Classic study, drawing from Shakespeare a large body of references to supernatural beliefs, terminology of falconry and hunting, games and sports, good luck charms, marriage customs, folk medicines, superstitions about plants, animals, birds, argot of the underworld, sexual slang of London, proverbs, drinking customs, weather lore, and much else. From full compilation comes a mirror of the 17th-century popular mind. Index. ix + 526pp. 5⅜ x 8½.
Paperbound $2.50

THE NEW VARIORUM SHAKESPEARE, *edited by H. H. Furness*
By far the richest editions of the plays ever produced in any country or language. Each volume contains complete text (usually First Folio) of the play, all variants in Quarto and other Folio texts, editorial changes by every major editor to Furness's own time (1900), footnotes to obscure references or language, extensive quotes from literature of Shakespearian criticism, essays on plot sources (often reprinting sources in full), and much more.

HAMLET, *edited by H. H. Furness*
Total of xxvi + 905pp. 5⅜ x 8½.   Two volume set, paperbound $4.75

TWELFTH NIGHT, *edited by H. H. Furness*
Index. xxii + 434pp. 5⅜ x 8½.
Paperbound $2.25

LA BOHEME BY GIACOMO PUCCINI,
translated and introduced by Ellen H. Bleiler
Complete handbook for the operagoer, with everything needed for full enjoyment except the musical score itself. Complete Italian libretto, with new, modern English line-by-line translation—the only libretto printing all repeats; biography of Puccini; the librettists; background to the opera, Murger's La Boheme, etc.; circumstances of composition and performances; plot summary; and pictorial section of 73 illustrations showing Puccini, famous singers and performances, etc. Large clear type for easy reading. 124pp. 5⅜ x 8½.
Paperbound $1.00

ANTONIO STRADIVARI: HIS LIFE AND WORK (1644-1737),
W. Henry Hill, Arthur F. Hill, and Alfred E. Hill
Still the only book that really delves into life and art of the incomparable Italian craftsman, maker of the finest musical instruments in the world today. The authors, expert violin-makers themselves, discuss Stradivari's ancestry, his construction and finishing techniques, distinguished characteristics of many of his instruments and their locations. Included, too, is story of introduction of his instruments into France, England, first revelation of their supreme merit, and information on his labels, number of instruments made, prices, mystery of ingredients of his varnish, tone of pre-1684 Stradivari violin and changes between 1684 and 1690. An extremely interesting, informative account for all music lovers, from craftsman to concert-goer. Republication of original (1902) edition. New introduction by Sydney Beck, Head of Rare Book and Manuscript Collections, Music Division, New York Public Library. Analytical index by Rembert Wurlitzer. Appendixes. 68 illustrations. 30 full-page plates. 4 in color. xxvi + 315pp. 5⅜ x 8½.
Paperbound $2.25

MUSICAL AUTOGRAPHS FROM MONTEVERDI TO HINDEMITH,
Emanuel Winternitz
For beauty, for intrinsic interest, for perspective on the composer's personality, for subtleties of phrasing, shading, emphasis indicated in the autograph but suppressed in the printed score, the mss. of musical composition are fascinating documents which repay close study in many different ways. This 2-volume work reprints facsimiles of mss. by virtually every major composer, and many minor figures—196 examples in all. A full text points out what can be learned from mss., analyzes each sample. Index. Bibliography. 18 figures. 196 plates. Total of 170pp. of text. 7⅞ x 10¾.
Vol. 1 Paperbound $2.00, Vol. 2 Paperbound $2.00,
The set $4.00

J. S. BACH,
Albert Schweitzer
One of the few great full-length studies of Bach's life and work, and the study upon which Schweitzer's renown as a musicologist rests. On first appearance (1911), revolutionized Bach performance. The only writer on Bach to be musicologist, performing musician, and student of history, theology and philosophy, Schweitzer contributes particularly full sections on history of German Protestant church music, theories on motivic pictorial representations in vocal music, and practical suggestions for performance. Translated by Ernest Newman. Indexes. 5 illustrations. 650 musical examples. Total of xix + 928pp. 5⅜ x 8½.
Vol. 1 Paperbound $2.00, Vol. 2 Paperbound $2.00,
The set $4.00

THE METHODS OF ETHICS, *Henry Sidgwick*
Propounding no organized system of its own, study subjects every major methodological approach to ethics to rigorous, objective analysis. Study discusses and relates ethical thought of Plato, Aristotle, Bentham, Clarke, Butler, Hobbes, Hume, Mill, Spencer, Kant, and dozens of others. Sidgwick retains conclusions from each system which follow from ethical premises, rejecting the faulty. Considered by many in the field to be among the most important treatises on ethical philosophy. Appendix. Index. xlvii + 528pp. 5⅜ x 8½.
Paperbound $2.50

TEUTONIC MYTHOLOGY, *Jakob Grimm*
A milestone in Western culture; the work which established on a modern basis the study of history of religions and comparative religions. 4-volume work assembles and interprets everything available on religious and folkloristic beliefs of Germanic people (including Scandinavians, Anglo-Saxons, etc.). Assembling material from such sources as Tacitus, surviving Old Norse and Icelandic texts, archeological remains, folktales, surviving superstitions, comparative traditions, linguistic analysis, etc. Grimm explores pagan deities, heroes, folklore of nature, religious practices, and every other area of pagan German belief. To this day, the unrivaled, definitive, exhaustive study. Translated by J. S. Stallybrass from 4th (1883) German edition. Indexes. Total of lxxvii + 1887pp. 5⅜ x 8½.   Four volume set, paperbound $10.00

THE I CHING, *translated by James Legge*
Called "The Book of Changes" in English, this is one of the Five Classics edited by Confucius, basic and central to Chinese thought. Explains perhaps the most complex system of divination known, founded on the theory that all things happening at any one time have characteristic features which can be isolated and related. Significant in Oriental studies, in history of religions and philosophy, and also to Jungian psychoanalysis and other areas of modern European thought. Index. Appendixes. 6 plates. xxi + 448pp. 5⅜ x 8½.
Paperbound $2.75

HISTORY OF ANCIENT PHILOSOPHY, *W. Windelband*
One of the clearest, most accurate comprehensive surveys of Greek and Roman philosophy. Discusses ancient philosophy in general, intellectual life in Greece in the 7th and 6th centuries B.C., Thales, Anaximander, Anaximenes, Heraclitus, the Eleatics, Empedocles, Anaxagoras, Leucippus, the Pythagoreans, the Sophists, Socrates, Democritus (20 pages), Plato (50 pages), Aristotle (70 pages), the Peripatetics, Stoics, Epicureans, Sceptics, Neo-platonists, Christian Apologists, etc. 2nd German edition translated by H. E. Cushman. xv + 393pp. 5⅜ x 8.   Paperbound $2.25

THE PALACE OF PLEASURE, *William Painter*
Elizabethan versions of Italian and French novels from *The Decameron*, Cinthio, Straparola, Queen Margaret of Navarre, and other continental sources — the very work that provided Shakespeare and dozens of his contemporaries with many of their plots and sub-plots and, therefore, justly considered one of the most influential books in all English literature. It is also a book that any reader will still enjoy. Total of cviii + 1,224pp.
Three volume set, Paperbound $6.75

THE WONDERFUL WIZARD OF OZ, *L. F. Baum*
All the original W. W. Denslow illustrations in full color—as much a part of
"The Wizard" as Tenniel's drawings are of "Alice in Wonderland." "The
Wizard" is still America's best-loved fairy tale, in which, as the author expresses
it, "The wonderment and joy are retained and the heartaches and nightmares
left out." Now today's young readers can enjoy every word and wonderful picture of the original book. New introduction by Martin Gardner. A Baum
bibliography. 23 full-page color plates. viii + 268pp. 5⅜ x 8.
Paperbound $1.50

THE MARVELOUS LAND OF OZ, *L. F. Baum*
This is the equally enchanting sequel to the "Wizard," continuing the adventures of the Scarecrow and the Tin Woodman. The hero this time is a little
boy named Tip, and all the delightful Oz magic is still present. This is the
Oz book with the Animated Saw-Horse, the Woggle-Bug, and Jack Pumpkin-
head. All the original John R. Neill illustrations, 10 in full color. 287pp.
5⅜ x 8. Paperbound $1.50

ALICE'S ADVENTURES UNDER GROUND, *Lewis Carroll*
The original *Alice in Wonderland*, hand-lettered and illustrated by Carroll
himself, and originally presented as a Christmas gift to a child-friend. Adults
as well as children will enjoy this charming volume, reproduced faithfully
in this Dover edition. While the story is essentially the same, there are slight
changes, and Carroll's spritely drawings present an intriguing alternative to
the famous Tenniel illustrations. One of the most popular books in Dover's
catalogue. Introduction by Martin Gardner. 38 illustrations. 128pp. 5⅜ x 8½.
Paperbound $1.00

THE NURSERY "ALICE," *Lewis Carroll*
While most of us consider *Alice in Wonderland* a story for children of all
ages, Carroll himself felt it was beyond younger children. He therefore provided this simplified version, illustrated with the famous Tenniel drawings
enlarged and colored in delicate tints, for children aged "from Nought to
Five." Dover's edition of this now rare classic is a faithful copy of the 1889
printing, including 20 illustrations by Tenniel, and front and back covers
reproduced in full color. Introduction by Martin Gardner. xxiii + 67pp.
6⅛ x 9¼. Paperbound $1.50

THE STORY OF KING ARTHUR AND HIS KNIGHTS, *Howard Pyle*
A fast-paced, exciting retelling of the best known Arthurian legends for young
readers by one of America's best story tellers and illustrators. The sword
Excalibur, wooing of Guinevere, Merlin and his downfall, adventures of Sir
Pellias and Gawaine, and others. The pen and ink illustrations are vividly
imagined and wonderfully drawn. 41 illustrations. xviii + 313pp. 6⅛ x 9¼.
Paperbound $1.50

Prices subject to change without notice.

Available at your book dealer or write for free catalogue to Dept. Adsci,
Dover Publications, Inc., 180 Varick St., N.Y., N.Y. 10014. Dover publishes more
than 150 books each year on science, elementary and advanced mathematics,
biology, music, art, literary history, social sciences and other areas.